Homeland Mythology

Biblical Narratives in American Culture

CHRISTOPHER COLLINS

The Pennsylvania State University Press
University Park, Pennsylvania

Publication of this book has been aided by a grant from
the Abraham and Rebecca Stein Faculty Publication Fund
of New York University, Department of English.

LIBRARY OF CONGRESS CATALOGING-IN-PUBLICATION DATA

Collins, Christopher.
Homeland mythology : biblical narratives in American culture / Christopher Collins.
p.   cm.
Includes bibliographical references (p.   ) and index.
ISBN-13: 978-0-271-02993-1 (cloth : alk. paper)
1. United States—Church history.
2. Bible—Criticism, interpretation, etc.
3. Christianity and culture—United States.
4. Christianity and politics—United States.
5. Church and state—United States.
I. Title.

BR515.C643 2007
973.01—dc22
2007018608

The Pennsylvania State University Press is a member of the
Association of American University Presses.

It is the policy of
The Pennsylvania State University Press to use
acid-free paper. This book is printed on Natures Natural, containing
50% post-consumer waste, and meets the minimum requirements of American
National Standard for Information Sciences—Permanence of Paper for
Printed Library Material, ANSI Z39.48–1992.

THIS BOOK AND ITS AUTHOR ARE DEDICATED
to Emmy

CONTENTS

PREFACE

Tracking Down an Old Story

In recent years, the world's attention has focused on one particular people and the extreme pronouncements of its spokesmen. What motivates them? How do they justify their policies? How would they change the world? Though religion is not universally practiced among them and a number of sects continue to vie for influence, one religious narrative does seem to offer insights into their global agenda.

According to this narrative, the spiritual ancestors of this people were ancient Middle Eastern tribesmen who long ago swept in from the desert, conquered city after city, and built themselves a glorious kingdom. Their descendants live today in expectation that a martyred leader in the royal lineage of these tribesmen will soon return from Paradise to help them wage their final holy war and lead them to world domination. When that day comes, fire and pestilence will be dropped upon the infidels, whose bodies will be reaped by a great sickle and crushed like grapes, the blood rising five feet high and two hundred miles across—or, as their holy book phrases it, "even unto the horse bridles, by the space of a thousand and six hundred furlongs."

To outsiders, these people have always been inscrutable. Despite their ferocity in battle, their faith is one of peace. Despite their reputation as wily traders, over the centuries they have also produced notable works of art, science, and philosophy. Despite the sacred texts that require every woman to cover her head while praying, "learn in silence with all subjection," and never "usurp authority over the man," in this culture women have been known to rise to positions of high esteem and prominence.

I refer, of course, to the American people. As for their narrative, I mean the biblical stories that for some four centuries they have adapted to explain and justify their conquest of North America and their hegemony abroad. *Homeland Mythology* is meant to serve as a guide to the foundational narratives of this people.

What do these people believe? Is there a national creed? A majority of Americans tacitly assume that God has blessed America above all other nations; that he has given her a mission to liberate the world from tyranny and crime; that, without seeking territorial gain, she strives to feed, clothe, and enlighten the less fortunate; and that, though evildoers will attack her, she will eventually defeat them and inaugurate an era of universal peace. Biblically schooled Americans have tended to believe that they are now the "peculiar people," a designation that Moses (in Deut. 14:2) conferred on the Israelites. When the American military goes forth into the world, men like Lieutenant General William G. "Jerry" Boykin, deputy undersecretary for defense, refer to it as the "army of God."[1] Especially in times of crisis, Americans rally around these articles of national faith, which non-Americans view as . . . well, *peculiar.*

Until recent years, few Americans and even fewer foreigners have realized that beneath the cultural heritage of the Enlightenment—with its ideals of free thought, personal liberty, and tolerance toward others—a more ancient worldview has persisted. According to this view, God had reserved this country to be the Promised Land for his True Church, his New Israel. The Puritans brought this exceptionalist mythology with them, and the early republic elaborated it. Manifest Destiny was understood as God's own compassionate plan, for it would have to be here, in this ample American homeland, that his Chosen People would someday establish for the benefit of all nations the millennial kingdom prophesied in the Book of Revelation. The latter text, however, added quite different elements to the American mythology. Revelation, the final book of the Christian Bible, speaks of the People of God as victims of unprovoked aggression, martyrs to the human agents of demonic malevolence—of pure evil. This apocalyptic prophecy has always braced Americans to accept the bitter and otherwise incomprehensible truth that, despite their righteousness and generosity, there would be those abroad who would regard them not merely as peculiar but as arrogant and selfish as well.

The word "homeland" has two main connotations: a homeland *of* and a homeland *for.* That is, we speak of the homeland *of* a particular human or animal population ("the homeland of the polar bear," "the homeland of the Maori"). We also speak of the homeland as a refuge set apart for a displaced people (Liberia as a "homeland for freed American slaves," Utah as a "homeland for the Mormons"). After the dispersal of a people from their ancestral region, the call for the return of this people combines both connotations: consider the homeland of/for the Palestinians, the homeland of/for the Jews, the homeland of/for the Kurds. As far as Europeans are concerned, America began as a homeland *for,* and only over time became a homeland *of.* American nativism—the Euro-American hostility to recent immigrants and the perceived threat of multilingualism—has always asserted the latter identity, an assertion that the events of 9/11 served to accentuate.

In contemporary usage, however, this word stands for a more complicated set of concepts. A "homeland" is a place of residence, but it also implies a destination marked by that potent word "home," a word that seems to alter subtly in accordance with the verbs attached to it. The phrase "come home (to)" suggests a return to an earlier set of values from which we may have strayed. In a decade of orange alerts and not-quite-cozy-enough basement safe rooms, "coming home" still brings to mind a simpler, more secure setting, a little house on the prairie, a time of quilts and comfort foods. "*Going home,*" on the other hand, can connote an involuntary return—at least when, in the imperative, it is addressed to Americans abroad. That "go home" has appeared on placards and in angry chants on nearly every continent, and it does not evoke the "home" intended by the phrase "American homeland." Americans may like to *come* home, but not to *go* home—much less "cut and run" (home). At any rate, they are certainly not likely to "go home" in an era of global markets and outsourcing, of cheap labor and materials.

As for that key phrase, "homeland security," there is something paradoxical (not to say Orwellian) about it when the word "security" has come to evoke its very opposite. No doubt "The Department of Homeland Anxiety" would have been more accurate but not have struck quite the right tone. Whenever we sense a gap—in this case, a very wide gap—between language and reality, belief and experience, we are entitled to analyze crucial words and question the motives of those who disseminate them. Here, an inquiry into mythic discourse begins to be useful.

In an oral society, a myth is a narrative believed important enough to be passed down from generation to generation. As a collection of such orally transmitted stories, a mythology constitutes the preserved wisdom of a people. When writing is introduced, however, "myth" comes to mean a story that may convey a valuable lesson but is factually untrue.

A body of written texts—a shelf of books, for example—we can peruse whenever we like. We can pick up a book and open it to any page. We can come together and debate the merits of this or that writer. But an orally stored text is quite a different form of knowledge. Someone retells a story that is already composed, completed, and not normally open to dispute, let alone refutation. The hearers' role is to suspend disbelief. In grammatical terms, the speaker (the *I*) is invested with absolute powers of speech and must not be interrupted; the hearers (the *You*) are obliged to believe, or pretend to believe, with perfect faith; and the persons spoken about (the *They*) are absent, which is a very good thing indeed because these narratives usually include superhuman beings with cruelly whimsical dispositions.

In my last book, *Authority Figures,* I proposed that authority, as the socially accepted right of some individuals to tell other people what to think and do, derives from the speech-situation, which in grammar is governed by the pronoun paradigm with its three classes of "persons." In its simplest, most primitive form, speech creates three concentric zones: that of the centralized speaker, the sound of whose voice extends to a secondary zone of hearers, beyond which lies the zone of those third persons who cannot, must not, or will not hear this voice. "Homeland" is a word devised to designate a social entity, the relationship of an *I* to a *You,* i.e., of a dominant speaker or class of speakers and a heedful populace, bound together in a relationship that explicitly excludes the unheeding *They.* Insofar as myth is the continually renewed bond between an *I* and a *You,* myth is the living medium of "homeland."

When we set about examining any myth, we usually isolate it as a significant narrative, a web of places, characters, animals, and plants that displays traditional motifs and plot characteristics. Just as an archaeological site is examined as an array of physical objects, a mythic narrative is often analyzed as an array of nouns. This is not, however, a fully adequate approach to this phenomenon. We need first to recognize that every mythic narrative that we examine was once a *narration*—a real person (re)telling a story to other real persons. This means that this structure of nouns was once also a function of pronouns, a speech-event in which a speaker (an *I*) told it to a hearer or group of hearers (a *You*). The structure of nouns, which is all we are left with now as the narrative artifact, was then, as it is now, an account of the behavior of third persons (the *They*), who were never around to hear themselves talked about in this social performance. Secondly, we need to recognize that this narration was not a one-time event. Not only was it a *re*telling of a familiar narrative, but it was also a *ræ*nactment of countless earlier gatherings in which narrators performed this narrative to the same or other hearers. We can be quite sure of this because, had it not been retold countless times, it would not have survived.

Once we define it as a public narration and the social context of its retelling as essential to its function, we realize that myth is a phenomenon not confined to purely oral cultures. Myth is a function of human sociality regardless of whether the narration occurs in a preliterate or a highly literate culture; whether it takes the form of an epic chanted in a mead hall, a ghost story told around a fire, or an anthem sung at a sports event; whether it is referred to in a sermon preached on Christmas morning or in a State of the Union address delivered before the assembled Congress and Supreme Court. Any public gathering at which a traditional tale is narrated, acted out, or in any way alluded to in songs is a speech-event that affirms a commonality.

The fact that oral culture has always been alive and well within literate cultures means that narrative, and the style of thinking associated with storytelling, also survives in written forms. Even the highly analytical work of mathematics and philosophy—the reasoning of Newton and Locke, for example—could be narrativized. In his *Postmodern Condition* (1979), Jean-François Lyotard proposed that certain narrative models, or master-narratives, had been used to explain the two founding concepts of Western modernism: science and liberty. One he called the speculative narrative, which popularized the notion of science as the noble pursuit of universally valid knowledge, an epic adventure of cosmic exploration. The other he called the emancipative narrative. As scientific speculation spoke a denotative language ("this is that"), emancipation spoke a prescriptive one ("you must do this") and popularized the cause of material and social progress. Both served to mobilize public opinion in favor of expansionist governmental policies and imperial ambitions. The time had come, Lyotard said, to expose and abandon these two dying paradigms, these two metanarratives that the Enlightenment had devised and upon which modernism had been founded.

In the early 1990s, the media theorist Jay Rosen applied this postmodernist theory to the way American journalists had come to package the news.[2] Thanks to his insight, by 2004 "narrative" had become a media buzzword. Commentators spoke of the presidential campaign as a war of competing narratives—among them the narratives of Vietnam service, blood for oil, revenge for the threat to a father's life, and the ongoing war against terror. After the election, the political strategist James Carville lamented that the Democrats had lost because they had a *litany* but no *narrative,* i.e., a list of facts and issues but no compelling story line to connect them. Litanies have little entertainment value. To the degree that our information is now mediated by radio and television, we have come to live in what Walter Ong called the "era of secondary orality," a postliterate world in which narrative logic once again determines public decision making.

How should we characterize the world we now inhabit? If, as Lyotard defined it, postmodernism is defined by an "incredulity toward metanarratives," the American electorate has not yet entered postmodernity. And if we consider modernism as founded in a pre-electronic age, when books and newspapers were read, quoted, and discussed, over the past half-century we may have become increasingly *de*modernized. Indeed, how significant are the differences between secondary and primary orality, the oral culture of preliterates? Insofar as we inhabit a global village of electronic storytelling, we inhabit a world that is neither modern nor postmodern. Despite our technological advancement, we now live and think in a *pre*modern age.

For Americans, the premodern roots of our culture are Puritan. The master narratives our cultural forebears brought with them and disseminated throughout the continent were, and continue to be, biblical. Though the Bible comes to us now in written form, it is infused with oral authority. In it we learn that a single divine speaker, Yahweh, first spoke the world into being, and later imparted his commands directly to Moses and the prophets, who then relayed them to the people, announcing "thus saith the Lord." Yahweh, in the fashion of an ancient King of Kings, is the first of all first persons, the *I* who, as the King James Version construes the Hebrew, refers to himself as the "I-am-who-am." In the world envisioned by biblical faith, the human hearers of God's word, the heedful *You,* remain in relationship with the Divine Speaker and are protected by him, but only so long as they remain within the speaking-hearing space with God at the center. When they turn away and no longer hear him, they enter the space of the *They,* those who are to be spoken not *to,* but *about*—behind their backs, as it were. To be third persons was, from God's point of view, to be cast off and abandoned: "if *ye* shall at all turn from following me . . . then I will cut off Israel out of the land which I have given *them* . . . and Israel shall be a proverb and a byword among all people" (1 Kings 9:6–7, italics added). In the biblical world, the addressees (the *You*) are subject to a pronominal anxiety. They must be classified as standing either with God or distanced from him, either second or third persons in this cosmic paradigm.

Each of the seven chapters that follow is an essay intended to shed light on "homeland mythology" at different stages in its cultural evolution and from different disciplinary angles—from anthropology and biblical studies to sociology, rhetorical theory, and literary analysis. Though I will often view my topic from a rather long perspective, my underlying focus throughout will be on contemporary issues, for it has been the present, not the past, that has prompted my venture into "Big History." When the anti-Clinton campaigns of the mid-1990s rose to a level of invective I could not then adequately explain, I began to jot down notes that linked this disproportionate vehemence to apocalyptic frenzy, that cyclical American phenomenon that by then, thanks to round-the-clock media coverage, had perhaps frothed over into politics. When Hillary Clinton complained in January 1998 that she and her husband had been victims of a "vast right-wing conspiracy," I was at first skeptical, but gradually came to understand that there was something other than Y2K hysteria afoot in the nation.[3]

The conspiracy, it turns out, involved the efforts of several conservative billionaires to find and fund several aggrieved women and of talk-radio hosts to accuse the Clintons of crimes ranging from small-time embezzlement to drug trafficking and murder. But it involved much more. It involved what political analysts now recognize as a strategic convergence of two heretofore divided factions of American conservatism: secular neoconservatives, intent on directing the American economic empire in a post-Soviet, unipolar world, and religious conservatives, intent on controlling American social institutions by rewriting the laws and realigning the Supreme Court. Here was a grand strategy that would call upon corporate American media to convert a cold-war rhetoric into a set of talking points calculated to recruit a fundamentalist Christian voting bloc. Once I realized this, I began to examine the political rhetoric of Christian conservatives in a biblical and historical context and found that there was little new in the cultural narratives their leaders trumpeted to the faithful. Moreover, there was little new in the cynical nimbleness with which a Machiavellian elite could exploit this sector of society.

In May 1999, during the run-up to the 2000 presidential campaign, George W. Bush portrayed himself as a "uniter, not a divider."[4] His administration has, by most estimates, polarized the nation, but perhaps his phrase was misinterpreted. In retrospect, his candidacy seems to have been designed to unite the Right by bridging the gap, such as it was, between economic and social conservatives—that is, between Americans who resent being taxed to support the general welfare of the less fortunate and those other Americans, many of them the "less fortunate," who resent having to tolerate the behavior of those they regard as immoral. After the Supreme Court decided to deny Florida voters a systematic recount and named Bush president, I shelved this project on religio-political rhetoric and turned to other research. But after the events of 9/11, as the patriotic emotions of Americans began to be channeled into that old, exceptionalist rhetoric and into those old, expansionist policies, I reconsidered the project. With that word, "homeland," something powerfully conflictive seemed to emerge into public discourse.

Here was a word that seemed designed to transcend a division that had deep roots in human history, a word that, to me, manifested a utopian ideal that four centuries of Anglo-European settlement of North America had struggled to articulate—an ideal that, now uttered by an imperial president, might prove to have profound consequences for the entire earth.

The "homeland," that harmonious union of virtue and power, has long existed as a utopian concept to which myths alone can lend a semblance of reality. Yet the myths that have always concealed its falsehood are less able to conceal the falsehoods of its proponents, who must lie again and again (and ever more loudly) to retain their dwindling base of true believers. In recent years, investigative reporters have amply revealed the disinformation disseminated by members of the current administration. Important as it was and still is to expose the lies that led us to the Iraq War and its ongoing consequences, it is also important, I submit, to expose the reasons why American voters were, and remain, predisposed to believe such lies. In short, the unexamined issue we now need most to explore is not the mendacity of the few but *the credulity of the many.*

This quest for the myths that underlie the American homeland I can summarize as follows. Chapter 1, "Homeland and Its Discontents," begins with an inquiry into the way in which some patriotic songs link the words "home" and "land." Then I step back, rather far back, from American cultural history to trace the inherent tensions that have always separated "home," as a local entity, from "land," as a centrally governed entity. The communal, or local, level relies on a code of behavior, an ethos with which the governmental level does not, and perhaps cannot, comply. The radical disparity between the two social levels lies in the fact that the communal level adheres to the principle that the end never justifies the means, whereas the governmental level pursues the policy that the end *always* justifies the means. Insofar as we claim membership in both social levels and are required to believe equally in two contradictory principles, we suffer an inner distress, a cognitive dissonance. It is this psychosocial disorder that civil religion (formalized expressions of governmental piety) attempts to treat through that oldest of all "talking cures," mythology. Chapter 1 concludes with a discussion of two kinds of myths, the heroic and the ethnic, and their relevance to recent presidential rhetoric.

Because the specific mythological resources available to this rhetoric are biblical, we must pause to consider how biblical writers themselves dealt with these dissonances when they encountered them. When we do so, we quickly realize that the writers of both the Jewish and Christian canons were as acutely concerned as we are with the conflict between the praxis of the state and the ethos of the community. Out of their experience with this problem, they devised a theory of history based on an ingenious theory of time. Chapter 2, "Biblical Time and the Full Narrative Cycle," begins with a discussion of several models of time and the methods of interpreting history that follow from them. The model that seems to have had the most effect on the biblical worldview, a model that most of us find challenging to conceptualize, likens time to a stream that emerges out of an unseen future and moves continuously toward us.

From our modern point of view, time carries us with it "forward" into the future, and so it seems strange that biblical time moves "backwards." Yet, given certain cultural premises, this directionality makes about as much sense as our own future-oriented "arrow of time." After all, does not every generation *follow* its predecessors? Does it not *pass* and take its place in the *past*? As for the future, which will someday become the present, might it not already be "there," and might not a mind superior to time know the future before it reaches us, confined as we are in our narrow present? Biblical metaphysicians believed not only that their god could know the future but also that he could easily share his advance knowledge with certain humans. This revelation (in Greek, *apokalupsis*) made it possible for Christians to visualize a pre-scripted future in which the dissonant connotations of "land" (as governmental territory or nation) and "home" (as shelter, family, and protective community) could be finally reconciled.

When the first English settlers arrived in America, they brought with them this profoundly biblical time line. As I show in Chapter 3, "Myths of Curses, Myths of Blessings," their leaders had convinced them that they were participating in the climactic events of world history. The prophesied final future was about to appear for all the world to see. Reading the book of Revelation, many of them grew to believe that they were themselves the army of God hemmed about by the forces of the Antichrist, which for them meant the Pope of Rome and his agents, the Spanish, the French, and the Indians—the first Anglo-American "axis of evil." The successes of these settlers both before and after their War of Independence reinforced their belief that their venture in the New World had been uniquely blessed and their nation destined to play a decisive role in world affairs. Some went even further: God had chosen them to combat an evil empire, destroy it in a worldwide conflagration, and then inaugurate the Millennium. Bible-based secondary narratives like this were devised to explain why and how God

had illuminated American leaders and led their followers to claim the country "from sea to shining sea" as their Promised Land. As we shall observe,
ethnic myths that use biblical parallels to account for inequalities among
races, classes, and religions have always held a prominent place in American
homeland mythology.

American clergymen and politicians, eager to justify governmental policies, have often appealed to these parallels. Some took the Church doctrine
that, when the Jews rejected Jesus, Christians became God's Chosen People,
and they stretched it to interpret all references to the Chosen Ones of the
Old Testament as being prophetic references to themselves as a covenanted
people in the wilderness. For example, the Israelites' divinely ordained conquest of the Canaanites prefigured, and therefore justified, the Americans'
expropriation of Indian and Mexican territories. Even chattel slavery could
be defended as God's will. As for the future, Americans would have little to
fear. As long as the nation continued to advance in virtue and to preach the
gospel to the heathen, it would infuse the world with Christ's spiritual presence and thus create the thousand-year kingdom of heaven, with America
at its center. Christ would physically return, of course, but only *after* the
Millennium concluded. (This belief is known as *postmillennialism*.) When
he returned then in power and glory, it would be to summon the living and
the dead to the Last Judgment. Having been evangelized by American missionaries, most then living on earth would promptly enter into their eternal
reward.

There was another tradition, however, that ran counter to this expansive
view. This other tradition, which I begin to explore in Chapter 4, "Narratives of the Night," rejects the notion that this earth could be anything other
than a place of testing, a dark vale of tears, and denies that any human effort
can ever reform humanity and create the Millennium. Not until the "midnight cry" is heard and Christ physically returns to purge this earth with
blood and fire could it be a Christian's genuine homeland. (Because Christ's
return must occur *before* the Millennium, this belief is called *premillennialism* and is shared by Christians who identify themselves as evangelicals,
dispensationalists, and fundamentalists.) Until then, "while the Lord tar-
ries," one's only true homeland is the spiritual realm of heaven, where the
weary are refreshed and the bereaved reunited with their lost loved ones.
This familiar theme of funeral homilies was the message of countless tracts,
including John Bunyan's allegory *Pilgrim's Progress*. While they describe this
otherworldly homeland in terms of light and peace, blossoms and music,
premillennialists look upon the earthly realm as a nightscape of unnatural

vices that richly merits the carnage, plagues, and conflagrations that God will visit upon it for seven years before the battle of Armageddon. The prospect of the Second Coming does not worry these believers, because most of them maintain that God will rescue them in the Rapture before the tribulation sets in. The thought of the fiery purging of the earth and the dispatching of the worldly-wise to eternal torment is, for them, a source of positive consolation.

Not too surprisingly, many of their Christian brethren—*nominally* Christian, premillennialists might say—take scant solace from this prospect, preferring instead to visualize the arrival of their Messiah not as the implacable judge of the Second Coming, but as the little prince of peace. To conclude this chapter, devoted to America's fascination with apocalyptic images, I note several annual festivals that serve to mask those end-time images and thereby mitigate their terror. The "traditional" Christmas, a narrative of the night that apocalypse-expectant Christians have always inveighed against, substitutes end-of-the-year merriment for end-of-the-world mindfulness. The Americanized myth of Santa Claus has gone even further: by concealing the figure of the grim avenger behind that of the jolly giver of goodies, it has converted an article of faith into a mere children's fable. Other carnivalesque seasonal festivals and ceremonies, too, elide the horrors of the tribulation and betoken the classless leisure of the Millennium.

In Chapter 5, "Abduction Narratives," I shift my focus from the terrors of end-time rhetoric to the more structured scenario that Christians understand as the Redemption, literally a "buying back" of an abducted person. The myth of a celestial hero who struggles against a monstrous villain in order to save his favored ones is an ancient story that, in America, has been updated in many ingenious ways. Science fiction projected this scenario into the distant future, but Christian futurists (both minor cultists and major televangelists) projected it into the very *near* future, retrofitting its supernatural weaponry with nuclear and space-age technology. Since 1945 the well-warranted fear of nuclear war has inspired innumerable escape scenarios, not only within established religions but also on and beyond their fringes, where visionaries rose up announcing the imminent arrival of extraterrestrials. Like Bible-wielding preachers who assure their congregations that both devils and angels will soon descend to earth, these New Age prophets warn that space aliens might either be evil abductors or compassionate saviors. Both Christian and New Age rapturists, yearning to take permanent flight from this doomed planet, thus weave their end-time narratives out of the same biblical skein and have more in common with one another than they readily admit.

I end this chapter by exploring some culturally significant American abduction/redemption narratives and point out that, like the myths of curses and blessings derived from Genesis, these narratives also dull the guilt that the beneficiaries of the fruits of raw aggression sometimes feel, thereby legitimating the Euro-American conquest of North America. By celebrating the virtuous victimhood of white Americans, these narratives, beginning with that of Mary Rowlandson, have diverted attention from the institutionalized mass abduction and enslavement of Native Americans and Africans from 1637 to 1865. They have also been used to characterize the status of American prisoners in foreign war zones.

The verb "to redeem" not only means to pay *for* the freedom of an abductee—it can also mean to pay *back* the abductor with retributive justice. As I go on to suggest in Chapter 6, "Homeland Nostalgia and Holy War," Americans who long for an avenger to appear envision a future that reinstates a past associated in their mind with righteous, wise, and heroic men. The process of human degeneration can stop, they believe, but only when a strict, godly government is put in place. This view of historical process they derive, directly or indirectly, from the Old Testament prophets and the prophetic writings in the New Testament, especially Revelation. The prophets, most of whom wrote after the fall of Judah to Babylon in 587 BC, never relinquished their vision of a restored kingship and a regathered Twelve Tribes that would someday reestablish the Law of Moses over the entire land that God had promised to Abraham. This orientation has inspired a number of American nostalgic attitudes, many of which indicate a communal resentment against what they perceive as a governing elite that does not share their own cultural values. Among these attitudes, I cite an idealization of rural life, a disdain for the city, a tendency to fortify the home from outsiders as though it could be a self-sufficient castle, and a longing for a homogeneous society, a racially pure, theocratic kingdom instead of a modern nation. At this point I discuss the emergence of a form of postmillennialism called Dominion Theology and assess its use in neoconservative imperialism.

Such American nostalgias have generated a number of diverse ethnic myths. One of them has it that the Nordic peoples are the Lost Tribes of Israel and that the present-day Jews are impostors. A related myth maintains that the white race is the true seed of Adam, that Jews are descendants of Eve and Satan, and that all other races are subhuman. According to this narrative, no sooner had the children of Adam found their final homeland in America than "Satan's Seed," the Jews, saw their opportunity to frustrate God's will. They first brought African slaves to America and then, in the nineteenth century, agitated to free them in order someday to destroy the Adamites' racial purity through miscegenation. As though to prove that myths of racial supremacy come in all colors, several separatist groups have arisen that preach that the only true Israelites today are African Americans. As such movements indicate, a little biblical knowledge is a dangerous thing: not only is membership in God's true, racially pure Chosen People a seductive recruiting gimmick, but so also are the uniforms and firearms that usually come with this membership.

Chapter 6 concludes with a brief look at a politically influential movement with a nostalgia of truly biblical proportions. It calls itself Christian Zionism and is led by a number of premillennialist evangelists who follow an interpretation of biblical prophecy known as dispensationalism. This movement supports the Israeli Far Right in its quest to ethnically cleanse the state of Israel and, by force of arms, to expand its borders to that of David's kingdom three thousand years ago. According to what they call God's "prophetic time table," only when the Twelve Tribes are regathered in their historical homeland and 144,000 of them accept Jesus as the Messiah will the tribulation commence. What happens to the rest of the Jews and indeed to all humanity when the final war of good against evil explodes in the Middle East? That will be for God to decide. As for the true believers, each will rise upward into bliss, their mission on earth completed.

New Agers are not the only non-Christians to construct their worldview out of biblical materials. Atheists, agnostics, deists—American secularists of every persuasion have regarded the Bible as a useful source of imagery and rhetoric. In Chapter 7, "Secular Modernism, Biblical Style," I examine four secular narratives that emerged during the Enlightenment: the two that Lyotard discussed, which I term here the narratives of nature and of freedom, plus two others, the narratives of progress and of judgment (the judicial system). For each narrative, I indicate the specific biblical master-narrative that authorizes it within American culture. In a literate era, when observable facts are foregrounded and issues are publicly debated, all such narratives have best operated in the background as ways to popularize ideas. Inserted in novels, poems, and essays, these narratives require a willing suspension of disbelief, but in a *post*literate, no-longer-modern era, in which disbelief in official "talking points" is deemed unpatriotic, narrative can be overtly presented as the simple truth. When this happens, *narrative becomes lie.*

The book concludes with several observations on Plato's myth of metals, a passage of ideological significance to neoconservatives. As told in the *Republic,* this scheme aimed to persuade the citizens of a state that the land in which they made their home was actually their mother, who, having assigned them one of four immutable classes and birthed them from her earthy bowels, henceforth forever claimed their absolute loyalty. Of course, this homeland myth was a lie. Yet as Socrates argued, it was a "noble lie," because it was a means to two good ends: it made citizens content with their social class, and it inspired a willingness to fight and die for the state. As the political philosopher Leo Strauss taught two generations of neoconservative thinkers, a government must propagate lies like this if it is to maintain public order. Only an intellectual elite is able to accept the reality that life has no transcendent meaning. Only they, like Plato's philosopher kings, can gaze directly into the wordless void. For the rest, there must be government-sponsored mythology.

As these chapter summaries suggest, this book has drawn information and inspiration from a wide range of sources. Apart from my references to them in text, notes, and bibliography, I ought to single out for acknowledgement several of those persons whose work I found especially helpful: Ernest Lee Tuveson, whose *Redeemer Nation* first revealed to me the religious pretensions of American exceptionalism; Paul Boyer, whose *When Time Shall Be No More* broadly updated Tuveson's book; Rev. Stephen Sizer for his Internet-posted analyses of Hal Lindsey's *oeuvre;* Rev. Barry Lynn, founder of Americans United for the Separation of Church and State, for his efforts to preserve religious and political freedoms by documenting the attempts of those who would blur the distinctions between sectarian and secular institutions; Shadia Drury, for venturing into the cave of Straussian political philosophy and training light into some of its darker recesses; Fr. Walter Ong, whose concept of secondary orality helped explain for me the function of myth in postliterate politics; George Lakoff, for demonstrating how conceptual metaphors, operating at the level that Fredric Jameson called the "political unconscious," can be manipulated to frame and constrain political discourse; and Brooks Kraft, the prize-winning photographer, who, in 2000, was present and precisely positioned in that Council Bluffs, Iowa, church to snap the picture that adorns the dust jacket of this book.

I also want to thank the scholars whom Penn State Press chose to review my manuscript. I am especially grateful to Jacqueline Bacon for her careful attention to the text and for reminding me that not all American Christians are social conservatives. In addition, I wish to thank Laura Reed-Morrisson for the insightful diligence with which she prepared my manuscript for publication.

Finally, I want to acknowledge my indebtedness to my neighbors in Pine Bush, New York, from whom and with whom I have learned the meaning of community; to Scott Marshall for his help in designing my diagrams and in overcoming my natural tendency to misunderestimate the monstrousness of the "New American Century"; to Susan Drucker-Brown of the Department of Anthropology, Cambridge University, who has encouraged me over the years in ventures like this; and to her sister, Emily, my wife, to whom this book is dedicated.

1

HOMELAND AND ITS DISCONTENTS

In the autumn of 2001, Americans began to hear their country referred to as the "homeland," a compound noun linked to other nouns such as "security" and "defense." "Homeland" was not a new word, of course, but after the devastating attacks on New York City and Washington, D.C., it seemed to connote meanings new to most of us—vulnerability, fear of strangers, retrenchment, territorial fortification. At the same time, the phrase "God bless America," which orators had long used as a mere perfunctory coda, took on a broad range of overtones, from defiance and reassurance to anxiety and supplication. As the months passed, words such as "home," "land," and "blessing" began to reveal some of the other concealed meanings that four centuries of Anglo-American history had packed into them.

Compounding a Problem

"Home" has a narrower meaning in American English than in British English. In Britain, the "home secretary," for example, attends to domestic (as distinct from foreign) affairs, and "home counties" means those shires bordering London. The American word "home," however, has as its primary meaning the house in which one lives. Only in its 1928 supplement did the Oxford English Dictionary, in its entry for "home," acknowledge this usage: "In U.S. and Canada, ['home' is] freq. used to designate a private house or residence merely as a building." Of course, the word connotes much more, but these notions of familial and communal protectiveness all seem to converge within the walls of a house or apartment. "Land," on the other hand, connotes a broad geographical and governmental entity and is roughly synonymous with "country." Thus, when Americans in the past used the words "home" and "land" in a single sentence, each word preserved its separate meaning.[1] In America's national anthem, "The Star-Spangled Banner," the phrase "the *land* of the free and the *home* of the brave" refers to two complementary, yet distinct, concepts and implies that during the British bombardment of Fort McHenry (September 13–14, 1814), the bravery of the local Baltimoreans had preserved the freedom of the entire nation.[2]

Like the "Star-Spangled Banner" (the anthem and the banner itself), most patriotic symbols strive to unite "home" and "land" by seeming to overcome the tensions that exist between the local and the national, the citizenry and the government. Patriotic songs provide ample evidence of this collective need. In 1906, during the second administration of Theodore Roosevelt, as American forces were beginning a three-year occupation of Cuba, George M. Cohan wrote the immensely popular song "You're a Grand Old Flag." In his one allusion to Francis Scott Key's poem, Cohan wrote: "You're the emblem of / The land I love, / The home of the free and the brave." The two concepts that Key had linked in juxtaposition, Cohan placed in apposition, so that once subsumed beneath this unifying emblem, "home" might become equated with "land."

The song most often heard following September 11, 2001, was neither the stately anthem nor the brassy show tune. It was the prayerful "God Bless America."

> God bless America,
> Land that I love.
> Stand beside her and guide her
> Through the night with a light from above.
> From the mountains, to the prairies,
> To the oceans white with foam,
> God bless America,
> My home, sweet home.

Irving Berlin wrote this song in 1918, one year after Cohan's "Over There" had encouraged American families to believe that their sons would quickly and painlessly subdue the Hun and two years after President Wilson had finally declared "The Star-Spangled Banner" the national anthem, a choice confirmed by Congress in 1931. Berlin's first two and last two lines put land and home together by a doubled apposition: America as *land*, and America as *home*. These lines also place the unified nation within the context of two clichés of American domestic piety. One was the popular embroidered sampler phrase "God Bless Our Home"; the other, also a sampler phrase, was "Home, Sweet Home."

As Berlin's audience would have understood, the latter phrase appeared on plaques and samplers because it brought to mind the best-loved sentimental parlor song of the nineteenth century, John Howard Payne's "Home, Sweet Home."[3] A comparison with Payne's lyric reveals how Berlin, when he wrote "God Bless America," had not only quoted it but also nationalized its meanings. "Home, Sweet Home" had been the very embodiment of domestic sentimentalism: "'Mid pleasures and palaces though we may roam, / Be it ever so humble there's no place like home!" The chorus to each of the stanzas reaffirms, "Home! home! sweet, sweet home! / There's no place like home."[4] Though the *grand monde* of the urbane and powerful may beckon, it can never satisfy our hearts as can the home we left behind. The next two lines explain why this is so: "A charm from the sky seems to hallow us there, / Which, seek through the world, is ne'er met with elsewhere." In popular lithographs of the time, this hallowing charm, a sign of divine blessing, was regularly depicted as a beam of light falling from an opening in the clouds and illuminating some scene of rural innocence. Berlin redirected this beam from a home to a land, from a domestic to a national benediction: "God bless America, land that I love / Stand beside her and guide her through the night with a light from above." Here America, personified as the woman Columbia, is the entire people that occupies the "land that I love / From the mountains, to the prairies, to the oceans white with foam." Thus unified, the people are guided "through the night with a light from above," much as the Israelites were guided through the wilderness by God's nightly pillar of fire.

The latter image connects with and draws energy from the widespread belief that America was indeed to be the new Promised Land toward which God continued to guide a New Israel, a persecuted people of faith. The history of America, accordingly, was not to be accounted for in economic, political, or social terms: nothing short of Divine Providence could explain its victories over the British Empire, its expansion in the face of Indian and Mexican resistance, and its rededication to union and liberty after its Civil War. Berlin's song, composed during the dark days of World War I and revived in 1938, as Americans watched Europe rearm, has ever since been caroled whenever the nation has faced the future with anxiety. When Kate Smith trumpeted it down through the decades from the Great Depression through the Vietnam War, "God Bless America" had a martial optimism to it, a sense of assurance, even a touch of triumphalism. Though the meaning of the first two lines seems to be "*May* God bless America" (as in the phrase "God bless you"), the meaning of the next two may easily be construed as a prayerful command addressed to the Deity: "Stand beside her." However we construe the grammatical mood of these verbs, command or wish, their context suggests another kind of mood, an apprehensive question: Might God someday choose *not* to bless America? Might he reclaim the land and send another people to possess it?[5]

As we see from this brief overview of patriotic sentiments, a national wish seems to link the words "home" and "land," but fusing these two words into a single compound noun poses a problem. This problematic wish is not unique to American culture. The separation of two terms has deep roots in human history and, as I will now propose, in human *pre*history.

A Problem with a Past

The deepest and oldest impressions that we carry with us we can barely recover, yet we know that upon these we began to build our personal view of ourselves, of others, and of the world that surrounds us all. This is also true when we turn our thoughts from our brief life span to the life span of our species.

Over a period of several million years, our ancestors extended the strength and skill of the human body by the invention of wood, stone, and bone tools. As they did so, their ability to feed, clothe, and shelter themselves improved, permitting them to live longer, have larger families, and survive in new and otherwise hostile environments. We are the beneficiaries of hard-won technical and cognitive skills—foraging and hunting, herding and farming, signaling and speaking. And because evolution is additive rather than substitutive, each older skill has remained for us to call up when we need it. With a little practice we can, for example, still learn to distinguish edible elderberries from poisonous pokeberries. We can hunt and fish. We can also easily slip into a prelinguistic mode, motion our intentions to a friend across a noisy city street, and even gesture gratuitously with a free hand when talking on the telephone.

Social structures had to have evolved, too, to keep pace with newly acquired skills. The course of social evolution is more speculative than that of technological evolution, certainly, but that it did occur is not in serious doubt. Most anthropologists assume that at some point in human evolution the extreme individualism inherited from primate societies, a behavior marked by aggressive displays and deceitful tactics, proved less successful than in-group trust and cooperation.[6] The individual survival instinct might be better served by sharing tasks and rewards than by struggling for dominance or by hoarding food and sex. Hunters working together could take down larger game with less expenditure of effort. The communal protection of childbearing women and the training of their offspring served to perpetuate this success.

The behavioral and cognitive traits that differentiate us from our primate cousins must have appeared at some point during those four million years of prehistory. Was the change gradual, as most Darwinians believe, or sudden, as some "catastrophe" theorists maintain? In either case, the earlier primate traits of aggressiveness and cunning have, in maladaptive forms, survived alongside the newer traits associated with tool making and language. The older and newer traits must have clashed from the beginnings of hominid speciation some million or so years ago, and, as we are all well aware, have clashed continually throughout the brief millennia of recorded history.[7]

Social evolution includes the evolution of religion, of course. In his introduction to *Varieties of Civil Religion,* which he co-edited with Phillip Hammond in 1980, Robert Bellah distinguished three phases in this evolution—the primitive, the archaic, and the historical. In the primitive phase of foraging and early agriculture, religion and politics were not differentiated into separate hierarchies. In the archaic phase, associated with the Bronze Age kingdoms of the second millennium BC, the figure of the divine king emerged.[8] The political and religious realms began to develop hierarchies. Their bases were separate, but they were firmly fused at the top in the person of the divine, or divinely appointed, ruler. A third phase, that of the "historical religions," emerged in the first millennium BC and continues down to the present. These religions promised direct access to the gods, unmediated by political authority, but they maintained a collaborative relationship with the secular state, to which they offered conditional legitimacy, receiving in turn conditional protection.[9]

While acknowledging that some aspects of the second (archaic) worldview have, from time to time, reappeared in the era of historical religions, Bellah did not consider the possibility that aspects of his *first* phase have also continued to operate. Even today, though we may survey the doings of nations, the rise and fall of scientific paradigms, the culture wars, and the clash of civilizations in our conscious thoughts, we still live out our physical lives well rooted in phase one of human social organization—the community. We do so whether we live in a small town, a suburb, or a city, and whether our local economy is privately or cooperatively managed. On the communal level, we require of our neighbors that they deal fairly with us in matters of life and property and that they assist us in our need. In return, we also allow that they have a right to demand the same behavior from us. Should we have disputes with any of them, we expect that at some point the community will intervene. We may also believe that unseen watchers monitor human behavior, rewarding and punishing individuals here or hereafter. Indeed, we may invoke these watchers in oaths to testify to our truthfulness.

Religion is the expression of the communal need for coherence. It creates a communion that, as the Latin noun *religio* implies, is both a bond that links and a restraint that binds separate individuals. The communal level has always been concerned with the individual—not with the individual's rights or well-being so much as his or her usefulness or danger to the community. This is the cultural level profoundly concerned with mores, or as we now phrase it, "appropriate behavior." Here, neighbors "look out for one another," and gossip is not only a major form of entertainment but also a means of generating shame for malefactors and cautionary tales for the young. Émile Durkheim put it well: "The only hearth at which we can warm ourselves morally is the hearth made by the company of our fellow men; the only moral forces with which we can nourish our own and increase them are those we get from others."[10]

Human communities of this sort, according to some estimates, may have existed for several *million* years already when—only a brief four or five thousand years ago—large, centralized, agriculture-based societies first appeared on the earth.[11] Today the original economy, that of hunter-gatherers, survives only in remote and forbidding terrain such as the Amazon basin, the Arctic, and the deserts of Australia and southern Africa. When inserted into the time line of human cultural development, agriculture and livestock raising have been a rather recent experiment. From their small beginnings some ten to fifteen thousand years ago, these activities have grown to claim the richest sectors of the biosphere and in the process have transformed humankind into the fallen Adam, driven him from the garden, and forced him to work the land to earn his bread by stoop labor and the sweat of his brow.[12] Those remaining societies that have not yet cut their forests down, or have no forests to cut, we have thought of as "arrested" in their development, as Arnold Toynbee put it—as dehumanized and brutish.[13] We have come to realize, however, that despite the harsh conditions in which they find themselves, they have retained a keen sense of communal relationship and an egalitarian ethos rarely found in agricultural economies. Dependent on one another, they have had to share information, work, risks, and rewards. Such societies, as Colin Turnbull pointed out, "frequently display those characteristics that we find so admirable in man: kindness, generosity, consideration, affection, honesty, hospitality, compassion, charity. . . . This sounds like a formidable list of virtues, but for the hunter-gatherer they are not. [They are rather] necessities of survival; without them [their] society would collapse."[14]

Agriculture can coexist with a hunting-gathering economy and help support a communal culture, but as soon as it dominates an economy, it requires guards and overseers. Walls are built to protect stored surpluses and those who rule over their distribution. Whenever and wherever that new level of social organization, government, is set in place, we have the moment that the old histories called the "dawn of civilization." (Nowadays, when outsiders impose this organization upon a people, current political analysts term the process "nation-building.") Boundaries are staked out and fortified; the concept of a land, as a fixed spatial entity, is established. At that point in evolutionary time, a new function is found for an old and unreconstructed personality type. A job opening appears that in the following basic form has been listed now for some five thousand years: "*Wanted:* an aggressive male of above average height; demanding respect, sensitive to a slight, and capable of intimidating others; secretive when necessary, suspicious of rivals; possessed of a resolute will and a strong sexual appetite." Of course, each ad would have to go on to list more specific requirements, for if only this boilerplate were published, we would not know whether the job opening were for a pharaoh, a Little League coach, a corporate CEO, a modern head of state, or an alpha male gorilla.[15]

With the emergence of agriculture-based kingdoms, the relation between the male who had once ruled through strength, aggressive displays, and cunning and the community that preserved the egalitarianism of hunter-gatherer culture was readjusted. Now at the governmental level, the privileged elite could indulge their regressive fantasies of domination while the officials of their court—administrators, scribes, priests, educators, and soldiery—could practice the collaborative skills that humankind had long found engrossing, if not always exhilarating. Cooperativeness proved more successful than strutting and bluster in the countryside and even in the court, but at the highest governmental level, it was the primeval alpha male behavior that became the dominant trait, and communal behavior the recessive.[16]

In this archaic phase, when agriculture first began converting the surface of the earth into real estate, religious rituals that had long been used on the communal level of family and clan to influence the beings that control the universe now needed to be raised to a national scale. In adapting these practices, it was of course to the advantage of the ruler and his literate elite to draw upon as many elements of local cult and myth as could be harmoniously accommodated.[17] Syncretic polytheism, perhaps the most conspicuous feature of archaic theology, may well have been a consequence of political expansion. Selected regional divinities could, for example, be adopted into the national pantheon by being declared members of a single divine family constituted through marriage and filiation.

The culture of kingship also called for the founding of sacred cities and houses of worship worthy of the gods and of the royal guardians of the sacred traditions. Because local rituals had always served to guide the moral interactions of interdependent individuals on the communal level, and because the vast majority of his subjects lived their lives at this level, a ruler needed to create the illusion that the conduct of the land (kingdom, empire) was governed by precisely the same principles as the home (neighborhood, region). Was not the monarch also an individual, a dutiful individual whom the god(s) had chosen to be "father of his land" and "shepherd of the people"?[18] And was he not obliged to protect his children, just as a shepherd protects his flocks from predators that skulk about the borders or infest the hinterlands? Once personified, the national government could then, through metaphor, be invested with moral agency.

Yet all such efforts to unify trade-related villages into a single kingdom using the religious traditions of the older communal culture were impeded by one simple, ineluctable fact: *the praxis of a nation contradicts the ethos of a village.* No entity motivated solely by self-interest and by a principle of sovereignty unconstrained by the judgment of peers can be said to act "morally." In this respect, nations resemble corporations, which, as Edward Coke memorably commented, "cannot commit treason, nor be outlawed, nor excommunicate[d], for they have no souls"—and, as Edward Thurlow added, having "neither bodies to be punished, nor souls to be condemned, they therefore do as they like."[19] Nations may form strategic alliances and within them establish codes of conduct, but so do competing robber bands and criminal syndicates. Honor among nations, as history testifies, is observed in the same spirit as honor among thieves. Nations exercise their sovereignty by war or its credible threat, and this "diplomacy by other means" brings with it the outlawry of plunder, enslavement, rape, and murder, those very behaviors that local communities are the most vulnerable to and therefore most rigorously prohibit. Communal religions envision gods that promote fertility and health, manage the economics of cyclic time, and requite individuals for their virtues or vices. National religions, on the other hand, must have additional divinities, warrior gods who wage war against alien gods, forge crafty alliances, and in the process manage the destiny of favored nations. The symbols of these gods are fittingly destructive—lightning, earthquake, volcanic eruption, flood, predatory beast, and carrion bird.

By the beginning of the first millennium BC, the peoples that bordered the Mediterranean had experienced a great growth in commerce and in such armaments as the war chariot and the iron weapon. Then, as more aggressive kingdoms spilled over into ever-wider empires, local populations that were not exterminated outright were absorbed or transplanted, their long-stable cultures shattered. Bronze and early Iron Age documents extol not only the righteousness and compassion of kings for their subjects but also their god-enjoined cruelty toward rebels and aliens.

Many of the lawgivers, philosophers, and religious leaders who appeared early in this era saw this social division and strove to overcome it by conceiving universal principles of justice. What would a righteous kingdom be like? they asked. Generation after generation, out of demoralized and restive populations there now arose persons who claimed to have access to beings whose power transcended that of this world's rulers. We are now most familiar with the prophets of the Hebrew Bible, but this movement was international in scope and comprised all manner of seers, shamans, sibyls, and mages, their new revelations each couched in the unforgotten cultural idiom of particular peoples, their master narratives or oral canon of myths.

The need of rulers, then and now, to deflect and channel this fundamental conflict is understandable. The more diverse the population, the greater the need for unifying symbols of moral authority. In a stable, homogeneous nation with a long-standing religious establishment, the distance between the governing elite and the yeomanry is spanned by hierarchical gradations that may seem organically evolved—but a culturally diverse population, the result of imperial conquest or open immigration, requires considerable social sensitivity and institutional engineering if it is to achieve any degree of harmony. In such stressful conditions, governing elites find it necessary to promote religious myths and rituals of sufficient generality that a sufficient percentage of the population may be willing to accept them.

Civil Religion—Some Internal Contradictions

It should come as no surprise that the conditions I have described over the last several paragraphs seem familiar to Americans. When asked whether the president can decide that, in the best interests of the nation, he can do something illegal, Richard Nixon answered, "Well, when the president does it, that means it is not illegal."[20] The clash between community-based traditional religion and government-sponsored religiosity outlasted the kingdoms and empires of antiquity and has continued in the nation-states and empires of the modern era. America is not uniquely troubled by the disparity between traditional values and governmental practices, but whatever it is that troubles the soul of the one and only global superpower ought now to be a matter of global concern.

From its very inception, the American republic has been a "nation with the soul of a church," as G. K. Chesterton observed.[21] But what kind of "church" has it been? Robert Bellah, who has been among those who have thought earliest and longest about the nature of America's churchly soul, has called it "civil religion," a sort of one-size-fits-all (or almost all) set of biblically styled beliefs concerning God and country.[22] If America is a nation with the soul of a civil-religious church, its soul is a generic one, compounded of innumerable separate churches. By constitutional law, the state must accommodate the free exercise of *all* religions. Immigration policies have been open enough to ensure that virtually all of the world's faiths are practiced here. Although some prohibit their members from participating in such rites of civil religion as the Pledge of Allegiance, oaths on the Bible, "traditional" Christmas, and observing Sunday as the Sabbath, most religious communities accept such behavior as an expression of "Americanism." Because the membership of every separate religion constitutes a minority, even the most powerful sects grudgingly recognize that they must tolerate every other sect.

Over time, the widening circle of American religion—which at first was restricted to several regionally separated Protestant sects—gradually enlarged to include all Protestant churches. The mid-nineteenth century saw the addition of Roman Catholics, and the circle closed on *Christian* America. By the mid-twentieth century, Judaism was invited to join, and America became a *Judeo-Christian* nation. As President Eisenhower then famously put it: "Our government makes no sense unless it is founded in a deeply felt religious faith—and I don't care what it is."[23] Finally, by the end of that century, religionists of non-European origin—such as Muslims and Buddhists—were uneasily admitted, and Americans were pronounced to be a *people of faith.*

It has been America's religious diversity that has necessitated the construction of a civil religion to express its national religiosity. Civil religion requires toleration of diversity, but toleration, after all, is neither easy nor unconditional: it requires delicate, ever-readjusted calibrations of goodwill, condescension, and forbearance. For their part, those who represent the governmental level (or whose economic interests are advantageously affected by governmental policies) are intent on representing those policies as expressions of the ethical ideals that prevail on the communal level.

Though, as Edward Thurlow said of corporations, a nation does as it likes, under a written constitution it is obliged to persuade its people that it does as *they* like. The meaningfulness of that compound noun "homeland" can be maintained only so long as the values of the *home* appear reflected in the laws of the *land*. Any clash between the moral code that operates on the communal level and the expedient policies of the nation must be mitigated by cultural spin, that is, by recourse to governmental narratives, newly minted myths that seem to accord with the myths that undergird the communal. In this way, social causes deemed disruptive to powerful economic interests—such as collective bargaining, expanded health care, environmental safeguards, and even public education—can be locally discredited. Even policies as abhorrent to communal ethics as slavery, expropriation of land, and genocide have been successfully promoted once an appropriate biblical text could be found and quoted.

Civil religion has evolved to cope with the sort of discontents that Sigmund Freud recognized as endemic to modern nations. In the 1930s, as fascism was rising in Europe, Freud returned to a topic he had pondered earlier in his career: social sanity and its alternatives.[24] In *Civilization and Its Discontents,* he associated *Kultur* ("civilization" in both the Riviere and Strachey translations) with reason, humane social attitudes, and technical ingenuity, traits to which we owe those modern comforts and conveniences that distinguish the civilized from the savage. The fact that *Kultur* is accompanied by *dis*comfort (*Unbehagen,* translated as "discontents") led him to ask if there might be such a thing as a cultural neurosis.[25]

According to Freud, civilization seeks to impose from above an altruistic ideal upon humans, who, left to themselves, are fundamentally aggressive and pleasure-seeking animals. He illustrates this view of the cultural id run amok by remarking on the atrocities committed by the Huns, Mongols, Crusaders, and most recently by those fighting in the First World War. In conditions of social chaos, unrestrained by law, individuals quickly revert to savagery. While this is certainly true, Freud also seems to credit national leaders and cultural elites with an interest in maintaining moral behavior.[26] He ignores the fact that *nations* are incapable of altruism, that they bully and humiliate other nations and encourage, indeed command, their citizens to perform acts of cruelty against designated neighbors and strangers. The Huns, Mongols, Crusaders, and twentieth-century European belligerents constituted nations, not neighborhoods.

Because each of us now exists in the two social domains that I have called the communal and the governmental—the *home* and the *land*—and because these two often conflict, most of us internalize this conflict. Citizens, for example, are regularly asked to support with taxes or even with their children's lives governmental policies that, if acted out on the street corner outside the window, would be condemned as criminal outrages. The sociologist Leon Festinger addressed this internalized conflict in his *Theory of Cognitive Dissonance* (1957). His basic hypotheses were: "1. The existence of dissonance, being psychologically uncomfortable, will motivate the person to try to reduce the dissonance and achieve consonance. 2. When dissonance is present, in addition to trying to reduce it, the person will actively avoid situations and information which would likely increase the dissonance."[27] Though it is similar in these respects to hunger, frustration, or disequilibrium, cognitive dissonance has origins that are neither somatic nor unconscious. Since by "cognition" Festinger meant "any knowledge, opinion, or belief about the environment, about oneself, or about one's behavior," cognitive dissonance is an inner conflict on the conscious level, usually triggered by societally transmitted information.[28]

The relevance of Festinger's theory to cultural issues becomes apparent when it is applied to a given group's attempts to assimilate two very different worldviews together with their associated narratives. This happens, for example, when children of immigrants try to harmonize their parents' beliefs and traditions with those of their culturally indigenous peers. This also happens when, for practical reasons, a population adopts certain approaches to problem solving that clash with traditional methods—as when Western concepts of infectious disease conflict with beliefs in black magic, for example. In both these instances, cognitive dissonance provokes cultural responses aimed at reducing or avoiding the uncomfortable conflict. In the immigrant situation, children may either reject their parents' traditions altogether, sequester themselves in an immigrant enclave, or, assuming a "hyphenated" identity, attempt to live in both worlds at once. In the case of the population new to Western medicine, persons may similarly choose to adopt it, reject it, or forge a compromise position.

Down through the centuries, certain religious groups and geographically sequestered peoples have thus succeeded in reducing this oldest and most profound of all cognitive dissonances, the clash between communal values and the authority of the state by attempting to ignore the latter. To the extent, however, that we participate in both social levels and claim, as it were, dual citizenship, we suffer the collective neurosis that Freud sought to identify. To mitigate this neurotic dissonance we require a special form of therapy: mythology, the oldest talking cure.

The Uses of Heroic Myth

Figure 1 depicts three areas of human organization as they are variously affected by two sets of instincts: the *egoistic,* which is concerned with individual survival and gratification, and the *altruistic,* which is concerned with the survival and well-being of the group. Though they both serve the purposes of human evolution, they do so in opposition to one another. The fundamental condition we share with all others, as this diagram shows, is individuality—each of us having, or rather being, a separate central nervous system accumulating its own memories and its own strategies for dealing with the world outside our skin. In addition to this inner realm, we belong to a social body, a communal level that includes family, friends, neighbors, and co-workers, the level at which the group oversees the behavior of individuals. Growing out from this is the government, the level at which a certain few individuals oversee the behavior of groups.

The Freudian model seems generally adequate to explain the conflict within the individual between the two sets of instincts. An internalized monitor (the superego), representing the will of society as expressed by parents, teachers, and other communal authorities, watches, advises, and sometimes punishes the self (the ego) for overindulging its desire for pleasure (the id). According to Freud, neurosis is caused by various extreme imbalances, an overassertive superego producing anxiety and, when the superego is underassertive, an overassertive id producing narcissism.[29] As the equally large lower arrows in the diagram suggest, the influence of superego and id is normally more or less equal and is kept in balance by conscious and unconscious speech. This "inner speech," monologic when it is advice from the superego, becomes dialogic when the ego responds, interceding for the id.[30] A dissonance, which we might term "sub-cognitive" or "preconscious," produces the sorts of *Unbehagen* that result in anxiety and wish-fulfillment dreams.

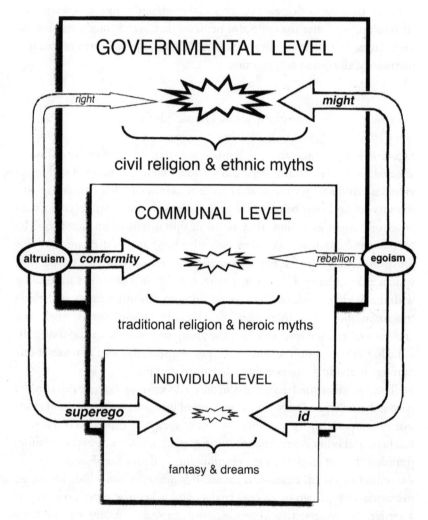

Figure 1.　Egoism and altruism in areas of human organization

My main concern, however, is with the upper two levels. On the communal level, the dominant factor (indicated by the thicker arrow) is the behavioral code that we designate as morality. In transforming the primate pack, long tyrannized by the alpha male, into a cooperative clan of families that uses speech, protects pregnant females, rears young together, and gathers food in common, human evolution favored those individuals who were able to maintain inherited beliefs and join with others to perform traditional rituals. We each recapitulate this transition as we move from childhood to adulthood. All children, presumably then as now, express the need to separate from parents and test the forbearance of the community: for them, the extended period of education is a gradual initiation into the communal level. Only a few preserve their behavioral independence into adulthood (hence the thinness of the egoistic arrow). Most of these, then and now, have fared poorly with the group and some have become outcasts, but others have supplied innovative elements vital to the survival of what would otherwise be a conformist society.[31]

Heroic myths have always moderated the conflict between the consensus-seeking group and the self-reliant individual, thereby allowing community members to imagine in safety their own repressed instinct to break the rules and dominate others. That is to say, the human tendency both to admire and fear transgression (and, conversely, to respect and despise obedience) creates a cognitive dissonance that certain narratives serve to reduce.

These narratives are hard to forget because they so strikingly contrast with standard behavior. They typically tell the story of a young man who grows up unmindful of the advice of his elders. Too headstrong to fear either the community or the dangers that lurk beyond it, a hero looks for and causes trouble. Even when he is *in* the community, he is not *of* the community. From a communal perspective, a hero seems so unlike his parents and siblings that some say his true parents must have abandoned him and that he was suckled by some wild thing. Or perhaps some god sired him, for anyone who does not share communal values (as Aristotle said in reference to individuals not belonging to a *polis*) must either be part-beast or part-god. This confrontation of a strong, independent person with his or her community has been a perennial theme of epic and tragedy. In Greek tragedy, the clash of id and superego was visually represented by the juxtaposition of a protagonist on the raised stage with the chorus in the orchestra.

Many of the world's traditional religions—Judaism, Christianity, and Islam, for example—were founded by men who are now remembered as heroes. Claiming a special relationship with a divine being, each stood out in opposition to the prevailing mores of his community and, except for Moses, promised to individuals an otherworldly state of bliss in return for curbing their selfish desires in this world. The belief systems and practices associated with these heroes reinvigorated the ethos of the community and reconfigured its relation to the heroic individual, now defined as the self-abnegating servant of God. Traditional religions thus built on heroic myths to reduce the cognitive dissonance generated by the clash of communal security with individual agency.

The old, communal conflict between altruism and egoism is transposed to a new key when it reemerges on the governmental level. Though the influence of communal ethos is diminished at this level, it is usually powerful enough to demand a degree of official respect. The stakes are high for all participants, but especially for those who are entrusted with the task of preaching the values associated with *home* to those who control the resources of the *land*. Communal principles are antithetical to the will of the sovereign state, but at this level they must not *seem* to be. Issues of right and might must be negotiated through quiet diplomacy. Failure to mitigate the clash between ethos and praxis would subject the populace to an intolerable cognitive dissonance and undermine all authority. In response to the criticism of communal spokespersons, government performs rites of civil religion and does so by promulgating a uniquely politic genre of narrative, a variety of the talking cure that I will call "ethnic myth."

The Uses of Ethnic Myth

Once we turn our attention to the institution of government, one of the first things we notice is that its very existence presupposes a partitioning of the communal level into groups variously defined—regionally, ethnically, religiously, and so forth.[32] Because such arrangements grow slowly and in response to real needs, it would be wrong to suppose that government began as a cabal of clever egoists. As agricultural and herding techniques improved and populations increased and consolidated, older ways of communal management became disrupted and formerly separate groups found themselves competing for territory. Disputes within an economy demand arbitration, so government was more likely a consequence than a conspiracy. But having acknowledged that, I must add that while governing may be a dirty job and somebody has to do it, the more clever, more egoistic, and more conspiratorial seem to apply for leadership positions.[33] Whatever its origins and howsoever its administrators perceive their role—as conciliating or exploiting differences—one thing is certain: no government can exist without these divisions. If it succeeds in persuading its people that these divisions are natural and immutable, it justifies its own authority as likewise natural and immutable. To this end it will cite references in communal religious traditions to argue that the gods had planned that distinct groups should exist and that certain of them (those currently in charge), being patently superior, have always been called upon to assume the obligations of noblesse. Once the egoistic ideal of the alpha male is reconstituted as a corporate entity, all individuals may be invited to partake vicariously in its charisma through patriotic pride.

This patriotic homeland ideal is, however, difficult to maintain on the individual level. As a member both of a nation and of a local community, each individual experiences the conflict between altruism and egoism on the communal and the governmental levels. That alone would account for considerable "discontent" in any "civilization," but these dissonances are further exacerbated by the fact that the strategies used to reduce the conflict on one level cannot be applied to the conflict on the other level. As difficult as it is for the communal group to persuade headstrong individuals to conform to its code of conduct, it is virtually impossible to constrain governmental authority. Consequently, its spokespersons must either content themselves by making moral compromises or choose to see no evil by gazing heavenward.

Though communal spokespersons can operate as a superego of sorts, a conscience that rulers cannot entirely afford to ignore, the latter do have a tactical response. Without altering their underlying policies, they can reduce dissonance between the moral claims of the community and their own pragmatic claims by borrowing from the community the talking cure of narrative, enhanced in this case by the promotional powers of the state. Through one narrative or another, the dignity of public office must be extolled, the axiom that power corrupts must only be applied to other nations' leaders, and the overriding notion that this government expresses the highest moral consensus of its people must be promulgated. In this enterprise, to paraphrase La Rochefoucauld, hypocrisy becomes the tribute that egoism pays to altruism.

Just as heroic myths have always served to harmonize the conflicted feelings the group harbors toward individuals, ethnic myths do so for the conflicted feelings that governing individuals have toward groups.[34] These latter narratives, which purport to account for the origins of "peoples" broadly defined, are used to justify the stance taken toward them by the government—

to explain why some groups are held back and why other groups deserve their benefits, but only so long as they agree to block those other groups from attaining similar benefits. When managed correctly, one set of ethnic myths can be used to stoke domestic divisions in times of peace; in times of war, when national unity is required, these myths may be damped while another set is fired up to demonize foreign populations.

Each level of religion selects, from an array of available narratives, those that best suit its current thematic needs. Civil religion builds upon ethnic myths in some of the same ways that traditional religion builds on heroic myths. Though its preferred narratives will come from traditional religion, pre-inscribed as they are with the moral authority of the community, a nascent civil religion will supplement them with historical narratives that it will proceed to reinterpret in order to prove that certain groups are wise, heroic, and patriotic, others are benighted and need to be converted, and yet others are innately vicious and need to be excluded or exterminated. Government must first unearth, cull, and shape ethnic myths and then rebury them to form the foundation upon which to construct its civil religion.

Unlike traditional religions, however, civil religion has the capacity to revise its "doctrines" and "rituals" quickly in response to emergent circumstances. In September 2001 the *volte-face* performed by the Bush administration—from isolationism and Christian-Right pieties to internationalism and the praise of "true Islamic values"—should have surprised no one. As Constantine the Great proved, the civil-religious conversion experience may be as sudden as it is superficial.

The discontents that provoke mythmakers to elaborate a civil religion are, as I have suggested, the cognitive dissonances generated by the clash of communal morality with governmental expediency. For example, suppose that a nation in need of certain raw materials sends its armies into its neighbor's territory, occupies it, and takes these goods. On the communal level, such an act would be the punishable crime of theft. On the governmental level, a civil-religious justification of this action might use one or several of the following premises: (1) God has made us stewards of his world; (2) we are therefore both innocent and invincible; (3) we have been provoked by a group who has made a pact with the devil; or (4) we have been invited by long-suffering groups who are seeking freedom to learn our superior way of life and to practice our religion. Absurd as these justifications sound, when artfully fabricated they have rarely failed, in the short term at least, to salve the communal conscience. A government that uses these premises must never spell them out as I have done, but it must be sure to imply the predatory instinct behind its guileless demeanor. A nation's statesmen, when they sport their sheep's clothing, must always do so with a certain lupine flair.

A second set of discontents arises when this attempted reconciliation of might with right reveals itself to be a sham. As soon as one or two of these tacitly accepted, myth-based premises proves false—when, for example, the invaders are repulsed, the subdued populace refuses to be converted, or the cost in lives and suffering undermines domestic morale—the radical incompatibility of the governmental and communal levels is again exposed. Out of the disillusionment that thereupon ensues, new cults may arise by a kind of spontaneous generation, and new myths may be cobbled together from old ones. Finally, to restore social equilibrium, a seemingly new civil religion must be inaugurated.

When a nation feels immediately endangered by external forces, however, these dissonances are likely to be ignored. The proclaimed interests of the governmental and the communal appear to converge in the overriding concept variously called the "motherland," the "fatherland," and the "homeland." When this happens, ethnic and heroic myths embed themselves in one another: ethnic stereotypes color personal accounts of bravery, while heroic episodes highlight xenophobic oratory. At such times, the merely local hero—the high school athlete, the risk-taker, the "hell-raiser"—may apply for a higher status. By entering military service, even the most wayward of such persons can redeem himself in the eyes of the community by committing himself to its two highest ideals, obedience and altruism. If he can be fully convinced that he is fighting not for the advantage of those that govern the "land," but to defend his communal "home," he can experience the deep, addictive passion of those who welcome the necessity of death, of killing and being killed, in order to preserve the lives of their kin. In the view of the community, this hero is the willing savior of his people. When the government identifies its own policies with this communal ideal, it portrays its own motives as likewise *salvational.*

When the first Bush administration tried to mobilize public opinion in 1990 to turn back Iraq's invasion of Kuwait, it packaged its appeal in mythic terms that the linguist George Lakoff then characterized as the "Fairy Tale of the Just War." In his article "Metaphor and War," posted on the Internet in January 1991, he explained how the metaphors that the hawks were then using had acquired resonance by evoking two versions of an ancient narrative featuring three characters: a victim, a villain, and a hero.

One version was the self-defense scenario: Iraq is the villain, the United States is the hero, the United States and other industrialized nations are victims, and the crime is a death threat (that is, a threat to economic health). The alternative scenario, he said, was the rescue scenario: "Iraq is villain, the US is hero, Kuwait is victim, the crime is kidnap and rape. The American people could not accept the Self-Defense scenario, since it amounted to trading lives for oil. The day after a national poll that asked Americans what they would be willing to go to war for, the administration settled on the Rescue Scenario, which was readily embraced by the public, media, and Congress as providing moral justification for going to war."[35] The self-defense scenario put the U.S. military in the role of heroes saving a victimized America: a madman had a "stranglehold" on its economy by threatening to cut off its "lifeline" to vital energy. Though this approach lacked sufficient appeal, it was not, however, repudiated. It became a subtext, a fallback justification, while the rescue scenario was brought center stage. (I will return to this theme in Chapter 5 and to Lakoff's analysis of political metaphor in Chapters 3 and 7.)

During the buildup to Gulf War II, George W. Bush's advisers floated a similar pair of scenarios. They revised the rescue scenario, this time making the victim the Iraqi people—many of whom, it was said, had been *literally* kidnapped and raped by Saddam Hussein's thugs. Americans were urged to support the liberation of this oppressed people, the sort of selfless action that most Americans believe has always been their historical duty to perform. The war was accordingly dubbed Operation Iraqi Freedom. But polls soon indicated that Americans were less moved by the prospect of freedom for Iraq than of freedom *from* Iraq and from those weapons of mass destruction (WMD) that they were told Saddam had secreted and would soon deliver to a resurgent al Qaeda. In the summer of 2002, spokesmen such as Vice President Dick Cheney began assuring Americans that the connection between the 9/11 hijackers and the Iraqi government was indisputable. The government was so successful in this "public diplomacy" that from fall 2002 through the war in the spring of 2003, an average of two-thirds of Americans polled believed that this connection was a fact that justified preemptive action.[36] During the 2004 presidential campaign and through most of 2005, polls indicated that a majority of Americans still believed that this connection existed and justified the invasion of Iraq.[37]

The scenarios that both Bush administrations used in their respective Gulf wars may, as Lakoff remarked, be read in terms of a fairy tale, but only if we understand that this tale is very culturally specific. American civil religion draws upon a historical narrative that portrays Americans as a good and invincible people, peculiarly blessed by God with the most perfect system of government on earth, a nation so universally admired that it is opposed only by evil and envious forces intent on enslaving mankind. This ethnic mythology, which heroizes the defenders of this exceptional nation, has over the years demonized, in different ways and for different reasons, a series of Others that has included Native Americans, enslaved Africans, Chinese and Mexican laborers, Catholics, Jews, Communists, and (most recently) Muslims.

Now, it may be objected that the current Bush administration has taken pains to distinguish mainstream Islam from "Islamist" extremism and, consequently, that a full-blown ethnic mythology—i.e., one that heroizes the governmental leadership and its supporters while broadly demonizing its opponents—is not fully in place. There do exist, however, subtle means to convey unsubtle concepts. Although every American president plays a central role in our civil religion, as a sort of *pontifex maximus* or, as Bellah said, our national theologian, he is not alone. In his entourage are self-appointed community spokesmen who speak out on political matters whenever they feel the Holy Spirit prompts them. Clergymen close to the Republican leadership, such as Jerry Falwell, Pat Robertson, and Franklin Graham, have proclaimed Islam to be an "evil religion" without incurring more than a mild presidential rebuke, if any.[38] The simple implication, which has not been lost on the Islamic world, is that these men have been licensed to voice certain sentiments with which the administration concurs but is, for the time being, too diplomatic to espouse publicly.

2

BIBLICAL TIME AND THE FULL NARRATIVE CYCLE

"Home" and "land" are concepts that we visualize in three-dimensional space. But before we can continue to explore the American homeland, we need to consider its fourth dimension: time. As St. Augustine remarked, "Time? If no one asks me, I know it, but once I have to explain it, I don't know it."[1] Every culture's members "know" what time is, but when asked to explain it, they are left with little more than analogies of movement.

In one of these analogies, the observer is in motion: he walks out of the past into the future, and as he does so, the future unfolds, present moment by present moment. Another analogy, one that is deeply embedded in the Bible, represents time as the moving force and events as literally following one behind the other from the future into the past. The observer can choose to turn his gaze toward the future or toward the past, but, as long as he lives, he remains fixed in the present while time—with its eddying, swirling changes—streams past him until, finally, he too is swept backward into the past. Let us call this the river metaphor. The present, the zone that separates the past from the future, is visualized as a space through which time moves. As the landscape through which the road winds or the river flows, it is distinguished by the stable objects *present* to the observer in an otherwise shifting vista.

Governmental leaders claim the present, the extended spatial here and now, but they must also embrace the full temporal range. Each successful American president has felt it necessary to prove himself connected to the past by following the traditions of his illustrious forebears while leading his people into the future. He must therefore appear to view history as though through the eyes of a biblically justified community, praising the values of a glorious past, decrying present moral failures, and offering to lead the populace onward to a better future. By directing his people's gaze backward into an idealized past, he may succeed in treating the discontents I spoke of in the last chapter. The reason why we feel dissatisfied and anxious now, he will in effect argue, is not because the governmental and communal levels are morally at odds, but because this *particular* era, compared with the past, is culturally degenerate.

Every American president, or presidential candidate, has had to convince his nation that he is capable of this Janus-faced performance and do so in a properly biblical manner. Once he convinces the electorate that it lives in a time of moral depravity within and mortal danger without, he can then offer himself as the Moses to lead his people into their future. To understand how presidents have used the concepts of past, present, and future, we will need to appreciate how a biblically based culture charges these abstract categories with specific values. To do so, we will need to delve a bit into the ancient documents and the historical movements they inspired.

Keeping Time in the Shadow of Empire

Judaism is imbued with a sense of temporal becoming, and Hellenic culture with the concept of cosmic being. According to this widely accepted contrast, we in the West inherit from biblical prophets our belief that history is a meaningful process of change, and from classical philosophers our belief that the universe is an intelligible structure of elements. While these generalizations may be true, the assumption that each culture arrived at its distinct orientation by simply unfolding some inward essence is open to debate.

If we understand time to be a relation between a retreating past and an approaching future and space as a relation among objects in the here and now, the distinction becomes one of absence (and lack) and presence (and plenitude). Translated into political terms, a culture focused on the past and the future is likely to be one that has been deprived of power over territorial space, whereas a present-oriented culture may be one that strives to maintain its power over space despite the forces that, over time, inevitably undermine it. If the Jews developed a belief in temporal dynamism, it was perhaps due to the fact that for some 2,600 years since the Babylonian captivity (sixth century BC), the Israelite nation has been reduced to a community scattered within a series of empires and nation-states. If the Greeks and Romans developed a concept of spatial connectedness, it may well have been due to the historical fact that for six centuries, from the fall of Persia to the rise of Byzantium, these northerners successfully asserted control over a band of formerly independent kingdoms from Gibraltar to the Persian Gulf. The Greco-Roman civilization assumed, moreover, a governmental character, while Judaism came to represent the claims of community. The business of government is always spatial control in the here and now. Community, if it contests the legitimacy of this control, will always define its own legitimacy with reference to a glorious past and a glorious future of governmental power.

As a set of books that reveal glimpses of God's own historical agenda, the Bible also preserves an interesting portrayal of the three phases of religious evolution described by Robert Bellah. The first eight books of the Bible deal with what Bellah called the primitive phase. Though kingdoms already existed (Egypt and Chaldea, for example), the twelve federated tribes of Israel on which these books focus were not yet consolidated. These twelve tribes—linked by their god, Yahweh, and by legends of a common ancestor, Israel—settled separate portions of Canaan. Despite their independence, these tribes could, in times of danger, be mobilized as a people though the temporary leadership of warlords whom they called "judges." The period of Judges, 1200–1020 BC, corresponded to the early Iron Age in this region, a time recalled in the Hellenic north as the heroic age made famous by the siege of Troy.

For the Israelites, the saga of the second phase, divinely appointed kingship and national religion, begins with 1 Samuel. Here we read how these tribes finally petitioned the prophet Samuel to select for them a king so that they might be ruled as other nations were ruled (a choice that later generations would question). Even after their invasion of Canaan and their adoption of the settled ways of agriculturalists, many looked back nostalgically to a simpler age when pastoral patriarchs and tribal judges spoke familiarly with God and his angels. Centuries after the time of Samuel, Saul, David, and the kingliest of all, Solomon, the writer(s) of this chronicle presented this crucial moment as the abandonment of a divinely sanctioned communal way of life in favor of governmental authority. Before he found them a king, Samuel explained to them what the consequences of this political reorganization would be. The passage (1 Sam. 8:11–18) is worth a close reading:

> *11:* And he [Samuel relaying the words of God] said, This will be the manner of the king that shall reign over you: He will take your sons, and appoint them for himself, for his chariots, and to be his horsemen; and some shall run before his chariots.

12: And he will appoint him captains over thousands, and captains over fifties; and will set them to ear [i.e., plough] his ground, and to reap his harvest, and to make his instruments of war, and instruments of his chariots.

13: And he will take your daughters to be confectionaries, and to be cooks, and to be bakers.

14: And he will take your fields, and your vineyards, and your olive-yards, even the best of them, and give them to his servants.

15: And he will take the tenth of your seed, and of your vineyards, and give it to his officers, and to his servants.

16: And he will take your menservants, and your maidservants, and your goodliest young men, and your asses, and put them to his work.

17: He will take the tenth of your sheep: and ye shall be his servants.

18: And ye shall cry out in that day because of your king which ye shall have chosen you; and the LORD will not hear you in that day.

A modern paraphrase might run something like this:

> The government will draft your sons and make them cavalry soldiers and guards; it will set up state-operated agricultural projects and weapons industries; it will employ your daughters in restaurants; it will expropriate your land by right of eminent domain and parcel it out to civil servants; it will tax you to pay for its bureaucracy; it will release your servants and employees from your authority, claim a tenth of your livestock, and make you its own servant class.

This passage has been traditionally read as a rejection of theocracy on the part of the Israelites and their acceptance of gentile secularism. Historical scholars have come to read it as an indictment of the excesses of Solomon's reign and those of the rulers of the breakaway Northern Kingdom. It may also be read, however, as a dramatic rendering of an inevitable shift from a communally organized society of independent households and rural hamlets to an urban society, centrally governed and retooled to deal economically and militarily with its neighboring kingdoms. This was clearly a moment when a loosely affiliated group of tribes saw the advantage of joining together and establishing defensible national borders. In that light, exchanging the benefits of home rule for those of collective security must have seemed irresistible. As the passage implies, however, this shift of power from the communal to the governmental was most painfully felt as an erosion of parental authority. It meant the decline of what we call today the "family farm" and the local economy. At any rate, the perceived ethical consequences of this socioeconomic shift would provoke the eloquence of later prophets such as Elijah, Hosea, Amos, and Micah.[2]

Having agreed to consolidate themselves under Saul's central command, the tribes, under David and Solomon, accepted Jerusalem as their capital. These kings' reigns were militarily successful, thanks largely to the weakness of Egypt and the preoccupation of Assyria and Babylonia with one another. Yet here was a small land precariously lodged between the two great river civilizations of Egypt and Mesopotamia. If God had planted a people here, ultimately he alone could preserve them from eradication—if they merited preservation. Chroniclers noted with foreboding, though, that with monarchy there had also come a slow decline in divine worship and public morality, and now God had seemed to turn his face away.

A river metaphor allows for a downstream and an upstream view of time. The downstream, or past-oriented, perspective of biblical time we may identify with the first two centuries of the first millennium before the Christian era (1000–800 BC). Despite internal divisions, the people of the twelve tribes could afford to rest peacefully upon the accomplishments of their heroic ancestors, but with the rise of Assyria to the north and, later, Babylonia to the northeast, the future became a source of increasing anxiety. The nation's gaze, serenely turned to its past for so long, was now reverted to the unsettling flow of events rushing down toward it from upstream. There was, of course, a crucial difference here. The past constituted a store of knowledge that grew day by day, year by year, but the future could not be known until, like a flash flood—too late to be averted or evaded—it cascaded into the present.

The period of the monarchy showed strains typical of all such consolidations, including the re-emergence of intertribal rivalries, resentment toward the governing elite and its appetite for taxes, and a sense that the old pastoral virtues were giving way to a tawdry cosmopolitanism. The nation split into two kingdoms in 928, four years after the death of Solomon and a mere ninety-two years after the founding of the monarchy. If, as Bellah maintains, the third stage arrives when religion institutionally detaches itself from politics in the first millennium BC, then the Bible preserves a record of one way by which this detaching could be effected: by diaspora abroad and colonial status at home. The northern fragment, Israel, was destroyed by Assyria in 721; the southern fragment, Judah, fell to Babylonia in 587. Though Cyrus of Persia, upon conquering Babylon, restored the tribe of Judah (or "Jews") to its southern homeland, the Jews' experience henceforth, for two and one-half millennia, was that of scattered communities—a religious minority living, and sometimes suffering, under gentile rule. (Until the founding of the state of Israel in 1948 they would be a people relegated to the communal level, a *home* without a *land*.)

This unhappy history impressed itself on early Christianity and, despite the fact that the Christian West has increasingly dominated the world since the eighteenth century, many conservative Christians still identify themselves as a beleaguered people of God. Reading their Bibles, they learn the stories of Moses and Pharaoh, Daniel and Nebuchadnezzar, Jesus and Pilate. To them every government is an occupying force, like the Romans. American Christians also learn the stories of the brave settlers who fought to free themselves from the imperial yoke of Britain. They have learned, in short, to regard empire as an intrinsically evil institution.

This biblically sanctioned anti-imperial attitude, which is also expressed in a general hostility to "big government," has often run counter to American foreign policy and has necessitated a good deal of rhetorical spin. What other nations have regarded as wars of economic expansion, American presidents have had to explain as campaigns of liberation. This has always been a difficult sell. For Americans whose Holy Land imagery comes from pious movie epics and Sunday-school illustrations of palm trees and bearded patriarchs, the recently televised images of American centurions breaking through doors and ordering about a long-robed populace must prompt a disturbing visual dissonance.

Conquest also creates problems for conquerors. For their part, the Babylonians, Persians, Greeks, and Romans each had to devise ways of pacifying their newly acquired territories. Unlike the centralizing process of archaic kingdoms, a sudden imperial expansion could not always be managed by the sort of religious syncretism that announces that "this god of yours is identical with that god of ours—we merely call him by a different name." These biblical empires were multiethnic and multilingual. If the vanquished were to cooperate to the extent of paying taxes and tribute monies, providing hospitality to foreign administrators, and serving to defend their new patrons from hostile forces on the imperial borders, they could not be allowed to become entirely demoralized. Of course, there would come events when they would be required to stand up (or, on occasion, kneel down) to profess their allegiance to the new regime, but in the interim their cultural identity would need to be minimally respected.

Gentile administrators overall were rather accommodating in matters of religious customs. If one ruled over many distinct ethnic groups, one might do well to respect their differences and profit by exploiting them. One could always rekindle smoldering animosities among old neighbors and let these peoples vent their resentments on one another rather than on oneself. Though brute force was always an option, a politic magnanimity was always the safer tactic. Thus, toleration could prove a more potent instrument of empire than persecution.

In the book of Daniel, set in Babylon of the sixth century BC but probably written under (and *about*) the Greek Seleucid occupation of the second century AD, one of several vivid episodes is the testing of Shadrach, Meshach, and Abed-nego. We are not told Nebuchadnezzar's reasons for erecting his monumental statue, whom it represented, or why he commanded his audience to kneel down and worship it, but the Jewish writer's interpretation suggests several points.[3] The assembled audience is wholly composed of government officials (Dan. 3:2). Because many were drawn from the provinces of the newly conquered territories, the assembly is multiethnic and multilingual (3:4). The non-native officials are not actually being required to convert to the conqueror's religion, but rather to acknowledge the sovereignty of the national pantheon (3:14). Though these officials must have been followers of other religions, they comply with the command to assume a worshipful posture toward the statue—all but the three Jews.

This test, which to second-century readers would have brought to mind the attempts of Seleucid occupiers to Hellenize their Phoenician, Syrian, and Judaic provinces, suggests a ritual of a civil religion. Those who acquiesced in it probably recognized it as a *pro forma* act of respect, knowing that in return they were permitted to practice their traditional religions in private.[4] These men, once the educated elite of sovereign kingdoms, had now become leaders of exile communities and, in order to secure a measure of autonomy for their people, were obliged to pledge their loyalty to the new ruler and his divine patrons.

The essential issue raised in this biblical tale is, of course, the old sanction against graven images. The familiar argument against idol worship is that it is simply stupid—how can a god of stone or wood be of any help to anyone? But the writer of the Wisdom of Solomon—a younger contemporary of the author of Daniel residing in Alexandria in the early first century BC[5]—offers another theory of idolatry along with some media implications for civil religion:

> graven images came to be worshipped at the command of despotic
> princes. When men could not do honour to such a prince before

his face because he lived far away, they made a likeness of that distant face, and produced a visible image of the king they sought to honour, eager to pay court to the absent prince as though he were present. Then the cult grew as those to whom the king is unknown are spurred on by the ambitious craftsmen. In his desire, it may be, to please the monarch, a craftsman skilfully distorts the likeness into an ideal form, and the common people, beguiled by the beauty of the workmanship, take for an object of worship him whom lately they honoured as a man. (14:16–20)[6]

When a kingdom expanded into an empire, the king had to find ways to exert control at a distance. To this purpose, carved words could represent his voice and a carved or molded likeness could represent his physical features. Multiple inscribed likenesses enabled him to be virtually present throughout his realm. This was a policy that, between 200 BC and 100 AD, especially rankled the Jewish and, later, the Christian communities: the foreign ruler's presence seemed to intrude everywhere, demanding allegiance and reminding them of their vassal status.[7]

Most religions require belief in absent beings that, through certain rites, can become present. If, as in most religions, visual representation is permitted, believers will display divine images prominently in public and at home. If they use writing, they will also preserve messages from this divine source. They may even call their special god "Lord" or "King," imagine him ruling some faraway realm, and, for his visits to his worshippers, build him a temple on the model of a royal palace with an inner throne room. Traditional religions may be rooted in the communal level of society, but the beings they worship have tended rather closely to resemble members of the governmental elite. It is a historical irony that religions, having borrowed the symbolic code of governments, should react with horror when rulers reassert their secular lordship by disseminating verbal and visual representations of themselves.

One potent means of distributing the ruler's image was the monetary system. Though it could hardly be mistaken for an object of religious devotion, a drachma or a denarius could remind sellers and buyers in the local marketplace that one faraway man was responsible for guaranteeing the exchange value of goods. This had important implications for Greco-Roman civil religion and was a potential source of controversy. A few days before Jesus's arrest, the Pharisees—hoping that he would utter treasonous words—sent agents of the collaborationist court of Herod to ask Jesus if it were religiously lawful to pay taxes to Rome. He asked for a coin: "'Whose is the image and the superscription?' They say unto him, 'Caesar's.' Then saith he unto them, 'Render therefore unto Caesar the things which are Caesar's: and unto God the things that are God's'" (Matt. 22:17–21). This simulacrum of the emperor had nothing, presumably, to do with the law of God, and so there was no conflict. The Herodians' question was based on the civil-religious premise that the secular state and the religious community were somehow seamlessly united. Jesus seems to imply, however, that the empire—lofty, remote, corrupt, and destined for God's wrath—was, for the time being, welcome to this meaningless symbol.[8]

Roman politics had always drawn upon local religious customs, but during the first century BC, as this swollen city-state struggled with civil war at home and empire abroad, a systematic civil religion evolved. It was centered on the hopeful belief that the Sibylline scrolls had predicted the birth of a leader who would usher in a second Golden Age, a Saturnian age of rural peace and virtue. After defeating Antony and Cleopatra at Actium in 31 BC, Octavian, the adopted son of Julius Caesar, began to craft a messianic public image. In 31 the Senate decreed that at every banquet, public and private, a libation should be poured to his guardian spirit, or *genius*. In 28 Octavian became *princeps senatus* (president of the Senate) and in 27 assumed the title *augustus,* a word that connoted a person ritually consecrated. In 13 BC he became the chief religious officer of Rome, the *pontifex maximus,* and his house became the Temple of Vesta, the national hearth, as it were. Then, shortly after the dedication of the Altar of Peace in Rome in 9 BC, the imperial cult was inaugurated in the eastern provinces—Greece, Asia Minor, Syria, and Egypt.[9]

This cult was a civil religion that harked back to what Bellah described as the archaic stage of divine kingship. In the more ancient civilizations of the East, the second millennium lived on in legend and in monumental ruins, which in the popular imagination testified to a rich and peaceful era ruled by kings who had conversed with gods. Through the first century AD, the Roman Empire crafted the civil religion and applied it to promote its authority over these provinces. Rome's policy was to tolerate all the religions of all its peoples, but it demanded that they acknowledge its divinely ordained mission to pacify the nations and, as Vergil had said, to spare the submissive while battering down the proud. The cult of the emperor involved certain public acts, such as praying for his health, crowning his statues with flowers, offering incense and wine to his *genius,* and sharing sacrificed meat. To proconsular administrators, participation in this civil-religious ritual was something of a loyalty test and for most provincials it was, no doubt, a perfunctory affair. For some Christians, however, and some observant Jews, Roman civil religion was an abomination. There was no way to render this to Caesar, no possible compromise. This conflict between the governmental and the communal led to civil disobedience and insurrection. It ultimately provoked the Roman destruction of the second Temple (70 AD) and the outlawing of Christianity as a subversive superstition.

The Once and Future Kingdom

Early Christians who had been schooled in the biblical master narratives had a special perspective on these cultural policies of Rome. Incorporating the Jewish books (as the "Old Testament") and, by the early second century, the Gospels, Epistles, and Book of Revelation (as the "New Testament"), the Christian Bible is much concerned with the two levels of social organization. In biblical history, what I have called the communal level precedes the development of the governmental kingdom and appears first as the pastoral family of the patriarchal age. Though this level, the community of true believers, historically continues to exist, its specific character becomes conditioned by its relation to the governmental level, which appears in three forms: the evil kingdom (e.g., Egypt, Assyria, Babylon, Rome, and the Northern Kingdom under Ahab); the good kingdom (Israel united under David and Solomon, and then Judah under several "good" kings, e.g., Hezekiah and Josiah); and the heavenly kingdom (the transcendent kingdom of God). Under an evil kingdom, the faithful are persecuted by the government. Under the good kingdom, the communal and the governmental levels are allied against external foes. In the heavenly kingdom, the divine homeland, they are united as in a perfect marriage, their bliss and peace eternal.

The Old Testament, especially Exodus through 2 Chronicles, focuses on the possibility that under divine auspices, a people can come together and create a just kingdom. The tale of how twelve fractious tribes defended one another in need and then merged as the royal kingdom of David was remembered as a glorious epic. Unfortunately, the good kingdom inaugurated at David's enthronement proved, as we have seen, short-lived. It soon divided in two and centuries of instability and disaster ensued.

Despite the mistakes and excesses of their reigns, later generations regarded the kingdom of David and his son, Solomon, as indeed a Golden Age. These kings, like the patriarchs and prophets of old, were men whom God had favored with his presence. This storied past, though as unreachable as the invisible Yahweh, was nonetheless radiant with his living spirit and powerful enough to draw every completed day at nightfall into its vast storehouse. In this ideal era, every present moment *followed* the moment that, having preceded it, belonged now to that past. Every generation took its place *behind* (in a spatial sense) and *after* (in a temporal sense) the preceding generation, which had now passed away to the sleep of the fathers and belonged to that permanent order of portentous, epochal events back toward which the living turned their gaze to understand their present circumstances. The living followed the dead, literally *following* the lessons of their lives; to address properly the events that streamed toward them out of the future, the living were obliged to turn continually to the experience of the past. Linguists have demonstrated by an analysis of the use of the Hebrew word *achar* (behind) and its cognates that the ancient Israelites experienced time in a way that most modern translations fail to indicate. For example, when we read in 2 Kings 14:22 that King Amaziah "built Elath, and restored it to Judah, after that he slept with his fathers," the phrase "after that" seems to us to mean some forward movement in time. What the phrase originally meant was that the king followed *behind* his ancestors and receded with them into the past.[10]

The biblical model of linear time that I have been describing, based as it was on the river metaphor, tended to focus on the flow of events downstream from us, a vista in which causes and effects could be charted after the fact and the lessons of history contemplated. In stable times the future was a fairly predictable matter, with little variation. We might imagine the river of time as rising beside the observer as a refreshing spring—a gift of life from the Giver of all good things—that gently overflowed and meandered downward from the present into the past. Yahweh, the Lord of Time, could be supplicated, and a careful compliance with his commandments could protect the people from the adverse impact of coming events, but, as I noted above in my thumbnail survey of bible history (p. 27) the eighth and seventh centuries demanded a more active inquiry into divine Providence.

The idea that God used foreign nations to chastise and lead to repentance this stiff-necked people, an idea that appeared in the seventh-century Deuteronomic theory of history, no longer seemed sufficient following the fall of Jerusalem in 587 BC. Increasingly, prophets dreamt dreams and saw visions of what they called the Day of the Lord (the Day of Yahweh), when he would turn on the foreign armies that had been his instruments and utterly destroy them (Isa. 49:22–26). He would also turn against the accusatory angel who had urged him to punish the Jews. This adversary (or *satan* in Hebrew) would be revealed as a false witness, a father of lies, and be destroyed along with the gentiles whom he had marshaled against Israel. Only Yahweh and his warrior angels could effect this. Human history had been nothing more nor less than a series of catastrophic wars, but the peace that would ensue after the Lord of Hosts destroyed Israel's oppressors would mark the end of history and the inauguration of a well-nigh unimaginable kingdom. Somewhere at the end of history shone the light of that great day, that homecoming of the living and the dead. The end of the time line was already there in the future, moving toward realization, but only God could now behold it. The momentary raising of the veil that concealed this future from the eyes of the living came to be termed a revelation (in Greek, *apokalupsis*). In the bitter years of humiliation, exile, and bondage, the prospect of an apocalyptic peaceable kingdom sustained this broken people.

The Day of Yahweh would be the ultimate deliverance of Israel, compared with which the earlier episodes of divine favor were mere foreshadowings. It was difficult, however, to envision this new age without employing the traditional master narrative—the escape from Egypt under Moses, the entering into and conquest of Canaan by Joshua, the long struggle with the Philistines, and the establishing of Jerusalem as the City of David, followed by Solomon's building of the first Temple. The apocalyptic future was modeled upon a miraculous past in which Yahweh, the divine "Man of War" (Exod. 15:3), journeyed with his warrior people all the way from Sinai, hovering above them or standing invisibly atop the Ark of the Covenant and dwelling within the tent constructed for it, the Tabernacle. The post-apocalyptic age to come would center on a New Jerusalem, the capital of the kingdom of God.

This biblical master narrative, broad enough to encompass world history and innumerable secondary narratives, conforms to a five-part pattern set forth by Tzvetan Todorov in his *Genres in Discourse* (1990). I have outlined this model, which recalls Gustav Freytag's dramatic triangle in some respects, in Figure 2.

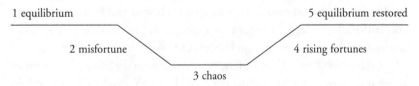

Figure 2.   The full narrative cycle

This represents the full narrative cycle, but, as Todorov notes, it is not always presented in its entirety:

One can imagine a tale that omits the first two elements and begins with a situation that is already deficient [e.g., comedy]; or a tale might omit the last two elements and end on an unhappy note [e.g., tragedy]. But we sense that these would be the two halves of the cycle, whereas here we have the cycle in full. Theoretical research has shown—and empirical studies have confirmed—that this cycle belongs to the very definition of narrative: one cannot imagine a narrative that fails to contain at least a part of it.[11]

If we regard this cycle as the supreme master narrative template, we might then consider secondary master narratives as deriving their power by indicating their relation to this all-inclusive narrative model.

As the diagram shows, this narrative cycle is symmetrical: 1 and 5 are identical; 3 is the inversion of 1 and 5; and 4 is the negative transformation of 2. This might also remind us of the ritual phases outlined by Arnold van Gennep in his *Rites of Passage*.[12] In a traditional society, when a person's status must change, the person moves from (1) a state of equilibrium through (2) a ritual of separation from the former state into (3) a liminal condition involving rites of transition, often painful and always bewildering. The person then moves upward to (4) rites of incorporation, which teach the person about his or her future status, and finally to (5) the successful entry into the new state of equilibrium.

This pattern, which I am calling the "full narrative cycle," may be found throughout the Bible. For example, the book of Job takes us through all five phases, though phase 3 is its primary focus. The parable of the prodigal son replicates this full cycle in miniature. A larger cycle is plotted out in the origin legends of Genesis: Adam's Edenic state (1) is followed by his Fall (2) and the descent of his progeny into a depth of wickedness that provokes the Flood (3), but God chooses to save Noah and his family (4), and subsequently God and Noah make their covenant (5) and give humanity a second chance. Christians trace an even larger cycle from Eden (1), through the gradual estrangement of God from his own covenanted people (2) and their conquest and dispersion by pagan nations (3), until God sends his own son to regather his people (4). Then, in the "fullness of time," the kingdom of God is to be established on earth (5) and the Edenic Tree of Life will feed and heal humanity.

Todorov suggests that the full narrative cycle is a human universal. But even if it should prove to apply only to agricultural societies or to cultures that derive from the eastern Mediterranean and Mesopotamia, its relevance to this present study is apparent. Whenever its structure is woven into the historiography of any culture, we should expect to find it used predictively: every rise is inevitably followed by a decline, and every decline by a rise.

This is illustrated in the early Christian uses of the Hebrew scriptures. The prophets had predicted the coming of an Anointed One, or Messiah, a "Son of David," and Jesus's words and deeds, his followers believed, had fulfilled these prophecies. But, besides proving the messiahship of their crucified leader, what was the value of the Jewish scriptures? When the resurrected and ascended Christ would return to earth to establish the kingdom of heaven, as his followers believed, would it be a restoration of the biblical past? Paul, a Jewish official who before his conversion had persecuted the followers of Jesus, hit upon an ingenious solution. The heavenly kingdom of the future would so transcend the biblical past that the past was now a mere intimation of this future. Past and future might be mirror images, but the past at best was a glass reflecting only darkly the reality of the world to come.

In the Epistle to the Hebrews traditionally ascribed to him, Paul says that Jesus is now the "minister of the [celestial] sanctuary," the true high priest of the "true tabernacle" (Heb. 8:2). The earthly priesthood of the Jews was but a "shadow of heavenly things," just as the tabernacle was a reproduction of the celestial holy place that Moses beheld on Mount Sinai (8:5). Just as earthly worship imitates the worship the heavenly hosts offer to God, the past glories of David and Solomon imitate the future glories of Christ's kingdom of heaven. The phrase "shadow of heavenly things" becomes "shadow of things to come" in Hebrews 10:1 and Colossians 2:17, but the meanings of these metaphorical formulas are virtually equivalent. The shadow is an insubstantial phenomenon—a figure, a figment—projected by a real entity not otherwise perceived. It is an indicator of something other than itself. We are familiar with this idealist shadow-model as Plato presented it in the *Republic* (Socrates' parable of the cave), but its temporalization in early Christian thought was a daring innovation. Earth was a created space that in its beauty would continue until the end of the world to reflect the heavenly space, but with the advent of Christ all preceding earthly time revealed itself to have been an imitation of the heavenly time to come, a shadowy parable of the kingdom of heaven.[13]

When Christ ascended from this earth, he returned to the realm of light. It is from this realm that he is now preparing to return, bringing with him (to use Todorov's model) the remaining segment of phase 4 and all of phase 5. During phase 4, the interval of history between his departure and his return, his shadow—as well as the shadows of all the personages of the end time—can be detected falling upon events and world leaders. The verb "foreshadow," when applied to apocalyptic time, does not refer to a shadow cast from past to future in chronological time, as we might mean when we say "John Brown's raid on Harpers Ferry foreshadowed the Civil War." The author of the First Epistle of John, traditionally assumed also to be the writer of Revelation, declared that "God is light" (1 John 1:5). It was God's light that, flooding heaven, cast the shadows of heavenly things onto the earthly plane spatially, as nature, and temporally—out of the future into the past—as history. These realities were the *eschata,* the ultimate things. Earthly history was mere shadow-play. We, who generally read history as a cause-and-effect sequence, find this model of time perplexing. To us it may seem like entering Alice's looking-glass world, but enter it we must if we are to understand this biblical master narrative.

These figurative anticipations of Christ, or types, were, as I have described, shadows of him cast before him as he approached humanity out of the divinely illuminated future. According to the Christian apostles (especially Paul) and the church fathers of the first three centuries, the Jews were never able to interpret their entire history as the profoundly detailed shadow-play that it was. The word "type," like the word "shadow," is a similitude for similitude itself. A type (in Greek, *tupos*) means the impression made by an object: by observing this mark, one infers that there has been a corresponding mark-maker, its antitype. Here again we must remind ourselves that in the future-to-past trajectory of biblical time, the type, or effect, always precedes the revelation of its antitype, or cause. Just as the person of Christ and his actions during his first coming are the antitypes that explicate the preceding Old Testament era, the prophecies of his *second* coming provide in advance the set of antitypes that unlock the meanings of the Christian era, which, like the Bible, is also a text composed of types.

God's schedule is teleological. That is, events are directed toward predetermined outcomes by a cosmic craftsman whose prior intentions lie embedded in all things as final causes governing their development and fulfillment. All things in this created world are fulfilled in their *eschata,* the ultimate state they attain before dissolution. Sky and ocean and mountain declare the glory of their creator, while the lilies of the field, who neither toil nor spin, he arrays more splendidly than Solomon in all his glory. Only Solomon and his errant successors neglect their assigned goals. When this happens, the one who embedded the goals and oversees their fulfillment enters the process and corrects its course. From those to whom he has revealed more of his intentions he will expect more compliance and, if he fails to get it, will use history to punish them. In this way only do humans affect the course of history. By provoking God they blindly prompt him to cause historical events to occur—events that, paradoxically, were already written in his book of time. Based on the notion of an indissoluble covenant between God and people, this was the theory of history developed by the prophets of Israel in the middle of the first millennium before the Christian era and adopted, with variations, by the early Church.

The master narrative I have sketched out here with the help of Todorov's model traces a true revolution, a turning back, and the restoration of an earlier, more righteous government, but on a higher plane. I turn now to two texts that were meant to prepare holy warriors for this ultimate revolution.

Apocalyptic Politics

The discovery of the scrolls at Qumran in 1947 revealed the institutional rules and beliefs of a sect of Jews that most scholars have identified as the Essenes. Having separated themselves from the urban, partly assimilated population to the west around 125 BC, they set up an all-male community overlooking the Dead Sea. According to the historian Josephus, the Essenes lived communally, observed unanimity of belief and uniformity of dress, adopted children whom they educated in their strict form of Judaism, renounced pleasures and amusements as evil, and looked upon all women as morally weak and as a dangerous source of temptation. They bitterly resented the influences of Hellenistic culture, which was first introduced by the Seleucids and later reinforced by the Romans. The latter finally succeeded in routing them from their caves in 68 AD, during the Jewish Revolt (66–70).

Regardless of whether this community actively participated in the rebellion, some of its teachings must have encouraged it. The battle lines were already drawn for these separatists: in the heavens, the forces of the satanic Belial confronted the forces of God; on earth, the children of darkness menaced the children of light; and in each man's soul, the spirit of perversity debated the spirit of truth. As many have speculated, this dualistic theme in Jewish apocalyptic may have been borrowed from Zoroastrianism either as early as the sixth century or since the late fourth century, when Persia and Judah felt similarly threatened by Hellenistic cultural imperialism.[14]

The brethren of Qumran believed that this opposition, which had always existed in human history, would soon be abolished. In the fragmentary "War of the Sons of Light and the Sons of Darkness," a document that might remind contemporary readers of the rhetoric of the Taliban and of al Qaeda manuals, the writer sets forth plans for a military campaign.[15] These plans aped Roman tactics in some respects but in other details were so fantastical as to have drawn laughter from a centurion, had he uncovered them—*and* had he been able to decipher the biblical code in which they were written. He might have altogether missed the fact that the Romans were designated as the principal enemies, because they are referred to as the Kittians, a term previously applied to the Greek Seleucid occupiers.[16] The non-Jewish client states of Rome, which are also given ancient names, will be the first to be attacked and "havoc shall then beset the descendants of Japheth," another code name for Greeks and Romans.

> [Streaks of lightn]ing will flash from one end of the world to the other, growing ever brighter until the era of darkness is brought utterly to an end. Then, in the era of God, His exalted grandeur will give light for[evermore,] shedding on all the Sons of Light peace and blessing, gladness and length of days.
>
> On the day the Kittians fall, there shall be mighty combat and carnage in the presence of the God of Israel, for that is the day which He appointed of old for the final battle against the Sons of Darkness. Thereon the company of the divine and the congregation of the human now engage side by side in combat and carnage, the Sons of Light doing battle against the Sons of Darkness with a show of godlike might, amid uproarious tumult, amid the war-cries of gods and men, in a veritable day of havoc. . . . For [with Thee] in heaven are a multitude of holy beings, and armies of angels are in Thy holy abode, to [serve as] Thy [legionaries]; and down on earth Thou hast [likewise] placed at Thy service the elect of an holy people. . . . Thou wilt muster an army of Thine elect, in their thousands and tens of thousands, side by side with Thine holy beings and Thine angels. . . . Warrior angels are in our muster, and He that is Mighty in War is in our throng. The army of His spirits marches beside us. Our horsemen come like clouds or like banks of dew, to cover the earth, or like torrential showers, to rain judgment on all that grows on it.[17]

To readers of the Gospels and the Book of Revelation, many of these details will seem familiar: the flash of lightning across the entire sky, the children of darkness and of light, the terrible carnage, the angelic auxiliaries (the heavenly host), the final battle (Armageddon), and the era of peace to follow. Like the "War of the Sons of Light and the Sons of Darkness," Revelation envisions a decisive war of terror in the very near future. Yet no actual catastrophe, no actual war in human history, has yet been able to measure up to the rhetorical extremes of either text. Perhaps for this reason the prophesied horror has always seemed to belong to some ultimate future. In the minds of believers, that which has not yet happened cannot be disproved.

Revelation holds a special place in the Christian Bible. It is the only book in which every successive generation of Christian readers may imagine themselves actually referred to. For over 1,900 years they have scrutinized the book of Revelation as though scanning a vast panoramic painting thronged with human figures (among whom they might recognize themselves). They could also place their neighbors and local clergy in the scene, and others, too—the lord in his manor house, the rich merchant in town, the distant emperor, and the pope of Rome. Were these contemporaries mere shadows of enigmatic figures such as the Two Witnesses, the Antichrist, and the heroic man on the white horse, or could they be the *real personages?* These could be the antitypes only if this present time was the time foretold in prophecy. Jesus, of course, had himself cautioned his disciples against such speculation. There would be scant warning. He would come like a thief in the night. They had better be prepared. Yet Revelation seemed to list a long series of preparatory signs, disasters both natural and political, and numbers that did indeed suggest a precise timetable. Though none could know the very day or the hour when the sky would crack open and the Eternal Judge appear in a blaze of light and a blare of trumpets, all Christians wondered—and not a few dipped pen in ink and calculated.

The Book of Revelation seems to have been most avidly studied when its consolatory message seemed most needed, as in times of religious persecution and among classes of Christians who felt aggrieved by social injustice. Apocalyptic texts in the first two centuries of the Christian era reassured Christians and Jews alike that the God of the Universe would soon requite their grief and their faith and satisfy their demand for retribution upon Roman authorities. But when persecutions became less frequent and severe, theologians such as Origen (ca. 185–ca. 254) sought to allegorize Revelation, and when Constantine and Licinius finally issued the Edict of Toleration in 313, some churchmen began to question the canonicity of this popular text. Even after agreeing to keep it in Christian scriptures, the Church sought ways to reconstrue its more destabilizing elements. Augustine, who is associated with this movement, taught that the battle against the forces of evil had already been fought and won by the resurrected Christ. Satan had been chained in hell (exactly where Dante was to find him centuries later), and with the founding of the Church, the millennial realm had been inaugurated. This City of God was a spiritual kingdom that would coexist until the end of the world with the City of Man, the secular, vice-ridden regime. Jesus, when he returned to judge the living and the dead, would then and only then separate the two forever, rewarding the one and punishing the other. In 431, at the Council of Ephesus, belief in some future earthly Millennium was condemned as a dangerous superstition.[18]

If the age of the Church was to be a thousand years, then the events that followed Revelation 20:6, that is, the temporary release of Satan, the final battles, and the Last Judgment (or Doomsday), would have to occur early in the second millennium AD. When this did not happen, speculation then focused on 1300 as roughly a thousand years after Constantine legalized Christianity. Even before this ominous century began, Christendom had not seemed to be much enjoying the last years of its Augustinian Millennium. The Vandals, Visigoths, and Vikings had terrorized Europe; then, in 1241, the Mongols defeated the Germans in Silesia and ravaged Poland and Hungary. The end-of-the-world hymn, the *Dies Irae,* was composed in 1250. By 1260, the year the prophet-monk Joachim of Fiore announced as the start of the Millennium, mass hysteria was sweeping across many regions and sending flagellants on processions of self-torment. All this was merely a prelude to the next century, which saw the bubonic plague, or Black Death, kill over twenty-five million Europeans between 1347 and 1351. Here at last was a catastrophe of truly apocalyptic magnitude.

This period of apocalyptic reawakening also coincided with Europe's confrontation with Islam over the sacred sites in Palestine. Persuaded by incendiary preachers (Joachim among them) that Muslim rulers such as Saladin were devils and Antichrists, and that the infidels had to be driven from Jerusalem before Christ could return in glory, troops of knights and unarmed peasants joined in the Crusades (1095–1291). Though these invaders were ultimately expelled from the Holy Land, their apocalyptic bigotry permanently affected the relations between the Christian West and the Islamic East—including the Jews, whom their Muslim rulers had generally tolerated. As Paul Boyer describes it, "Further acting on their end-time beliefs, the lower ranks of the Crusaders before embarking for Palestine sometimes conducted murderous campaigns against European Jewry. In the folk eschatology of the period (reinforced by some prophecy writers), Jews and Muslims alike were demonic agents of Antichrist. Indeed, it was widely believed that Antichrist himself would be a Jew—a conviction occasionally still found among post-1945 prophecy writers."[19] It should be recalled that the role of the Jews in apocalyptic conjectures has always been of central importance. If Christ could return only when Jews ruled Jerusalem and had converted to Christianity, those Jews who chose to reside in Christian Europe and obdurately follow their old religion could only be prolonging the reign of the Antichrist and the sufferings of the true believers.

The fifteenth century saw rising unrest among the poor of Europe, the Holy Land being now closed as a safety valve and the new continents of America not yet opened. As ever, the Book of Revelation provided the peasant revolutionaries with a dramatic structure and a justifying agenda. From Bavaria to Bohemia, small bands of rebels rallied around fiery preachers whom, they believed, God had sent to prepare Christians for the last onslaught of Satan and his human minions. The lofty rich would need to be pulled down and the humble exalted. The young Martin Luther, whose concept of social reform was less radical, was dismayed by these anarchist sects and in 1522 condemned this apocalypticism. He even went so far as to dismiss Revelation as "neither apostolic nor prophetic," relegating it to an appendix of his German translation of the Bible.[20] On the other hand, he recognized that communal resentment could be usefully diverted extraterritorially. Instead of raging against local authorities, these restless populations could learn to regard the pope of Rome as the Antichrist, the First Beast of the Apocalypse.[21] Joined in this extreme position by John Calvin in 1544, Luther inspired an interpretive tradition that over the past five centuries has identified the Catholic Church as a satanic conspiracy and the Vatican as the prophesied Babylon.

The use of Revelation to attack the papacy may also be viewed as one ploy in the long-term struggle of secular states to achieve absolute sovereignty. The notion of a "Holy Roman Empire" as the kingdom of God on earth and its emperor as divinely selected was used to support claims of monarchical independence from, and even superiority over, ecclesiastical authorities. The "divine right" of kings, with its enthronement rituals and anointings, was a civil-religious concept that drew upon the narratives of King David and of the heroic man on the white horse (Rev. 19:11–16), that messianic king who would win the battle of Armageddon, dispatch the Antichrist to hell, and inaugurate the Millennium. For those who applied this end-time narrative to current affairs, the apocalyptic logic was quite simple: if a current ruler was to be this hero, and a pope opposed him, then that pope must be the Antichrist. The only issues left in doubt were whether King X or

Emperor Y was indeed God's final champion (and Pope Z his satanic antagonist). As for Rome, there could be no doubt: she continued to be Babylon the Great, the Mother of Harlots and Abominations of the Earth.[22] What if the final pope, the *real* Antichrist, has not yet made his dramatic entrance? His type has preceded him upon the stage of history countless times. Historical persons and nations have been the multiple manifestations of the shadow of Antichrist, the shadow that he has been casting into time from that unique point in the final future when he will physically appear to perform his abominations, for like the messianic Judge, the Antichrist, too, is backlit by the glory of God.

As literacy spread in this new age of proliferating texts, rhetoric became a more powerful instrument of public policy. In Tudor England the apocalyptic narrative that had helped support the monarchy against the papacy's claims now mobilized the anti-Catholic sentiments of a people terrified by the prospects of a Spanish invasion. The defeat of the Armada in 1588 only intensified the popular belief that England had been divinely designated to enact the final struggle of the saints against the Babylonish empire of the Beast.

The Puritans, who regarded themselves as the vanguard of the cleansed Church and perhaps indeed the army of the Apocalypse, called for a holy war against the papacy that would end with the city of Rome sinking in flames into the Mediterranean. In 1593, John Napier, inventor of logarithms, the decimal point, and the mechanical calculator, scanned his numbers and reckoned that the tyrant of the triple tiara would be cast into hellfire in 1639, an event that would be followed by Judgment Day between 1688 and 1700. Thomas Brightman in 1602 assigned the year 1650 for the fall of Rome and the conversion of the Jews and the year 1686 for God's sentencing of the Antichrist. According to Brightman and other hopeful Puritans of the early seventeenth century, the Millennium actually began in the 1300s with the first stirrings of the Reformation, that century when many earlier Christians had expected it to end. Sown like mustard seed in England with the first translations and preachings of John Wycliffe (1320–1384) and later nourished by the blood of martyrs, the kingdom of God would soon blossom forth in England for all the world to see.[23]

The English Civil War (1642–48) was popularly promoted by apocalyptic tracts that identified King Charles as the Beast and Parliament as the victorious army of saints whose duty it was to execute the wrath of God. With the beheading of the king, the euphoric saints under Oliver Cromwell envisioned the slaying of *all* kings and the forcible inauguration of the millennial kingdom. But even Cromwell soon began to question the extremism of the millennialists. They would freely use apocalyptic rhetoric to vilify anyone, even a patriotic English Protestant, who expressed a differing opinion. As Luther had done a century earlier, Cromwell moved to divert his country-men from further fratricide in the Lord's name by refocusing their bellicosity elsewhere—once again toward Catholic Spain.

Earlier that century, repressive ecclesiastical policies had prompted some of the more intransigent Puritans to migrate to New England. In their mind, the Anglican episcopacy, its antipopery protestations notwithstanding, was a creature of Satan, and Old England had become the newest conquest of the papal Antichrist. Though the Puritans and Separatists who settled New England were steeped in apocalyptic speculation, their leaders were well aware of the socially disruptive consequences of individual interpretations of this scripture and carefully directed their apocalyptic hatred safely beyond their own borders.

In 1633, John Cotton sailed for New England in the company of other like-minded Puritans, including Thomas Hooker. Cotton moved into the settlement that, in his honor, would be named for the small coastal town on the Wash where for twenty years he had served as vicar: Boston, Lincoln-shire. Nine years later, at the height of the Puritan insurgency in England, he published *The Churches Resurrection, or the Opening of the Fift and Sixt Verses of the 20th Chap. of the Revelation.*[24] In it he argues that the Millennium could not have occurred during the thousand-year period 300–400 to 1300–1400 AD, because this was not a "comfortable time" for the saints (5). Nor could it have occurred during the early Reformation, for, though men like Luther and Calvin had as individuals risen out of moral death, the churches they established had "administrations . . . deaded [*sic*] with the inventions of men" (19). The Millennium could only come after the Anti-christ and Satan were fully put down.

To characterize Cotton's use of Revelation as polemical is to put it mildly. The resurrected martyrs of Revelation he identifies as the early persecuted Protestants. These martyrs will return to rule the Church for a thousand years as the "house of *Israel* rising out of their graves of Ignorance and Apostacie, to a Church estate" (9), where they will with Christ pass judg-ment upon the "workers of iniquity" (10). This is the time, not far off, when "the Saints that hate Popery, and have suffered against Popery, and have borne witnesse to the word in their times, sit upon Thrones; This Reformation of Churches is the first Resurrection [i.e., the Millennium]" (16). In Cotton's view, as expressed in his later tract *An Exposition Upon the Thirteenth Chapter of the Revelation* (1655), the insufficiently reformed English Church, as long as it retained diocesan and parochial structures, was the veritable image of the Beast, the pope of the "Roman Catholick visible Church" (7, 16–21). As for those in New England who thought that they might return to their old country, they were like the Israelites who yearned to return to Egypt: England was still a place of spiritual bondage as long as the popish traditions remained. And as for those popes, "(as their storyes do record) they were witches, and gave their soules to the Devil, that they might obtaine the Popedome" (225).

From their snug enclave in eastern Massachusetts, the transplanted Puritans scanned a chessboard where every skirmish, palace coup, and natural disaster bespoke a divine strategy. The Turks, for centuries a favorite candidate for the role of collective Antichrist, could now be made unwitting instruments of God if they could somehow move into southern Europe and destroy "Popedome." One New England divine predicted in 1738 that this invasion would occur sometime before 1900, thus permitting the general resurrection of the dead by the year 2016.[25]

Unfortunately, as this calculation was being published, circumstances nearer home were taking on a troubling aspect. Even as the Turks were imagined on the road to Rome, the French and Indian agents of the Beast were encircling God's own plantations in the New World. As usual, this development helped bring the sometimes-fractious colonists together as their leaders redeployed biblical language and ethnic mythology to demonize this enemy. John Burt described the French as the "Offspring of that *Scarlet Whore, that Mother of Harlots,* who is justly called *the Abomination of the Earth*" (a pungent denunciation, yet restrained for biblical invective: the French are only the *children* of the Whore of Babylon). For Jonathan Mayhew of Boston, however, the French in 1754 were nothing less than the seven-headed, ten-horned Antichrist himself, intent on enslaving British colonists and dispossessing these "free-born subjects of King GEORGE of the inheritance received from their forefathers." This attitude changed abruptly when, in 1776, the American rebels began to call George's royal grandson the Antichrist and to receive military aid from Catholic France—an irony not lost on the Tory Loyalists.[26]

The ironies of apocalyptic politics took yet another turn when end-time observers tried to descry the significance of the French Revolution. Its leaders were by all accounts professed atheists, yet, like those devils the Turks, they attacked the privileges of the Catholic Church. To Protestants of the Puritan persuasion, this curious inconsistency posed a moral dilemma. Should

Christian America support the French Revolution because the ancient Antichrist was now being assaulted by the anticlerical Jacobins? Or should it make common cause with that erstwhile Antichrist, the British Crown, to help crush the head of this serpent of atheism?

Such nice moral conundrums are fortunately not for us to trouble our heads about. Another rhetorical question, however, does propose itself. How could anyone, except an ignorant bigot, identify the Antichrist and the Whore of Babylon with so many different persons, nations, and institutions? Was it because this was an age when the pen, or rather the printing press, was competing with the sword and when vituperation had risen to the height of a low art? That might do for one answer. A more fruitful solution to this question may be to observe that this political exploitation of Revelation is actually very much in the spirit of John's text. If, as most interpreters agree, he refers to contemporary political events and personages using older appellations, e.g., the emperor or emperors as the Beast, Rome as Babylon, and the Roman state as his Babylonian whore, then John the Revelator is the very paragon of all Christian polemicists, his book a masterly recension of the great biblical master narrative.

Two Visions of the Millennial Homeland

The book of Revelation proved a highly adaptable text as well. We have seen how it could lend its authority to any number of ethnic myths by identifying contemporary nations and churches, some with the servants of Satan, others with the saints of God. It could also console its readers with visions of an ultimate state in which government no longer harasses the community of true believers but has merged with that community and become the kingdom of God, the millennial homeland. Revelation, read in this light, narrates the final episodes in a quest that began in Genesis 12, the story that three world religions know so well: a man hears a voice that tells him he must leave his father's home and travel to another land that will be for him and his descendants an everlasting homeland.

By the time St. Paul retells this story, however, the destination of this journey seems to have changed from an earthly to a heavenly homeland:

> By faith Abraham, when he was called to go out into a place where
> he should after receive for an inheritance, obeyed; and he went out,
> not knowing whither he went. By faith he sojourned in the land of

promise, as in a strange country. . . . For he looked for a city which hath foundations, whose builder and maker is God. . . . [His descendants] all died in the faith, not having received the promises, but having seen them afar off, and were persuaded of them, and embraced them, and confessed that they were strangers and pilgrims on the earth. For they that say such things declare plainly that they seek a country. And truly, if they had been mindful of that country whence they came out, they might have had opportunity to have returned. But now they desire a better country, that is, an heavenly: wherefore God is not ashamed to be called their God: for he hath prepared for them a city. (Heb. 11:8–10, 13–16)

The medieval Church offered to its believers citizenship in this celestial city, theological statements and hymns referring to it as a *patria,* a fatherland, ruled over by a Heavenly Father. This world was merely a place of sojourn; Christians, in effect, were "resident aliens." Only gradually did royally governed nation-states assume the status of *patriae* and demand the moral allegiance of their people. Promoting the merits of this or that duchy or princedom or bourgeois democracy proved a difficult task in light of the vision of a transcendent, otherworldly kingdom of heaven waiting to welcome home the weary pilgrim.

As an article of belief, the concept of two polities—a temporal City of Man alongside an eternal City of God, the one a place of sojourn, the other an everlasting homeland—has a kind of bold elegance to it. But the twentieth chapter of Revelation complicates matters by introducing the notion of a third polity, an earthly Millennium, a thousand-year reign during which Satan will be prevented from deceiving the nations and the faithful will rule with Christ in the "beloved city." This kingdom, founded after the terrors of the tribulation and the carnage of Armageddon, would not be the otherworldly transcendent kingdom but the kingdom of heaven on earth, a true theocracy, a government ruled directly by God yet placed among alien, secular states. These three polities roughly correspond to the three kingdoms I referred to earlier in this chapter. The City of Man is the evil kingdom; the City of God is the transcendent heavenly kingdom; and what we might call the Millennial City is the good kingdom, the harmonious theocracy. This homeland, reserved for those who had "overcome" and braved martyrdom, became the focus of increased speculation as European governments took shape in the centuries following the great migrations of the early Middle Ages.

Not all Christians accepted this interpretation of John's Revelation. Catholics were taught that the Millennium had already begun, either at the founding of the Church or at the end of Roman persecution. According to this doctrine, known as preterism, the events prophesied in the first twenty of the twenty-two chapters of Revelation have already transpired. As Tyconius, an early church father, asserted, the "millennium" simply refers to the period between Christ's first and second advents.[27] For Protestants who identify themselves as premillennialists, this is not the case. The opening of the sealed scroll, the four grim horsemen, the mayhem, famine, pestilence, earthquake, and fire from the skies, the satanic dragon, the great beast out of the sea, the false prophet, the great whore, the army of saints led by the returned Messiah, the battle of Armageddon, and the total devastation of an evil empire—all this is yet to come.[28]

All those who locate their present moment in historical time somewhere between chapters 1 and 20 of Revelation and look forward to entering into and enjoying the thousand years of earthly bliss are termed millennialists (alternatively, millenarians, or chiliasts). From the time of Augustine through the sixteenth century, most political establishments viewed such promises with considerable apprehension. But as printing presses throughout northern Europe produced more and more Bibles and religious tracts, there was no stemming the tide of millennialist speculation. Joseph Mede was among the first English scholars to revive the belief that the martyrs would rise from their graves and together with Christ rule the earth a thousand years before its final destruction.[29] His work encouraged theologians like John Cotton, and in the seventeenth and eighteenth centuries politicians, tradesmen, and even renowned scientists such as Isaac Newton and Joseph Priestley pondered the prospects. Newton, in fact, wrote more words about the prophecies of Revelation than about the nature of the universe, leading Voltaire to quip: "Sir Isaac Newton wrote his comment[ary] upon the Revelation to console mankind for the great superiority he had over them in other respects."[30]

The first emergence of millennial controversy within American Protestantism is itself controversial. Some scholars place it in the decade following the Civil War; others, in the decade following the Revolutionary War.[31] Such dating suggests that during times of crisis, such debates are kept in abeyance. Until the close of the eighteenth century, American millennialists were generally united in their hostility toward those who, like Voltaire, scoffed at their "enthusiasm" and toward those who held the insufferable notion that the Millennium had already begun and was being adequately administered by an ecclesiastical hierarchy. Among themselves they could identify doctrinal differences, but for the time being chose to tolerate them.

The conditions that permitted these differences to emerge, however, were already established in America. When the first English came to New England, they brought with them two translations of the Bible. One, the Geneva Bible (1560), was consistently Christocentric. The Old Testament, whenever possible, was interpreted in marginal notes as constituting types of Jesus and his ministry.[32] According to Harry Stout, "in this interpretive framework, the Old Testament language of national covenant, judicial laws, or temporal rewards and punishments was uniformly spiritualized and interpreted as 'signs' or 'figures' of the Messiah."[33] But coming out of Cambridge and Oxford in the early seventeenth century was another view of the Bible, a covenant theology that required believers to regard the Israel of the Old Testament as a practical model in itself. While the spirit of the Geneva Bible was the covenant of grace and of faith proclaimed in the New Testament, that of the new Bible translation, the King James Version (KJV) of 1611, was in effect the covenant of works. As Stout argues, while the "Geneva Bible and its marginalia served well the purpose of an embattled religious minority with its thoughts fixed firmly on martyrdom and the world to come, it was less useful in fashioning binding principles of social organization and order in the world."[34] As Puritan influence grew, the significance of the Old Testament grew as a document every bit as important for Christians to meditate upon as the New. Moreover, because the KJV was devoid of explanatory notes, most Christians required a learned clergy to explicate it, thus greatly enhancing the status of this professional class.

In America, the Plymouth Pilgrims retained their fondness for the Geneva Bible, but the Puritans of the Massachusetts Bay Colony embraced the newer translation and used it to preach the notion of a holy people.[35] Giving equal standing to the Old Testament, the KJV highlighted God's relationship to an ethnically identified people at the expense of the New Testament, which in the Gospels and Epistles is international in scope and spirit. John Winthrop's famous words are resonant with Old Testament theocratic particularism: "We shall find that the God of Israel is among us, when ten of us shall be able to resist a thousand of our enemies, when he shall make us a praise and glory that men shall say of succeeding plantations: 'The Lord make it like that of NEW ENGLAND.' For we must consider that we shall be as a city upon a hill. The eyes of all people are upon us."[36]

In Boston, however, there emerged two notable dissenters: Anne Hutchinson and her brother-in-law the Reverend John Wheelwright. Despite the earnest admonishments of the church elders, these two refused to accept the civil magistrates' right to enforce particular issues of faith. As Stout points out, during the "antinomian" controversy, their critics drew upon the KJV, but Hutchinson and Wheelwright quoted from the Geneva Bible. They were banished from Massachusetts and sought refuge in Rhode Island, where Roger Williams—a like-minded believer in the covenant of faith and for that reason also banished—had settled the previous year. He too, incidentally, preached from the Geneva Bible and, like Hutchinson and Wheelwright, opposed the Old Testament model of the theocratic state. As he declared in *The Bloody Tenent of Persecution* (1643), the function of government was to maintain order and protect the people, but not to compel their consciences.

The faith versus works debate was already centuries old. Which is the more important trait of the justified Christian? Both would be necessary for salvation, of course, but which would be essential? The division between the two parties in seventeenth-century New England underlay the later doctrinal division between postmillennialists, who stress the covenant of works, and premillennialists, who support the covenant of faith. Beneath these two positions, we can recognize an even older division: that between those who identify their interests with strong, central governmental authority and those who distrust this authority and advocate communal independence.

Though such issues may sound to some like the minor details of a divinity school debate, the differences between the two positions have had, and continue to have, profound implications for America. The postmillennialist believes that American Protestants have been assigned by God the task of ushering in the Millennium, a thousand years of spiritual and material progress, and that Christ will physically return only *after* the Millennium in order to quell the last resurgence of Satan and pronounce final judgment on the living and the dead. This view has been opposed with increasing vehemence over the years by those who maintain that Christ will intervene physically, extract his elect from the end-time tumult of vice, pestilence, and war, and then punish the unsaved—accomplishing all this *before* the Millennium begins, during which time the saved, in their glorified bodies, will rule the earth with Christ, their king.

Though both millennialisms anticipate the coming kingdom of God, American postmillennialists believe that it is their duty to make their nation a worthy location for it. For them, the Jeffersonian ideal of a perpetual revolution was best phrased by Ezekiel's God when he decreed that "iniquity shall have an end. . . . [E]xalt him that is low, and abase him that is high. I will overturn, overturn, overturn" (Ezek. 21:25–27). Once evil leaders were removed and evil institutions abolished, America could finally act upon the words of Isaiah, the words that John the Baptist later used to announce the first coming of the Christ: "The voice of him that cryeth in the wilderness, Prepare ye the way of the Lord, make straight in the desert the highway of our God. Every valley shall be exalted and every mountain and hill shall be made low: and the crooked shall be made straight, and the rough places plain. And the glory of the Lord shall be revealed, and all flesh shall see it together; for the mouth of the Lord hath spoken it" (Isa. 40:3–5). In the American narrative, the wilderness, which in the Bible had been the place of temptation that one had to traverse before entering the Promised Land, became identified as the great North American continent. The road across it ("the way of the Lord") had to be laid down and walked upon before the glory of the Lord could be revealed. Here was a commandment to build the millennial kingdom in which Christ, having returned *in spirit* to the hearts and souls of the faithful, could rule the world through his chosen people.

In contrast, premillennialism emerges out of a historical pessimism that favors isolationist policies. As a human government, America has no grand national mission such as leading the world's "march to freedom." Churches that say so and preach a man-made Millennium ruled by the invisible spirit of Christ have ignored the plain literal message of Revelation. America is a place of sojourn only. Even here, the true believers are strangers and pilgrims yearning for a distant heavenly homeland. If American Christianity is Protestant, for the most part biblically based, and relatively free of popish influences, so much the better, but salvation is a matter of individual souls preparing themselves in fear and repentance for the imminent return of the master. The moment he returns, he will lift the saved into the sky—an event called the "Rapture"—and leave the damned below to wallow a few more years in their filthy ways, fully earning their eternal damnation, before he destroys them utterly.

This view of history was supported by an interpretation of the Bible set forth in the mid-nineteenth century by John Nelson Darby, an Anglican curate in Wicklow, Ireland. Darby attacked all "spiritual," or allegorical, readings of biblical prophecy, especially those that interpreted the end times in postmillennialist terms. Instead, he devised a theory of world history according to which God has preordained six ages, or dispensations. During each he has tested humankind under six distinct conditions. The six dispensations are as follows: Innocence (Adam and Eve in Eden); Conscience (after the Fall); Human Government (Noah and his children); Promise (Abraham); Law (Moses); and Grace (the Church Age). The seventh dispensation, the

Sabbath of rest in this cosmic week, will be the Millennium, or Kingdom Age, a period that for the elect will be one of reward rather than testing. According to Darby's American follower, Cyrus Scofield, these dispensations—each with its own special requirements—should not be confused with covenants, those unconditional and everlasting promises that God makes at certain points along this time line.[37]

In American culture over the past two hundred years, the popularity of these two millennialisms has oscillated in pendular fashion. Postmillennialism is a biblical frame of reference that has accompanied reform movements, periods characterized by a hopeful attitude toward future possibilities and a confidence in organized political action. Premillennialism has reasserted itself when these hopes seem unfulfilled. It represents a backlash against the ideals of the preceding era. Then, when premillennialist movements overstate their predictive powers or economic conditions begin to improve, postmillennialist optimism is rekindled.[38]

On the broad cultural battlefield, the two millennialisms clash over Enlightenment values and meanings. As scientific inquiry and liberatory politics began to transform Americans' view of nature and the individual, the world represented in the Bible seemed to slip further and further into the historical past. The term "modernism" emerged to characterize what was called the "march of the mind" out of medieval darkness into the new dawn. Postmillennialists sought to bless modernism and work it into their endtime agenda as the means by which the spirit of Christ would triumph over paganism. Premillennialists, however, saw modernism as paganism itself, an idolatrous turning away from God toward a worship of human inventiveness. The rise of fundamentalism a century ago was fueled by preachers who denounced modernism in all its manifestations, especially what they called "Christian modernism."

As theories of history, the two American millennialisms also reflect the conflicting interests of the two social levels I outlined in Chapter 1. Premillennialism, for example, is community based. Though it defines itself in opposition to government (which, associated in the biblical tradition with Egypt, Babylon, and Rome, is the oppressor of the True Church), premillennialism is not a unified communitarian movement wholly antagonistic to the governmental level. Its current adherents support national defense, homeland security, and some social programs, as long as these do not override local authority in matters of belief and behavior. Though they regard themselves as patriotic, they reject as presumptuous the notion that America might somehow postpone, much less avert, God's wrath upon a sinful world by espousing a "rational" foreign policy, by "saving the environment," or by adopting any other "humanistic" stratagem. America loses its divine protection by permitting abortion and extending civil rights to homosexuals. Using the river metaphor, premillennialists believe that a divinely planned punishment for sin is hurtling toward the world out of an obscure future and that, by the time it arrives, it will already be too late for nations (including America) to repent. The timing of this cosmic ending is wholly in the hands of God. Only those who absolutely trust his utter sovereignty can ever hope to enjoy his free gift of salvation in the millennial kingdom. As for mythology, this communally based culture focuses on heroic narratives of repentance, virtue rewarded, self-sacrifice, and law enforcement.

By contrast, postmillennialism supports the governmental level. It assumes that God, while not a respecter of persons, is indeed a respecter of nations and, as the one-dollar bill confidently asserts, "has approved our undertakings" (*annuit coeptis*). As Americans walk forward into the future on the road of time, they collaborate with God in preparing the world for the global millennial kingdom. John F. Kennedy concluded his inaugural address in a typically postmillennialist fashion: "let us go forth to lead the land we love, asking His blessing and His help, but knowing that here on earth God's work must truly be our own." Unique among the world's elected heads of state, American presidents radiate the aura of anointed rulers. Be their origins ever so modest and their retirement years ever so obscure, during their years in office they are the veritable vicars of God. Moreover, despite their personal failings, the flawed men who have risen to this highest of governmental offices are believed to have been granted God's empowering grace *ex officio*.

The Judgment of George W. Bush

The full narrative cycle, concretized in Judaic and Christian historiography, has always offered assurance to believers and advantage to politicians. At the beginning of the twenty-first century, President George W. Bush—in the words scripted for him by his chief speechwriter, Michael Gerson—exploited the possibilities of biblical time in unprecedented ways. By representing himself as the champion of the traditional values of the American past, as opposed to the current climate of moral relativism, he linked himself with a down-home brand of premillennialist antimodernism. At the same time, he took on the postmillennial agenda, standard for all American presidents, by declaring his right to extend American traditions abroad and, as the leader of the "civilized world," to project his model of the American past into the world's future.

But Bush went further. Not only did he attempt to shape the future, but he also implied that he *knew* the future. On January 28, 2003, in the State of the Union address in which he warned of Saddam's weapons of mass destruction and his ties with al Qaeda, he concluded with these words: "We Americans have faith in ourselves, but not in ourselves alone. We do not know—we do not claim to know all the ways of Providence, yet we can trust in them, placing our confidence in the loving God behind all life, and all of history."[39] (*All* the ways of Providence? As Bush was once quoted as saying, God had wanted him to be president,[40] yet God had apparently not yet revealed to him *all* his plans for the future.) As a professed believer in the relevance of biblical prophecy to world history, Bush hereby conveyed to a sizable sector of his Christian constituency that he, along with them, has a clear general understanding of the future—and that it will be a God-blessed future if only the children of light uncompromisingly wage war against the children of darkness, wherever they lurk.

It was as a postmillennialist commander in chief of the Redeemer Nation that he sought to assure the newly elected Palestinian prime minister, Mahmoud Abbas, in June 2003 that he could and would shape the political future of the Middle East. The Palestinians would get their own state. He would personally see to that. God's will, he implied, had all along directed his administration's foreign policy: "God would tell me, 'George, go and fight those terrorists in Afghanistan,' and so I did, and then God would tell me, 'George, go and end the tyranny in Iraq,' and I did."[41]

It was as a premillennialist, however, that Bush in the summer of 2004 journeyed to the antimodernist heartland of Lancaster, Pennsylvania, to woo the traditionally nonvoting, pacifist Amish. On July 9, at a gathering of some fifty locals in Smoketown, he highlighted his social-conservative agenda, asked for their votes and their prayers, and concluded: "I trust God speaks through me. Without that, I couldn't do my job."[42]

A man who claims that God speaks *to* him may be excused should he sometimes misinterpret the message. (Those who believe that in prayer we can commune with a higher power generally allow for human error.) But when George W. Bush asserts that God speaks *through* him, that what he says is nothing less than the utterance of the Almighty, he cannot possibly misinterpret the words he directly relays. But who *is* the President's source? Whoever this is speaking through him (and in phrases sometimes difficult to comprehend), one thing is sure. This deity must have had very limited prewar intelligence-gathering capabilities —and an overly optimistic view of the post-invasion consequences.

As I proposed earlier, a successful government justifies itself by dominating the spatial here and now. It occupies phase 5 in the full narrative cycle. History, once it is written by the victor, is now no longer a perilous, ongoing process but rather a monumental inscription. Confident that it has fulfilled the promises of the past and mastered the present, such a government tends to project its current status into a future that its leaders sometimes claim to know.

In its temporal rhetoric, the early Bush administration looked backward toward the past generation of statesmen who, under Ronald Reagan and George H. W. Bush's leadership in the 1980s, had forced the implosion of the Soviet state and the end of socialism. This past, indeed mere prologue to this present, had inevitably led to the "unipolar moment" when it was America's turn to reshape global politics to its own advantage. To accomplish this, the Pentagon would train an all-volunteer military, arm it with high-tech weaponry, and then, thanks to the provocation of 9/11, insert it surgically into the center of the oil-rich Middle East—Iraq. From the perspective of the war planners, the future was substantially knowable.

To report the pacification of Iraq, reporters, embedded with the military, were expected to send back to America instant accounts of mopping-up operations, interspersed with images of grateful, smiling, liberated villagers. Views such as these did dominate the news during the first weeks following the invasion begun on March 20, 2003. Then, as time passed, the euphoria cooled and accounts of American losses at the hands of insurgents (then called "diehards") began to grow. With the *present* increasingly out of control and the *future* in doubt, voices began to be heard that questioned the recent *past*—namely, the evidence that Bush, Cheney, Donald Rumsfeld, and Condoleeza Rice had laid out for the invasion and for the optimistic assessments they had offered to the Congress and the American public.

Rice, in response to the critics, began to speak of them in early June as purveyors of "revisionist history," though it was uncertain what version of events she had assumed was already "history." Two weeks later, the president himself complained: "This nation acted to a threat from the dictator of Iraq. Now there are some who would like to rewrite history—revisionist historians is what I like to call them."[43]

In 2004, during ten months of presidential campaigning, the president's critics continued to question the historical narrative used to promote the war, while Bush and his cabinet tried to convince voters that fighting "them" over there was preferable to fighting them here in the homeland. But after Bush's narrow electoral victory, the administration sought, early in 2005, to reclaim the history theme by broadening it to mean an age-old struggle between tyranny and freedom. The president had already invoked this traditional American-exceptionalist view of history, especially following 9/11 and during the public diplomacy that preceded the invasion of 2003, but this new campaign, which used the catchphrase "the history of freedom," seemed aimed at diverting attention from the political and economic motives that lay behind the current invasion.[44]

By fall 2005, as support for the war and for this "wartime president" plummeted, Bush found that he needed to revisit the issue of historical revisionism. Addressing troops at the Tobyhanna Army Depot in Tobyhanna, Pennsylvania, on Veterans Day, he explained: "We didn't ask for this global struggle, but we're answering history's call with confidence and with a comprehensive strategy. . . . While it's perfectly legitimate to criticize my decision or the conduct of the war, it is deeply irresponsible to rewrite the history of how that war began. (Applause.) Some Democrats and anti-war critics are now claiming we manipulated the intelligence and misled the American people about why we went to war. These critics are fully aware that a bipartisan Senate investigation found no evidence of political pressure to change the intelligence community's judgments related to Iraq's weapons programs."[45]

A long view of historical time must have seemed the perfect message for a public with a short attention span. During a White House press conference on December 19, 2005, President Bush again invited his audience to place current difficulties in Iraq in proper perspective: "Think about what has happened in a brief period of time—relatively brief. I know with all the TV stations and stuff in America, two-and-a-half years seems like an eternity. But in the march of history, it's not all that long." The press corps, however, proved less interested in the march of history than in the president's last five years in office. When John Dickerson asked, "What would you say is the biggest mistake you've made during your presidency, and what have you learned from it?" Bush answered, "The last time those questions were asked, I really felt like it was an attempt for me to say it was a mistake to go into Iraq. And it wasn't a mistake to go into Iraq. It was the right decision to make. I think that, John, there's going to be a lot of analysis done on the decisions on the ground in Iraq. For example, I'm fully aware that some have said it was a mistake not to put enough troops there immediately—or more troops. I made my decision based upon the recommendations of Tommy Franks, and I still think it was the right decision to make. But history will judge."[46]

"History will judge"—here, the future tense marked a significant rhetorical shift by means of which he could project himself and his critics into a future that would supposedly vindicate his actions. This projection of his presidential legacy into a kinder, gentler future had apparently comforted him for some time already. Two years earlier, Bob Woodward interviewed Bush and later recalled: "We got up and walked over to one of the doors. There are all of these doors in the Oval Office that lead outside. And he had his hands in his pocket, and I just asked, 'Well, how is history likely to judge your Iraq war,' . . . And he said, 'History,' and then he took his hands out of his pocket and kind of shrugged and extended his hands as if this is a way off. And then he said, 'History, we don't know. We'll all be dead.'"[47]

It is "deeply irresponsible" for us the living to question the commander in chief instead of waiting until we are "all dead," when historians will be able to unseal the presidential files and with 20/20 hindsight render judgment on the forty-third president. This, at least, is one way to interpret the administration's stance toward its critics. At any rate, this seems to have been what Secretary of State Condoleeza Rice meant when, speaking at a town hall event in Sydney, Australia, on March 16, 2006, she suggested that we are too close in time to judge this president's actions:

> Sometimes when you look at the grand sweep of history you have to step back and you have to remark at how much has happened. When you get as old as I am, you have a grander sweep of history to look at, and that's an advantage. . . . So yes, the President has done some tough things, some of which were not popular. But as I said to the young man in answer to his question, I think that the outcome, the judgment of all of this, needs to await history. I'm a student of history. I know very well that things that seemed like brilliant strategies one day or maybe for one week or maybe for one year or maybe even for five years turned out to be disastrous strategies in terms of history. And I know that strategies that seemed at the time to be fraught with mistakes and fraught with errors turned out to be very good for human history.[48]

Bush's invocation of history was, in itself, not new. In the address he delivered at the United Nations eight days after 9/11, he identified history as God's book of time. "We are confident," he declared, "that history has an author who fills time and eternity with his purpose. We know that evil is real, but good will prevail against it. This is the teaching of many faiths.

And in that assurance, we gain strength for a long journey. It is our task, the task of this generation, to provide the response to aggression and terror. We have no other choice, we did not ask for this mission, yet there is honor in history's call."[49]

Over the next five years, as we have seen, his references to history became darker and less confident. In Todorov's narrative model, once equilibrium is lost, the government breaks down, the long journey turns inevitably downward, and only the hope for that once and future kingdom sustains the wanderers. In the biblical version of this universal master narrative, this future kingdom, this ultimate homeland, is won at great cost: not until pestilence, famine, and the bloodbath of Armageddon have ravaged the earth will the author of history render his Last Judgment.

3

MYTHS OF CURSES, MYTHS OF BLESSINGS

America was settled and its republic founded by Europeans steeped in a biblical theory of history, a belief that the final age was dawning and that the kingdom of heaven would soon appear on earth. If we may judge by their rhetoric, the leaders of this enterprise assumed that their work had been inscribed in God's providential book of time and had not only temporal consequences but eternal ones as well. Patriotic clergy preached that if Americans were *truly* Christian, Christ would manifest himself in their lives in a manner so palpable that the entire world would follow their example. Then, working through his believers, he would soon complete his redemptive mission. Even before postmillennialism was theologically defined, this belief that the ultimate nation had at last appeared had become the mythical premise of the United States.

Leaders of government appreciated the advantages of this myth. English settlers had always been quick to discern the features of the Antichrist and his minions in the pope, the Spanish, the French, the Indians, and later the English king—any current enemy of theirs—because his appearance in the time line of history made it possible for them to fancy themselves the army of saints on their march to the Millennium. Of course, the founders of the republic did not, for the most part, believe this epic narrative, but few were inclined to chill the zeal of those among their countrymen who did.

American millennialists, however, needed more than properly vilifiable enemies. They had to practice an intense religious regimen of scripture readings, good works, and close observation of God's signs in their souls, in nature, and in current events to prove to themselves that they, and no others, were the true millennial people. They also had to find ways to justify a number of activities that appeared similar to those of other, less godly European invaders of the New World. When necessary, they, too, needed to launch preemptive military attacks on the native populations, destroy their natural resources, extirpate their culture, and take their land. They found it increasingly profitable, moreover, to import Africans as slave laborers to help build their peaceable kingdom. Whenever their actions seemed to clash with their ethics, their troubled consciences sent them to the Bible for master narratives that might legitimate their actions.

The Peculiar People of Deuteronomy

Toward the end of his sermon aboard the *Arbella,* having outlined his biblical model of Christian government, John Winthrop proceeded to "shut up this discourse with that exhortation of Moses, that faithful servant of the Lord, in his last farewell to Israel." What followed was a paraphrase of a text from chapter 30 of Deuteronomy that must have been quite familiar to his fellow voyagers. In it, having detailed God's conditions for their possession of the Promised Land, Moses added these blunt words: "I have set before you life and death, blessing and cursing: therefore choose life that both thou and thy seed shall live" (30:19).

Deuteronomy, the "second law," was an elaboration on the covenant code received by Moses on Mount Sinai (Exod. 20). Since its reported discovery in a wall of the Temple in 621 BC, this book has been admired for many reasons: its ideals of social justice (but not for most gentiles), its moral vehemence, its majestic eloquence, and its importance to the development of monotheism. It was also the book from which Jesus most often quoted. But why the English colonizers of North America so often referred to it is not immediately apparent. One might sooner expect them to have found in Exodus, Joshua, and Judges closer resemblances to their enterprise. Those epic narratives did indeed provide homeland mythology with much of its vivid imagery, but Deuteronomy, with its lists of blessings and curses, provided its fundamental ideology.

Deuteronomy grounds this ideology firmly in a set of traditional narratives derived from the second, third, and fourth books of the Bible (Exodus, Leviticus, and Numbers). This, the fifth book of the Pentateuch, might therefore provide us with a model of narrativized thinking and rhetoric. A thumbnail outline of some of the key Deuteronomic themes will suggest how important this text was in the development of America's own master narratives, especially those that have come to be associated with postmillennialism. It will also suggest how Deuteronomy may have served to justify certain frequently attributed tendencies in American culture.

Exodus   See Deuteronomy 6:20–25, 7:18–19, 8:14–16. The Puritans' and Separatists' escape from the control of a pharaonic papacy and from a hostile English monarch, the crossing of the Atlantic Ocean as a crossing of the Red Sea and of the Jordan River—all this replicates the Israelites' journey. Hence America as a land of *religious freedom.*

Covenant   True believers constitute the New Israel, chosen by God as a "peculiar people" and subsequently bound to him by a national covenant: "The LORD has chosen thee to be a peculiar people unto himself, above all the nations that are upon the earth" (Deut. 14:2; see also 7:6 and 26:18). Hence *American exceptionalism.*

Wilderness   The "howling wilderness" passage (Deut. 32:10) is probably the Deuteronomic text most frequently quoted in the seventeenth and eighteenth centuries (see also 8:2–5). North America, to English colonists a wilderness, an undeveloped wasteland echoing with the devilish chants and whoops of savages, awaited its transformation into God's intended Promised Land. Hence the equation of progress with the *exploitation of nature.*

Promised Land   Canaan prefigures North America, and so English Protestants, as the new Israelites, had a divinely countersigned deed to the continent. This meant that they had the right to oust nonbelievers (Indians, French, and Spanish) and, if necessary, kill them. (See Deut. 11:23–25.) Hence *Manifest Destiny.*

Backsliding   As their nostalgia for the "fleshpots of Egypt" testified, the chosen people were not inherently more virtuous than any other people. Unless the law of God is publicly and regularly preached, Israelites may fall away from their covenanted duties (Deut. 4:2 and 9:5–24). For his famous sermon, "Sinners in the Hands of an Angry God," Jonathan Edwards chose Deuteronomy 32:35 as his text: "their foot shall slide in due time." Americans will need moral guidance. Hence *a strong central government.*

Reform	Because of the moral weaknesses even of the chosen people, periodic "awakenings" and revivals are required. Deuteronomy, as the "second law," is a document of religious reform that underscores the people's need to return to earlier, purer practices (Deut. 5–6:5). Hence *traditionalism.*
Idolatry	This preference for the visual image over the word of God was specifically cursed with death. The Puritan condemned religious icons and distrusted the visual arts and the visual imagination. Idolatry was equated with "following other gods"; no rival religions could be tolerated in the land of Israel (Deut. 13). Compromise is not an option for God's "peculiar people." Hence *cultural intolerance.*
Invincibility	"[T]hou shalt smite them, and utterly destroy them; thou shalt make no covenant with them, nor shew mercy unto them" (Deut. 7:3). One Israelite could, with God's power, "chase a thousand, and two put ten thousand to flight" (32:30, 33:28–29). This spiritual power to which Winthrop alluded in his sermon was materially enhanced by English musketry. Hence *military triumphalism.*
Curses	These fall on Israelites who transgress the laws of the covenant and may thereby tempt God to abandon his people (Deut. 27:14–26, 28:15–68). Though many of them fall on individual malefactors, they are related to earlier inheritable curses, e.g., the curses of Adam and Canaan. In the context of an ethnic myth, a curse could therefore explain the lower social and economic status of some groups, e.g., Africans and American Indians. Hence *racism.*
Blessings	Obedience to the covenant of works would bring material benefits (Deut. 23:5, 28:1–14, 30:3–10). Divine approval could therefore explain national prosperity and legitimize the preceding nine premises. Hence *materialism.*

Deuteronomy is anything but an action-filled narrative. An old preacher assembles his congregation, delivers a monologue that refers to past events, and thirty-four chapters later climbs a mountain and dies. Yet to political and religious leaders, men who relied on their oratorical prowess, this book must have been a special favorite. Its speaker, a man to whom God had directly spoken, was the paragon of preachers. He had personally led his congregation from bondage until, after forty years of wandering in a howling wilderness, they were on the frontier of their Promised Land. This was the sermon of an inspired lawgiver and, as a detailed legal document, was a political constitution of sorts.[1] As for consequences, on the one hand there was the curse, and on the other, the blessing. Drawing meanings from a rich traditional history, this was also a moment of high drama: the heroic prophet stood poised between a past visible as the wasteland to the south and a future in the form of the rich hillsides and valleys to the northwest, a vista he was to glimpse from atop Mount Nebo as he drew his last breath. The curses of slavery and deprivation lay on one side of this historical divide; the blessings of prosperous nationhood awaited on the other.

In the mind of biblically schooled English settlers, however, this moment in sacred history had yet other meanings. Crossing over the Jordan marked their transition from homeless wandering, but it also signified the resurrection of Jesus. His name, a later form of "Joshua," linked him typologically with the man whom God had chosen instead of Moses to lead his people across Jordan and into the Promised Land, the new dispensation of grace. Moses and his law had been insufficient. Only Jesus could effect this transition from the Old Testament to the New.[2] Interpreted anagogically, i.e., in terms of the soul's journey of life, crossing Jordan meant dying a Christian death and entering heaven. (This was the central trope in John Bunyan's *Pilgrim's Progress*.) Finally, it might also have broader historical significance. It could mean the transition from the long ages of human pilgrimage to the new age, the millennial kingdom of heaven on earth, a moment in time that many felt was swiftly approaching.

This latter interpretation, of course, required that both the prophecies of Revelation as well as contemporary events be read into the drama of Deuteronomy.[3] In a sermon delivered in Cambridge, Massachusetts, in 1673, Urian Oakes chose for his text Deuteronomy 32:29 ("O that they were wise, that they understood this, that they would consider their latter end!").

> As the words of my text respect the body of a nation, even Israel, that were sometimes the peculiar people of God, so give me leave to direct my exhortation to the people of New England . . . and to persuade the New England Israel to . . . consider what will be the latter end of your sinful ways and unworthy deportments before the Lord. . . .
>
> God has sequestered you from the rest of the world, allured you into this wilderness . . . that you might set up this way and worship in the purity and gospel-glory of it. . . . If we cast up the account

and sum up all the mercies and lay all things together, this our commonwealth seems to exhibit to us a specimen or a little model of the kingdom of Christ upon earth. . . . This work of God set foot and advanced to a good degree here, being spread over the face of the earth and perfected as to greater degrees of light and grace and gospel-glory, will be (as I conceive) the kingdom of Jesus Christ so much spoken of. When this is accomplished, you may then say . . . [that] you have been as a city upon a hill, though in a remote and obscure wilderness, as a candle that gives light to the whole house. You have to a considerable degree enlightened the whole house (world I mean).[4]

Jonathan Edwards, the most eminent American theologian of the eighteenth century, believed that America would indeed be the place in which the millennial kingdom would be founded. At the outbreak of the War of Independence, his grandson, Timothy Dwight, addressed his fellow graduates at Yale's commencement ceremonies:

the empire of North America will be the last on earth. . . . Here the progress of temporal things towards perfection will undoubtedly be finished. Here human greatness will find a period. Here will be accomplished that remarkable Jewish tradition that the last thousand years of the reign of time would, in imitation of the conclusion of the first week [of creation], become a glorious Sabbath of peace, purity, and felicity. . . .

From every deduction of reason as well as from innumerable declarations of inspired truth, we have the best foundation to believe that the continent will be the principal seat of that new, that peculiar kingdom, which shall be given to the saints of the Most High, that also was to be the last, the greatest, the happiest of all dominions. . . . Here shall a king reign in righteousness whose kingdom shall be everlasting and whose kingdom shall not be destroyed.[5]

Deuteronomy and Revelation are in some respects similar documents. Both aimed to correct religious abuses, viewed history as a struggle between God's chosen people and a hostile world, and prophesied a new era of blessings for the persevering faithful. Ezra Stiles asserted a commonly held belief when, in 1783, he told his congregation that Deuteronomy was "allusively prophetic of the future prosperity and splendor of the United States." It was no mere coincidence that as "God's American Israel" fought for independence, it had reached a population level of "three million of people," the same number that stood and heard that great discourse of Moses. Now led by Washington, that "American Joshua," and having crossed over into the new era, America was prepared to go forth and convert the heathen: "great things are to be effected in the world before the millennium. . . . I doubt not this is the honor reserved for us."[6]

Many Americans understood that the Promised Land story prefigured the end-time narrative of Revelation. It had been the end-time drama of the Apocalypse that had passed its long shadow over world history and was the final key to understanding all previous world events. Could it not be possible that the founding of the United States was necessary for the fulfillment of John's prophecy? If the patriots of 1776 were *like* the battle-ready Israelites assembled by Moses upon the plain below Mount Nebo, were they not perhaps *in actuality* the army of saints described in Revelation? If so, the resemblance should be reversed: the Israelites poised to cross over Jordan were like the stalwarts of the new republic. At any rate, America was beginning to see the Promised Land and Revelation narratives as type and antitype, fading one into the other and constituting a single epic written by God himself, the last episodes of which it was their destiny to enact.

When the Saints Go Marching In

People who identify themselves with the godly ones in the Promised Land and the Apocalypse narratives see themselves as warriors—like those who, with Joshua, "fit the battle of Jericho" and who will, at the end of time, "go marching" into the New Jerusalem. But what kinds of actions do these traditional American spirituals really allude to? When the walls of Jericho did "come a-tumbling down," the book of Joshua tells us that "the people [i.e., the army] went straight up into the city, every man straight before him, and they took the city. And they utterly destroyed all that was in the city, both man and woman, young and old, and ox, and sheep, and ass, with the edge of the sword" (6:20–21). And before the saints can go marching into the millennial kingdom, blood has to flow "even unto the horse bridles, by the space of a thousand and six hundred furlongs" (Rev. 14:20), which for the literal-minded amounts to a pond of blood two hundred miles across and five feet deep. The carrion birds are then invited "unto the supper of the great God [to] eat the flesh of kings, and the flesh of captains, and the flesh of mighty men, and the flesh of horses, and of them that sit on them, and the flesh of all men, both free and bond, both great and small" (19:17–18).[7]

What kind of warriors are these saints? In the words of another popular hymn, "Onward, Christian soldiers, marching *as* to war," an aspect of this militarism is professedly metaphorical. The Christian term "crusade," like the Islamic term *jihad,* may mean "moral struggle." Yet the formula "living religiously is like fighting a war" (battling one's own tendency to sin) is easily reversed to become "fighting a war is like living religiously" (battling the tendency of others to resist our power and reject our exculpatory myths).

This raises a significant technical issue. In his theory of metaphor, George Lakoff, together with his colleagues Mark Johnson, Mark Turner, and Zoltán Kövecses, formulated what he has called the "invariance principle."[8] According to this principle, the second term of a metaphor, the source (or vehicle), transfers only as much knowledge over to the first term, the target (or tenor), as is consistent with the properties of this target. For example, when Romeo exclaims "Juliet is the sun!" only certain aspects of the source (the sun) apply to the target (Juliet), e.g., warmth, light, and importance, but not gaseousness or rotundity. A corollary to this principle is metaphor unidirectionality: the flow of meaning normally goes in one direction only, from the source to the target. If, for example, in some other context he saw the sun and, reminded of Juliet, proclaimed "The sun is Juliet," this would convey a wholly different set of thoughts, and the sun (now as main topic) would be extravagantly anthropomorphized. Similarly, the metaphor "The Lord is my shepherd" becomes totally changed when it is reversed: "The shepherd is my Lord."

The broad cultural terms "religion" and "war" may, in any order, be paired in metaphors, as long as their semantic differences are respected. If in rhetorical practice they are regularly reversed, those necessary differences become effaced. When this happens, the metaphor breaks down and all that remains is an equation—a false and abusive equation. This is especially the case when the two terms are fundamentally antithetical, "religion" suggesting communal ethos and "war" suggesting governmental praxis. (Metaphor reversal, a topic I will return to in my final chapter, may have even further significance: if it is a factor capable of fusing opposites, it may precede the formation of such compounds as "homeland.")

These two concepts, religion and war, which had for so many centuries taken turns allegorizing one another, had become by the eighteenth century dangerously interchangeable. One passage will suffice to exemplify the "religion = war" formula. These are the words of Joseph Bellamy, a student of Jonathan Edwards:

Hail, noble heroes! Brave followers of the Lamb! Your General has sacrificed his life in this glorious cause, and spoiled principalities and powers on the cross, and now he lives and reigns! . . . Your predecessors, the prophets, apostles, and martyrs, with undaunted courage, have marched into the field of Battle, and conquered dying, and now reign in heaven! Beyond, ye are risen up in their room, are engaged in the same cause, and the time of the last general battle draws on, when a victory is to be won![9]

Now, for an example of the "war = religion" formula, consider David Austin's 1794 visionary bluster and note how it revises Cotton Mather's promise of sending a light "to be darted over unto the other side of the Atlantic":

Behold, then, this hero of America, wielding the standard of civil and religious liberty over these United States!—Follow him, in his strides, across the Atlantic!—See him, with his spear already in the heart of the beast!—See tyranny, civil and ecclesiastical, bleeding at every pore! See the votaries of the tyrants; of the beasts; of the false prophets, and serpents of the earth, ranged in battle array, to withstand the progress and dominion of him, who hath commission to break down the usurpations of tyranny—to let the *prisoner out of the prison-house;* and to set the vassal in bondage free from his chains—to level the mountains—to raise the valleys, and to prepare an highway for the Lord![10]

If these sentiments remind us of the neoconservative voices raised in support of Operation Iraqi Freedom, it only demonstrates how susceptible Americans still are to this myth-based rhetoric.

This hero's mission is twofold: on the one hand it is to liberate, and on the other, to coerce. These two functions, essential to all governmental systems, he shares with the biblical Deity who blesses and curses. The Bible promotes this most troubling but powerful combination because its single god is the ultimate giver of life and death, of good things and evil things. Having no divine siblings to share in the allotting of fates to humans, this god is the one source of all destinies. He is the first and last speaker of the world, thus issuing what to humans must sometimes seem mixed messages. For Christians, his son shares his nature and equally combines this bipolar ambiguity, thanks to the inclusion of Revelation alongside the Gospels in the New Testament. It is troubling to conceive of a mysterious, unvisualizable

God the Father lovingly creating humankind (on Sunday, October 23, 4004 BC, according to Bishop Ussher),[11] and then 1655 years later repenting of his venture and drowning his human "children" like a litter of unwanted puppies. Many Christians have found it even more troubling, however, to visualize a human god—one who preached the Sermon on the Mount, saved the adulterous woman from being stoned to death, healed sick children, and forgave his crucifiers—coming back to earth, mounting a white horse, and slaughtering hundreds of thousands of infidels with a sword that shoots from his mouth. The Messiah of the Gospels and the book of Revelation seems indeed to be two persons in one divine nature, a "good cop" and a "bad cop." Those early churchmen, Augustine among them, who opposed the inclusion of Revelation in the biblical canon must have been disturbed by this contrast. This duality produces not merely a cognitive but also an emotional dissonance in his worshippers, a condition that might clinically be described as a "double bind."

Theologians remind us that the invisible God of the universe is not human and should not be bounded by the metaphorical language used to portray him. Such human attributes as male gender, age, and royal demeanor are culturally specific signifiers of wisdom and authority. God is only *likened* to, they say, but not *equated* with, a secretive, all-powerful, "oriental despot" of the first or second millennium BC. Those who insist on reading metaphorical language literally tend to mistake the human descriptors of this similitude (the source domain, or vehicle, of this metaphor) and fashion from them a verbally constructed icon, an idol they worship as the divine embodiment of government.

The kingdom of God, as an apotheosis of the governmental level, is inherently dissonant with the ethos of the communal level. Here, where individuals and their families are personally held to account for the consequences of their actions, the end never justifies the means. Only a rash egoist would assume otherwise, and this sort of person would eventually be punished or banished from the group. Like the destructive forces of nature, however, the gods, especially the single gods of monotheisms, have always been exempted from this rule. Either they did as they pleased or their providential designs were simply beyond human comprehension. At any rate, for the immortal and invulnerable gods, the end *always* justified the means. They alone could sanction the spilling of blood, both human and nonhuman. This was a sacred, or taboo, action, a *sacri-ficium*. Conversely, mortal rulers became "godlike" when they claimed eminent domain over not merely the property but also the very lives of their subjects. According to the civil-religious model of divine kingship, once a god or gods chose a "shepherd" to guide a human flock, the sheep could never fully comprehend their destined end. On this point, communal ethos and governmental praxis sharply diverge. (As for foreigners, mass deportation or annihilation might serve as a salutary object lesson to others.)[12]

David Austin's postmillennialist sermon, excerpted above, presents us with a mythic American hero who has fully absorbed the divine ambiguities of the Christian Messiah and is now fully prepared to apply them in the field of power politics. Though the personality of Austin's freedom-loving avenger may appear ambiguous, his own moral consciousness is not. He knows who the evil and the righteous are: the first he will cut down to size as one might level a mountain, and the second he will raise up as one might fill in a valley. Then, over this level space, he will build a highway for God to use to enter his millennial kingdom. This passage alludes to Isaiah 41:3 as well as to the gospel accounts of John the Baptist's exhortations (see especially Mark 1:1 and Luke 3:4–5), a strategic blurring typical of postmillennialist mythology. Narrative thinking is essentially paralogistic. The American hero *is* the avenging Messiah and at the same time *is not* this Messiah, but rather a new John the Baptist, a voice crying out in the American wilderness, preparing the way for the Second Coming. Thanks to this ambiguity, America is tasked with the duty of leading the world to the Millennium both *as* Christ and *like* Christ.

The words Austin italicizes also come from Isaiah:

> I the Lord have called thee [the Messiah] in righteousness, and will hold thine hand, and keep thee, and give thee for a covenant of the people, for a light of the Gentiles;
> To open the blind eyes, to bring out the prisoners from the prison, and them that sit in darkness out of the prison house. (Isa. 42:6–7)

This image brings to mind the representation of an Egyptian or Mesopotamian king holding the hand of a god and receiving a divine commission to rule the people. A messianic government effectively becomes personified in that ruler and is invested by God with the duty of world empire, which includes within the protective aspect of its authority the duty to free the unjustly imprisoned. This liberatory message of postmillennialism helped inspire the American War of Independence, abolitionism, temperance and civil rights movements, child labor laws, women's suffrage, antiwar and antinuclear campaigns, and countless other collective reforms. It has also provided rhetorical cover for less altruistic freedoms, such as free enterprise, free trade, right-to-work laws, and the support of designated "freedom fighters."

The road metaphor (the "highway of the Lord") of postmillennialism gave a martial character to all manner of reforms. The very word "movement" indicates that the image of such reform is of an army moving forward to meet the foe. It has been difficult to engage Americans in cooperative public action without recruiting them into a "crusade" or a "war"—a "war on poverty," a "war on drugs," a "campaign against illiteracy," even a "march of dimes." More recently, President Bush has characterized the Iraq War with the phrase "Freedom is on the march."

Postmillennialism has provided America the template of a national epic in the form of a mythicized history. Though no single literary text has emerged as *the* American epic, the epic spirit of postmillennialism has animated countless poems, short stories, novels, and films. Not one genuine *epos,* perhaps, but thousands of *epyllia.* Children learned to sing patriotic songs that, like Julia Ward Howe's "Battle Hymn of the Republic," embodied epic themes. They were also catechized in a single story that demonstrated those themes in action. According to this familiar historical narrative, America was founded by Pilgrim Fathers and their beleaguered families, a people persecuted for their religious faith. They fled into the American wilderness and thanked the God who saved them by inviting the friendly—noble but backward—Indians to the first Thanksgiving. Then, when the arrogant armies of mad King George tried to reassert the rule of tyranny, their descendants resisted. A militia of volunteers drove the greatest empire in the world back across the Atlantic in defeat. The liberated colonies, augmented by new immigrants who had fled to freedom from the evil feudal kingdoms of the Old World, could now face westward. As the pioneers began their trek over the Appalachians and into the great green prairies beyond, they and their families were menaced and sometimes massacred by hostile Indians and cruel Mexican soldiers. But, trusting in God, America confronted every challenge and prevailed.

This was the mythic history that Herman Melville imbibed in the first half of the nineteenth century and gave voice to in 1850, one year after Mexico was forced to cede its territories north of the Rio Grande. Though in the middle chapters of *White-Jacket* his subject is flogging in the United States Navy, his passionate attack on this time-honored practice reveals both the rhetoric and the logic of postmillennialism. His place of bondage is "the Past, . . . the foe of mankind . . . the Past is the text-book of tyrants; the future the Bible of the Free. Those who are solely governed by the Past stand like

Lot's wife, crystallized in the act of looking backwards, and forever incapable of looking before."[13] (The past thus becomes the city of Sodom.) He then proceeds to identify America with Israel on its way to the Promised Land: "Escaped from the house of bondage, Israel of old did not follow after the ways of the Egyptians. To her was given an express dispensation; to her were given new things under the sun. And we Americans are the peculiar, chosen people—the Israel of our time; we bear the ark of the liberties of the world." In accord with liberatory postmillennialism, Melville seems to insert the Declaration of Independence and the Constitution into the new Ark of the Covenant alongside the Ten Commandments.

> Seventy years ago we escaped from thrall; and, besides our first birthright—embracing one continent of earth—God has given to us, for a future inheritance, the broad domains of the political pagans, that shall yet come and lie down under the shade of our ark, without bloody hands being lifted. God has predestined, mankind expects, great things from our race; and great things we feel in our souls. The rest of the nations must soon be in our rear. We are the pioneers of the world; the advance-guard, sent on through the wilderness of untried things, to break a new path in the New World that is ours. In our youth is our strength; in our inexperience, our wisdom. At a period when other nations have but lisped, our deep voice is heard afar. Long enough have we been sceptics with regard to ourselves, and doubted whether, indeed, the political Messiah had come. But he has come in *us*, if we would but give utterance to his promptings.

We have been given this vast land (he does not so much as allude to its indigenous population) in order to be an example to the "political pagans," a curious politico-religious locution that becomes meaningful in the context of postmillennialist discourse. We not only have the Word, we *are* the Word Incarnate. When we speak *ex cathedra* to the political pagans of the world, we speak infallibly, because the "political Messiah" has returned and his indwelling spirit now prompts our utterances: "And let us always remember that with ourselves, almost for the first time in the history of earth, national selfishness is unbounded philanthropy; for we cannot do a good to America but we give alms to the world."[14]

Another nineteenth-century seagoing novelist, Joseph Conrad, employs similar rhetoric. His narrator in *Heart of Darkness,* Charlie Marlow, describes a conversation with his aunt, who has enthusiastically pulled strings to get him a job commanding a steamer on the Congo River for a Belgian company in the ivory trade. In her eyes, however, he is to be

> something like an emissary of light, something like a lower sort of apostle. There had been a lot of such rot let loose in print and talk just about that time. . . . She talked about "weaning those ignorant millions from their horrid ways," till upon my word, she made me quite uncomfortable. I ventured to hint that the company was run for profit.
> "You forget, dear Charlie, that the laborer is worthy of his hire," she said brightly.[15]

Marlow's aunt would have applauded Melville's statement, except that for her, all those who bore the white man's burden—not only Americans but also Englishmen and King Leopold's Belgians—bore also the cross of Christ the king, who had already returned to dwell in their hearts. In her civil-religious vision of the world, selfishness had also become fully compatible with philanthropy. The impulses of egoism and altruism, the rhetoric of might and right, and the values of land and home had all become comfortably reconciled.

Cursed Be Canaan

The Promised Land myth includes the escape from the "house of bondage," which Melville alluded to in his first sentence, but it also includes the conquest of Canaan under Joshua, which he delicately skirted in his biblical allegory. The attempted enslavement, the expulsion, and the near genocide of the native populations of North America were justified in the minds of postmillennialists by the American nation's need to reenact the God-blessed subjugation of Canaan by the wandering twelve tribes of Israel. Following this, the citizens of the New Israel would begin the last act of the cosmic drama: the Millennium.

The name "Canaan" refers both to the region later conquered by the Israelites in the twelfth century and to its eponymous ancestor. According to their version of the story, Canaan's grandfather, Noah, had pronounced the words "Cursed be Canaan" two thousand years earlier to punish with the penalty of slavery the obscure misconduct of Canaan's father, Ham, through all this branch of Ham's line. American settlers thus had at their disposal two scriptural precedents: (1) Noah's curse on Ham's progeny and (2) its historical application to Joshua's subjugation of the land of Canaan. Here I will consider the latter narrative as mapped onto the campaign to expel the Indians from their lands, and in the next section, I will take up the Noachic curse as a justification for the enslavement of Africans.[16]

To the Puritans, who viewed themselves as the army of saints, the Indians who did not convert were (together with the witches) part of Satan's conspiracy to destroy them and to preserve the devilish darkness that had covered the Western Hemisphere before their arrival. Here was a master narrative that could survive the dawn of the Enlightenment almost intact. Timothy Dwight had spoken for many in the new republic when, in his poem "America," he described the sorry state of the pre-Columbian continent:

> Sunk in barbarity, these realms were found,
> And Superstition hung her clouds around;
> O'er all, impenetrable Darkness spread
> Her dusky wings, and cast a dreadful shade;
> No glimpse of science through the gloom appear'd;
> No trace of civil life the desart chear'd;
> No soft endearments, no fond social ties,
> No faith, nor justice calm'd their horrid joys:
> But furious Vengeance swell'd the hellish mind,
> And dark-ey'd Malice all her influence join'd.
> Here spread broad plains, in blood and slaughter drown'd.[17]

Translated into contemporary neoconservative political speech: the Indians lacked the skill to develop their natural resources and, animated by pure evil, felt only hatred toward the civilized world. Only English settlers, Freedom's emissaries, could make this baleful "desart" bloom.

> To these far-distant climes our fathers came,
> Where blest NEW ENGLAND boasts a parent's name.
> With Freedom's fire their gen'rous bosoms glow'd,
> Warm for the truth, and zealous for their GOD:
> With these, the horrors of the desart ceas'd.

(4)

When William Penn pacified the natives for a while, they seemed to slip away into the vast uncultivated continent, a concept of native evanescence—the "vanishing red man" theme—that we find wishfully restated again and again in later decades.

> Peace rul'd [Penn's] life; to peace his laws inspir'd;
> In peace the willing savages retir'd.
> The dreary Wilderness, with glad surprise,
> Saw spacious towns and golden harvests rise.
>
> (5)

In Dwight's view, these rootless, shiftless savages were incapable of building towns and raising crops, but not incapable of destroying them. They had, apparently, a confoundedly un-English fondness for "desarts."

Despite their hostile neighbors, the colonists built and prospered:

> Happy they liv'd, while Peace maintain'd her sway,
> And taught the furious savage to obey,
> Whilst Labour fearless rear'd the nodding grain,
> And Innocence securely trod the plain:
> But soon, too soon, were spread the dire alarms,
> And thousand painted nations rush'd to arms,
> War's kindled flames blaz'd dreadful round the shore,
> And hills and plains with blood were crimson'd o'er,
> Where late the flocks rov'd harmless on the green,
> Where rising towns and cultur'd fields were seen,
> Illimitable desarts met the eye,
> And smoking ruins mounted to the sky.
>
> (5)

Dwight here refers to the long decades of hostility on the frontiers of the English colonies during the French and Indian Wars (1689–1763), a period of great interest to him and most other New Englanders who saw in it the struggle of true Christianity to survive in the New World. For him, these had been "good" wars, successfully concluded, that had brought the world a step closer to the glorious Millennium.

Dwight had already begun writing an American epic about this long colonial conflict. Rather than dealing with it in eighteenth-century dress and settings, as James Fenimore Cooper was later to do, he decided to place it in the biblical era of Joshua and called it *The Conquest of Canäan*. Before he could complete his epic, however, the Revolution supervened and obliged him to work some of its themes and motifs into the manuscript. The final product proved not a great literary success. Its rhymed couplets sounded old-fashioned—like Alexander Pope's, but without Pope's wit. Transparently about American history, his allegory failed to focus on what by then had come to seem the defining event, the War of Independence. Still, this overgrown narrative, humorous in its humorlessness, reveals much about the postmillennialist struggle to justify the conquest of North America.

Dwight was aware that most thoughtful Americans from time to time questioned the justice of one people's invading another people's territory. What justified the unprovoked conquest of a peaceful land and the uprooting and extermination of its inhabitants? His implied answers to such questions were, first, that it was not a peaceful continent but a land of violence, where vengeance was the highest moral principle, and second, that its inhabitants were rootless wanderers who by natural law had no claim on particular plots of land. By book 3, already far into the invasion of Canaan, he appeals to the covenant myth. The "Maker claims his own" and gives the land to whom he chooses:

> By him bestow'd, a righteous sword demands
> These flocks, these cities, and these promis'd lands,
> Yet not 'till crimes, beyond long-suffering great,
> Had fill'd their cup, and fix'd their changeless state,
> Would Heaven permit our race its gift to claim,
> Or seal the glory of th' almighty Name.
>
> (3.171–76)[18]

The Canaanites, in resisting the Israelites, have violated the laws of nature and of nature's God, but they will not be finally overthrown until the enormity of their crimes provokes God's retributive justice. This justification echoes Deuteronomy 9:4: "for the wickedness of these nations the Lord doth drive them out."

The couplets quoted above are put in the mouth of a young Israelite captain, Prince Irad, who, with the patience of a Miltonic Adam instructing Eve on the reason for night and starlight, explains to his betrothed, Selima, why the slaughtering of Canaanites is a sacred duty. Concerned about collateral damage, she is not at first convinced. She acknowledges that Canaan, as "nation" and "race," bears the stain of "black guilt." Yet she argues, "But not alike are all from virtue driven; / Some, more than others, claim the sword of Heaven; / Yet undistinguish'd falls the general doom, / The best, the worst, we destine to the tomb" (3.181–86). The next town marked for destruction must contain, she opines, "young, beauteous fair-ones" (3.193), more beauteous than she herself and betrothed to youths similar to Irad, albeit "less wise, less virtuous, and less fair than thou" (3.196).

> Shall this bless'd train, so young, so fair, so brave,
> Fall, with black wretches, in a firey grave?
> Or round wild regions must they hapless roam,
> Exil'd from joy, and forc'd from cheerful home?
> To hunger, thirst, and sorrow, sink and pray,
> And breathe, with lingering death, their lives away?
>
> (3.199–204)

And what if he, Irad, should

> To some lone hamlet loosely wandering come,
> Where simple swains had built their peaceful home,
> Where care in silence smoothly pass'd away,
> And home-bred happiness deceiv'd the day;
> Should there sweet, helpless children meet thy view,
> Fair as young rosebuds look thro' early dew,
> With infant wonder, on thine armour gaze,
> And point, with artless hands, the steely blaze:
> Say could thy heart one angry purpose know,
> Or doom such cherubs to a single woe?
>
> (3.209–18)

Colonial writers had used these very images again and again to portray the mindless cruelty of Indians in raids on isolated farm settlements. The final charge against George the Third in the Declaration of Independence was: "He has excited domestic insurrections amongst us, and has endeavoured to bring on the inhabitants of our frontiers, the merciless Indian Savages, whose known rule of warfare, is an undistinguished destruction of all ages, sexes and conditions." During the war that followed this Declaration, Americans, urban and rural, had also been brutalized by British invaders. They vividly remembered the price paid for insurgency and resistance. Dwight had used Selima to pose his spokesman a difficult question. But Irad rises to the occasion:

> The Prince replied, Bless'd gentleness of mind!
> The grace, the glory of a heart refin'd!

When new-born, helpless beings meet our eyes,
In noble minds, such thoughts resistless rise:
Even brutes, when young, our tender wishes try,
And love forbids the infant whelp to die.

(3.235–40)

This "kindest impulse of the soul," however, may run counter to God's plan.
The angels in heaven must applaud Selima's generosity of spirit,

But once as fair, as young, as soft as they,
As white with innocence, with smiles as gay,
Were those black throngs, whose crimes as mountains rise
And wipe out pity from th' all bounteous skies.

(3.247–50)

Those harmless babes are like asp eggs that, if left untrampled, will grow into
huge reptiles. For a moment Dwight's hero waxes Vergilian in his description of the crested, spiry serpents, and he then proceeds with a plea for godly
infanticide. "Harmless once," they grow "athirst for sin" and are lured to
every possible crime.

There the sot reels, the murderer prowls for blood;
There the starv'd orphan sues in vain for food;
For man man burns, with Sodom's tainted flame,
And the world sickens with incestuous shame.

. . . .

Should then these infants to dread manhood rise,
What unheard crimes would smoke thro' earth and skies!
What hosts of demons sin's dark realm would gain!
How hell gape hideous round Canäan's plain!
This sea of guilt unmeasur'd to prevent,
Our chosen race eternal justice sent,
At once the bright possession to reclaim,
And 'gainst its victims point the vengeful flame,[19]
Thus crimes their due and dire reward shall know.

. . . .

But, O unrivall'd maid! The kindest doom
These babes may destine for an early tomb.
To manhood risen their guilt, beyond controul,
Would blot their names from life's celestial roll.

Now, in fair climes, their souls, forever bless'd,
May bloom in youth, and share immortal rest;
And hail the boundless grace, that snatch'd its foes
From sins unnumber'd, and from lasting woes.

(3.265–68, 273–81, 285–92)

What Selima had thought a brutal act was really an act of mercy. By killing small Canaanite (read: Indian) children, the Israelites (read: Americans) will prevent a flood of criminality and demonstrate that "thus crimes their due and dire reward shall know"—in *advance*. This policy of preemptive war will also save the babes from eternal damnation. Dwight might have agreed with later Americans that "the only good Indian is a dead Indian," but he would have added the proviso, "only if he is killed as a child." (The argument lends historic resonance to that phrase from the 1960s, "better dead than Red.") What an image of cherubic felicity, those "Canaanite" babes in heaven hailing the "boundless grace" of those on earth who massacred them to save their souls! That is, to save their souls *and* "the bright possession to reclaim," for we ought not forget that these laborers are worthy of their hire. Selima, overcome by Irad's superior reasoning, acknowledges her error.

All gentle Youth! Selima soft replied—
How well thy words from falsehood truth divide!
With what sweet tenderness, thy voice displays
The truth, the lustre, of th' Eternal ways.

(3.299–302)

The presumption that God had preferentially blessed the New Israel is casually suggested by a journal entry John Winthrop made on July 5, 1643. A sudden gale, perhaps a small tornado, had struck eastern Massachusetts: "it blew down multitudes of trees [and] lifted up their meeting house at Newbury, the people being in it. It darkened the air with dust, yet through God's great mercy it *did no hurt,* but only killed one Indian with the fall of a tree."[20] As time passed, Americans sought to eliminate reminders of the people they had conquered by transforming them into romantic legends. In 1855 Henry Wadsworth Longfellow published his *Song of Hiawatha.* In 1856 Walt Whitman listed the names of fifteen Indian tribes and rhapsodized that "they melt, they depart, charging the water and land with names."[21] Consciously, unconsciously, or coincidentally, Whitman echoes the prophecy of Moses in his triumphal song, "all the inhabitants of Canaan shall melt away"

(Exod. 15:15). Only two years later, in 1858, a vignette appeared in *Godey's Lady's Book* entitled "An Indian Tale." It began: "The red men of America are rapidly becoming extinct. The grand old forests whose solemn stillness once echoed their tread now resound with the strokes of the woodsman's ax, or have given place to cities and villages, whose spires and domes, reared heavenward, mark the advent of another race. . . . Those children of the forest, whose places we have usurped, are passing away; but they leave behind them many a history and tradition."[22] By 1860 the U.S. government had succeeded in forcing most Indian nations westward across the Mississippi.

Cursed Be Ham

The Promised Land myth represented America's goal as the building of a "city upon a hill," a homeland for the righteous, a messianic Sion. There was, however, another Old Testament narrative that also provided America with powerful lessons. This was the story of Noah, the story of a cataclysm (literally a "washing away"), the sort of destruction that befalls an agricultural settlement that farms rich bottomlands. For Bible-reading settlers of the Appalachians and the floodplains of the Mississippi and its tributaries, it was an apt image of uncontrollable disaster.

What could have provoked God to send the original Flood? Something pertaining to sex and marriage, the context implies. Chapter 6 of Genesis tells us that the "sons of God saw the daughters of men that they were fair; and they took them wives of all that they chose" (6:2). The next verses suggest that God has been "striv[ing] with man" and is losing patience. Then they tell us: "there were giants in the earth," the offspring of the aforementioned unions, and these were "mighty men which were of old, men of renown. And God saw that the wickedness of man was great in the earth," and he resolved to destroy all beasts, birds, and humans (6:4–7). "Wickedness" covers many vices, but ingenious interpreters have always tried to probe this passage to ascertain precisely *what* God so vehemently abominated.

One theory had it that the "sons of God" were angels who lusted after mortal maidens, an idea that recalls many a pagan fable. From the point of view of comparative religion this is quite plausible, but believers in the textual purity of scriptural transmission understandably reject this interpretation. Cyrus Scofield was offended by the thought that angels are sexual beings. He chose to believe that the sin that had so incensed God was the intermarriage of the "godly line of Seth and the godless line of Cain."[23]

An anonymous pamphlet published on the eve of the Civil War, entitled *African Servitude,* gives a slightly different inflection to the human inter-marriage theory. God was furious because "the sons of God, or godly men, rejected the counsels of their fathers, and allied themselves with the wicked families of the earth, so that soon all were estranged from God."[24] Divine estrangement was a direct consequence of the primary sin of disobeying God's vicar within the family, the father. When sons treat their fathers with disrespect, they also spurn the Fatherhood of God, who then responds with appropriate fury.

This, as Stephen Haynes has demonstrated, was the dominant interpretation of the Noachic myth among proslavery writers.[25] The events immediately following the Flood have been thought to reinforce this theme. Ham's discovery of his drunken father provokes Noah to differentiate his sons and their descendants into masters, allies, and slaves. Why? The patriarchal theory has it that Ham dishonored his father by gazing at his nakedness and inviting his two brothers to do the same. Instead of mocking their father, however, Shem and Japheth cast a robe over him. When Noah gathered his wits again and learned that Ham had been guilty of disrespect, the very same crime against patriarchy that had incurred the punishment of the Flood, he became inspired by God to prophesy that Ham, in the person of his son, Canaan, should be cursed with perpetual servitude "unto his brethren."

The wording is puzzling. Why, if Ham was the offender, should Canaan be cursed? Some supporters of slavery felt that the biblical text needed emending: for Noah's prophecy to be fulfilled in America, it must be Ham, the ancestor of the black race, who is destined for servitude, and not Canaan, the ancestor of the native inhabitants of Palestine. The original text must have read: "cursed be Ham the father of Canaan."[26] Those unwilling to rewrite Genesis 9:25 asserted that by "Canaan," Noah simply meant all Ham's descendants, including those who settled in North and sub-Saharan Africa.

Thomas Virgil Peterson's *Ham and Japheth: The Mythic World of Whites in the Antebellum South* draws together an impressive collection of documents. They indicate that the use of this proof-text to legitimize African slavery in America went back at least to the beginning of the eighteenth century but reached its climax in the thirty years prior to the outbreak of the Civil War. According to one version of this myth, the descendants of the three sons of Noah, having wandered apart for thousands of years, had finally come together in America, the land where Providence had determined that all biblical prophecies were to be fulfilled. The color-coded logic may be summarized as follows:

1. The original color of humans was red ("Adam" is the Hebrew word for "red").
2. Noah's favorite son, Shem, the progenitor of the Semitic race, was red-complexioned, as was his father.
3. His son Japheth was colored white (his name was believed to mean "fair" or "beautiful").
4. His son Ham, however, was born the appalling color of night (his name was said to mean "hot" in Hebrew and "black" in Egyptian).
5. After Ham is cursed (whether personally or through his son, Canaan), Shem receives the primary blessing, but his descendants lose their blessing when the Jews (the principal line of Shem) reject Jesus and become a dispersed people.
6. Japheth, represented by Christian Europe, inherits Shem's blessing and fulfills the prophetic words "God shall enlarge Japheth" when his descendants leave their cramped countries and colonize the globe, especially North America.
7. Here they encounter the eastern branch of the Semites who had wandered across Asia, along the way becoming the Mongols, Chinese, and Japanese and, having crossed over the Bering Strait into America, are now known as "Indians."
8. The prophecy that Japheth "shall dwell in the tents of Shem" is now being fulfilled as the white race occupies the former dwelling places of the red race.
9. When the descendants of Ham are transported to America to perform their prophesied duties to the benefit of their Japhetic masters, the Noachic family of man is at long last united.
10. Aided by the docile Ham, who is fully aware of his inferiority, Japheth now directs the building of his righteous kingdom.

This astonishing set of premises leads to some equally astonishing conclusions, such as these written by Samuel Cartwright and published in Vidalia, Louisiana, in 1843:

> No sooner did Japheth begin to enlarge himself, and to dwell in the tents of Shem, than Canaan [here interpreted as the children of Ham] left his fastnesses in the wilds of Africa, where the white man's foot had never trod, and appeared on the beach to get passage to America, as if drawn thither by an impulse of his nature to fulfill his destiny of becoming Japheth's servant. Japheth did not go into

the wilderness and African deserts to look for Canaan and tear him from the home of his fathers. How did he get hold of Canaan? Ask the Hebrew verb from which the name of Canaan is derived and it will tell. *Submisit se;* Canaan *submitted himself.* Japheth even made him *servant* of *servants* by putting him under the delegated authority of overseers and others.

. . . Canaan came forth and became the good and faithful servant of Japheth, when he could easily, by leaguing with Shem, still powerful and lurking around the tents he had been driven from, have exterminated the race of Japheth in America. But it is contrary to the first principles of his nature for Canaan to league with his master's enemies.—He cannot do it, be they British, Indians or abolitionists. He is bound by the decree to be true to his master.[27]

The fulfillment of this prophecy marked the beginning of God's peaceable kingdom on earth, the millennial homeland, the final age before the physical return of Christ to judge the living and the dead. At this point, Japheth's mission was to preach the gospel to all the nations while developing the material resources of the earth. As Samuel Davies Baldwin wrote in *Dominion; or, the Unity and Trinity of the Human Race* (1857), Japheth "is the Divinity-inaugurated president of the world, adjured to maintain its national constitution inviolable [i.e., its racial hierarchy]. He must place all countries under tribute, [especially Ham's descendants] in Africa, Australia, and India."[28]

The South's view of America's destiny was no less imperialistic than that of the North. Despite their economic differences, both regions had endorsed for the republic a postmillennialist agenda, a typically American mix of Enlightenment serenity and apocalyptic fervor. They had also scoured the scriptures for prophetic references to themselves. Both the North and the South drove away the Hamitic bearers of a curse—the Indians who were the cursed Canaanites blocking their settlement of New Israel's Promised Land. But the South actively imported the bearers of that curse. In 1852 William Gilmore Simms, a South Carolinian novelist and historian, wrote that "the African seems to have his mission" and, unlike the Indian, "he does *not* disappear," for he was "designed as an implement in the hands of civilization always."[29] Japheth, as another writer argued, is "not to blame for this condition of servitude abiding upon Ham; and if there is any advantage in receiving his service—as it seems there must be, for it is pronounced by Noah as a blessing—they have, for the honor and obedience they rendered to their parent, a right to it given them by the Almighty."[30]

American slavery was a diverse blessing. As the beneficiary of Ham's labors, Japheth had been blessed through Ham's curse. That was apparently true. But Japheth, as the "Divinity-inaugurated president of the world," had labors far more onerous than Ham's. (And, for all his labors, Japheth was indeed worthy of his hire.) Furthermore, Ham had received a greater promotion, an inestimably greater blessing, for if it had not been for the holy institution of slavery, Ham could never have had the chance to save his soul. As for his body, this was bound to the service of Japheth, but what a minor payment was this for the gift of salvation!

Blessed Be Japheth

In biblical thinking, blessings and curses are complementary opposites. A blessing, like a good spell, counteracts a curse, and a curse reverses the effects of a blessing. In a culture that honored the rule of primogeniture—sometimes in the breach—the distribution of rewards was a zero-sum game. For some to have honor, others must have *dis*honor. For some to garner divine or paternal blessings, others must go unblessed—and sometimes expressly cursed. Thus Shem received Noah's primary blessing, Japheth was allied with Shem, and Ham (through Canaan) was cursed with slavery. To inherit honor is to be trusted as a morally responsible agent; to inherit dishonor is to be morally deficient, shameless, and degraded.

Because both blessings and curses, as we have seen, were inheritable through all descendants of an original recipient, nations, understood as extended stem families, could either be blessed or cursed collectively. As the Israelites under Moses were massing their forces on the borders of Moab, King Balak, seeing his men outnumbered and his land in peril of invasion, asked the prophet Balaam to obtain from God a curse to be laid on the invaders. Balaam could not obtain a curse from God, and in a trance he delivered instead a blessing beginning with the words, "How goodly are thy tents, O Jacob, and thy tabernacles, O Israel!" (Num. 24:5). Thus at the very verge of their entry into Canaan, this issue of divine justification was again linked to a blessing that averted a curse.

To many of their descendants, this passage seemed to prefigure the arrival of the English Protestants to their new Promised Land of America. Timothy Dwight exploited that parallel and implied that the American Indians bore the curse of Canaan. Later mythmakers, as we have seen, went back to the early chapters of Genesis and identified this people as the descendants of the red-complexioned Shem, descendants who were prophesied to share their tents with Japheth. Whatever their biblical identity, the Indians were foreordained to be dispossessed, and white Christians, to be masters of their land. For their part, the victors inherited a double blessing: in spirit, as the New Israel, they were descendants of Shem, while in body, they were descendants of Japheth.

Yet beneath America's assurance of divine blessings lay its fear of a divine curse. English settlers, with the help of smaller groups of Europeans, drove off or killed the original population of the North American continent in a two-centuries-long invasion. As I proposed earlier, a conflict between the values of right and the privileges of might produces within a society a cognitive dissonance, which in turn prompts the composition of a set of ethnic myths drawn from traditional sources. On the communal level, murder and robbery are dreadful crimes, but when those acts are performed by a government divinely chosen to build the Millennium, they become "unbounded philanthropy." When Melville spoke of "national selfishness," he implied that an entire people, when it acts *nationally*, cannot be held morally answerable for its action; some higher power leads it. The Deity makes it do it.

There is something surreal about America's homeland mythology. Europeans, Robert Bellah has written, regarded the American continents as a "state of nature," a blank screen: "Upon that screen they projected certain fantasies, dreams, and nightmares long carried in the European tradition but seldom heretofore finding so vivid and concrete an objective correlative."[31] "The American Dream as European Dream," Douglas Robinson adds, "was fundamentally a Protestant dream of historical apocalypse—a dream *of* history *in* history that would consummate and so give meaning *to* history."[32] In a dream we witness a series of images, and in American history, we likewise encounter the recurrent images of biblical types, overlapping sometimes in condensations of multiple meanings. We also experience displacements: things normally associated with certain feelings or meanings appear to represent other things, often their opposites. The relation of curse to blessing is one of the notable transformations of this collective dream.

In postmillennialist parlance, which over the years has became the dominant civil-religious rhetoric of America, the word "blessing" has shifted from the *cause* (divine words) to the *effects* (the material objects). The Anglo-American New Israel, like its biblical model, has always feared losing the blessing that had justified the conquest of its Promised Land. Quaint as it may seem to us, the Puritans and the citizens of the early republic had rituals of collective anxiety that they called "fasts" and "humiliations." Presidents, beginning with John Adams, proclaimed days of repentance to remind Americans of their national covenant with God.[33] Like ancient Israel, this peculiar people had to be collectively blessed, lest it be collectively cursed. The more frequently the phrase "God bless America" is heard or displayed, the more apprehensive seems its tone.

Thanksgiving, the national holiday that commemorates the Pilgrims' first successful harvest, has come to signify the unconditional blessedness of America as the millennial Promised Land. Malediction—the traditional complement of benediction—plays no part in this event. The curse that might otherwise have fallen on invading conquerors is nullified in the imagery of this ritual by the presence of Indian guests at the festive table. The curse of Canaan that later generations would apply to Native Americans does not descend on these men, who lower their eyes in prayer alongside their English hosts. The scene recalls the traditional harvest-home feast at which the laborers join with the farmer's household to feast as equals. Reenacted in a similar spirit of solidarity, past grievances temporarily laid aside, extended families reassemble each year on this day to contemplate their blessings, symbolized by the variety and quantity of food they are ritually obliged to ingest.

To celebrate the grandeur of America as a collective inheritance, to revel in its beauty and wealth, is, according to the logic of postmillennialism, to assert it as a gift from God to its present owners. Not only are the blessings that Americans are said to possess justified, they *justify their possessors,* because God would not have lavished them on an undeserving nation. Over the last hundred years or so at least, postmillennialists would prefer not to speak of Native Americans as cursed by God but rather of themselves as *blessed* by God.

Yet God's blessings, apparently, must also be fought for. If the Old Testament could be used to legitimize settlers' claims on Indian lands, the Book of Revelation could serve to excite young men into battle. In the early 1770s, pamphleteers and preachers could allude to colonial governors as false prophets enforcing allegiance to a Nero-like (or pope-like) tyrant. Tax stamps, too, were marks of the Beast. The embattled farmers of Lexington and Concord and the wretched patriots at Valley Forge—these were the army of the Elect. The redcoats, on the other hand, wore the colors of the Whore of Babylon and of the Red Dragon whom a new St. George had come to slay. The conflict was a war of good against evil, the good by a hero atop a great white horse, the evil forces led by a madly ravenous Beast—George and Antigeorge, like Christ and Antichrist at the battle of Armageddon.[34]

According to one national myth, the dark days of the War of Independence, the time that had tried men's souls, had been the final tribulation.

There could be no more revolutions (Thomas Jefferson's radical opinion to the contrary notwithstanding).[35] The Beast had been defeated; the Millennium had commenced. This, according to postmillennialists, was now to be a period of gradual but progressive moral reforms, culminating in Christ's physical return to preside over the Last Judgment. America was the harbinger of the Second Coming, a voice crying out in the wilderness. The Millennium was being made in America and would soon be exported hence for the salvation of all humanity. At the Last Judgment, the damned would only comprise those few individuals and nations that had resisted the moral influence of this missionary nation.

Public ceremonies associated with Independence Day had an apocalyptic aspect from the very beginning. John Adams, looking into the future, got everything right except the date (the motion for independence was indeed passed on July 2):

> The Second Day of July 1776, will be the most memorable Epocha, in the History of America.—I am apt to believe that it will be celebrated, by succeeding Generations, as the great anniversary Festival. It ought to be commemorated, as the Day of Deliverance by solemn Acts of Devotion to God Almighty. It ought to be solemnized with Pomp and Parade, with Shews, Games, Sports, Guns, Bells, Bonfires and Illuminations from one end of the Continent to the other from this Time forward forever more.[36]

By calling the first Independence Day an "Epocha," Adams meant that it would be the initial date in a new chronological system. As one of the images of the Great Seal of the United States announces, 1776 marks a *novus ordo seclorum*, a new series of centuries. This allusion to Vergil's "messianic" Fourth Eclogue was clear: Independence Day marked the birthday of a world savior. The years that followed should be numbered accordingly. Abraham Lincoln expected his audience to understand this trope when, at Gettysburg in 1863, he said, "Fourscore and seven years ago our fathers brought forth on this continent, a new nation, conceived in Liberty." All human children are conceived in sin because they bear the curse of Adam, but this blessed child, parthenogenically brought forth by "our fathers," is the corporate embodiment of the millennial era—the "political Messiah," as Melville called him.

Yet the final struggle of good versus evil was not to be the War of Independence. The antebellum apologists of chattel slavery in the South had argued that the "peculiar institution" of slavery was a blessing to both Japheth and Ham. To many in the North, however, it was the final evil that needed to be overturned before America, as a "peculiar people," could cross over into the promised Millennium. When John Brown sat in Ralph Waldo Emerson's parlor and discussed *his* biblical mission, he declared: "Better a whole generation of men, women, and children should pass away by a violent death than that one word of either [the Golden Rule or the Declaration of Independence] be violated in this country."[37] Despite the fact that the author of the Declaration had been a slaveholding Virginian, the statement that "all men are created equal and endowed by their Creator with certain unalienable rights," including liberty, seemed to have acquired the binding power of a covenant with the Almighty. America, it seemed, would now need a second Armageddon before its millennial kingdom could commence.

In the late 1850s the looming conflict revealed itself to many Christians, both black and white, in the North (and to some in the South) as the prophesied final battle of good against evil. Apocalyptic language was there, as it had always been, to inflame moral and political passions. In her conclusion to *Uncle Tom's Cabin*, Harriet Beecher Stowe had directed herself to an audience saturated with Bible verses, an audience that would respond fervently to anyone who could pack a paragraph with them: "O Church of Christ, read the signs of the times! Is not this power the spirit of HIM whose kingdom is yet to come, and whose will is to be done on earth as it is in heaven? But who may abide the day of his appearing?"[38]

Perhaps no single postmillennialist document reveals the juncture of military mayhem and moral meliorism more succinctly than Julia Ward Howe's "Battle Hymn of the Republic."

> Mine eyes have seen the glory of the coming of the Lord:
> He is trampling out the vintage where the grapes of wrath are stored;
> He hath loosed the fateful lightning of his terrible swift sword:
> > His truth is marching on.
>
> I have seen Him in the watch-fires of a hundred circling camps;
> They have builded Him an altar in the evening dews and damps;
> I can read His righteous sentence by the dim and flaring lamps:
> > His day is marching on.
>
> I have read a fiery gospel writ in burnished rows of steel:
> As ye deal with my contemners, so with you my grace shall deal;
> Let the Hero, born of woman, crush the serpent with his heel,
> > Since God is marching on.

He has sounded forth the trumpet that shall never call retreat;
He is sifting out the hearts of men before His judgment-seat:
Oh, be swift, my soul, to answer him! Be jubilant, my feet!
                                        Our God is marching on.

In the beauty of the lilies Christ was born across the sea,
With a glory in his bosom that transfigures you and me:
As He died to make men holy, let us die to make men free,
                                        While God is marching on.

The first three verses (or stanzas) begin with the assertion that the poet, like the prophet John, has had a vision of the Apocalypse. Unlike John, however, she had seen the preparations for Armageddon in an actual military encampment, that of the Army of the Potomac in 1862. Now, with the eyes of a visionary, she sees the Lord himself treading the wine press (Rev. 14:19–20) and presumably releasing a deluge of human blood. She sees him too in the marching men and in their weapons. The chorus, or refrain, emphasizes the image of the marching and asserts that the Day of the Lord—not Sunday but the apocalyptic day of divine vengeance—is also "marching on." But in this road metaphor, this day is not marching toward us out of the future but with us as we, the army of saints, march with it *into* the future. We, with our God, are jointly accomplishing the apocalyptic agenda and preparing the Millennium.

The images of Revelation are thus superimposed on this Civil War panorama, which now becomes legible as a scriptural text. The sword of verse 1, line 3, is the sword of the Word of God that issues from the mouth of the man on the white horse (Rev. 19:13–15). "His righteous sentence" is his doomsday judgment on the Antichrist and his followers, and his "fiery gospel" is the dreadful complement to the consoling gospel of his first coming. This second gospel is fiery indeed: now they who live by the sword and die by it receive divine grace when they wreak vengeance on the scorners of the incarnate Word, that Hero who, as the Second Adam, finally crushes the satanic snake (Gen. 3:14–15).

The hymn is, in effect, an exhortation to young men to kill and be killed. Christ in his first coming died to make men holy—and now the holy, the saints, are encouraged to die to make men free. The later popular addition to the chorus, "Glory, glory, Halleluja!" is drawn from the one and only place in the KJV in which this Hebrew word (which means "Praise Yahweh!") appears, chapter 19 of Revelation. Here it is shouted by "much people in heaven" (19:1), the already martyred saints.

This document represents the ideals of the northern form of American postmillennialism, the form that, since Appomattox, has grounded the presidential rhetoric of the nation. In it we can locate five narrative themes:

1. *God needs human warriors to fight for him.* He will not physically intervene at this point but instead is still testing our readiness to die for our faith. He will be present in our midst spiritually, but only the prophetic visionary will see him and only the eye of faith will sense him in this struggle, which is a spiritual struggle that must eventually be fought out with fire and sword.
2. *The warriors' mission is to liberate a people.* Somewhere in the world there are people being persecuted, enslaved, or imprisoned, and America, as the nation destined to build God's millennial kingdom, is obliged by its covenant to liberate them. When it does so, the liberated people will embrace America with profound gratitude, emulate its ideals, and share with it the prosperity of its peaceable kingdom.
3. *Their enemy is the tyrannical Antichrist.* The motive of the enemy is to enslave humanity—to deny men and women the blessings of Christianity and the material progress that only Christianity can create and to render their lives nasty, brutish, and short. America, as the defender of Christianity, is obliged to destroy this irredeemable enemy.
4. *This war is the final war in human history.* Every American war is advertised as the "war to end all wars" because it is understood to be the battle of Armageddon, the ultimate showdown between the children of light and the children of darkness.
5. *Heaven and the Millennium follow the victory.* The saints who die in this final war go on to heavenly bliss. Their survivors, who gratefully memorialize them in their purged homeland, now enter into the Millennium, a new world order ruled by Christians—that is, American Christians.

The destruction of the plantation system of the Old South deprived it of its uniquely mythologized millennialism. People who lose a war cannot soon again believe that the God of Battles has authorized them to build the earthly Millennium. A religious conservatism that saw paternal authority crumbling, moral chaos on the rise, and only God himself able to wrest the righteous from the clutches of Satan found fertile ground in the postwar South. Premillennialism and the evangelical churches that promoted it grew in the South and in the big-city "missions" of the North and Midwest, while postmillennialism remained enshrined in American civil religion and was used to unify the homeland through the Progressive Era, the Great Depression, and the two World Wars. But with the impasse in Korea and the defeat in Vietnam, the postmillennialist narrative lost much of its nationwide persuasiveness.

The comings and goings of these two millennial master narratives have been a kind of shadow-play within a collective dreamscape, a repository that Fredric Jameson has called the "political unconscious." As he said in his foreword to the English translation of Jean-François Lyotard's *Postmodern Condition,* the "great master narratives" of the past are always available "as a way of 'thinking about' and acting on our present situation."[39] In the 1970s, the present situation seemed to call upon many in America to reconsider the Bible-based narrative the defeated South had used a century earlier, the ancient narrative that portrays the world as a place of darkness and exile and the one true homeland as a far-off shining kingdom in the sky.

4

NARRATIVES OF THE NIGHT

Night, that time not merely of peace and renewal but also of dreams and danger, provides a powerful setting for a number of traditional narratives. This darkness between two days is a liminal time that can serve to represent any transition between two states of being or activity. If we apply Tzvetan Todorov's narrative cycle to this day-night-day pattern, the upper phases of equilibrium (1 and 5) each correspond to days, phase 3 to the night, and phases 2 and 4 to sunset and dawn, respectively.

In terms of end-time scenarios, the postmillennialist believes that the night having passed and the new day begun, Christ has returned spiritually and now works within Christians to build his millennial homeland on earth, after which (*post millennium*) he will return physically to judge the living and the dead. The premillennialist, however, believes that the world is still benighted in sin and false doctrines and, with the exception of the few true believers who are still vigilant, all are sleeping deeply. As the premillennialist narratives warn, this night will end abruptly for these sleepers.

Though this dark scenario is deeply rooted in the cultural unconscious of Americans, it is not their only narrative of the night. Several others are regularly told and reenacted and have earned their places in what we might call our civil-religious liturgical calendar. The Fourth of July, Halloween, and Christmas each contain significant nocturnal components. Though they are counter-apocalyptic in spirit, these rituals and the narratives that accompany them reveal some provocative resemblances to the Night of Wrath.

Cult, Myth, and the Thief in the Night

A people's founding narratives (its myths) and its ritual practice (its cult) help individuals achieve solidarity among themselves. But myth and cult are not totally separate cultural expressions. Every myth has some cultic (i.e., ritual) elements attached to it. Even national myths that entirely reject supernaturalism may revere the burial places of public leaders and celebrate certain days with religious solemnity. For its part, every cult also makes some reference to a myth. Even if its sole focus is on reuniting the individual soul with the cosmic soul, it will have a story to tell about how the two became separate. Myth is used to explain aspects of cult—why, for example, we do X or Y on this particular occasion—and cult is used to intensify and personalize a mythic image or episode, as when worshipers are asked to meditate on the meaning of a particular biblical event.

Because a main concern of American Protestantism is the preparation for the Second Coming of Christ, eschatological issues dominate both myth and cult and bulk large in its doctrinal debates. When mythic elements are adapted for cultic purposes, as they are most intensely by premillennialists, they undergo significant changes in emphasis—in the spirit, if not the letter, of the scriptural text.

This use of a sacred narrative has, of course, a long history in Christian devotional practice, as indeed it has in all religions that preserve such narratives. In the Christian tradition, such narratives are true either as historical facts, as typological signs ("shadows of things to come"), or as both. But they are also given to us, it is said, as "food for the soul," as sustenance as we pass through the experiences that test our faith on our way toward death and judgment. Biblical passages, therefore, have applications that must be prayerfully sought. In some denominations this special work of preachers often forms the central act of worship.

Whatever meaning may be assigned to a given passage, the use of apocalyptic myth for cultic practice has always tended to allegorize the literal in order to generate further meanings and applications. When, for example, the events prophesied in the Book of Revelation are redirected to cultic applications, the text becomes a manual of spiritual combat: this focuses the mind on the coming of Christ into the soul, his role as warrior against the congregated evils of this world, and his followers' need to persevere on the path of pilgrimage and die to this world in order to be reborn in the heavenly kingdom. This was the traditional use of this book from the third century until the reemergence of apocalyptic movements in the late Middle Ages, and it remains a major interpretive approach to the book among Catholic and liberal Protestant denominations.[1] (Even Puritans tolerated a certain degree of such allegorizing for cultic purposes, without neglecting its literal meanings.)

As I suggested in Chapter 1, heroic myths recount the clash between group order and individual will and feature the exploits of tricksters, rebels, tragic protagonists, and similar centers of disruptive energy. Jesus described himself as a disturber of the status quo when he said: "Think not that I am come to send peace on earth: I come not to send peace, but a sword" (Matt. 10:35). The Gospels depict him as an individual hero at odds with his own community, but, when Revelation reintroduces him, it is as the leader of his own people, waging an international war against evil kingdoms ripe for ruin— "Babylon," "Gog," "Magog," and all those other unnamed "nations." In effect, the intracommunal heroic myth of Rabbi Yeshua that we read in the Gospels becomes a cosmicized ethnic myth when he returns as governmental leader to separate the blessed from the accursed.

America's biblically grounded culture has given its politics a scriptural dimension. Its central question has been: What constitutes a just society, or, as I characterized it in Chapter 2, the *good* kingdom? Those inclined to trust centralized government have believed that, in its dealings with communities and foreign governments, it can behave, with proper oversight, in a just and godly manner and lead the world to a millennial age of peace, freedom, and prosperity. On the other hand, those who have felt most secure in a local, religiously defined community have looked toward the divine establishment on earth of a transcendent heavenly kingdom and regarded no humanly governed country as a Christian "homeland."

Premillennialism, this latter view, reflects American Protestant culture as it exists on the communal level. When ministers lead their congregations in joyously visualizing the sudden catastrophic return of the Messiah, they are in effect exulting in the destruction of the governmental level of society, assuming it to be the evil kingdom. When this longed-for event occurs, no worldly power can save any one of us. Only the just community, the True Church, can offer salvation. Membership in this body is the only way to reserve a place in the good kingdom of the Millennium and its transcendent model, the heavenly kingdom.

The religiously constituted community draws not only upon profound cultural resources but also upon instinctual elements, including our felt need to belong to protective groups (family, band, clan, tribe) and to accept the identity that such membership confers. If, as I suggested in Chapter 1, these needs were accentuated in the hunter-gatherer stage of human evolution, the possibility of separation here and hereafter from some communion is a deeply troubling prospect. To find oneself left behind and lost in a dark wood harks back to a more-than-allegorical terror. One must therefore never stray from the fold. To abandon this community or to be banished from it (to be *ex*communicated) is to perish.

Death, one radical form of separation, has always been regarded as a kind of sleep—a deep night, a cessation of consciousness, a balm, as the old proverb says, that cures all diseases. Death is the common end of all living beings. But otherworldly religions have attempted to narrativize mortality. Death may be one ending, but the Christian doctrine of the soul's immortality establishes three more "last things"—judgment, heaven, and hell—thereby enhancing our fear of death by supplying a variety of never-ending, infinitely contrasting activities. Someday the death of the individual and of all humanity will coincide, and the entire universe will face doom in one single terrifying instant of time. Yet even after this, something of us will somehow remain, some conscious, psychic identity, that is either forever rewarded or forever punished.

The most vivid natural imagery of punishment is the condition of a human being, with no hope of reprieve, suffering the onset of a trauma that will end with death. At a time when public execution—hanging, burning alive, pressing under stones, beheading, and the more grisly varieties of avulsion—were regular events in the larger towns, no one had to rely on preachers to summon up images of the pains of hell and the howls of the damned. They did need their divines, however, to assure them that in one respect the suffering of the damned would be different from that of these wretches in the public square. The throes of the damned would never end in the peace of physical death but would continue for all eternity at the purest, most convulsive climax of terror, humiliation, despair, and torment. Not only that: their eternal torments would be viewed from afar by God's elect, one of whose chief delights would be this spectacle of God's executed justice.

Given that, what else could traditional religion add to capture the attention of the indifferent? They would certainly need to be told to reform their attitudes, redirect their lives, and prepare their souls for eternity. But would there be time for repentance and conversion? Peter had said, "the day of the Lord will come as a thief in the night" (2 Pet. 3:10). Now this is an image that all can appreciate: the end of the world is like the sudden entry of a thief who robs sleepers of their possessions and, by implication, of their lives. This terrifying image of the thief appears twice in Revelation, where Jesus uses it, referring to himself.[2]

As the verse goes on to tell, this is the night "in which the heavens shall pass away with a great noise, and the elements shall melt with fervent heat, the earth also and the works that are therein shall be burned up." Though what happens in the end is here made fully known, this image of the terrible night visitor asserts that the precise time of the end of the world and of all human life cannot be known. What more could add to the terror of that sudden ending? Nothing, perhaps, but the knowledge that this deliberate, premeditating killer, who will later break into the house in the dark of night, is also the person who, elsewhere in Revelation, declares his personal love for humans. This speaker says of himself that he is now at the door asking to be let in for dinner: "Behold, I stand at the door, and knock: if any man hear my voice and open the door, I will come in to him, and will sup with him, and he with me" (Rev. 3:20)—a sublimely loving offer, remarkable in its simplicity, but all the more powerful as a dissonant image to that of the thief in the night. As noted earlier, the terrible power of Christian apocalyptic lies not so much in its vengeful cruelty as in the antithetical mix of sweetness and fright evoked by the returning Christ.

This suddenness is an essential condition of his return. Premillennialism's defining doctrine is that Jesus will physically return to execute the wrath of God after the 144,000 saved are taken up from the earth in the Rapture. On the biblical time chart, as most premillennialist preachers read it, the world totters at this very moment upon some particular verse in Chapter 7. The first six seals have already been broken; the "signs of the times" are plainly displayed to the faithful, and only the unregenerate remain blind to them. The moment when the seventh seal of the scroll is to be opened is at hand. Those to be saved are now soon to be rescued, after which the full wrath of God will be poured forth on the earth. This will capture the attention of those who find themselves left behind, realizing too late that the season of mercy has given way to the season of justice. *Now,* however, in the scant time before the avenging Messiah returns, the very knowledge that for fearless worldlings his return will be a complete surprise is, for the God-fearing, a salutary knowledge. The more they can fear in advance, the less they will need to fear when that actual day arrives.

Long before premillennialism defined itself in opposition to postmillennialism, preachers narrated the sudden terrors of the end times to rouse Christians from their moral torpor. Even if one believed that the Millennium had begun with the resurrection of Jesus, at the end of the Roman persecutions, or at the start of the Reformation and trusted that all that remained now was for the living and the dead to be summoned before the Judge to receive their sentence (Rev. 20:11–15), *that moment,* as Michelangelo's Sistine altar-piece depicts it, was quite terrifying enough. Devout Romanists and Anglicans alike supposed that Christ was already present to them in the sacrament of Eucharist and that they were either enjoying now, or progressing toward, that glorious kingdom at the end of which Christ (in his glorified body) would appear in the sky to judge the world. From a Puritan point of view, however, this comfortable gradualism blunted the one emotion indispensable for conversion and perseverance in the faith: the fear of God. If Christ was to appear *after* establishing his blissful, spiritual kingdom, all reasonable humans would have ample occasion to observe the fruits of his grace and could repent at their leisure. If his return were to occur *before* that, only those who held to the faith could enter the kingdom of God. This proved to be the issue that later defined the division between post- and premillennialists.

Dreams of Terror

There is something very dreamlike about the apocalyptic narrative in John's prophecy. Besides the metamorphosing Lamb, the hybrid and freakish Beasts, the flying and sinking movements, and the sheer terror of carnage and flaming devastation (chapters 4–9), there is a strange interlude in chapter 10, followed by a repetition of events (chapters 11–22) that reminds one of a failed attempt to wake oneself out of a nightmare.[3]

When Michael Wigglesworth published his long poem *The Day of Doom* (1662), he told his readers that it had in fact come to him as a dream. It may well be that this was how it came to him. It was also customary that, as the narrator of a dream, a Christian author could take some liberties with a biblical text. In this poem, for example, there is no series of portents and no references to an earthly Millennium. Whatever his reasons, Wigglesworth's chosen sequence renders his narrative starkly dramatic. The physical reentry of Christ, the Judge of the living and the dead, comes as a complete surprise to the ungodly—who, despite their pleas, are straightaway sent to hell, before the righteous get to enjoy their heavenly reward. The writer of this "incongruously bouncy ballad about the last judgment," as one reader irreverently styled it,[4] seems intent on achieving two objectives: justifying the apparent cruelties of the returned Christ and inspiring his readers with holy terror.[5]

"Still was the night, serene and bright / when all men sleeping lay." This narrative begins with a brief evocation of a world utterly at peace. But soon all heaven breaks loose.

So at the last, while men sleep fast
    in their security,
Surpris'd they are in such a snare
    as cometh suddenly.

For at midnight breaks forth a light,
    which turns the night to day,
And speedily an hideous cry
    doth all the world dismay.

                (stanzas 4–5)[6]

This scene seems to be the moment before the seventh seal is opened and the Last Judgment begins, for Jesus suddenly appears on his throne in the middle air. This dreamlike poem also has the structure of a rite of passage. The persons, in this case all humanity (living and dead), must first undergo a separation from their former condition, their beds for some, their graves for others, and enter the liminality of their ordeal. Drawn by some elective affinity, perhaps, the saved assemble to the Judge's right, and the unsaved, to his left.

The first to be condemned are the hypocrites, Christians—including Protestant clergy—who had always assumed that they would be saved, despite their tepid faith. They had not answered when Christ came to their doors and all his "knocks withstood like blocks / and would not be advised" (lines 119–20). They now involuntarily confess their sins and then try to argue extenuating circumstances, but this sitting Judge is the only person in the court with acceptable arguments. After the hypocrites, the apostates approach the bar, and then the heathens to whom the gospel was never preached. Each group is bested in a legal debate and uniformly sentenced to eternal torment. Finally, those infants who had not lived long enough to commit a sin, but whom God had predestined to hell anyway, approach the bar of justice.[7] If Adam had not sinned, they plead, they would not now be resurrected from the dead only to be hurled live into the burning lake. And Adam, they point out, appears now in the ranks of the blessed. Being contended with by such a rout of captious babes seems to chafe Wigglesworth's Savior. Suffer the little children, indeed! His free gift of grace, he explains, would not be free, if it were compelled by mere justice (stanza 177).

Whom injure I? Will you envy,
    and grudge at others' weal?

> Or me accuse, who do refuse
> > yourselves to help and heal?

(stanza 178)

Their innate sinfulness, he says, they cannot deny, although he must admit that their sin is much less than that of adults. But, he instructs them, "every sin's a crime," even inherited original sin.

> A crime it is, therefore in bliss
> > you may not hope to dwell;
> But unto you I shall allow
> > the easiest room in Hell.

(stanza 181)

Such arguments seem so correct that even the damned are persuaded: "all mouths are stopped, / sinners have nought to say, / But that 'tis just, and equal most / they should be damned for aye" (lines 599–602). As for the white-robed saints, not even the brothers, wives, husbands, and parents of the damned feel sorrow or pity for them now. For example:

> The pious Father had now much rather
> > his graceless Son should lie
> In Hell with Devils, for all his evils,
> > burning eternally,
>
> Than God most high should injury
> > by sparing him sustain;
> And doth rejoice to hear Christ's voice
> > adjudging him to pain.

(stanzas 199–200)

The poem ends with the final sonorous incorporation of the damned into hell and the saved into heaven—the damned where "they lie, and wail, and cry," the saved where they "praise with sweetest lays / and hymns that never end" (stanzas 218, 220). In an age before the Gothic novel, before the Marquis de Sade and Edgar Allan Poe appeared, there was perhaps a need to experience vicarious terror or, in this case, to contemplate the terrors of others. At any rate, this book sold out quickly in 1662—1,800 copies, which, if they reached only New England, would have been owned by one out of twenty settlers, or one out of forty-five if they reached the rest of the English colonists. Some of its admirers memorized it *in toto.* Women stitched selected verses into quilts and samplers. Ministers wove them into sermons. It was not what another age would call a "literary" or "aesthetic" success, but this was of minor concern. It had been intended, explained Cotton Mather, for the "edification of such Readers as are for plain Truths, dressed up in Plain Meeter. These Compositions have had their Acceptance and Advantage among that sort of Readers." *The Day of Doom,* he cheerily adds, has been so popular it "may find our Children till the *Day* itself arrive."[8]

There are, of course, other, more direct ways to arouse the fear of death. The stripped quick of mortal terror is sooner touched by simply pointing out the chalk-white skull beneath the rosy cheek than by conjuring up images of red dragons or many-headed beasts or by calculating the numbers in Daniel or Revelation. Living in the end times and witnessing the world destroyed in a climax of plagues, wars, famines, and meteoric acts of God is a fearful prospect indeed, but dying as a result of disease, injury, poverty, or natural disaster is a far more likely event and one for which a Christian must also be prepared.

Less spectacular than *The Day of Doom,* but of far more lasting influence on American readers, was John Bunyan's *Pilgrim's Progress* (1678). Like Wigglesworth, Bunyan uses the dream format. As he "walk'd through the wilderness of this world," he lay down once and had this dream. What follows is the allegory of "Christian," a man who has discovered that he has two problems. He carries a "burden that lieth heavy" on him (his individual accumulation of guilt), and he is "for certain informed that this our City will be burned with fire from Heaven" (the fire foretold in Revelation, which, however, is not an event included in the narrative).[9] When Christian cannot convince his family members that they are in the same desperate condition, he becomes even more despairing. The more he reads in his Bible, the more he cries out, "What shall I do to be saved?" In his mind, there could be no sacramental means of loosing his burden and no shelter from the "fire from Heaven" through membership in any church.

When "Evangelist" appears and asks why he is in such distress, Christian answers, "I perceive by the Book in my hand, that I am condemned to die, and after that to come to Judgment, and I find that I am not willing to do the first, nor able to do the second." Death and judgment are at once individual (everyone dies and is judged) and collective events (fire is to fall, and all humankind judged, when Christ returns), and both are imminent. Bunyan's dream condenses the two events into one overdetermined process so that the terror of cosmic conflagration intensifies and magnifies the terror of death. His only recourse, according to Evangelist, is to "fly from the wrath to come"—to separate himself from all those who dwell in the "City of Destruction," including his wife and children.[10]

Christian sets off for "eternal life," but it is clear that he is less driven by the hope for bliss than by the fear of damnation. Here Bunyan assumes an empiricist stance: through experience we know more of earthly pain than we know of heavenly bliss, and so we can conceive of an eternity of punishment with more vividness than we ever could its opposite. As Hopeful, his eventual companion, says: "I do believe, as you say, that fear tends much to men's good, and to make them right at their beginning to go on Pilgrimage." Christian replies: "Without all doubt it doth, if it be right; for so says the Word, *The fear of the Lord is the beginning of Wisdom.*"

Bunyan's tale, typical of the communal level, is a heroic myth. It begins with repentance, proceeds with perseverance, and ends with reward. Yet the only community that ever presents itself in this narrative is the unchurched *worldly* community against which Christian must contend and to which he seems a dangerous agitator. The pilgrim progresses, but into his own future only. Like Wigglesworth, Bunyan may be termed a proto-premillennialist. Here is no march of a self-defined New Israel, overturning evil institutions one after another as it journeys to the millennial kingdom. No nation, no churchly establishment, constitutes the chosen people. Though his hero encounters human types, they are not the stuff of ethnic myth. The elect, predestined for salvation, are individuals who have had a conversion experience. Theirs is a lonely path on which one is lucky ever to link up with a fellow pilgrim. This is a lifetime deliberately directed toward its inevitable negation, death, and beyond that to a life eternally free from the fear of death and that far worse fear, the eternal death agonies of hell, which Revelation calls the "second death" (2:11; 20:6, 14; 21:8). The chosen and the unchosen do not have to wait for the end of the world to have their individual judgment day. The stark terrors of the Apocalypse attend the passing of every man, woman, and child.

Jonathan Edwards's celebrated sermon, "Sinners in the Hands of an Angry God," is even less overtly apocalyptic than Bunyan's allegory, yet it, too, strategically alludes to the doomsday narrative to focus upon the individual the burning rays of the Almighty's spectacular rage. The death of the sinner is, for him or her, the "day of wrath," the individual's *dies irae*. Up to that point he or she enjoys the "day of mercy," corresponding to the "Church Age" prior to Christ's Second Coming.

Edwards deftly deploys these two antithetical images of God's attitude toward humankind. He first evokes a damned soul in hell who remembers that in life, he "never intended to come here": death "came upon me unexpected; I did not look for it at that time, and in that manner; it came as a thief; death outwitted me." In Revelation, as mentioned earlier, Christ says: "Behold, I come as a thief" (16:15; see also 3:3), but here it is death who is the otherworldly visitant, the being that in the Middle Ages came to be depicted in a hooded robe and bearing a reaping hook (or a scythe or a sickle). This image is also identified with Christ as reaper of humankind: "And I looked, and behold a white cloud, and upon the cloud one sat like unto the Son of man, having on his head a golden crown, and in his hand a sharp sickle" (Rev. 14:14). Edwards's second allusion is to Christ not as the midnight marauder, but as the missionary of mercy (Rev. 3:20): "And now you have an extraordinary opportunity, a day wherein Christ has flung the door of mercy wide open, and stands in the door calling and crying with a loud voice to poor sinners."

These juxtaposed visitations of Christ create an unsettling logic of metaphor. If in Revelation Christ is both deadly thief and loving guest at the door, and in Edwards's sermon Death is the thief and Christ the guest, then in this sermon the personae of Death and Christ become eerily merged. The knocking of Christ at someone's door is a prelude to his taking that person away with him, as in the consolatory expression "The Savior came for Grandfather and took him."[11] As both thief and guest, Christ comes out of the future toward an individual who is either asleep or "watching." Edwards reiterates that for the complacent sleeper, Christ's coming brings disaster: "Your damnation don't slumber; it will come swiftly, and in all probability very suddenly upon many of you." To complicate matters, along with Christ and Death, there could be other nocturnal abductors—angels and devils. Wigglesworth's postscript to *The Day of Doom* threatens that God might become so exasperated as to say, "This night shall Devils fetch thy Soul away."[12]

A full generation before Edwards's classic sermon, Wigglesworth used the image of a person dangling above a fire. This image, derived from actual penal practices, helped reinforce the notion of God—not Satan—as chief torturer. There below gapes the "flaming Pit of Hell":

> Consider well the greatness of thy danger,
> O Child of wrath, and object of God's anger.
> Thou hangest over the Infernal Pit,
> By one small thread, and car'st thou not a whit?

There's but a step between thy Soul and Death;
Nothing remains but stopping of thy breath,
(Which may be done tomorrow, or before)
And then thou art undone forevermore.
Let this awaken thy security,
And make thee look about thee speedily.[13]

If Edwards's congregation in Enfield, Connecticut, on that July 8th in 1741 could only see themselves as God sees them, they would see themselves as objects of revulsion, dangled by the Almighty "over the pit of Hell, much as one holds a spider, or some loathsome insect, over the fire." In reusing Wigglesworth's dangling trope, Edwards succeeds in presenting to all the assembled members of his congregation an image that applies only to the separate, desperately helpless individual, for there can be but one spider, one Christian, to each thread.

These early texts, which anticipate the urgency of premillenialist preaching, reveal three contrasts with postmillennialism. First, the midnight return of Christ is to be sudden and catastrophic, not gradual and ameliorative. Second, the relation of humankind to this return will be that of immobilized persons either vigilantly waiting or heedlessly sleeping (not moving forward in time to encounter the returning Messiah and to help him create his kingdom). And third, the message of wakefulness must be preached to individuals, not to any nation or institution capable of mediating between sinners and an angry God. The premillennialist adaptation of the millennial myth for cultic purposes thus requires individuals to contemplate the possibility of being separated from the community, persuades them that they are in a liminal condition (either vulnerable to fire from heaven or dangling helplessly over the pit of hell), and urges upon them a transformative experience as their only hope for survival.

Gathering the Elect on Doomsday Eve

As premillennialist preachers tirelessly declare, the end times will be relatively sudden in their onset and short in their duration, a matter of no more than seven years. This ending of earthly time would come, especially to the unsaved, like a sudden unexpected death by drowning or apoplexy or murder. The prospect of sudden death, such as Bunyan and Edwards evoked, was addressed to individuals, but individuals in the aggregate. The one, after all, was a popular writer with an immense readership, the other a revivalist who during the 1730s and early 1740s addressed scores of thousands of rapt auditors. It was inevitable, therefore, that later premillennialists, even those who professed an aversion to churchly establishments, began to think collectively, to identify groups of potential converts and form them into congregations, albeit loose ones.

Out of this tendency grew the social phenomenon of the apocalyptic sect, to which older Christian sects would apply the word "cult," here as a term of disapproval and derision. Such a sect, usually formed from a schism in an older sect, is likely to center on a charismatic preacher who claims to possess prophetic insight as to the time of Christ's return, or "second advent." Because this return will be sudden, such privileged knowledge will be of supreme value to the unregenerate who fear damnation. Collective and individual death will hang like a single sword over the entire world, as myth and cult together reach a transfiguring climax. The fervor of the converted, which will rise as the fateful day approaches, will spread to others and the gospel of Jesus will be preached to multitudes. Regardless of whether these preachers believe in their prophetic calling, merely indulge in learned speculation, or cynically manipulate the credulous, the power of such a narrative in a deeply millennialist culture can be profound.

Indeed, reading the "signs of the times" has always been a path for ambitious but politically excluded persons—an exceedingly perilous path to power. As Norman Cohn has documented in his studies of medieval millennialism, almost every religious revolutionary from Eudes de l'Étoile in the mid-twelfth century to Thomas Münster in the mid-sixteenth century claimed prophetic powers. As Europeans traveled further afield and printing presses multiplied, what we now call "news" became a proliferating commodity. To corroborate their private revelations they had only to refer to the comets, meteor showers, earthquakes, wars, famines, plagues, and teratological sightings that seemed from year to year to be more frequently reported.

As the world grew older, it seemed to begin to collapse upon itself and veritably bristled with omens. In 1665, the London plague caused the death of 75,000, and in the "year of the Beast," 1666, the Great Fire destroyed most of the city. In America, Cotton Mather, whom James West Davidson aptly called "one of God's most strenuous creations," declared 1697 to be the year the entire world would be consumed in flames. (He then designated 1716, and finally 1736.)[14] Many Protestant clergy, John Wesley among them, interpreted the earthquake and tsunami that leveled much of Lisbon in 1755 as the opening of the sixth seal of Revelation ("and, lo, there was a great earthquake; and the sun became black as sackcloth of hair, and the moon became as blood," 6:12). New Englanders gazed upward apprehensively when, due to forest fires in the West, the sun and moon were veiled (May 19, 1780, and November 12, 1807), and yet again when a solar eclipse darkened the day (June 16, 1808).

On November 13, 1833, the annual Leonid meteor shower was extraordinary. As one observer reported: "At Niagara the exhibition was especially brilliant, and probably no spectacle so terribly grand and sublime was ever before beheld by man as that of the firmament descending in fiery torrents over the dark and roaring cataract."[15] In the early hours of that very morning, William Miller, a farmer living in upper New York State and for many years an assiduous student of biblical prophecy, gazed upward into the night skies and recognized at once the wrathful "fire from heaven." Here, finally, was the fulfillment of the apocalyptic prophecy: "And the stars of heaven fell onto the earth, even as a fig tree casteth her untimely figs, when she is shaken by a mighty wind" (Rev. 6:13). Already, two years earlier, Miller had announced that Jesus would return "sometime in 1843" to destroy the world and bring the living and the dead to judgment. Commonsensical Americans were not so impressed by private revelations of this sort, and, when Halley's Comet reappeared as scheduled in 1835, it stirred little apocalyptic interest. But when a heretofore unknown comet suddenly flared in February 1843, visible in daylight and seemingly about to plunge into the sun, many of those who had scoffed at "Father Miller's" prediction now had second thoughts. Miller now announced that Christ's return would commence the next month, on March 21, and be completed in exactly one year.

Needless to say, no miraculous intervention appeared during that twelvemonth period. When a younger colleague recalculated the biblical numbers and arrived at October 22, 1844, Miller wearily acquiesced: the night of October 21 and the morning of the 22nd would have to be the moment. On the 22nd, an otherwise uneventful October day lightened in the east, and the Millerites—whose numbers had grown to about 50,000 committed members and perhaps an equal number of sympathizers—were devastated. "Our fondest hopes and expectations were blasted and such a spirit of weeping came over us as I never experienced before," one follower later recalled. "We wept, and wept, till the day dawned."[16] This unexceptional sunrise became known among Millerites, or Second Adventists, as the "Great Disappointment."

Established churches, most of them postmillennialist in their interpretation of Revelation, felt vindicated by the Millerite fiasco, but doomsday rhetoric and itinerant revivalism continued unabated through the 1850s and

1860s. The temptation to set a precise date for the Second Coming now had to be strictly avoided, but as if to compensate for the loss of that minatory tool, premillennialist preachers intensified the horrors of hell and the urgency of being rescued from its flames. Dwight Lyman Moody (1837–1899) was typical of post-Civil War revivalists when he declared: "I look on this world as a wrecked vessel. God has given me a life-boat, and said to me, 'Moody, save all you can.' God will come in judgment and burn up this world, but the children of God don't belong to this world; they are in it, but are not of it, like a ship in the water. This world is getting darker; its ruin is coming nearer and nearer. If you have any friends on this wreck unsaved, you had better lose no time in getting them off."[17] The imagery is confusing, what with the burning and the drowning, the wrecked vessel and the children of God like a ship on the water, but his point is clear. As Timothy Weber explains, glossing Moody's feverish rhetoric: "Premillennialists viewed the world as a sinking vessel whose doomed passengers could be saved only by coming one at a time into the lifeboats of personal conversion. Since the course of the world was downward, only souls, not societies, could be saved from certain destruction."[18] We humans are not all in the same boat, evidently. Most are clinging to the sides of a sinking hulk, while a few are bobbing along in Rev. Moody's lifeboat. No longer belonging to a world destined for destruction, these few are prepared to be physically plucked from the seething surface of this planet when, at any moment, Jesus returns.

This premillennialist focus on the physical return of Jesus and the sudden ending of the world became one of the five cornerstones of the Christian conservative movement generally known as fundamentalism.[19] This narrative-inspired movement was in large measure a response to the compromises that mainstream Christian churches felt forced to make with the natural sciences, especially geology and biology. These two fact-based sciences had wreaked the most havoc on biblical chronology and, augmented by the theory of human evolution, had lent support to the postmillennialist claim that the human species had actually improved over time. To fundamentalists, the spread of such ideas was just one more sign of the end times, the coming tribulation from which the born-again would be physically removed, leaving behind the unsaved "modernists" to sink into the everlasting magma.

Perhaps inevitably, this intense meditation on the apocalyptic scenario— a meditation that sought answers to every question readers posed—found somewhere in scripture the answer to the question, "What will be the status of the True Church when Jesus Christ executes God's wrath on the unsaved?"

Premillennialists found their text in Paul's First Epistle to the Thessalonians. At the moment of Christ's return, the True Church (first the dead, then the living) "shall be caught up together with him in the clouds, to meet the Lord in the air" (1 Thess. 4:17), an event that has come to be called the Rapture. This feature of the end time was not a new finding; Increase and Cotton Mather had already expounded it.[20] Yet it became more and more appealing as the catastrophism of twentieth-century fundamentalist discourse began to appall even the born-again.

That unique midnight, when, as Wigglesworth's *Day of Doom* describes it, Christ appears in the sky and the goats are separated from the sheep, was now expanded to a seven-year tribulation of increasing earthly torment. At some point in this period, the unsaved, in their frantic search for solace and respite from pain, will look about and find that individual neighbors, fellow workers, and perhaps family members have all vanished.[21] If they had seen them go, they might have seen them rising into the air and disappearing into the sky. At last, the individuals left below will realize that now it is too late. Their hearts had remained unsoftened by the prayers of their Christian spouses, parents, and children, and they will now never see their loved ones again. Jesus has called his sheep home. Now only the wicked are left behind. Satan's hostages have been liberated, and God's full wrath is to be poured out on their former captors and deriders.

We see "salvation" here neither as a spiritual assurance of God's promise of a blissful eternity nor as a state of grace merely—indeed, not as a "state" at all, but as an *action*. It is a dramatic rescue of certain individuals as from a sinking ship or a burning building. But for some to be "saved," there must of course be a catastrophic act of God from which others are not saved. The traditional apocalyptic division between the blessed and the cursed must be maintained. This climactic scene, which made Wigglesworth's poem a colonial bestseller, has recently done the same for Tim LaHaye and Jerry B. Jenkins's *Left Behind* series of books and films. Yet one problem in this narrative remains: the executor of these opposite judgments must be one person. The very person who rescues the individual survivors has to be the one who has himself engineered the catastrophe—torpedoed the ship, as it were, or torched the building.

Assurances that the Day of the Lord, with fire and brimstone, death and damnation, was fast approaching could in itself produce unease in Americans, but could not fully fix their attention. Only precise calendar dates could do that. But this was risky business. As Stephen O'Leary remarks, "the history of prophecy and its interpretation is littered with chronological calculations performed with the feverish energy of moths circling a flame, continually tempted and finally burned by predictive overconfidence."[22] The lessons of the Millerite "Great Disappointment" proved lost on some Salvationists.

One prominent apocalyptic sect has, over the years, been notably tempted. In 1934, Joseph F. Rutherford, the second president of the Watchtower Society (or Jehovah's Witnesses), recalled no fewer than three disappointments: "There was a measure of disappointment on the part of Jehovah's faithful ones on earth concerning the years 1914, 1918, and 1925, which disappointment lasted for a time."[23] This organization, which grew out of post-Millerite Second Adventism in the late nineteenth century, had announced that Christ had invisibly returned to earth and that 1914 would mark the end of the "Gentile times"—the age of secular governments that had commenced with the Babylonian captivity of 587 BC—and the inauguration of Jehovah's theocracy on earth. Charles Taze Russell, the organization's founder, had proclaimed this as early as 1874. The cosmic week was approaching its final day and the seventh millennium soon to begin. The year 1914, certainly a fateful year for Europe, would be the end of forty years of tribulation. When 1914 came and went, it was declared that in 1918 the "old heavens and earth, having been disposed of, this wicked world, which has been in its 'time of the end' since 1914, will come to its final end."[24] Much indeed did come to an end in 1918 on the battlefields of Europe, but this wicked world rolled on and soon was preening itself for the similarly wicked 1920s.

In 1920 Rutherford announced that Abraham, Isaac, Jacob, and eight other Hebrew patriarchs would be resurrected in 1925. This, in retrospect, was the third "disappointment" to which he later alluded. Yet despite the patriarchs' non-arrival, the Watchtower Society went ahead and built them a home, Beth Sarim ("House of the Princes"), in San Diego, California, in 1929. To date, the Witnesses' last millennial prediction was made in 1966: the kingdom of Jehovah would be finally established in the fall of 1975. The most notable event of 1975, however, was neither the arrival of Jehovah nor the embarrassment of his Witnesses. It was the fall of Saigon and the ignominious departure of American military forces from Southeast Asia. The Korean War had ended in a stalemate, but never in America's history had its military been defeated and expelled—and by a small third-world nation. This debacle and the aftermath of the Watergate investigation, that is, Richard Nixon's forced retirement and the convictions of his top aides, overshadowed the Witnesses' fourth disappointment and shielded it from the measure of public derision it would have otherwise provoked. Ironically, though, the major news stories of 1975 could be used—and were used—by the Witnesses and other apocalyptic sects as signs that confirmed their prophetic message. Whether these setbacks for America meant that the infernal forces had been unleashed and Armageddon was fast approaching or that America had lost its vaunted messianic mandate, it had become clear to many that the post-millennialist dream of progress had finally been exposed as a false gospel.

Assigning a specific date for Christ's apocalyptic return has proven to be a risky tactic. Other events—his birth, his death, his resurrection, his ascension—these could be assigned specific days and commemorated within the yearly cycle. This culminating event could not be commemorated because, obviously, it has not yet happened. Nevertheless, the Apocalypse has inserted itself within the Christian-American commemorative cycle in fragmentary and disguised forms. I will conclude this chapter on narratives of the night with some thoughts on how certain holidays, religious and secular, have incorporated apocalyptic themes and motifs.

Christmas, the American Un-apocalypse

A nation's calendar of holidays reveals a great deal about its major preoccupations. In European Christendom, the official series of holidays included the holy days of the liturgical year, commemorating the major events in world history as seen from a Christian perspective. This year begins in late November with the season of Advent, recalling the Jews' waiting for the Messiah, which culminates in Christmas. The twelve days following December 25th, six in December and six in January, were thought to hold portents for the twelve months of the New Year. New Year's Eve and Day were thus considered part of Christmastide. From Epiphany (January 6) to Easter, the liturgy commemorates the life and ministry of Jesus, then his ascension into heaven, and finally the descent of the Holy Spirit at Pentecost, which is called the "birthday of the Church." The Sunday readings through the summer and fall, a period that symbolizes the growth of the Church and its harvest of souls, lack the biblical chronology of the first half of the calendar. In world history, only the Second Coming of Jesus remains to occur. Though no one day of the year is specifically assigned to it, it is apprehensively alluded to on the last Sunday before Advent.

Puritans and other apocalyptically focused groups have always regarded this calendar as a stratagem of the "official" religion, the "visible church," crafted in the spirit of the Second Beast, the False Prophet. According to this view, it was all well and good to commemorate the events recounted in the New Testament, but the impression this liturgy gives is that God's engagement with human history was long ago and far away. Moreover, too many nonbiblical traditions, some of them borrowed from pagans, have crept into these celebrations over the centuries. (December 25, for example, is not the true birthday of Jesus, but merely a concession by timid churchmen to sun-worshipping pagans.) The Jesus *they* understood was the resurrected Lord who was soon to return and vindicate their faith. Christmas was, at best, a veil of pleasant images woven to conceal from Christians a fiery future that would soon burst upon them. If Christmas were to be celebrated at all, its publicly acknowledged focus should be on the birth of Christ, the redeemer and ultimate judge of humankind—not on some vague, ecumenical spirit of peace and goodwill.

Civil religion, on the other hand, has always taken a somewhat tolerant view on the end-of-year festivities and is, in principle, hostile to apocalypse. After all, no liturgy encouraged by secular authorities is ever likely to solemnize the imminent destruction of the state. Instead it will draw people's thoughts to how God, who has wrought great things for them in the past, continues to shower them with blessings in this rich and well-governed land. Instead of threatening them with the curses of Doomsday, it will assure them that they have earned blessings through obedience to some national covenant. The challenge for American civil religion has always been how to adapt this broad message to a deeply apocalypticized culture.

Long before the invention of the modern Christmas, the holiday seems to have absorbed a number of apocalyptic features that, while overtly negated, are covertly acknowledged. From the Middle Ages on, the few similarities between the first coming and the second were seized upon—and others invented—to help cushion the impact of the disturbing images of the Apocalypse by substituting the more reassuring ones of the Nativity. Here, depicted in the familiar manger scene, extending his hands to bless the world, is a divine infant, not a wrathful god returning to massacre unbelievers. Representatives of humanity, Jew and gentile, native and foreign, commoners and kings, are all reconciled in their adoration of this little Prince of Peace, not divided into hostile and eternal categories. On this night all sounds of conflict are stilled throughout the world. Even oxen and asses gaze with soulful eyes and rapt attention. In short, the Christmas narrative was traditionally reenacted in words and images taken from the millennial era *following* the end-times catastrophe.

The actual scriptural texts from which this millennial version was derived tell a somewhat different story. For one thing, the "wise men from the east" never meet the shepherds at the manger but visit the family at a house in Bethlehem (Matt. 2:11). They are not kings, but *Magoi* (Zoroastrian priests); they are not three, but an unspecified number; none of them is black. If, as I am suggesting, we read this bit of folklore as part of a process of substituting consoling images for disturbing ones, we may recognize these "kings" as masking the dreaded "kings of the east" whose way is prepared to cross the Euphrates and ravage the civilized world (Rev. 16:17). (We must recall that, for a full thousand years after the empire crumbled, the "kings of the east"—Huns, Moors, Mongols, Vikings, Turks, and others—had terrified western Europe as agents of the Apocalypse.) As the "kings of the earth" (cf. Rev. 17:18), they might in medieval iconography be represented as the racial descendants of Shem, Japheth, and Ham. As worshipers of the infant "King of Kings" (Rev. 19:16), these agents of destruction now become images of peace. Revelation predicts that "the kings of the earth do bring glory and honor unto it" (the millennial Jerusalem of the Lamb). As for the animals in the stable, the gospel texts mention neither animals nor stable, though these may be inferred from the word "manger." On the other hand, animals do bulk large in the *second* Advent text: in the end times, angelic beasts (*zoa*) worship the mystical Lamb, and diabolical beasts (*theria*) terrify humankind. The beasts imported into the Nativity scene may be comforting replacements of the above, but seem rather like the fauna of the pastoral age to come, the peaceable kingdom (Isa. 11:6–8).

Another detail in the popular tradition also suggests a wish that the first advent narrative of the night was meant to be inscribed over the second. Most Christians believe that angels sang "Alleluia" on that first Christmas night. Countless hymns reinforce this assumption. The sky in Luke's account is briefly thronged with angels praising God, but when they appear, they do *not* sing "Alleluia." The only place in the entire New Testament (Greek, Vulgate, and KJV) in which this Hebrew expression ever appears is chapter 19 of Revelation, when heavenly voices four times praise God for destroying "Babylon." The displacement of this word from a context of vengeful gloating to one of "peace, goodwill to men" muffles its catastrophic import. It is also significant that most Christians have accepted for their Christmas story a version of the angels that ignores their actual role as warriors. The angels in Luke are designated as members of the army of heaven (the "heavenly host"), certainly not androgyne singers in flowing robes. In fact, Luke never said that they sang at all. They *spoke* their praise of God. The same warrior angels will reappear in Revelation, where their job description again does not include singing. This restyling of the angels as benign choristers on a silent night seems one more instance of an unconscious wish to re-veil Revelation and divert the mind from its terrifying imagery.

This cultural superscription of the millennialized Nativity over the Apocalypse seems to have been a factor in the history of Christmas. In the sixteenth and seventeenth centuries, the English Puritans and their Presbyterian allies in Scotland inveighed against the "keeping of Christmas." Wherever they took control, they severely punished those who celebrated a holiday that had either distracted believers from the imminent return of Christ or, worse, seduced them into a lawless saturnalia. They saw no godly reason why fifty-two Sabbaths a year were not rest enough for their bondservants, apprentices, and hired workers. But as Calvinism lost its dominant position first in Old and then in New England, the traditional observance of Christmas revived and once again the rich and the poor, like kings and shepherds, met in a year-end ritual of equality. The well-to-do would open their homes to their less prosperous neighbors and give them food and gifts. For a period of from one to twelve days, the barriers that all year separated the social ranks would be removed, usually with the help of that universal solvent, alcohol. This custom survives with similar effect as the Christmas, or end-of-year, "office party."[25]

By the early nineteenth century, however, the Christmas open house began to decline as an institution in the larger cities of America. The population had become so mobile, poverty and public drunkenness so common, that one simply could not tell whom one was throwing open one's doors to anymore. So, as one by one the doors were closed and the silverware preserved, Christmas became what it is today, a domestic holiday.[26]

As children, taking the place of the "less fortunate," became the main recipients of their parents' munificence, the nuclear family in the nineteenth century came to model itself on the Holy Family—the father as the dutiful, patient, protective, strong Joseph; the mother as the loyal handmaiden, the chaste spouse, the ever-faithful Mary; and the child as the veritable gift of God, the Christ Child.[27] By contrast to this idealized scene, the Apocalypse presents the image of a dysfunctional family. The children who murdered, or tried to murder, their father's favorite son now await the return of this son who, with the father's approval and with the help of his father's servants, will slip back "like a thief in the night" into the house his father built, wreck it, attack these children, and torture them all forever except for those few who have been predestined to get to gloat upon their siblings' groans and spasms. For those who yearned in the "spirit of Christmas" for a universe motivated by familial love, yet knew full well what the book of Revelation had promised, here was a cognitive dissonance of profound proportions.

Long before 1823, when Clement Moore supposedly wrote *A Visit from Saint Nicholas,* a figure dressed as a bishop would visit homes in Holland and, somehow knowing who had been naughty and who had been nice, distributed toys and switches accordingly.[28] The shift of this "mini-version of the Last Judgment for children"[29] from the feast day of Sinterclaas (December 6) to Christmas Eve completed the domestication of Christmas as an end-of-the-year children's festival associated with the coming of the hoped-for new age. Finally, in a marvel of mythopoeic role reversal, the thief in the night was converted into a "jolly old elf" who, instead of routing the sleeping children out of bed to execute judgment upon them, quietly filled their stockings with toys and sweets.[30] This was more than the covering up of the second advent by a revised version of the first. This was the invention of the American un-apocalypse.

This Christmas poem, as Steven Nissenbaum has pointed out, starts with what sounds like a parody of Wigglesworth's still-remembered *Day of Doom.* The latter poem began: "Still was the night, serene and bright." But, as we soon learn, this nocturnal peacefulness is illusory:

> For at midnight breaks forth a light,
>   which turns the night to day,
> And speedily an hideous cry
>   doth all the world dismay.
>
> Sinners awake . . .
>
> .   .   .   .
>
> They rush from beds with giddy heads
>   and to their windows run.
> Viewing this light, which shines more bright
>   than doth the noon-day Sun.

(stanzas 1, 2, 5)

Compare this to *A Visit:* "'Twas the night before Christmas and all through the house / Not a creature was stirring, not even a mouse. Their children safely tucked into bed, the parents "settle [their] brains for a long winter's nap."

> When out on the lawn there arose such a clatter
> I sprang from the bed to see what was the matter.
> Away to the window I flew like a flash,
> Tore open the shutters and threw up the sash.

The moon on the breast of the new-fallen snow
Gave a lustre of mid-day to objects below.

(lines 9–14)

This narrative soon took the traditional Christmas spirit of generosity and permanently converted it into a handy hook for retail advertisers. But there was more to it than that. First popularized in New York City, then throughout the republic, this poem has from the start held a curiously tenacious grip on the American imagination.[31] Just as Puritans had failed to take Christmas out of Christianity, traditionalists wishing to "put Christ back into Christmas" have never succeeded in banishing St. Nick, or Santa Claus, along with his entourage of reindeer and pointy-hatted elves, to the land of merely childish make-believe.[32]

As a children's story of no particular literary merit, this narrative has permanently inserted itself in America's seasonal consciousness. It fascinates young children, perhaps because it relieves that universal childhood fear of a stranger who breaks into their room at night and, grimacing hideously, steals them away or devours them. Even adults, in the retelling, may recollect their own childhood belief in a magical stranger who watches their behavior, enters their home in the darkness, and rewards them if they have been good. As they grew older, they no longer believed in Santa, but in a Christian culture they learned about another figure that they were told they *must* believe in, the mind-reading midnight intruder of the Apocalypse. American adults, even those who have come to identify with an un-apocalyptic worldview, still have their own monstrous cultural fantasies to repress—those of a devil-haunted earth and a wrathful, all-knowing judge who appears suddenly in the night sky. In the act of transmitting the Santa narrative, adults participate in a fiction that magically recasts that deeply rooted, anxiety-provoking belief as a narrative that only a small child could ever believe. The same adult who was once told that soothing story of the kindly intruder thus achieves a measure of cognitive consonance in retelling it. The apocalyptic narrative, subtly implicated in this fable, is thereby simultaneously acknowledged and denied.

Civil Liturgy and the Apocalyptic Model

Government has always taken a special interest in public celebrations, because mass gatherings can get out of hand. Moses asked the pharaoh to "let my people go"—not out of slavery, or to some far-off homeland, but simply to celebrate a three-day religious observance east of the Nile (Exod. 3:18). The pharaoh, who might have reasonably concluded that a gathering on this scale by a hostile minority could have destabilizing consequences, denied the request.

Unauthorized celebrations may pose challenges to the state, but authorized ones, if carefully scripted, can promote national cohesion. During the first century of the Christian era, Roman officials required citizens of the empire to pledge their allegiance by participating in ceremonial feasts to honor the emperor. When Christians refused, as did the Jewish nationalists in Palestine, they were viewed as subversives. In the fourth century, when Christianity itself became the state religion, a new civil-religious calendar was instituted in which Christian holidays were superscribed on earlier non-Christian observances. Ritual time off was now structured by, and dedicated to, a new master narrative. Most notably, the celebration of the birth of Christ replaced that of the sun god, who, unconquered by wintry mists, was said to be reborn on December 25. One can easily imagine some Roman traditionalist urging his neighbors to honor the old-time religion by "putting Sol back into Solstice."

Vigorously suppressed though they were, those old beliefs attached themselves in seemingly innocent forms to the new religious calendar, and missionaries unwittingly spread them along with the doctrines of vicarious atonement, the resurrection of the dead, and the end of the world. All Saints Day (November 1), followed by All Souls Day, appropriated the Celtic festival now best known by its Gaelic name Samhain (pronounced "sawan"). This was the time when livestock that would not be wintered over were ritually slaughtered. (Northern peoples called November "Blood-Month.") The scent of the blood of Samhain sacrifices was believed to attract the spirits of the dead back to feast with the living. The meat that was not consumed was salted away for the long dark months ahead.

As a vestige of this great festival, All Hallows Eve, or "Halloween," has come down to us in America as a narrative of the night when the dead are allowed to leave their place of confinement and rejoin the living. According to Christian doctrine, a one-night resurrection of this sort could only be diabolically contrived (with God's permission, of course), because the saved are either in heaven already or sleeping the sleep of the just, awaiting Judgment Day. The eve of All Saints Day therefore became the night of the damned, a type of the brief uprising of Satan, who "must be loosed a little season" (Rev. 20:3) after the Millennium to work his futile mischief before the Messiah's Final Judgment of the world. The participants in this folk ritual were traditionally disguised not merely as the generic dead up from the graveyard, which would be frightening enough. These night stalkers were for the most part the *resentful* dead, such as witches, pirates, hostile Indians, and hoboes, the dead who continued to have a score to settle with the living. But, like the Santa festival, this enactment of apocalyptic themes is a carnivalized re-veiling of Revelation. The fact that the maskers who parade about as these evil sprites are actually children helps exorcise the uncanny, effectively taking the devil out of this deviltry.

Samhain and Halloween, like many other festivals celebrated throughout the world, are times meant to be somehow separate from ordinary, rule-governed time. In some cultures, the periods that fall between one annual cycle and the next are often regarded as "extra," or intercalary, days. During these times, members of the lower class are permitted to imitate the manners of the upper class, assume aristocratic titles, hold court, consume conspicuous amounts of food and alcohol, and exhibit all the hauteur and license they associate with the elite. Yet when Saturnalia or Carnival or Mardi Gras or Twelfth Night is over, they are expected to return to their underling status with equanimity. Such rituals function to provide a resentful underclass with a symbolic revolution—and thereby preserve the status quo ante.

Mikhail Bakhtin defined the "carnivalesque" as "the temporary suppression of all hierarchic distinctions and barriers among men," but a carnival can also be a ritual of social inversion that temporarily creates new hierarchical distinctions.[33] Adults may then cater to the whims of children, beggars wear the robes and crowns of royalty, and masters serve their slaves, which, as Nissenbaum has noted, was the practice in the antebellum South on July 4 and on Christmas. The specific commemorative or liturgical structure of a given festival helps contain and direct the anarchic energies of the celebrants, but may be less important than the general function of carnival—that is, the servants' temporary, symbolic promotion in rank and the demotion of masters.

In many cultures, carnivalesque rituals of social inversion symbolize the completion of the full narrative cycle, the coming age in which justice reigns, virtue is rewarded, and arrogance punished. The Greeks and Romans associated this renovation of the world with the return of the Golden Age ruled over by the god Kronos, or Saturn, the god of the harvest festival.[34] In the Christian tradition, this just realm is announced by a "voice crying out in the wilderness, Prepare ye the way of the Lord, make his paths straight. Every valley shall be filled, and every mountain and hill shall be brought low" (Luke 3:4–5).[35] The valley and mountain imagery is traditionally interpreted in terms of social inversion. More to the point, Jesus declared: "Verily I say unto you, That a rich man shall hardly enter into the kingdom of God. And again I say unto you, It is easier for a camel to go through the eye of a needle, than for a rich man to enter the kingdom of God." Then, moments later, when Peter asks what the lot of Jesus's followers will be in the coming age, Jesus says: "When the Son of man shall sit in the throne of his glory, ye also shall sit upon twelve thrones, judging the twelve tribes of Israel. . . . [M]any that are first shall be last; and the last shall be first" (Matt. 19:23–24, 28, 30). This promise is repeated in Revelation (3:21): "To him who overcometh I will grant to sit with me in my throne." Then, after the fall of Babylon, the corrupt city of the rich, John sees the kingdom of God where the righteous do indeed sit on thrones, enjoy a splendid marriage feast, and reign with Christ for a thousand years (Rev. 20:4).[36]

The more we examine American holidays, the more we find apocalyptic, carnivalesque elements lurking beneath the surface. Doomsday motifs lie concealed not only in the traditional and secular observances of Christmas and Halloween but also in the national nativity celebration of Independence Day.[37] When the American War of Independence ended and the enemy was sent back across the sea, the language of Armageddon that still clung to recent events now needed to be tempered and a liturgy devised to redraft the "Spirit of '76" in peaceful, millennial terms. The leaders of the new republic needed a national birthday party, but they were well aware that those sectors of the population who were dissatisfied with the fruits of revolution needed to be kept busy on that day with a series of carefully scheduled events.[38] These formalities seemed especially needed in cities such as Boston, New York, and Philadelphia, where for workingmen a day off other than the Sabbath was a day dedicated to John Barleycorn and Demon Rum. Painstaking efforts were therefore made so that the national nativity day did not become the occasion of actual social inversion and lower-class libertinism.[39] The well-regulated militias that paraded through the streets presented colorful entertainment but also supplied merchants and landlords with protection from freelance revolutionaries.

As we have seen, the traditional Christmas and its American Santa-fied version transformed some of the more anxiety-provoking passages of Revelation by blending them into the imagery of a harmonious millennial homeland. At the opposite end of the American liturgical calendar, the Fourth of July also blends sunny millennial themes with darker reminders of Armageddon and Judgment. The happier elements conform to the civil-religious belief that with the founding of the republic, the "political Messiah," as Melville called him, was reborn in America. This belief, in turn, conformed to the post-millennialist view that, thanks to the spread of Christianity, the world was improving. Humans were now, after all, virtuous enough to govern themselves—or, at least, white, property-owning American males were.

During Fourth of July celebrations, the principal oration gave a popular speaker the opportunity to inveigh against those whom Melville called the "political pagans" and thereby direct the rum-inspired imagination of the populace away from domestic discontents and toward vaguely defined foreign threats. The following passage from an oration delivered in 1796 gives us a sense of this rhetorical strategy. A day of reckoning was fast approaching when the United States of America would impose its Christian will on the evildoers of the entire world and effect a worldwide social inversion. In these concluding words, we hear the rumblings of Armageddon as the speaker proclaims the millennial destiny of the new republic. Then, soaring over the conquered world, the four angels of the Apocalypse transform themselves magically into the angels of Christmas:

> For behold, ye who have been exalted up to heaven, shall, ere long, be cast down to hell! The final period of your crimes is rapidly approaching. The grand POLITICAL MILLENNIUM is at hand, when tyranny shall be buried in ruins; when all the nations shall be united in ONE MIGHTY REPUBLIC! When the four angels, that stand on the four corners of the globe, shall, with one accord, lift up their voices to heaven; proclaiming PEACE ON EARTH, AND GOOD WILL TO ALL MEN.[40]

I have saved for the very last the most important of all genuinely American holidays. It is now celebrated no less than 109 days per year. It is the American weekend—an exported custom so culturally specific that even the French, to their chagrin, are obliged to refer to it as *le weekend*. Based on the institution of the Sabbath, which in Hebrew means a "rest" or "cessation" from some activity, the weekend now bridges both the Jewish Sabbath, beginning Friday at sundown, and the Christian Sabbath, Sunday. In expanded form, as a "long weekend," it now also includes the Monday observances of Martin Luther King Day, Presidents' Day, Memorial Day, Labor Day, and Columbus Day. Even the Fourth of July or Christmas, when it falls on a weekend, is officially observed with a day off on either Friday or Monday. The longest of all weekends, of course, begins on the final Wednesday of November as Thanksgiving Eve.

Granted, there are nonreligious reasons for this calendrical custom—e.g., a shortened workweek and a desire on the part of retailers to attract customers to sales—and granted, the phrase "Thank God it's Friday" is not associated with pious sentiments. Weekend activities, whether they are partying, sports, excursions, cookouts, or merely relaxing, do tend to be merely self-indulgent. Yet even self-indulgence may have religious significance. At any rate, whenever an entire society engages in a similar, synchronized behavior, we may infer that a ritual of some sort is being performed, a ritual that may well be the enactment of a myth.

Once again, it seems to me, we have a ritual expression of the apocalyptic master narrative. Of course, there are no precise rubrics for the observance of this ritual, but, with its vigorous "letting off steam" on Friday and its more placid "kicking back" on Sunday, the end of the weekly cycle broadly resembles that of the biblical end of the cosmic cycle. The Cosmic Week, some early theologians speculated, is a series of six 1,000-year "days," followed by a single 1,000-year Sabbath. This was the time scheme that Timothy Dwight alluded to as "that remarkable Jewish tradition that the last thousand years of the reign of time would, in imitation of the conclusion of the first week [of creation], become a glorious Sabbath of peace, purity, and felicity."[41] The fact that the seventh day of the week was also called "Saturn's Day" added support to the Cosmic Week theory, because (as the pagan messianist Vergil had prophesied) Saturn was to preside over the new Golden Age.

If the American weekend derives its religious significance from the apocalyptic myth, it follows that its self-indulgent character is a ritual enactment of the pleasures of the millennial kingdom. This condition will not be one of guilty hedonism but of divine entitlement, the reward awaiting those who will have fought the good fight and overcome at last. In the religious imagination the Millennium is portrayed as a glorious morning following a horrendous night. Bathed in sunlight, groups of friends and family members, young and old, wander among flowers, praising God and smiling blissfully on one another. It is both a Canaan and an Eden, a classless land that is finally home to all God's people equally. The weekend customs of cookouts and picnics and of visits to public parks, beaches, and family recreation sites reflect, albeit mundanely, this millennial expectation. This is a time when American presidents are filmed playing touch football, fly-fishing, or cutting brush on the ranch. The special weekly festival ritually reaffirms the homeland myth of a classless society and proclaims the millennial "morning in America."

The plot structure that qualifies as the ultimate master narrative may well be, as Todorov suggests, a revolutionary myth. Despite cultural modifications, this narrative of falling and rising fortunes may be found throughout the world, expressed by storytelling and by dramatic reenactment. The master narrative represented in the Bible achieves "full cycle" only with the fulfill-ment of apocalyptic prophecy in the violent (re)establishment of the divine kingdom. As we have seen, though, this narrative has been superscribed by other narratives—parodic and carnivalesque versions of the doomsday denouement.

5

ABDUCTION NARRATIVES

The biblical time line, superimposed on Tzvetan Todorov's narrative model, characterizes phase 3 not only as a long night but also as a period of bondage. The Hebrew Bible (or, as Christians call it, the Old Testament) records two such periods. One began with the voluntary migration of the Children of Israel to Egypt and the eventual enslavement of their descendants under a repressive regime. In this account, beginning in Genesis and continuing through the next four books, the Israelites under Moses escape bondage and make their way to the border of the land their god has promised them.

More historically detailed, though less miraculous, is the bondage story that begins with the deportation of the 4,500 Judeans who had survived the Babylonian siege and destruction of Jerusalem in 587 BC. They were taken from their homeland to Nippur, a city in southeastern Babylonia (modern Iraq), where they remained for almost fifty years until the Persians under Cyrus liberated them and sent them back to Judah. For later Jews, Babylon remained the symbolic land of exile in which the dispossessed yearned for their lost homeland. Christians subsequently interpreted this mass abduction and military detention as a type, a symbol of humankind's thralldom to sin, and they aligned Babylon with the temporary triumph of "the World" and its prince, Satan.

The possibility of rescue, the function and person of the rescuer—these are implicit details of this or any abduction narrative. In the Christian tradition, the more familiar terms for this rescue and this rescuer are "redemption" and "redeemer." As the word is used in the KJV, the first meaning of "redemption" is "ransom," the act of paying someone to release a captive; the second meaning is "revenge," the act of "paying back" the captor for his crime. Christians interpret Jesus's redemptive mission to suggest that he was the ransomer *and* the ransom payment by which humankind was freed from satanic bondage. As God, he had the power to intervene in history and rescue its victims, but as Man, he physically partook of their victimhood by substituting himself for them in his sacrificial act of atonement. As Christians came to understand his mission in the prophecy of Revelation, however, it was as that other redeemer, the avenger who would come to punish the evil Babylon for abducting and tormenting his chosen people.

Abduction, including kidnapping and hostage taking, can also entail imprisonment, slavery, torture, and sexual abuse. Little wonder, then, that such narrative themes produce powerfully emotional responses. Reduced to its simplest structure, an abduction narrative is a three-person plot, featuring a villain, a victim, and a hero: the villain acts by taking the victim, the hero acts by retaking the victim, while the victim functions as the passive object of exchange. In a patriarchal culture, not surprisingly, the victimized abductee is often a woman fought over by two males. This female abductee is passive only in the sense that, once captured, she cannot free herself. Up to that point she actively resists the abductor and, during her captivity, though passive, she is never *im*passive: she fervently believes that she will be rescued and is ever vigilant for the arrival of her liberator.

As Christian symbolism has it, the abducted people of God, the Church, is the "bride of Christ" for whom he will return to earth, rescuing her from Satan and his henchmen. Standard premillennialist doctrine holds that the bridegroom, when he comes, will spare her the perils of the seven-year tribulation and the climactic battle of Armageddon. He will first cause her to ascend into the sky and meet him in the event they call the Rapture. Only after that will he pour forth his wrath upon the earth.

The abduction narrative is not unique to biblical history or myth or to American culture. Tales of tender damsels, queens, princesses, and goddesses spirited away by evildoers and saved by heroes abound in world mythology.[1] Yet the Bible and the Christian theory of history extrapolated from it sank its impress so deeply into this narrative that, even when it appeared in non-Christian contexts, it seemed to radiate a moral, almost a sacral, intensity.

In the last chapter I traced the development of the premillennialist narrative and suggested how and why this apocalyptic scenario so powerfully affected American culture—even secular culture. This chapter explores some spin-offs of a closely related narrative, fantastical products of the Christian imagination that most Christians would regard as either nonreligious or heretical. Some of these focus on the episode of capture and abduction, which usually involves, or suggests, forced sexual intercourse. Others concern themselves with the circumstances of the captive and her yearnings to be rescued; still others depict the confrontation of the avenging hero with the abductor. In earlier variants of this basic narrative, the hero is granted superhuman powers, magical or miraculous, but over the past half-century his powers are usually explained in terms of technological know-how. This does not totally alter the role of the individual hero, who must still be resolute and courageous, but it does tend to associate his powers with cultural superiority. I conclude this chapter with an inquiry into several abduction narratives that have emerged out of white Protestant Americans' historical confrontations with alien cultures from colonial times to the present.

The Abductors Arrive

A belief that superior, deathless beings dwell in the remote regions of the sky is a nearly universal myth.[2] Linear time and gravitational space lead mortals inevitably toward the grave, but primitive religious thinking has always contended that eternal beings, like the lights of the firmament, are exempt from all this. Just as their powers of foreknowledge make them superior to earthly time, so, too, their powers of flight make them superior to earthly space.

The book of Genesis (6:1–4) preserves an intriguing legend, one that in some form appears in most ancient mythologies. (I mentioned it on page 79 in a different context.) It tells of a superior race of beings (the "sons of God") who are sexually attracted to human women (the "daughters of men") and sire through them a superior race ("giants" and "mighty men which were of old, men of renown"). Because the "sons of God" is a phrase associated with the "host of heaven," Yahweh's angelic army visible as the stars in the night sky, these would, in effect, be visitors from outer space. The ubiquity of this myth in ancient texts has led some modern writers to speculate that it somehow must be based in fact.

Now, if the activities of such beings have manifested themselves in the sky, they must have been visible to other mortals, not simply to the Hebrew tribesmen to whom their significance was communicated. Ancient myths and artifacts from Greece, Egypt, Mesopotamia, India, China, Polynesia, Mesoamerica, and Peru should describe or depict flying beings and their vehicles. Under the assumption that all ancient texts and inscriptions are equally inerrant (with a little tweaking), a theory developed that the "gods" are dimly remembered astronauts, visitors from outer space who, beginning 40,000 years ago, taught technology to our slow-witted ancestors.

Charles Fort, a collector of scientific anomalies who is sometimes called the father of science fiction, introduced this idea in the 1920s. It was Erich von Däniken, however, who popularized it in the 1970s with his best-selling *Chariots of the Gods? Unsolved Mysteries of the Past.* Suppose, he said, astronauts from earth were ever to visit a planet whose inhabitants were still in the Stone Age. They would "seem like almighty gods to these primitive people!" Despite their best efforts to disabuse the natives of these notions, these visitors would ever afterward be remembered as divine beings possessed of terrifying powers.[3] (If these primitives could have identified the visitors as "gods," the word "gods" and the concept it stood for must have preceded the first arrival of the spaceships, but why quibble?)

To prove his premise that the "gods," or the "sons of God," were visiting spacemen, von Däniken points to the fact that all over the world, there are images and legends of larger-than-life beings with powers to fly and to wield terrifying weapons. In a footnote, which reveals to us just about all we need to know about his logical method, he tells us: "'Giants' haunt the pages of almost all ancient books. So they must have existed."[4] The "giants" and the "sons of God" that Genesis 6:4 refers to as angels were, of course, spacemen, and their commanders were the "gods." Our ancestors never forgot the exploits of these visitors, who in various places around the world, using local labor, built massive stone structures and landing fields and cowed the natives with pyrotechnic displays. The destruction of Sodom and Gomorrah (everybody's favorite object lesson) was one of them. Von Däniken writes, "Perhaps . . . the 'angels' simply wanted to destroy some dangerous fissionable material and at the same time to make sure of wiping out a human brood they found unpleasant."[5] Other biblical wonders are similarly explained. Touching the Ark of the Covenant could electrocute a man, because the astronaut commander atop Sinai had shown Moses how to build a several-hundred-volt electrical conductor and how to use it to transmit and receive information from his spaceship. As for the chariot Ezekiel saw, it was obviously a helicopter with wheels capable of adjusting to uneven terrain.

These apparently benign marauders from a higher civilization were in contact with earthlings for tens of thousands of years. But what were they doing on earth in Paleolithic times? These spacemen—they were, it seems, only male—combined their two main interests, sex and livestock breeding, by inseminating "a few especially selected women. . . . Thus a new race would arrive that skipped a stage in natural evolution."[6] This they would do over and over again, apparently, until they got it right. Here again we encounter the standard story of a divinely chosen people, specially instructed by "gods," but in this case having the additional advantage of direct kinship with these higher beings.

We have a very obvious racial narrative here, an ethnic myth. Leaving aside questions of why alien beings should be anatomically like and genetically compatible with Paleolithic humans, we might ask what von Däniken means by "race." It turns out that these astronauts' genetic experiments were not all equally successful. The periodic destruction of humans, which all peoples have memorialized in their legends, was the work of extraterrestrial eugenicists, but for some reason they sometimes chose not to eliminate the misfits: they "either destroyed the unsuccessful specimens or *took them to settle other continents.*"[7] Which continents? Europe . . . ? Or perhaps he means sub-Saharan Africa, Australia, and the Western Hemisphere. The racial mythologies of Ham and Japheth and the even more fanciful ones of Pre-Adamism and Christian Identity thus appear written between the lines of what has now come to be called "pre-astronautics," or the "ancient-astronaut theory."

The broad contours of von Däniken's cosmic narrative reproduce the familiar biblical arc. Visitors from a superior realm generate human beings, hoping that the new creatures will imitate them. Some do and are blessed with the gift of a higher consciousness; others degenerate and are either destroyed or survive to live in enmity toward the chosen people. As this arc rises again, some of the elect, the nations or races that most resemble their extraterrestrial forefathers, raise themselves to a level of true equality with them, which for von Däniken is technological equality. (One gathers from the author's adulatory references to him that Wernher von Braun represents the apex of human evolution.) Thus the end of human history will witness the same level of technology that appeared at its beginning, that is, nuclear power and space travel. The monumental past, dimly preserved in myth and glyph, now briefly reappears on earth before some of us—the technologically elect—rapture ourselves to other planets and thereby escape the Malthusian tribulation to come.

Not surprisingly, the Book of Revelation has been a favorite of ancient-astronaut theorists. Interpreting it as a UFO alien abduction narrative, William Bramley in *The Gods of Eden* (1993) explains that the person John thought was Jesus (Rev. 1:13–17) was really a spaceman, "garbed in a one-piece body suit extending from the neck down to metal or metal-like boots. The creature's head was described as 'white like wool, as white as snow,' indicating an artificial head covering or helmet. . . . The 'two-edged sword' protruding from the creature's mouth easily suggests a microphone or breathing pipe."

John, like countless others before and after, was taken up into a spaceship and given a message beyond his capacity to comprehend. What he reported as a "trumpet talking with me" was a loudspeaker; the "lightnings" were television monitors. The vision of Revelation 4:1–5 would certainly not have perplexed any contemporary abductee: "A modern-day human might well describe the experience this way: 'Well, yes, I was lifted up into a rocket-ship. There I confronted the seated crew in their white jumpsuits and helmets. They had some radio or TV reception going.'"[8] Later, John ingests a scroll given him by an "angel" and reports a series of many-headed beasts and monstrous combats. Bramley has no doubt that that scroll was saturated with a hallucinogen.[9]

Ideologies that use explanatory narratives to attract believers compete for that same pool of persons for whom a story is always more persuasive than a sifting of evidence. Like storytellers and balladeers in an oral culture, these ideologues are quick to recognize an effective element in a rival's repertoire and work it into their own. When they do this, however, they must carefully show that the newly borrowed narrative element belongs to and subserves their own established narrative. In other words, their own story is the ur-text that helps explain selected elements in their rivals' narratives.

So, if ancient-astronaut theory can use UFO phenomena to rationalize Christianity, Christians can use the same rhetorical strategy to coopt this rival variant. "UFOs are astonishingly angel-like in some of their reported appearances," mused Billy Graham.[10] Angel-like? Hal Lindsey, the popular purveyor of biblical futurism, thinks *not:* "To be blunt, I think they are demons."[11] In 1996 Pat Robertson, then head of the politically influential Christian Coalition, issued a "fact sheet" on UFOs. After citing a variety of opinions, he concluded that they are spiritual phenomena that somehow alter a person's sense of reality: "That's precisely why many theologians suggest that the UFO phenomena are demonic and caution people to avoid them whoever and whatever they are. Standards to live by."[12]

A year later, Robertson had a much sterner message for his followers. He quoted from Deuteronomy to the effect that if anyone is found to have worshipped "either the sun or moon or any of the hosts of heaven. . . . Then you shall bring out to your gates that man or woman who has committed that wicked thing, and *stone that man or woman with stones.*" He then added:

> Now, that's what Moses said to the children of Israel about those
> who worship the sun and the moon and the hosts of heaven, because
> these things, at best, are lifeless nothings, or, if they are intelligent,

they're demonic. . . . Can a demon appear as a slanty-eyed, funny-looking creature? Of course he can, or it can. Of course they can deceive people. . . . And God says, 'My covenant says you won't do this. And if I find anybody in Israel,'—which is his pure nation—'If I find anybody in Israel that's doing this sort of thing, then I want you to take him out and *dispose of him.*'"[13]

There is yet another biblical strand to weave into this updated, tabloid apocalypse, that ever-useful passage from Jesus's last formal address to his followers, the Olivet Discourse: "as the days of Noe [Noah] were, so shall also the coming of the Son of man be" (Matt. 24:37). What was Jesus referring to as the "days of Noe"? Proslavery, segregationist, and Christian Identity spokespersons have often identified it as the passage in Genesis that mentioned the "sons of God" who sought out the daughters of men, practices that God abominated and sent the Flood to end.[14] *If* Jesus were referring to these passages (and the next two verses of Matthew prove that he was *not,* but no matter), then one of the irrefutable signs of the end times would be the arrival of space-devils intent on abducting vulnerable humans. Such randy E.T.s, unlike von Däniken's ancient astronauts, have no beneficent purpose in mind. A blurb for a recent collection of abduction stories captures the lurid character of this fantasy: "Perhaps you have wondered what it would be like to make love with an extraterrestrial? Maybe you have even fantasized about the landing of a flying saucer. Heart pounding, you rush over to get a glimpse of the occupants. With a hissing sound the hatch opens. Out walks an ethereal extraterrestrial beauty with one thing on his or her mind—sex!"[15]

Sexual encounters with uncanny beings constitute, of course, a very ancient mythic theme. The "sons of God" whom ancient Hebrews imagined as wayward members of Yahweh's court and Greeks imagined as gods, Christians imagined as devils, demonic shapeshifters who could be anywhere, especially at night. In unsanctified lands they might sire monstrous hybrids (Shakespeare's Caliban was one of these), but in Christendom their modus operandi was more surreptitious. A devil, having assumed the appearance of a woman (a succubus), would receive a man's semen, then soar off and, in the guise of a lusty male (an incubus), deposit it in a woman's womb. This helped explain how a virtuous virgin or widow could get pregnant—and how her child might bear a striking resemblance to the miller's lad or the parish priest.

Devils might also abduct their victims, flying off with them through open windows. Some men and women were believed to do so voluntarily, having been promised miraculous powers in return for serving their captors' lecherous purposes. Fairies, an order of spirits independent of the infernal empire, also abducted humans, hiding them for days or even years in their own magical kingdom. When their abductees returned, suffering from what we would call partial amnesia, they usually reported having experienced physical powerlessness and undergone bizarre sexual rituals, the details of which bear considerable similarity to UFO abduction narratives.

The antiquity and universality of uncanny abduction accounts, if we follow von Däniken's logic, would prove that uncanny beings do indeed abduct humans and require us to go on to the next question, "Why do they do it?" But since a talking animal (to cite only one example) is also a universal and ancient folkloric motif, we might do better seeking explanations elsewhere than to posit erotomaniacs from outer space.

Some investigators have suggested that UFO abductees are reliving episodes, real or fantasized, of childhood sexual abuse, now masking the original perpetrator (often a family member) in space-age comic-book panoply. Moreover, the "coming-to-get-you" theme of witches, ogres, ghosts, wolves, and similar child abusers, always a staple of children's stories, never fails to make an impression on young imaginations. Regardless of whether child abuse—sexual or otherwise, real or fantasized—is the principal source of the abduction motif, all narratives of abuse and abduction involve the relation of a powerful agent and a powerless victim. The action of the rescuer in many ways mimics that of his evil double, the abductor, and thus the two figures can seem to blend into one another. This powerful agent can choose to hurt, even destroy, but can also, without diminution of power, choose to comfort and save the victim.

In the Christian tradition, the mating of the divine and the human is decorously veiled. There is none of the intrigue and tumultuous pursuit that marks the amours of the Olympians, none of the genital experimentation that appears in UFO abduction narratives. Nevertheless, the Christian Bible tells a story that is no less centered on selective breeding than is Ovid's *Metamorphoses* or von Däniken's *Chariots*. Consider the following summary:

> A powerful being from deep space, assisted by an army of couriers, creates a planetary system, and on one planet he creates a set of living things, the last species of which resembles him in some way. On their own his extraterrestrial couriers (or "sons" or "angels") participate in this process, mating with the females of this species and producing a more advanced hybrid strain. At one point this higher being (or "Yahweh") decides that his genetic experiment is flawed

and destroys all but a handful of specimens. From these he chooses a particular lineage, which he carefully oversees and trains preparatory to inseminating one of its females and producing his own hybrid. This superior creature is called Jesus.

As a human, he lives, suffers, and dies, but as a being from a far more evolved world, he performs miracles and teaches humans how they may also do them. The greatest miracle he teaches is the way to rise from the dead and ascend into the sky. Because only a human who, like him, is a "son of God" can perform this feat, he teaches his disciples how to become adopted sons through a rebirthing process. If they undergo this process and agree to regard as their primary family their adoptive extraterrestrial kin (Jesus as their brother and his father, Yahweh, as their father), they too will one day rise from their graves and fly off to join him in his starry realm.

This promised miracle will occur, however, only after he returns to this planet to settle scores with his and their enemies. At his return he will find his adopted brethren, the spiritual hybrids known as "Christians," confined and mistreated. At this point they will no longer be spoken of as his brethren: according to the prophecies, the condition of this people will be that of a *bride,* espoused by a prince, but still suffering as an abused daughter in an evil household.[16] When he returns he will abduct his people from the earth, unite with them as a bridegroom with his bride, and then celebrate his marriage feast. Though it is not mentioned, this union will presumably produce a yet more highly evolved race of beings who then populate a new heaven and a new earth.

Rapture I: The Seekers

To view oneself as radically different, as cut off and misunderstood by others, is a common experience of adolescence. But prolonging this sense of separateness into adulthood can lead one to desperation and alienation unless one finds others who share this feeling. Coming together for mutual support, such persons can draw comfort from a theory that explains why they do not, cannot, and should not fit in with their neighbors and co-workers: they do not fit in because their true homeland is elsewhere. One response to the inevitable question, "Then why are we here?" is an abduction narrative, which may become the foundational myth of a freestanding cult.

Members of such a group exchange their outsider status for that of insiders. They now belong to a circle centered on one person, a leader who interprets this narrative. The more unequal the relationship between the center and the circle, the more likely the group will be organized in a military fashion. And the more incredible the narrative, the more likely it is that the believers will be derided by family and erstwhile friends and will therefore be enjoined to keep the narrative hidden from the uninitiated. Particularly isolated circles become even more exclusionary, and members meet frequently to reinforce the narrative belief upon which their new insider identity is based.

Membership in an abduction-myth cult is only the first act in the liberatory drama, for while it offers comfort within, it provokes hostility from the larger society outside it. Its leader warns the faithful to expect to be mocked and even persecuted for their beliefs. Only the intervention of a higher power can ultimately rescue them from the dangers that encircle them.

Most of the recent Christian and non-Christian abduction narratives focus on the escape, or Rapture, episode (phase 4 in the diagram) and assume nuclear war to be the final act in the drama of human history. While premillennialists see the bomb as God's way for the armies of the Antichrist to annihilate themselves, New Age channelers tell a somewhat different story: the nuclear explosions of the 1940s first alerted the more advanced intelligences in the universe to take their spacecrafts to this little blue planet to save the savable. This was the message of a series of "flying saucer" contactees in the early 1950s.[17] It is worth reminding ourselves that in 1953 the Rosenbergs were executed, the USSR announced that it had detonated a hydrogen bomb, and the McCarthy hearings were in full swing. At the height of the cold war, expectations of imminent nuclear conflict were on the rise.

The first UFO rapturists to be closely studied by nonbelievers belonged to a small group, the Seekers, active in the Upper Midwest in 1954. We know of its inner workings because several social psychologists, most of them graduate students under the direction of Leon Festinger, joined the Seekers and kept careful records of their group dynamics before and after the disconfirmation of their doomsday prediction. The book that emerged from this study was *When Prophecy Fails*.

Their story began when a middle-aged housewife confided to a small circle of friends that she had, through automatic writing, come into contact with some higher being, a Jesus figure who had identified himself as "Sananda." From him she had learned that a cataclysmic flood would occur on December 21 of that year. The North American continent would split apart from Hudson Bay to the Gulf of Mexico, and the sea would inundate Middle

America from the Rockies to the Appalachians. As the day approached, the group, now numbering twenty to thirty, began to receive messages from Sananda's father, the Creator. These messages, channeled through another woman, tended to corroborate Sananda's words. The Seekers, and others like them, would be saved by alien spacemen sent in flying saucers to pick them up before that fateful day. Each was issued a "passport," a blank sheet of paper and a three-cent stamped envelope, and was given a password for the spacemen: "I left my hat at home."[18]

As Festinger and his colleagues observed, this group felt ambivalent about announcing their prophecy to the world. On the one hand, they were eager to share with others their miraculously garnered knowledge; on the other hand, when the news did get out, the public greeted it with something less than seriousness. This, they decided, was a matter of God's choosing. No one can simply take cognizance of one's situation and then assent to the reasonableness of the Divine Word. One's inability to believe the messenger simply means that one is not the intended addressee of the message. Election always precedes faith. A spokesman for the Seekers put it this way during a press conference on the evening of December 16:

> I'll say to you that all of you who are interested in saucers are in a special category. Now, you don't know that but you are, because it seems that the people around the world who have been having a special interest in saucers are people who have had that interest because they had something within themselves that goes back to things they have forgotten. Therefore there is something within you that returned to life. So don't be surprised within the next weeks and months ahead, regardless of where you happen to find yourself, if you find you have an unusual experience in relation to spacemen or saucers or something of this kind. Because I think I can say this to you—and it's no secret—that spacemen have said that they are here for a purpose and one of these purposes is to remove certain of their own people from the earth.[19]

"Certain of their own people": this is a significant claim. The Seekers, and all those in that room whose interest in flying saucers implied an actual past experience, a recoverable memory, were being watched over by benevolent kin from outer space prepared to rapture them from an impending cataclysm.

Five days later, when the saucers failed to arrive, the group was dispirited—but then, as North America had not been split down the middle and submerged, they rejoiced. The Guardians, they concluded, had been test-ing them and, because of their perfect faith in Sananda, his Divine Father had saved the earth from disaster.[20] Their response *to* the narrative had now qualified them to be inserted as major characters *in* the narrative. Buoyed by this happy thought, they promptly went forth to preach the Guardians' gospel to the world—a world that had, by then, transferred its fickle atten-tion to other news.

Rapture II: The Total Overcomers

The Seekers' spokesman had ended his press conference by addressing a list of questions to his audience: "begin asking yourself, why saucers? Will you ask yourself why saucers? Why now? Why in my lifetime?"[21] That voice of one crying out in the desert of the Middle American 1950s was answered in divergent ways over the next several decades. One set of answers was prom-ised by a notice posted in September 1975 around the seaside town of Wald-port, Oregon:

UFO'S
> Why they are here.
> Who they have come for.
> When they will leave.

NOT A DISCUSSION of UFO SIGHTINGS
or PHENOMENA

> Two individuals say they are about to leave the human level and literally (physically) enter the next evolutionary level in a space craft (UFO) within months! Followers of "THE TWO" will discuss how the transition from the human level to the next level is accomplished, and when this may be done.
> This is not a religious or philosophical organization recruit-ing membership. However, the information has already prompted many individuals to devote their total energy to the transitional process. If you have ever entertained the idea that there may be a real, physical level beyond the earth's confines, you will want to attend this meeting.[22]

A few days after this lecture at the Bayshore Inn, which 150 people attended (a quarter of the town's population), twenty of them disappeared with The Two and their band of followers.

The Two had formerly been known to friends and family as Marshall Herff Applewhite and Bettie Lu Nettles. Applewhite, once a Presbyterian seminarian and later a locally successful concert singer, met Nettles in a Houston hospital where he had gone for heart treatment. She, a nurse, had cared for him there. Applewhite recognized in her a soul mate, or, more precisely, a spiritual guide. Together, they persuaded themselves that their bodies had recently been taken over by the spirits of two higher beings. They had become that couple mentioned in Revelation 11:3–12, the Two Witnesses, who after three-and-a-half years of preaching are executed by the Beast, left unburied, and then, after three-and-a-half days, are reanimated and rise to heaven in a cloud. As identifying names, The Two now chose "Bo" and "Peep," alluding apparently to the nursery-rhyme character who had lost her sheep but was assured that they would eventually "come home." Over the next several years, the couple crisscrossed the country announcing themselves to those who, like them, might have been "deposited" in human bodies in order to learn to overcome temptation. Their West Coast missionary work, which culminated in Waldport, was to complete their three-and-a-half years as the Two Witnesses—but instead of accepting their prophesied fate of martyrdom, they and some followers went "undercover" between 1975 and 1990.[23]

Peep died in 1985, but Bo carried on the work. Alluding to the musical scale, he now called himself "Do," and his discarnate teacher, "Ti." To his followers, Do had become the "Older Member," the "Representative of the Evolutionary Level Above Human," who had come to earth to lead them through their "transitional process" and effect their "ascension," terms that correspond roughly to "tribulation" and "rapture." Since Ti's departure, however, Do had come to realize that he and she had *not* been the Two Witnesses after all. The body that had belonged to one Marshall Herff Applewhite had been taken over by the same being that Christians call "Jesus," who, when he had last appeared on earth two thousand years ago, had issued from a spaceship and taken over the body of a Galilean carpenter at the moment of his baptism. Bettie Lu Nettles's body had been the recent vehicle taken over by the Messiah's Heavenly Father. His work was now to travel about gathering disciples who *themselves* had also come from outer space, entering the bodies of specially "prepped" or "tagged" persons. (The source for this eerie belief may have been no more esoteric than the 1956 movie *The Invasion of the Body Snatchers*.) His mission now was to bring these lost sheep back by teaching them how to live together, male and female, as though they were already in the kingdom of heaven, where "they neither marry nor are given in marriage" (Matt. 22:30). In this regard, his "monastery" closely resembled a Shaker commune. (The Shakers' founder, Mother Ann Lee, also identified herself with the returned Jesus.)[24]

According to some reports, the only reading Do's students were permitted was the "red letter" edition of the New Testament, wherein the words of Jesus (Do in his previous visitation) are printed in red. There they would read that the meaning of their new name, "The Total Overcomers," derived from the words of Jesus when, in John 16:33, he said he had "overcome the world." In Revelation, he promised that "he that overcometh shall not be hurt of the second death" and "to him who overcometh will I grant to sit with me on my throne, even as I also overcame, and am set down with my Father on his throne" (Rev. 1:11, 3:21). From the currently incarnate Jesus they would learn that being called on to "overcome" meant that they must conquer all the instincts associated with earthly evolution—the instincts to preserve the body, to enjoy food and sex, and to trust the nurturing instincts of parents. This latter task would be difficult. Do, in his earlier incarnation, had warned those who were then his students how painful it would be: "Think not that I am come to send peace on earth: I came not to send peace, but a sword. For I am come to set a man at variance against his father, and the daughter against her mother, and the daughter in law against the mother in law. And a man's foes shall be they of his own household. He that loveth father or mother more than me is not worthy of me" (Matt. 10:34–37). These sayings—which most Christians read as hyperbole, assuring themselves that Jesus really *did* love peace and family values—the Total Overcomers read quite literally. Like their leader, they accepted as axiomatic the premillennialist view that peace is mere acquiescence to an unredeemable world, to a sinking ship (to use Rev. Moody's simile). Those, such as their families, who would call them back to that ship would have them drown along with them. The "Older Member" was now their true parent, and they, his children.

Without knowing it, the bewildered families they had escaped from were actually in league with the airborne forces of Satan, the "Luciferians," who

occupy the near heavens as what humans refer to as "space aliens." They also burrow in bases underground and participate in genetic manipulation and hybridization with humans, and attempt to recruit (while remaining among the "unseen") those humans with souls who are unstable or weak in their pursuit of the Kingdom of

Heaven. These "Luciferians" (for the most part from the "unseen" world) started all religions and masquerade as "gods" to humans [a clear response to von Däniken's theory]. They offer to humans (who are unknowingly praying to them) whatever material gains they desire. These "Luciferians" and their devotees preach "Heaven on Earth," "Peace among men," and a long and healthy life in the human condition, and are determined to take the steps to make the inhabitants of the planet subservient to their "ideal" mammalian ethic—destructive to the natural evolutionary processes, and abhorrent to the Kingdom Level Above Human. . . . Since this is the close of the Age, the battle in the Heavens with their servants on Earth will be the means of that closing and spading under of the plants (including the humans) of this civilization. "Weeds" are now getting rid of weeds—from gang wars to nations involved in ethnic cleansing. This is simply a part of the natural recycling process which precedes a restoration period of the planet in preparation for another civilization's beginning.[25]

As one of Do's students explained this doctrine, deliberate channeling was unnecessary: the Luciferians are always out there, eager to make contact. Schizophrenia, multiple personalities, and demonic possession are caused by spirits competing to possess a single human "container."

These are extreme situations. Most individuals house several compatible spirits that have worked out a sort of time-share agreement. They work together for the most part and make up the characteristics of the personality. Emotional outbreaks are often caused by the invasion of discarnates wanting physical sensation. You lose control and an influence uses your body. Anything from sensuality to depression can give discarnates the feelings they crave. A lot of people become addicted to feeling certain ways because of these invaders.[26]

The various postings and position papers of the Heaven's Gate group (the name the Total Overcomers assumed via the Internet) give a sense of its effort to situate itself in the context of New Age issues and beliefs. The members' decision not to engage in channeling for fear of contacting unknown "discarnates" must have set them at odds with the "mainstream" (I use this term advisedly) of New Age apocalyptic cults, particularly those that have

made the Southwest their Holy Land. Compared, for example, with the
Ashtar Command cult, which was founded in 1951 by George Van Tassel
and featured a being also called "Sananda" surrounded by a whole pantheon
of Greek gods and cabalistic angels, the Heaven's Gate folk seem like *sola
Scriptura* fundamentalists.

They did, however, share most of their articles of faith with the larger
New Age community. Their idea that the earth is periodically "recycled" by
forces external to it echoed the catastrophism and armchair archeology popularized by Immanuel Velikovsky and his disciple Zecharia Sitchin.[27] They
also shared with many New Agers a demonology of extraterrestrial abductors. As "documented" by Whitley Strieber in *Communion: A True Story,* these
beings first creep into a victim's home, then rush him out and violate him
in aerial labs, either to extract genetic materials or merely to gratify their
depraved appetites.[28] As for conspiracy theories, they accepted the notion
that the United States government allows these ETs, or "grays," to experiment
on its citizens in return for their advanced aerotechnology, and that the pact
between the two forces aimed to create a Luciferian one-world empire.

On March 27, 1997, after thirty-nine members of this cult (including its
leader) were found dead, having ritually poisoned themselves, Americans
wondered how this could have happened. Had they been mesmerized by
the computers they worked on daily and lost their souls in cyberspace? Had
they overdosed on *Star Trek* and *X-Files,* television programs that they watched
religiously? Had they been twisted by the fabled weirdness of Southern California, brainwashed by a delusional leader, maddened by sexual deprivation
to the point of surgical castration? Commentators pondered these possibilities. Dan Rather, to whom many Americans looked for explanations, seemed
particularly perplexed. These cult members had to have been confused about
Christianity, he told his viewers, because they spoke reverently about Christ
but criticized Christian churches—as though Christians had not consistently
done exactly this ever since the day Peter met Paul.[29]

The cult members killed themselves (or discarded their "undercover cos-
tume," their "borrowed bodies," as they would say) for reasons that were
undoubtedly more complex than their faith in their leader's version of Apocalypse. Do was in failing health. Their numbers had dwindled. More than a
thousand persons, according to some estimates, had joined their group over
the years; now barely forty remained. Their attempts since 1994 to proselytize
over the Internet had been met with ridicule. Like others before them who interpreted rejection as a mark of election, they still hoped to make common
cause with other disaffected persons. A sign that one has been "deposited"

in a human vehicle and is really from the Next Evolutionary Level could, they believed, be recognized in

> an individual's lack of motivation or rebellion against the world, or "system," and what it has to offer. In their futility, many of these individuals turn to the corrupt devices that are most anesthetizing. You will *not* find them with the so-called mainstream righteous, but more likely with your social dropouts or even as addicts or criminals—as your so-called "sinners." Another manifestation of worldly dissatisfaction can be seen in the current movement of radical separatists—patriot/militia types—who clearly recognize the corrupt condition of today's governments (particularly the dominant governments of the Western world). It is for *those* that we have come again—to give them a way out of this corrupt human kingdom, which was never designed to work or be satisfactory unto itself.[30]

On their Web page, they began to express a fear of government persecution (their two leaders had voiced similar apprehensions some twenty years earlier). On September 20, 1996, a message was posted on the alt.conspiracy Usenet group. Its title was TIME TO DIE FOR GOD? OR ARMAGEDDON— WHICH SIDE ARE YOU ON? In it the writer includes among the elect those who have *mentally* connected with Do. This covers "a broad spectrum"— from the Weavers at Ruby Ridge, the Branch Davidians at Waco, the Unabomber, the Order of the Solar Temple, Aum Shinri Kyo of Japan, and the Freemen of Montana to UFO believers and others: "Many like these are still in hiding, while others take the form of the patriot/militia movements, Farrakhan and the Nation of Islam, the many other Islamic movements, and countless groups that are simply rebelling from the system, the 'norm,' and WANT TO GO TO GOD, OR LEAVE THIS CORRUPT WORLD, at any price."[31]

If they expected a wave of recruits eager to join the "away team," they were sadly mistaken. Neither imagined friends nor imagined foes seemed to take their mission seriously, a fact that Do interpreted as a further "sign of the times." Then, when he heard that the newly sighted comet Hale-Bopp had a mysterious companion, which a "remote-viewer" said was a spaceship full of aliens, Do told his flock that if they would "lay down" their bodies, this ship, commanded by his Older Member, Ti, would come to rescue their souls before the comet devastated the earth. The coincidence of this supposed unnatural fact with the vernal equinox and the pre-Easter Holy Week was the sign for which they had waited.[32]

God's Nuclear Option

Before the twentieth century, the notion that sounds and images could fly through the air or that humans could travel faster than sound and even enter outer space was, for most educated persons, simply beyond belief. Only faith could maintain that the laws of nature, as they were then understood, could be suspended. Faith alone could allow religionists to believe in the miracles of the past and the miraculous future yet to be. But by the middle of the twentieth century, science and the history of its terrifying applications had caught up with biblical prophecy. Finally, preachers could supply a skeptical audience with contemporary evidence. The events that appeared in the morning tabloids and nightly on CNN and the Fox News Channel could be cited in the Sunday-morning sermon and over the Christian Broadcasting Network.

In a world in which rival governments and quasi-governmental organizations can wage war by targeting one another's noncombatant populations, the perennial tension between the governmental and the communal levels rises a notch. Homeland security, the bond that holds home and land together, seems to weaken not only in America but in every other nation as well. Myths, then, need to be created—narratives that explain why injustices, massacres, famines, plagues, tsunamis, hurricanes, and genocide happen and, above all, tell how some of us can escape them.

Most modern abduction myths share the belief that power reveals itself in events of catastrophic fury. Whether they believe they will view the Great Tribulation from what one preacher called the "heavenly grandstand" or fight it out in the trenches, this God-directed spectacle will be awesome. As the Bible suggests, the invisible creator of the world, withdrawn into his heaven, might easily be ignored even by his chosen people unless he periodically appears as a destructive force. Only through acts of violence, it seems, can he assert his existence and demonstrate to a complacent humankind that he is still a force to reckon with. This appears to be the theology of those who use natural and humanly engineered misfortunes as sermon texts. The Reverend Jerry Falwell reminded Americans on September 13, 2001, "God will not be mocked." When the citizens of Dover, Pennsylvania, voted out of office a school board that required the teaching of "intelligent design" in science classes, the Reverend Pat Robertson warned them, "You just rejected God from your city." He added that they could now no longer be protected from disaster. Such theologians apparently see no contradiction in an intelligent designer behaving as a cosmic poltergeist.[33]

Less bellicose premillennialists may sometimes ask why there are not other, equally effective ways in which God might manifest himself, but they do have to admit that when things seem to operate efficiently, his presence seems less apparent. Only when something terribly mysterious happens do humans suspect the hand of some superior intelligence. God may work in mysterious ways, yet even then—even when something really mysterious does happen—no one, not even believers, can actually observe him doing anything. Why? Because Satan, by inducing Eve and Adam to sin, converted God's creation into what scripture calls "The World," a spiritual space that Augustine referred to as the "region of unlikeness."[34] Nature now represents a barrier between God's realm and Satan's, a wall reinforced, according to many American Christians, by two other walls: the one between church and state, and the other between scripture and science.

Satan's claim to be prince of this world is, however, provisional. God permits him to hold humanity hostage only to test the elect. When Christ returns to redeem his abducted bride, the reign of Satan will be finished, and with it the illusion that the material universe is the bedrock of reality. All humans, even the damned, will then understand that nature exists within supernature, as a lower is subsumed within a higher dimension.[35] Then they will realize that there is no real conflict between the two kinds of knowledge. Contradiction seems to enter only when the inductive methods of science are exalted above the authority of scripture, in the heresy of scientism, or when so-called facts are set in opposition to God's revealed master narrative.

End-time signs loom large in the minds of premillennialists for several important reasons. The most crucial is that if these prophesied phenomena can be proved to be occurring, then biblical inerrancy will be vindicated, together with the three christological principles of fundamentalism: the virgin birth, the vicarious atonement, and the physical resurrection of Jesus. Each of these depends on the Bible's freedom from error.

Observable end-time signs would also refute those biblical scholars who, for over two centuries, have been uncovering the culturally motivated, all-too-human ways in which this ancient anthology has been composed, transmitted, and redacted.[36] The view that every verse of every book was dictated by the Holy Spirit and written down by inspired amanuenses has become more and more difficult for educated Christians to accept. Fundamentalism, grounded on the premise that the scripture alone (*sola Scriptura*) is the source of Christian doctrine, has therefore had to intensify its efforts to find empirical evidence that the final biblical event, the rescue of the persecuted Church, is now in progress. If such evidence could be found, it would confirm the narratives that ground all Christian beliefs. The supernatural simply must intersect the natural plane in some demonstrable way. Real-world events must occur that science cannot explain. In short, a series of *un*natural facts must appear for all to see.

Before we can comprehend this last concept, we need to project ourselves back in time for a moment, a time before the invention of the "natural" and the "supernatural." In a purely oral information economy, the fundamental distinction among phenomena lies between the extraordinary (unpredictable, astounding, memorable) and the ordinary (usual, understood, forgettable). What we now call scientific observation, with its disinterested desire to discover predictable patterns in the world, actually emerged out of a more ancient desire to discover *un*predictable events. The fixed stars, for example, needed to be located before the significant movements of the planets, or "wandering stars," could be plotted and astrology developed. For early observers, the predictable behaviors of sun, moon, stars, weather, beasts, and birds provided a blank background upon which the gods could inscribe anomalies, *monstra* (Latin for "indicators"). Far more compelling than the need to learn the "laws of nature" was the need to read the monstrous messages sent by beings superior to these laws.[37]

In the sixteenth century, Europe's craving for the monstrous was fed by travelers' accounts of wondrous beasts and beastly humans sighted in the newly discovered Western Hemisphere. The apocalyptic fervor of the Protestant Reformation drew heat, if not light, from what some declared to be sure signs of the wrath to come. Stephen Batman's sixteenth-century bestseller, *The Doome: Warning All Men to the Judgement,* crammed with woodcuts of multiheaded men and more-than-quadrupedal beasts, was typical of the publications that satisfied a growing appetite for the ominously bizarre.

By the end of the seventeenth century, this fervor had somewhat cooled. The work of men like Galileo, Bacon, and Newton had shrunk the realm of the anomalous. Even the sky, that most august of all God's theaters, was now becoming mapped and scheduled. Comets had long resisted natural explanation, but they were now believed to orbit the sun and return at regular intervals. Using Newtonian calculations, Edmund Halley announced in 1682 that the comet visible in the twilight sky was actually the same body that had appeared in 1531 and 1607. Some found this news troubling to their faith. The next year, the ever-alert Increase Mather condemned this trend of reducing all physical events to secondary causes: "natural philosophers" had to draw the line somewhere and leave comets to the First Mover's sovereign will.[38]

For a while it seemed that science was a demonstrable mass of knowledge that anyone with common sense and an elementary education could understand and apply. The early nineteenth century then confronted the paradoxical nature of electromagnetism and other physical phenomena. Now, two centuries later, seeing is no longer believing, and every new scientific fact seems counterintuitive. The layperson faces a hyperdimensional universe more mysterious by far than that spirit-thronged cosmos of the Middle Ages. The very word "lay," which once meant the nontheologian, now regularly designates the nonscientist. Physics, especially astrophysics and cosmology, has supplanted theology as the queen of sciences.

As a new source of mystification for the laity, science furnished late twentieth-century apocalypticists with fresh resources. The old signs were still sought. But from a global vantage point, floods and earthquakes were local natural facts that no longer resonated as end-time portents. Weeping statues and backwoods glossolalia, apparitions and prophetism—these, too, would no longer suffice. Even if they *were* signs of the ongoing struggle between God and the Enemy, they might well be diabolical manifestations engineered to delude the faithful. More pertinent to apocalyptic preachers now were the products of applied science as they affected world politics, for in the nuclear age, even skeptics must attend to these factual phenomena.

Here, a fascination with weapons of mass destruction and a fixation upon apocalyptic prophecy converge. A contemporary weapon or delivery system is not in itself a supernatural instrument, but suppose it existed in image form some 2,500 years ago. Suppose—just suppose—God displayed it to a Jewish ecstatic. This would contradict everything we think we know about time. But suppose history is a scroll upon which God has already written his complete narrative. Why could he not also have unrolled a little section toward the end to show an Isaiah or a Zechariah one illustration of a helicopter gunship, a Stealth bomber, a mobile rocket launcher, or a laser-targeted missile? The prophet could only gaze at such images but, of course, would not know how they worked. All he could know was that these flying vehicles and WMDs served God's miraculous, interventionist purposes.

"The Bible is ahead of science," commented one premillennialist, comparing the effects of the atomic bombs on Hiroshima and Nagasaki to 2 Peter 3:10: "The heavens shall pass away with a great noise, and the elements shall melt with fervent heat, and the earth also and the works that are therein shall be burned up." Another reminded his readers of Zechariah's question, "For who hath despised the day of small things?" (Zech. 4:10). The answer: those who had overlooked the awesome power of the atom. Yet another pointed out that the Greek verb for "melt" that Peter had used also could mean "unfasten" or "release," and that the Holy Spirit had surely been referring to the nuclear fission of the elements uranium and plutonium.[39] Hal Lindsey explained that what the prophet John interpreted in one of his visions as "fire and brimstone" could only be the effects of tactical nuclear weapons. The "falling stars" must be warheads launched from space platforms. As for the "stinging locusts," these were no doubt Cobra helicopters spraying nerve gas.[40] As biblical futurists assure us, the images of fighting (which make Revelation one of the bloodiest books ever written) and the images of flight (which make it one of the most phantasmagoric) are now on the verge of complete realization as natural facts of geopolitics.[41]

Until geopolitical developments anchor this airy web of inferences and speculations, the notion that God needs Jews to be ingathered in the state of Israel remains largely a matter of faith. But for evangelical dispensationalists, matters of faith need to be *acted* upon. They therefore support the work of the International Christian Embassy in Jerusalem and endorse the Bible-based claims of the ultraorthodox rabbinate and the Settlers' Movement to national boundaries that existed during the reigns of David and Solomon three thousand years ago. They call for the rebuilding of the Temple on Mount Moriah and the reinstitution of animal sacrifice. They goad Palestinians and their Muslim allies to adopt desperate policies toward both Israel and the United States. Unless its enemies continue to threaten Israel with annihilation and all peace plans fail, the prophecies will have to be reinterpreted, and the popular authority of these evangelists will weaken.[42]

The prophecies *must* be fulfilled—that is, the prophecies that dispensational premillennialists have carefully selected and interpreted according to the system devised by John Nelson Darby in the mid-nineteenth century.[43] According to those who, like Lindsey, profess to be Christian Zionists and friends of Israel, the final crematorium in which two-thirds of the Israeli population—some three to four million men, women, and children—must soon perish will be nuclear fueled. Who knows? Perhaps the Jews themselves will set off the blast in a suicide bombing of stupendous proportions. In 1998, Lindsey referred to this scenario as the Samson Option, named after that Israelite hero who killed three thousand Philistines and himself by toppling the pillars of their temple in Gaza (Judg. 16:23–30).[44] Then, at long last, Judaism will be eradicated from the world, because the only remaining Jews will, he says, be "Hebrew Billy Grahams" and their fellow converts to Christianity.

These preachers constantly repeat that God has shown exactly how the prophecies will be fulfilled. God did not simply have foreknowledge of nuclear fission; *he had invented it.* He had, for example, undoubtedly used such weaponry to destroy Sodom and Gomorrah, and for nearly four thousand years he had kept such secrets to himself. Then, in the 1940s, American scientists began to catch up with celestial technology. The God portrayed by apocalyptic popularizers is no longer the inscrutable sovereign of the universe so much as a parent watching his children play with toys, a parent who knows that some day they will learn to use grown-up instruments. Or, to sharpen the analogy, this God appears to be a demolitions expert approvingly watching his little ones graduate from matches and gasoline bombs to laser-guided nuclear warheads.

The Politics of Victimhood

Americans' special fascination with the abduction narrative began quite early in colonial history. The American frontier, that dangerous, shifting space between the European settler and the indigenous Other, lay a mere thirty miles west of Boston's North Church when, on the morning of February 10, 1676, the villagers of Lancaster were awakened by loud cries and gunshots. A band of Indians belonging to the insurgency led by Metacomet (whom the settlers knew as "King Philip"), sachem of the Wampanoags, had begun the process of massacring the villagers and burning their houses. Among those few taken prisoner were Mary Rowlandson and her two children. Her captors, accompanied by their own women and children, fled west toward the Connecticut River. As becomes apparent in Rowlandson's tale of her abduction—*A Narrative of the Captivity and Restoration of Mrs. Mary Rowlandson*—the insurgents had taken a handful of settlers to protect themselves from the English militia and to exchange them, at some point, for ransom payments. Three months later, after twenty hasty decampments or "removes," Rowlandson and several other abductees were indeed ransomed (or, as she said, "redeemed").[45]

In her account of the attack and abduction, published in 1682 at the behest of Increase Mather, there is not the slightest mention of the Indians' motives in attacking Lancaster, abducting her family, and then releasing them. No reference is made to the expropriation of the Indians' tribal land. (They were not forest wanderers, after all: an estimated 90,000 of them had been living as farmers, as well as hunters, in central and coastal New England in the first decades of the seventeenth century.)[46] The only explanation a reader can infer is that the attackers—"hell-hounds," as Rowlandson called them—

were driven solely by senseless malevolence. Actions such as sharing with Rowlandson the little food they had, seeing to it that she was kept dry and warm, and sparing her the "least abuse of unchastity" are never attributed to their common humanity but instead to God's special providence. Mather, who would publish his own *Remarkable Providences* two years later, had a long-term interest in conveying a Deuteronomic message to his fellow Puritans: God had judged them harshly for their backsliding by sending the smallpox and the Indian scourge but, in response to their repentance, had also shown his providential care for his New Israel.

First proclaimed one century after the raid on Lancaster, the Declaration of Independence listed among its grievances the assertion that King George had incited "the merciless Indian Savages" to attack frontier settlements (see page 76 above). Indeed, as a corollary to the Treaty of Paris of 1763, England had agreed to convert the open colonial frontier into a legal boundary line. This treaty, which ended the seventy-four-year conflict of Britain and France for North America, proclaimed as "Indian country" the land from the western Alleghenies to the Mississippi. In the mind of those colonists who had borne the brunt of what they called the French and Indian War, this clearly seemed an attempt by the Crown to hem them in and use these frontier tribes to limit their economic growth. When Rowlandson's *Narrative* was republished in 1773, it helped incite both anti-Indian and anti-British fervor.

At the height of the centennial celebration of 1876, a full two centuries after the Indian raid on Lancaster, reports arrived east that the Sioux, under Sitting Bull and his young lieutenant Crazy Horse, had wiped out an entire cavalry commanded by George Armstrong Custer at the Little Bighorn in the Montana Territory. Coming two days after the festivities of July Fourth, concentrated on the Philadelphia Exposition, the news cast a pall over the nation—and the mood soon turned to angry calls for revenge.

Typical of the renewed anti-Indian sentiment that followed Custer's disaster was the popular "half-dime" novel *Plucky Phil, of the Mountain Trail* by Thomas Chalmers Harbaugh. Very much at the level of melodrama, this book told the story of the brave, pure, right-thinking young trailsman Phil Steele and his search for Nora Dalton, a young woman who, two years earlier, had been taken captive by the Sioux after her family and the rest of their wagon train had been massacred only a few miles from Custer's battlefield. First the possession of Coyote, a "squaw-man" (a white man who had been married to an Indian woman), the abducted girl then fell into the hands of none other than Sitting Bull himself, who, supposing her the daughter of a "big white chief," hoped eventually to exchange her for ransom money. In this abduction narrative, the villainous Sioux places Nora, his "White Flower," in the custody of "Ape," a deformed half-human who proceeds to imprison her—sometimes bound, sometimes unbound—in a series of desert caves. The narrator's regular refererences to this creature as a "Caliban" slyly implies Ape's lustful designs on this Miranda of the West.

Throughout the novel, we are aware that the U.S. Cavalry is somewhere out there in hot pursuit of these hostile tribes. We learn this through an old trail guide, Policy Pete, who passes as a "half-breed" with the Indians (thanks to a supply of red paint) but is actually a scout for the cavalry. While the authorial voice refers to the Indians as "scarlet fiends," sheltered in "grotesque tepees," Pete regularly calls them "red niggers" and expresses surprise that "this kentry is alive with red-skins. . . . I told you the kentry was full of red niggers!"[47] After furious struggles and hairbreadth escapes, the novel ends with Phil's rescue of Nora. Thanking their friend Policy Pete for his help and advice, they finally turn their backs forever on "Siouxdom" and return east as "Mr. and Mrs. Steele."

On its surface, an abduction (or captivity) narrative has the structure of a heroic myth. An evil person or group invades the communal space of a peaceful, innocent person or group; a crime of theft, abduction, and captivity is committed; a hero then appears who rescues the abductee(s), punishes the evildoer(s), and vindicates the community's values. But below the surface, an ethnic myth may function as a master narrative. In the Rowlandson narrative, which maintains the victim's point of view, and the story of *Plucky Phil,* told mainly through the rescuer's point of view, we are asked to admire the courage and perseverance of the embattled heroines and heroes, empathize with their fears and griefs, and despise the injustice of their captors. But we are also expected to understand that these abductees and rescuers represent "civilization," which implies reason, compassion, and divinely legislated order, while their enemies represent a condition that has satanic and even prehuman aspects.

Yet other historical factors—hidden in plain sight, like Poe's purloined letter—may shed light on this national obsession with abduction narratives. From the mid-seventeenth to the mid-nineteenth century, by far the most abductees held captive in the English-speaking colonies and, later, the United States *were non-Europeans.* In 1637, following the Pequot War, approximately 500 of the captured survivors, mostly women and children, were enslaved— either distributed among rival tribes, given to English settlers, or transported to the West Indies, where they were either sold or exchanged for African slaves. The same policy was followed after King Philip's War (1675–76), when an estimated 400 Abenaki from southern Maine were sold to Caribbean plantation owners.[48] In the southern colonies, somehere between 24,000 to 51,000 Indians (the recordkeeping was informal) had been enslaved between 1670 and 1715. Those captured after the Tuscarora War (1711–13) were removed from their towns in North Carolina and sold as slaves from Pennsylvania to Florida. Those who had been able to elude capture or had later escaped from their masters migrated to northern New York, where the Tuscaroras became the last of the six-nation Iroquois Confederacy.[49]

Only after it became clear that American Indians could not be reliably enslaved on their native continent did the colonists begin the large-scale abduction of captives from another one. By 1800, an estimated 1.2 million chattel slaves of West African origin labored in the southern states. By 1860 their number had grown to almost 4 million, most of them third- and fourth-generation slaves.

First Native Americans and then Africans: here was abduction and captivity on a massive scale. Of course, these statistics do not make the English colonies and the republic that succeeded them unique in world history. The Spanish enslavement of the Indians of Mexico and the Pacific coast, from California to Peru, has been well documented. Of the 12 to 15 million Africans who were transported by ship to the Americas, only about 500,000 landed in the southern colonies. The rest had been sent to Cuba, the West Indies, and the Atlantic coast of South America.[50] What was unique about Anglo-American slavery was that those who practiced it regarded their culture as conscientiously righteous. Traditional English freedoms, expressed as individual rights and duties, and the belief that government is justified only through a covenant with God had led the New England Puritans and, to varying degrees, the other English colonists to hold themselves to a lofty moral standard. This meant that when it seemed expedient to invade, steal, and enslave others, many of them had to have suffered considerable cognitive dissonance. Faced with this conflict, how would they be able to preserve their *ethos* and the profits of their *praxis*? How would they maintain their communal values, centered on the home, while they governed a land they had stolen from Native Americans and enriched through African slave labor?

As I proposed earlier, the sovereign remedy for this and every other conscience-localized distress is the cultural narrative that we know as myth. Abduction narratives, which represent vulnerable white Protestant Americans targeted by hostile aliens, allowed readers troubled by their nation's history and its ongoing policies to preserve, intact, both their moral principles and their ill-gotten gains. By representing the Indians' resistance as unprovoked aggression, they vindicated their Christian principles; then, having projected this evil onto its actual victims through popular narratives, they could portray themselves as innocent. Let us call this variant of the abduction narrative the invader-as-victim narrative.

This version of the story helped legitimate the Anglo-American possession of the continent and establish the basis for America's homeland mythology. But in this process there was more than a simple projection of guilt. The subsequent use of the invader-as-victim narrative suggests that a thoroughgoing ethnic role reversal had occurred, one in which the white invaders, in order to portray themselves as innocent, narrated their own historical experience *as though it were the historical experience of the Indians.* Consider how, over the past hundred years, white America has fabulated a fearful narrative that, at certain points, mirrors what it guiltily knows to have been its treatment of the Indians.

1. Americans, who at first generously welcomed the oppressed, the storm-tossed refugees of conscience from across the seas, later found themselves overwhelmed by an invasion of economic immigrants. (White Americans' fears that their homeland may be overrun by aliens takes an ironic turn when those identified as such are Native Americans of Mexican nationality.)
2. Whenever they find themselves outnumbered and surrounded by these covetous others, they are subject to unprovoked attack, and their right to arm and defend themselves is undermined by federal laws.
3. Their women and children are every day vulnerable to assault and abduction by men of nonwhite races.
4. Their birth rate in decline, they are becoming a minority in their own country and are now in danger of losing their traditional culture, i.e., their history and language.
5. Most important, the open practice of their religion has been outlawed by the judiciary.

When Americans travel abroad to vacation or conduct business, the seventeenth-century colonial confrontation is restaged. They again are the visitors who must be wary of the natives and, once again, though they mean well, they are often misunderstood and targeted by shadowy forces of evil. When Americans go abroad not to vacation or conduct business but to invade, occupy, and subdue a foreign population, the abduction narrative that helped their forebears justify their conquest of North America is again

invoked to grant them the moral superiority of victimhood. Native insur- .
gents continually commit acts of aggression against the occupiers who, if
captured, must expect to be severely abused at the hands of a barbaric enemy.

American administrations understand how useful the abduction narrative can be in rallying domestic support for foreign military ventures. In
1969, when Richard Nixon and his defense secretary, Melvin Laird, sought
to "stay the course" in the face of rising opposition to the Vietnam War, they
reclassified the troops listed as KIA/BNR (killed in action/body not recov-
ered) to simply MIA (missing in action). As H. Bruce Franklin argued in
MIA: Mythmaking in America, this was calculated to give several thousand
families the false hope that their sons, brothers, husbands, and fathers had
been captured somewhere in the jungle or had been moved to Laos or Cam-
bodia, and that continued U.S. engagement in the war might reunite them
with their loved ones. These families, quickly organized into the National
League of Families, served to blunt the antiwar movement and thus assisted
in Nixon's landslide reelection in 1972.[51] On January 23, 1973, when Nixon
announced to America that an agreement had been signed in Paris to end
the war, he ended his Peace with Honor speech with this grateful acknowledgement: "In particular, I would like to say a word to some of the bravest
people I have ever met—the wives, the children, the families of our prisoners of war and missing in action. While others called on us to settle on any
terms, you had the courage to stand for the right kind of peace so that those
who died and those who suffered would not have died and suffered in vain,
and so that, where this generation knew war, the next generation would
know peace." Following Nixon's forced resignation in 1974 and Saigon's fall
in 1975, when pitifully few of the MIAs returned, their families still could not
bring themselves to abandon the narrative they had been told, preferring
instead to blame its disgraced narrator for abandoning his missing troops.

The peace of the next generation was at best a troubled peace. By the
end of the 1970s, another abduction crisis had burst on the media—this time
focused on the Middle East. Militant students stormed the U.S. embassy in
Tehran and took sixty-six Americans hostage, hoping to pressure the United
States to return the deposed shah to face Iranian justice. A new folk custom
suddenly sprang up in the United States: yellow ribbons tied about the trunks
of trees symbolized patriotic support for American prisoners abroad.[52] When
Operation Eagleclaw—the attempt to send airborne commandoes to free
the hostages on April 24, 1980—failed, President Jimmy Carter's administration was dealt a crippling blow. In the final weeks of his administration,
Carter had agreed to unfreeze eight billion dollars of Iranian assets and was

promised the release of the embassy staff. The Iranian government chose not to finalize the deal, however, until an hour after the inauguration of Carter's successor, Ronald Reagan.[53]

On October 23, 1983, in Beirut, Lebanon, a suicide bomber crashed his pickup truck into a Marine barracks and killed 241 sleeping Americans. The American troops had been stationed there to help separate the antagonists in that civil war. Two days later, Reagan responded by invading the small Caribbean island of Grenada. The primary reason he gave was the need to rescue several hundred American medical students who, he said, might find themselves in danger because of a recent government coup. The plan had been sketched out two years earlier after a Grenadian government friendly to Cuba came to power, but the timing of this invasion, dubbed Operation Urgent Fury, conveniently distracted public attention from the carnage in Beirut.[54]

Since the Vietnam War, television has become the acknowledged American storyteller. Historians credit TV news photographers for exposing the American public to the terrifying violence and the dismal consequences of that war and for turning public opinion away from the victory-at-all-cost policies of the White House and the Pentagon. With that in mind, President Reagan decided to bar independent news media from his assault on Grenada, lest photos of American dead and wounded find their way onto the evening news.[55] All that viewers at home would get to see would be images of victorious U.S. troops and young Americans safely returned to the homeland. This foreign incursion was the first, though not the last, in which an American commander in chief sought to control the entire visual narrative.

For the last in this series of politicized abduction narratives, let us recall the capture and recovery of Pfc. Jessica Lynch in the Iraq War. On March 23, 2003, just three days after the ground invasion of Iraq began, American forces sustained their first setback when a supply convoy of trucks was ambushed in Nasiriyah. In the ensuing firefight, the Iraqis killed eleven soldiers and captured six others, including Lynch. On April 3, the *Washington Post* broke the story of her capture and subsequent rescue.[56] According to an unnamed Pentagon source, Lynch "fought fiercely and shot several enemy soldiers . . . firing her weapon until she ran out of ammunition [and] continued firing at the Iraqis even after she sustained multiple gunshot wounds. . . . 'She was fighting to the death,' the official said. 'She did not want to be taken alive.'" She was also stabbed, the official said, and taken to a hospital where she was interrogated around the clock and physically abused by her captors. As the *New York Daily News* reported in a follow-up story, word that a female American was being held at the Saddam Hussein Hospital in Nasiriyah "set off a daring nighttime rescue that involved the highest levels of the Pentagon and the most elite fighting forces of the U.S. military—all to ensure the safe return of a teenage private from West Virginia." Then, after a pause so that New York readers could fathom the depth of the Pentagon's concern for a low-ranking teenager from a rustic fly-over state, the article concluded: "Pfc. Jessica Lynch, prisoner of war, would not be left behind."[57]

But of course, Private Lynch was not just any prisoner of war. She was a cute nineteen-year-old volunteer whose rescue, the first such rescue behind enemy lines since World War II,[58] was filmed live and, in a well-edited five-minute video, immediately broadcast on national television. This encouraging story came along at a time when Americans were first beginning to hear dismaying news of Iraqi resistance—not the sort of reaction Vice President Dick Cheney had promised just two weeks earlier, when he declared that "we will be greeted as liberators."[59]

By mid-April, however, the Pentagon story began to unravel. The Iraqis who ambushed her convoy had taken her to the hospital, where the medical staff saved her life. She had not been shot or stabbed but had suffered multiple fractures when her truck crashed. By the time the hospital informed the U.S. military of her presence, the insurgents had left the area. In her account, published later that year in the book *I Am a Soldier, Too,* she thanked the hospital staff for the care she had been given and denied that she had been abused. She candidly acknowledged in a television interview with Diane Sawyer in early November 2003 that she disliked the exaggerated account of events: "It does [bother me] . . . that they used me as a way to symbolize all this stuff. . . . It's wrong." Reminded of the *Washington Post* headline of April 3, "She Was Fighting to the Death," she told Sawyer that her weapon jammed and she had not fired a single shot. The earlier story of her emptying her automatic weapon into the sinister shapes of lunging, mustachioed Fedayeen was as much a public relations fantasy as the woodcut ordered for the title page of Mary Rowlandson's *Narrative* had been when the book was reprinted in 1773. That picture showed a woman standing in profile at her door, firing her musket into a column of tomahawk-wielding Indians. In her account, Rowlandson makes no mention of having a firearm or of putting up any resistance to her attackers.

The Lynch narrative diverted Americans' attention from what they had been led to believe would be an abduction narrative on a far grander scale. As its name signifies, Operation Iraqi Freedom was to be a rescue mission—not of captive Americans, but of captive Iraqis. When President Bush landed his Navy fighter jet on the flight deck of the USS *Abraham Lincoln* on May 1, 2003, he announced the end of major combat operations in Iraq and declared:

> In this battle, we have fought for the cause of liberty, and for the peace of the world. . . . the tyrant has fallen, and Iraq is free. . . .
> . . . We thank all the citizens of Iraq who welcomed our troops and joined in the liberation of their own country. . . .
> In the images of celebrating Iraqis, we have also seen the ageless appeal of human freedom. Decades of lies and intimidation could not make the Iraqi people love their oppressors or desire their own enslavement. Men and women in every culture need liberty like they need food and water and air. Everywhere that freedom arrives, humanity rejoices; and everywhere that freedom stirs, let tyrants fear.

Bush concluded by reminding his audience of the troops who died to achieve the underlying purpose of this war:

> Their final act on this Earth was to fight a great evil and bring liberty to others. All of you—all in this generation of our military— have taken up the highest calling of history. You're defending your country, and protecting the innocent from harm. And wherever you go, you carry a message of hope—a message that is ancient and ever new. In the words of the prophet Isaiah, "To the captives, 'come out,'—and to those in darkness, 'be free.'"[60]

Jessica Lynch's invader-as-victim narrative, like that of Mary Rowlandson and the fictional Nora Dalton, was one in which the invading force is represented by an innocent woman, "treated in the most barbarous and cruel Manner by those vile Savages," as the caption beneath the musket-shooting image of Rowlandson had declared. Bush's closing comments, in what is popularly called his Mission Accomplished speech, referred to another abduction narrative—one that we may call the invader-as-rescuer narrative, according to which a foreign country, seized by a vicious tyrant, is a victim yearning to be rescued by an altruistic America. (See pages 19–20 for George Lakoff's discussion of what he calls the rescue scenario.)

The genealogy of these cultural narratives is complex, however. Both the invader-as-victim and the invader-as-rescuer models are abduction master narratives authorized by what Jean-François Lyotard called the "emancipative narrative," the story line supporting the belief that individual rights and social progress are now an irresistible historical trend. This modern secular master narrative, I maintain, is itself authorized by a *pre*modern religious master narrative that we may call the "redemptive narrative." Accordingly, the American abduction narrative, in all its variants and manifestations, is charged with the powerful patriotic emotions of the emancipative narrative, which, in turn, is infused with the profound aspirations of this older redemptive narrative.

The efficacy of the invader-as-rescuer narrative lies in its rhetorical blending of premodern with modern master narratives. The premodern redemptive narrative represents the victim not only as persecuted Christians, but also as the heathen, to whom the gospel has yet to be preached. According to the modern emancipative narrative that evolved from it, the abducted victim is a populace ruled over by an oppressive system. The villain in the older biblical account is Satan, the prince of this world who has enslaved humankind in sin and now, through his demonic and human agents, compels them to honor him. In the modern political version of the story, he is the ruthless despot maintained in power by a palace guard and a secret police. In the biblical master narrative the hero is Jesus Christ, the Son of God, who seeks to redeem humanity from Satan's prison of sin; in the political master narrative, he is a human emancipator, the freely chosen leader of an enlightened people, a Redeemer Nation.[61]

The process by which the victim is rescued in the premodern narrative is the preaching of the gospel, i.e., the good news of the millennial kingdom of heaven, first proclaimed by the messianic hero himself, then by his apostles, and now through his Church and its missionaries. In the modern narrative, it is the "gospel" of democracy that must be preached to the world through print and other media, a doctrine that may eventually have to be transmitted through military force. At this point the commander in chief sends a liberating army to break down the prison walls and rescue the captive nation. This struggle has its biblical parallel in the battle of Armageddon; the rescuing troops, like missionaries pledged to martyrdom, are themselves subject to the victimhood of capture, torture, and death. But those to whom this happens will not have suffered and died in vain, for the cause they uphold is the sacred cause of freedom—sacred because in the modern emancipative narrative, the word "freedom" has claimed for itself the profound power of the hallowed *pre*modern word "salvation."

6

HOMELAND NOSTALGIA AND HOLY WAR

Any nation's homeland mythology will include, among its cultural narratives, certain accounts of its founding that do not simply magnify its achievements but also reduce its cognitive dissonance. Its founding myths and epics will attempt to take historical events, which usually involve an aggressive seizure of land and the scattering, enslavement, and/or genocide of its former inhabitants, and bring them into at least partial conformity with communal ethics.

American homeland mythology, as I have been examining it, emerged out of the unique circumstances of a large-scale transatlantic invasion that drew upon the Bible for its legitimacy. This was the source book that answered such questions as: How do we earn blessings, not curses, in this stolen land? How do we understand our status among other races? What is our national purpose in world history? More to the point, how can we continue to enjoy our material *and* our moral superiority?

In the last two chapters I explored American narratives that evolved out of premillennialist readings of end-time prophecy. The "narratives of the night" represented the "last things," the *eschata*, as suddenly bursting upon a sleeping world. Abduction narratives dramatized the night as a prison house, a place of bondage in which an abducted victim awaits the rescuing hero. This heroic redeemer would not merely pay for the release of the captive. He would also pay *back* the abductor for his crimes. In this chapter I will focus on the hero in his relation to the villain.

Christians are called upon to imitate Christ and, faced with difficult choices, ask themselves "What would Jesus do?" The biblical master narrative helpfully casts Christ in two roles: as the regatherer of the lost sheep of Israel, the Good Shepherd of the Gospels who lays down his life for his flock, and as the avenger of Revelation who blasts his foes and plunges them into the everlasting fiery lake of hell. There are, therefore, times when Christians must imitate the suffering Jesus, but at other times their *imitatio Christi* calls them to be "soldiers of Christ"—liberators of the unjustly imprisoned and instruments of divine judgment.

The warriors of Christ the King have a lost kingdom to restore. This is the world God planned before Satan suborned humans to corrupt it. The process necessary to lead the true believers from phase 3 of the full narrative cycle to phases 4 and 5 entails a cosmic war against evil forces—those forces responsible for the spiritual descent from the innocence of Eden and right-eousness of the patriarchal age to the current state of darkness and bondage. Motivated by a sense of collective nostalgia, this reascent from 3 to 4 to 5 becomes a paradoxical progression backward into the future. For the premillennialist, this transition, effortless and sudden, is effected by the Rapture, but for the *post*millennialist it is an arduous climb of many stages. The earthly Millennium does not simply *happen*. It somehow requires human agency. Before the reign of Christ begins, Christians will play a role in which armed combat, rather than prayer, teaching, or preaching, will be the dominant activity. Without this, the true believers can never be securely regathered in their rightful homeland.

In this chapter, we will see how the postmillennialist narrative has inspired a number of different apocalyptic movements, each with its own vision of this long-lost homeland and of the violent means necessary to achieve it. But before we explore some of the nostalgias that have beset American political culture over the past century and a half, we must consider some of the ways in which orality shapes narrative discourse, predisposing it to a nostalgic representation of the past that it projects as a utopian vision of the future.

Narrative Logic in the No-Fact Zone

Golden Ages, with their mix of fabulous events and idealized persons, grow naturally from the soil of oral cultures. Long after literacy is introduced, cultures still tend to revere political myths that derive from collections of tales transcribed from oral sources several thousand years old. As for those that derive from Hebraic sources, much of the content of the first seven books of the Bible appears to have been preserved for many generations and transmitted by word of mouth, for the features familiar to us from transcriptions and performances of oral material abound in these books—formulaic and syntactic repetitions, extraordinary content, and narrative form.[1]

For verbal information to survive in an oral culture, it must be retold. This means that it has to remain in the memory of the hearer long enough to be communicated to others and be interesting enough to them to warrant retelling. Certain lexical patterns and rhythms are useful mnemonic devices, but the content of an oral text has to be extraordinary enough to stand out against the background of routinized village life and compete successfully with other oral texts to garner a niche in the communal memory.[2] This means, for example, that if two variants of the same story are current—one in which the hero escapes from a giant by slipping away under cover of night, and another in which he escapes by donning a helmet that renders him invisible—there is little question which variant would survive longest in oral transmission. Mythic hyperbole in preliterate societies is not an aesthetic adornment. It is there simply because it is one of the best available means of preserving extended verbal compositions.

Because the extraordinary nature of its details is a principal means of its survival, what we call the "content" of a myth is virtually impossible to disentangle from its other built-in mnemonic devices, such as formulas and iteration. Paper, ink, and typeface are elements necessary to the survival of information in a print culture; likewise, magic, gods, and monsters are key to its survival in an oral culture. The oral message is dependent on the oral medium. Can there ever be a message, then, distinct from this medium, a factual content with truth-value that is extricable from the necessary format in which it is conveyed? If the Greek word for truth (*alêtheia*) has any bearing on this discussion, the question of truth embedded in the husk of fable is meaningless in an oral culture, for, in the absence of the critical habits that literacy promotes, the "true" is simply the unforgettable (*a* = not + *lêth-* = forgetting). What we generally refer to as "mythology" is thus the genre of discourse that memory-dependent, oral transmission naturally engenders.

A series of merely extraordinary events, however, would be as forgettable as a dream quickly becomes upon waking unless it possesses the sequential form of narrative, a feature that is both mnemonic and familiarizing. It is mnemonic in that it imposes a before-and-after, cause-and-effect structure on these items of information. It is familiarizing in that it uses the linear format of everyday speech and memory retrieval, thereby transmitting a series of episodes as though they had been somehow experienced by the narrator.

If the earliest materials in the Bible derive from oral sources or have passed through phases of oral preservation, then they were probably not only shaped by the mnemonic requirements of extraordinary detail and narrative sequence but also intended to satisfy a popular need to reinforce communal beliefs.

That is to say, the Homeric epics, the German *Märchen,* the English folk ballads, the tall tales from the American frontier, contemporary "urban legends," and every other oral artifact must have been shaped by tacit cultural assumptions and have survived only because people found them meaningful and enjoyed repeating them. When we find that certain oral texts survive over time, we may conclude that forgettable and cognitively dissonant portions were edited out until what remained fairly corresponded to the moral, political, and aesthetic preferences of the community.[3]

Spontaneous oral discourse also reflects and reinforces shared assumptions. As a way for members of a community to show respect and form alliances with one another, Robin Dunbar has speculated, it may be a carryover from prehuman, primate grooming behavior.[4] Oral narrative—gossiping, telling jokes, sharing secrets—was, and for the most part still is, an intracommunal discourse that presupposes a social context of trustful interdependence.

Once literacy is introduced, social, face-to-face discourse continues, of course, but is no longer absolutely necessary. The Egyptians, Sumerians, and Chinese, who first mastered the technology of writing, learned to send and receive information across distances and issue commands from a central authority.[5] At this point we have the emergence of what I have called the governmental level and, with it, new modes of thinking that often conflict with the sequential logic of narrative. As a spatial format, a written text permits the reader's eye to move backwards and forwards and compare one passage with another. As an outside-the-brain means of verbal storage, it also permits *un*extraordinary data to be stored for future retrieval, so along with writing came into being those finite kernels of knowledge we call "facts." One of the first uses to which writing was put was the transcription of oral compositions, certainly, but the most frequently encountered samples of early writing are lists of words and numbers, records and property deeds, tax accounts, and the like—the sort of information that was difficult to retain in memory. Literacy also led to the syllogism, the method of reasoning by assessing the relation of three sentences, and to the collection of observations from which general conclusions may be derived. As philosophy, history, and natural science developed out of the medium of writing, analytic thinking began to diverge from the narrative modes that had defined preliterate culture and that now continued, alongside writing, to be practiced within literate culture.

The persistent differences between oral and literate modes of thought begin to blur in the postmodern age of electronic media, which Walter Ong has called the age of secondary orality.[6] Though radio, television, and film are as centrally produced and disseminated as print media, by the nature of their formats they conform to the preliterate logic of narrative. For example, if news broadcasts increasingly entertain more than they inform, they do so by yielding to the tendency (inherent in oral narrative) to "stroke" the audience, an expression that appropriately calls to mind the grooming rituals of our primate cousins. Audiovisual media, as directed by corporate elites, inevitably efface the distinction between the communal and the governmental, blending the ethical values associated with *home* with the realpolitik associated with the *land.* In this age of secondary orality, the government explains itself through parables and argues its moral rectitude through narrative logic.[7]

From a literacy-based point of view, a narrative never has the persuasive weight of facts and logical demonstration. From an orality-based point of view, a narrative may convey a "higher truth." The following five characteristics will serve to typify "narrative logic."

1. Oral narratives rely on vivid episodes that appear to confirm preestablished beliefs rather than merely illustrate them.
2. These culturally shared beliefs, when they concern social groups, are usually ethnocentric and xenophobic in their moral judgments.
3. Oral narrative presents simple recognizable characters of little psychological depth. Any character who considers more than two options for action or suffers from cognitive dissonance is consigned by narrative logic to the status of a weakling or a fool.[8]
4. Narrative thinking tends to equate priority with causality: if event A precedes event B, A is assumed to have caused B. Accompanying this tendency is a belief in the intentionality of outcomes: if C is the ultimate result of A's acting upon B, the entire sequence had to have been designed by the initiator of A.
5. Finally, narrative thinking has a great tolerance for internal contradiction. Being a linear discourse that unfolds over time, it may present a character doing or saying X and later on doing or saying something quite opposite (Y). The inconsistency is usually ignored because of the distance between passages, but, when a contradiction is too glaring to ignore, some rationalizing episode may be inserted to bridge the gap between X and Y, e.g., he was under a spell, drank a potion, or was misled by a deceiver. Factual, as distinct from behavioral, inconsistencies are of least importance in narrative logic, because facts are treated as interchangeable modules of information—elements of form, not of substance.

To exemplify the political uses of narrative logic in the age of secondary oral-ity, I will cite some typical and currently all-too-familiar rhetorical gambits.

Anecdotal evidence	The use of vivid, often emotional illustrations to support a policy position. ("I received a let-ter just the other day from a widow who asked why she was being forced to contribute a por-tion of her taxes to finance health care for un-documented immigrants." "I want to point out and ask to stand up for a moment a man in the audience whose story of bravery says so much more than I could ever hope to say about [the topic at hand].")
Group stereotyping	A simplification of issues, motives, and char-acter traits that confirms the preexistent beliefs of the audience. ("No loyal American needs to fear NSA wiretaps." "The enemy we face just hates our freedoms.")
Character simplification	Heroic characters always have easily understood positions. ("The man I have the honor to intro-duce today is resolute and unwavering." "My opponent is a compromiser, a clever Washing-ton politician.")
Post hoc ergo propter hoc	A preceding event causes a subsequent event. ("Saddam's defeat in 1991 led him to conspire with jihadists to attack the World Trade Cen-ter in 2001." "Our decision to bring the battle to the enemy over there has made Americans more secure.")
Tolerance for factual inconsistency	Consistent characters render inconsistent facts negligible. ("The British government has learned that Saddam Hussein recently sought signifi-cant quantities of uranium from Africa." "Re-ports that Iraq obtained bomb-grade uranium from Niger have not been substantiated.")

These five rhetorical gambits may be used rationally as means of misin-forming the uninformed, but, even for users, they are not harmless ploys. As a striking example of how overexposure to them may also infect their users with magical thinking, consider the following account, from an article written by Ron Suskind and published in the *New York Times Magazine* in the fall of 2004:

> In the summer of 2002, after I had written an article in *Esquire* that the White House didn't like about Bush's former communications director, Karen Hughes, I had a meeting with a senior adviser to Bush. He expressed the White House's displeasure, and then he told me something that at the time I didn't fully comprehend—but which I now believe gets to the very heart of the Bush presidency.
>
> The aide said that guys like me were "in what we call the reality-based community," which he defined as people who "believe that solutions emerge from your judicious study of discernible reality." I nodded and murmured something about enlightenment principles and empiricism. He cut me off. "That's not the way the world really works anymore," he continued. "We're an empire now, and when we act, we create our own reality. And while you're studying that reality—judiciously, as you will—we'll act again, creating other new realities, which you can study too, and that's how things will sort out. We're history's actors . . . and you, all of you, will be left to just study what we do."[9]

If this spokesman for the president brings to mind Steven Colbert's character on the television program *The Colbert Report,* it may be because his rant against the "reality-based community" expresses the essence of "truthiness." This word, which Colbert introduced in his very first broadcast on the Comedy Central cable channel, circulated quickly through the "blogosphere" and the alternative press. In January 2006, it was voted "Word of the Year" for 2005 by the American Dialect Society, which defined it as "the quality of preferring concepts or facts one wishes to be true, rather than concepts or facts known to be true."[10] Later that month, Colbert (the reality-based person, not the right-wing pundit impersonator) explained what he meant by the term:

> It used to be, everyone was entitled to their own opinion, but not their own facts. But that's not the case anymore. Facts matter not at all. Perception is everything. It's certainty. People love the president because he's certain of his choices as a leader, even if the facts that back him up don't seem to exist. It's the fact that he's certain

that is very appealing to a certain section of the country. I really feel
a dichotomy in the American populace. What is important? What
you want to be true, or what is true? . . .

Truthiness is: "What I say is right, and [nothing] anyone else
says could possibly be true." It's not only that I feel it to be true,
but that *I* feel it to be true. There's not only an emotional quality,
but there's a selfish quality.[11]

In an oral information system, truthiness, like the primitive Greek *alêtheia,*
becomes an accepted representation of reality simply by its being repeated.
This faith-based mindset can then insulate believers from the cognitive dissonance produced whenever hope and knowledge stand opposed. Its logic,
embedded in narrative, cushions the distress they experience when, inevitably, they collide with extra-creedal reality. "History's actors" and their super-
numeraries have sometimes gone quite far before discovering that the only
realities they have created for themselves are unintended consequences.

In this vein, I might briefly mention Colbert's appearance at the White
House Correspondents' Association Dinner of April 29, 2006. First instituted
in 1920, this ritual of social inversion allows the president and his family to
own up to the foibles and annoying mannerisms that, over the past year,
have become all too apparent to the press corps and the citizenry. Comics
and raconteurs are hired to perform mildly needling monologues, to which
the president is expected to respond affably.

On this night, the 2,700 well-fed and -wined correspondents and assorted
guests, plus a national C-SPAN audience, first got to witness President Bush
paired with the Bush impersonator Steve Bridges in a curious point-and-
counterpoint debate that the guests found uproarious. Colbert rose next.
After formally acknowledging President Bush, the First Lady, and the other
distinguished guests, he introduced himself and, without mentioning "truthiness," began to apply its meanings to the president and his administration:

> . . . my name is Stephen Colbert and it's my privilege tonight to
> celebrate this president.
>
> We're not so different, he and I. We get it. We're not brainiacs
> on the nerd patrol. We're not members of the "Factanistas." We go
> straight from the gut, right sir? That's where the truth lies, right
> down here in the gut. (Do you know you have more nerve endings
> in your gut than you have in your head? You can look it up. I know

some of you are going to say, "I did look it up, and that's not true." That's 'cause you looked it up in a book. Next time look it up in your gut. I did.) My gut tells me that's how our nervous system works. Every night on my show, *The Colbert Report,* I speak straight from the gut. Okay? I give people the truth, unfiltered by rational argument. I call it the "No Fact Zone." (Fox News, I own the copyright on that term.)[12]

By the end of Colbert's monologue, the President's smile was gone. He immediately rose as soon as Colbert concluded and vanished with something like the haste of King Claudius in Act 3 of *Hamlet.* Ironic truthiness—"'Tis a knavish piece of work, but what of that?"

Historical Fantasies and the Angry Man

There is yet another important aspect of narrative logic, one that primarily derives from oral transmission. It is the notion that in the past, the world was more wonderful than it now is, and people were wiser, stronger, and more virtuous than they now are. From this perspective, the people of today are dwarfish, shabby replicas of their ancestors. The ancestors to which every living generation looked for guidance seem more extraordinary than their degenerate descendants, because of course only extraordinary persons and events, real or fabricated, can survive the test of time and be enrolled in the remembered past. As the Bible demonstrates, an oral culture preserves a miraculous past: angels mate with mortals, giants range the earth, God himself speaks familiarly with men, sun and moon hover motionless in the sky, and prophets rise to heaven in fiery chariots. Not so in more recent times. Even before the prophets, it was known that, as generation had followed generation, God's allotment of life to humans had grown smaller. The antediluvian patriarchs had regularly lived over nine hundred years, but those from Abraham to Moses could not outlast two hundred years. King David, despite God's remarkable favors, grew "old and stricken with years" and died in his sixties. Again, nostalgia is common to all cultures that depend on or continue to revere their oral heritage. For them, as descendants, time is indeed a *descent.* Homer and Hesiod, contemporaries of Isaiah and Jeremiah, arrived at similar conclusions: the Age of Heroes was over, and an Iron Age had begun.

Writing, on the other hand, can and does preserve a past of facts—of banal events and unheroic, albeit more recognizably human, personages, as the books of Kings and Chronicles amply demonstrate. Compare, for example, the characterization of David with that of Noah or Moses or Joshua. Readers see David's humanity vividly portrayed, whereas that of the earlier heroes they must imaginatively reconstruct. The contrast between the narratives contained in the first seven books of the Bible and those in the later scribal histories further reinforced the notion that latter-day generations lacked the grandeur of the past. Now, as the medium of writing proceeded to modify the message, God no longer seemed to visit his favorites. His voice grew so still and small that it became audible only to prophets. Then, at length, it was heard no more. To the extent that a utopian project shares a biblical nostalgia for the past, it will express a longing to hear once more the thunderous, authoritative voice of the Divine Father speaking to his mighty men as of old.

The persons most susceptible to nostalgia and retrospective utopianism are usually those whose lives have been disrupted by social changes, especially those workers who have lost their livelihoods. In nineteenth- and early twentieth-century America, they were preindustrial farmworkers who found themselves in an industrial nation. In the last half of the twentieth century, they were industrial workers in a postindustrial nation. In the early twenty-first century, their ranks now swell with white-collar workers whose jobs have been outsourced to Southeast Asia. Though they are of every race and ethnic background, the most numerous and therefore most worrisome displaced workers are white and male. Demographers sometimes refer to this type as the "angry white male," but I will refer to him simply as the "angry man."

A "baby boomer" growing up on Kennedy's New Frontier, he was not always angry or confused. Once the proud, independent supporter of a respectful and cooperative family, or so the nostalgic story has it, he ruled wife and children with kindness and wisdom. He patiently put up with the arrogance of bosses and the incompetence of peers at work, but when he returned home to his family, he left that world behind and resumed his God-designated status as husband and father—a kind of biblical patriarch on a modest scale. Conditions had improved, he had done his bit to make them better, and he would create an even brighter future for his children.

Now, however, everything has changed. He finds himself having more and more to compete with women, blacks, and recent immigrants, both legal and illegal. No longer indispensable in the workplace, his wages stagnate or drop. His wife is forced to seek employment. His children have less after-school supervision, use drugs, and engage in casual sex. His status as ruler of the family has now become a cruel joke. He senses that some evil influence has corrupted his family and begins to search for objects of his anger. Feminists, blacks, immigrants, Jewish bankers, homosexuals, welfare recipients, moviemakers, journalists, and environmentalists—somehow these groups are all implicated in the decline of the family. He feels unappreciated both on the job and in his own home. Some days his only friend seems to be his favorite radio talk-show host, a man who also seems to have lost his patience with the prevailing culture. His life becomes, like Christ's, a vicarious atonement. *He* didn't enslave the blacks or send the Jews to the gas chambers; *he* respects his wife and daughters; *he* gives everyone a fair shake. But because of his gender and the color of his skin, he is reviled and spat upon, a man of sorrows and acquainted with grief.

Being an American, it is difficult for him to step outside the millennial paradigm. He sees, moreover, a reflection of his own rage in the story of the Apocalypse. The last spectacular event in world history, he learns, is enacted by two angry males, a father and a son who return to a place where they had been mocked and abused and destroy almost everyone in sight in what can only be called a planetary mass killing.

This does make sense to him. Something has gone terribly wrong and only some drastic measure, some intervention by a Divine Angry Man, can rectify matters. There is no doubt about it: conditions have deteriorated. The young have lost respect for their elders. People act like animals. Reacting against his former progressivism, he visualizes the trajectory of human time as sloping downward from a more glorious, more virtuous past, a *monumental* past, toward a steadily worsening future. This view of the slippery slope of history makes perfect sense to the angry man, whose life has now become a series of steps down, not up, the great stairway of success.

Yet there are moments when he glimpses a brighter vista, a way up and out of the impasse of his life. The upward path toward this perfect homeland is a reversal of history. His imagined future appears as a palimpsest upon which three previous cultures are written—the agrarian, the feudal, and the monarchical. The angry man, in other words, has three simultaneously available archives of idealized imagery to represent his yearned-for condition and to explain, by contrast, the degeneracy of the present. These three are represented by images of the farm, the castle, and the kingdom.

The Farm

Independent family farms still exist in America, though their number diminishes every year. As their economic importance steadily decreases, however, their cultural importance grows. The most modest farm substitute, though increasingly difficult to afford, is the single-family home. In the American Dream fantasy, i.e., American millennialism at the level of the family unit, this home must have a fenced-in yard enclosing those minimal symbols of agrarian culture, an animal and a garden.

Most angry men are not likely to become farmers, even if they were given farms to work. The agrarian ideal, remember, is a fantasy. Like all such obsessive daydreams, it exacerbates the fantasizer's anger to the extent that it eludes his grasp. Even if a single-family home may be beyond his reach, some form of self-employment intrigues him as a symbol of agrarian independence. Economic conditions now make this more possible because corporations, large and small, are less likely to offer long-term commitments to employees and prefer to engage them as "independent contractors." Thus the ideal of the rugged independent farmer—or, to add a related fantasy, the footloose cowboy—serves to compensate him for his lack of health benefits and economic security. At least he no longer has to pay union dues and, if completely self-employed, he can ask his clients to make out their checks "to cash" and so pays little or no tax on his income.

According to the agrarian ideal, independent farmers are happier, healthier, and more virtuous than city folk. Rural families depend on God's bounty and their own honest labor, while city folk depend on the farmer's bounty and their own dishonest wits. "Those who labor in the earth," wrote Jefferson in 1785, "are the chosen people of God, if ever he had a chosen people." Corruption has never been associated with "cultivators," he asserts. Then, using another biblical allusion, the apocalyptic mark of the Beast (which even deists felt entitled to deploy), he says that corruption "is the mark set on those, who not looking up to heaven, to their own soil and industry, as does the husbandman, for their substance, depend for it on the casualties and caprice of customers." As for manufactured goods, let the cities of Europe produce them for us, and, as for the wage slaves who make them: "the mobs of great cities add just so much to the support of pure government, as sores do to the strength of the human body."[13]

The Bible endorses this antiurban bias. The first mention of a city appears in Genesis 4:17, when Enoch, son of Cain, built one. The next city builder, after the Flood, was Nimrod, whose city was the wicked city of Babel (10:8–10). After that, the next mention is of the "cities of the plain," Sodom and Gomorrah (13:12). The biblical chronicle of human cities ends in Revelation with the fall of Babylon, a city associated with Babel (Rev. 14:19).[14] The hatred of the City of Man reaches a crescendo in chapters 17 to 19 of Revelation.

"And I saw," John reports, "the woman drunken with the blood of the saints, and the blood of the martyrs of Jesus." Presently an angel announces, "Babylon the great is fallen, is fallen. . . . How much she hath glorified herself, and lived deliciously, so much torment and sorrow give her. . . . And the kings of the earth, who committed fornication and lived deliciously with her, shall bewail her, when they shall see the smoke of her burning. . . . And the merchants of the earth shall weep and mourn over her; for no man buyeth their merchandise any more. . . . For in one hour so great riches is brought to nought." Then the prophet hears the voices of martyrs in heaven crying out "Alleluia. And her smoke rose up for ever and ever. . . . Alleluia: for the Lord God omnipotent reigneth."[15]

Should these vindictive and gloating sentiments bring to mind the responses of al Qaeda sympathizers following the destruction of the World Trade Center, we should recall that prior to that event, many otherwise patriotic Americans had expressed similar ill will toward New York City. *New York Times* reporter David Rosenbaum summarized Richard Nixon's sentiments, tape-recorded in 1972, after they were released in the summer and fall of 2003: "Mr. Nixon is contemptuous of cities in general and New York in particular. 'Goddamn New York,' he says, adding that it is filled with 'Jews and Catholics and blacks and Puerto Ricans.' There is a 'law of the jungle where some things don't survive,' so, Mr. Nixon says: 'Maybe New York shouldn't survive. Maybe it should go through a cycle of destruction.'"[16] For various other reasons as well—e.g., Wall Street, media and publishing, and the United Nations headquarters—New York has long been regarded as the City of Destruction, the Babylon of John's prophecy.[17] One premillennialist calculator, Jerry R. Church, announced that the letters in "New York City" could add up to 666, the mark of the Beast.[18] In 1983 the popular Christian broadcaster Jack Van Impe declared that New York City would undoubtedly be the Antichrist's capital, making it the prime target for God's incendiary wrath.[19] The saved would be raptured, of course, even out of New York, but there would be precious few of them rising upward through the smoke.

The Castle

If we step behind the façade of a smiling, friendly, small-town, farming America, there is another movie set that appeals to the angry man in search of his homeland. This fantasy projects him yet further back in time to a medieval panorama of castles and knights. While farmers, though self-employed, still must sell their produce to purchase other needed goods (even Jefferson allowed for that), the feudal system and its later forms, the British manor, the southern plantation, the multi-thousand-acre western ranch, and the large northern estate, minimized that need. Here the lord had not only his own wheat fields but also his own mill and bakery, not only his tools and weapons but also forges to make and repair them. Here was a situation far superior to self-employment, if, that is, one was fortunate enough to be the lord or a member of his comitatus. Here was autarky and, besides complete economic self-sufficiency, there was self-protection, for the castle was also an armed fortress.[20] The economic self-sufficiency of his demesne allowed him and his knights, when endangered, to cross the moat, pull up the drawbridge, and hold off an army of besiegers for weeks and months.

The angry man into whose fantasies these images insinuate themselves does not really expect to lord it over some labor-intensive fief. Instead, his *home* is his castle, an expression that is more than folksy hyperbole. To protect this castle of his, he may buy elaborate surveillance and alarm systems and act out the chivalric ideal by purchasing several guns and joining the National Rifle Association and a local sportsmen's club. He may also join a militia-like group that drills and goes out on weekend maneuvers. (The right to bear arms, wear military regalia, and belong to a comitatus was always a knightly prerogative.) If he lives near a major city, he expects that sooner or later a disaster will strike that city—a nuclear missile attack, a terrorist release of lethal gas or bacteria, a race war—and hundreds of thousands of refugees and looters will then stumble out of the rubble and overrun the outlying counties. With this in mind, the angry man may begin storing water and canned goods in a fortified part of his house—a basement, perhaps, the modern equivalent of a castle keep. He may even construct a backyard bunker.[21]

The convergence of religion, politics, racism, and private weaponry was made clear on September 19, 1998, during the Christian Coalition's "Road to Victory" conference in Washington, D.C. The keynote speaker was Charlton Heston, who earlier that year had been elected president of the National Rifle Association. After praising Rev. Pat Robertson, who chaired the conference, Heston began to identify gun ownership with a particularly embattled class of Americans: "Finally the message begins to get through. Heaven help the God-fearing, law-abiding Caucasian middle class—Protestant or even worse evangelical Christian, Midwest or Southern or even worse rural, apparently straight or even worse admitted [heterosexual], gun-owning or even worse NRA card-carrying average working stiff, or even worst of all, male working stiff. Because not only don't you count, you're a downright obstacle to social progress."[22]

The angry man could not then, nor does he now, trust federal or state governments to protect him. The taxes they collect from him, he is convinced, buy him absolutely nothing. Far from protecting him from the evils associated with the city, government *is* the city, the government of this world, the Babylonian state of which the Bible speaks. His reading of the Bible and the tracts that purport to explain it inform him that behind the liberal media (which constitute the False Prophet) stands the tyrant (which is the Beast, or Antichrist), and behind him, authorizing all the governments of the world, stands Satan himself. In these ways the angry man identifies the objects of his fears, resentments, and rage, using as his guide the cosmic conspiracy theory found in the Book of Revelation.

The Kingdom

Ultimately there is to be a showdown between God's militia, composed of white Christian American males, and a multicultural, multiracial, multilingual horde of invaders who owe allegiance to some international government, some evil empire. An "empire," after all, is defined as an international government ruled from an autocratic center. It tolerates diversity—and, to the angry man, diversity is impurity and toleration a vice. A kingdom, on the other hand, implies a single people with a single language and a single culture, living in a fortified homeland, and led by a divinely anointed sovereign. From the beginnings of English settlement in America, this evil empire was believed to be the Church of Rome, that international expansionist cabal of the triple-crowned Antichrist. Catholic immigration began to alter the religious demography of the nation in the mid-nineteenth century, however, and anti-Catholic hysteria slowly abated. By the end of that century, a fresh but anciently convenient danger began to appear on America's shores: the Jews, who now began to be associated with two very different and mutually contradictory evil internationalisms, European banking and European socialism. Then, for most of the twentieth century, the satanic enemy was identified with international communism directed by the Kremlin.

Since the economic collapse of the Soviet Union, this imperial enemy has revealed itself to some as the Trilateral Commission, to others as the European Union. Yet the favorite of most right-wing mythologists is the United Nations. One reason why Americans who view current events through biblical lenses are so easily persuaded that the United Nations is a dangerous conspiracy is that they associate the word "nations" with the enemies of God's people.[23] This is the word used to translate the Hebrew *goyim* and the Greek *ethnoi* (gentiles).

George Bush Sr. intended to sound statesmanlike when he hazarded the "vision thing" to announce the beginning of a "new world order" in which the United Nations would play a more active role in peacekeeping and mediating international disputes.[24] The upshot of this remark was the defection of the ultra-right fringe of his Republican Party, whose members heard this as a concession of national sovereignty to a sinister one-world government. His son promulgated a new "vision thing," but without multilateral assistance. For him, the imperial foes have become the "enemies of freedom," shadowy international groups who "hate us," groups not limited to followers of Islam but conveniently characterized by them. On August 1, 2005, evading senatorial objections by using his recess-appointment authority, he made John Bolton—whose credentials as an angry man and an antagonist of the UN were impeccable—America's ambassador to the world body.

To those who hold to a premillennialist political agenda, the position of the elder Bush was wrong. Not only did it invite the satanically infiltrated UN to take precedence over Christian America, but it also seemed to favor *peace.* After all, the ultimate satanic illusion *is* world peace. The angry man, insofar as he interprets geopolitics in premillennialist terms, understands that before the Kingdom Age (the Millennium) can begin, the world *must* be plunged into horrendous misery climaxing in a final catastrophic war. Satan knows that his reign as prince of this world will end at Armageddon, so he will stop at nothing to improve the living conditions of the poor and prevent war. Extreme Christian Right ideologues spell out the specifics: programs to alleviate famine and disease, control population growth, inoculate children, stem the AIDS pandemic, educate women, and reduce illiteracy only play into the hands of Satan and his vicar, the Antichrist, who is soon to appear on the world stage.[25] At this point, any attempt to control the manufacture and distribution of armaments, especially nuclear weapons, is a futile (not to mention damnable) attempt to stay the arm of an angry God who has decreed that Satan's world empire will incinerate itself and the entire biosphere in a nuclear firestorm.[26]

Race: A Single Homeland Myth

All Christian millennialists believe that the end times will be marked by the pouring forth of God's wrath upon the unrepentant and their supernatural leaders, but premillennialists believe that when this happens, the elect will constitute a very small, persecuted community. Postmillennialists, on the other hand, believe that after they preach the gospel to all nations, most humans will convert and prepare to welcome their returning Messiah. Some "angry men," whom I profiled as disillusioned with postmillennialist optimism and susceptible to the sterner message of premillennialist conservatism, have gone on to become disillusioned with the standard premillennialist doctrine. Inflamed by the warlike imagery of a glorified past, they find it hard to leave all of the wrath to God and float up to heaven just when the real excitement begins.

There is, however, a premillennialism customized especially for those who like their Apocalypse spectacularly violent and want a role in the score-settling of Armageddon. It is called posttribulational premillennialism. According to this narrative, the saved will not be immediately raptured (if at all), but will last out the seven-year tribulation, which they will survive only if they maintain strict discipline within their ranks and defend themselves against the evil powers of this world. Then as now, they will not be able to trust the government to protect them. The civil authorities will either stand by and permit the Antichrist to persecute the True Church or actively take part in this persecution. If there is a Rapture, it will happen only after they have fought off the agents of Satan from their sacred compound. Some of these extreme posttribulationists go further and declare that the doctrine of the Rapture is itself a satanic hoax, a ploy to immobilize conservative Christians at the very time they must arm themselves for battle.[27]

In Pat Robertson's novel, *The End of the Age* (1995)—a lurid tale of lechery, greed, betrayal, and Satanism—the elect are obliged to survive the seven long years of tribulation.[28] Led by John Edwards ("Pastor Jack," a lineal descendant of Jonathan Edwards), described as "a man in his seventies with the lean, muscled torso of a prize fighter," the remnants of the True Church hide out in the mountains of northern New Mexico. Like Robertson, Pastor Jack is a televangelist who, by means of radio, television, and Internet transmissions, somehow inspires Christians worldwide to struggle against the Antichrist, a suave New York politician of Clintonesque ambitions who eventually comes to rule the world. Robertson's "posttrib" novel is a weave of ethnic myths, not unlike those deployed in the past by mainstream postmillennialists. Sinister foreigners abound—Hindu and Buddhist Satanists and Muslim assassins. There are also representatives of groups whom Robertson, head of the then powerful Christian Coalition, had publicly arraigned: homosexuals, media (reporters for the *New York Times* and *Washington Post*), Marxists, peace activists, and feminists, for example. As we will see later in this chapter, posttrib premillennialism and postmillennialism share the belief that their Christianity must be well-armed and vigilant.

Robertson and other churchmen anxious to promote a warlike religion can appeal to ample American iconography. These holy warriors have not only the images of farm, castle, and kingdom to represent a longed-for security but also a set of specifically American role models. One of these is the icon of the armed separatist: the "Pilgrim Father" in his somber uniform of black, his blunderbuss in one hand, his Bible in the other, and his perfect nuclear family clustered close, all on their way to Sabbath worship. The Pilgrim icon blends imperceptibly into those of the minuteman, the frontiersman, and the pioneer. Having separated from a corrupt tyranny, this composite figure makes his last stand in the wilderness of America, his predestined homeland, his millennial kingdom.

In their notion of a covenanted people defending themselves by force of arms from hostile neighbors, the more militant members of the religious Right have come to resemble those early fire-breathing postmillennialists who saw the young republic as a messianic hero, God's instrument in this world. Some of these deny the authority of the current state and federal governments and choose instead to transform their own community into a governmental entity with a supreme leader, a vertical chain of command, and a strict set of rules. They may refuse to pay taxes, giving tithes instead and even donating their property to this community, which, if it presents itself as a religious institution, may itself be legally tax-exempt. Like any government, this group also generates ethnic myths to situate its members within a civil society that, in a self-fulfilling prophecy, they predict will be hostile to their "nationhood." One organization, the Christian Exodus Movement, has called upon like-minded persons to migrate to South Carolina and, using the ballot box, take over the state county by county.[29]

To justify their belief that they, and only they, are divinely commissioned to be the pilgrim soldiers of the wrathful Jehovah (or "Yahweh," as many call the Deity), these latter-day separatists have needed to read themselves back into biblical prophecy. Like all apocalypticists then and now, they need to assume that their teachers are divinely inspired when interpreting scripture. This usually means that at the center of each "church" stands a charismatic leader capable of persuading his followers that they are indeed God's own militia, and their enemies, God's own enemies. To accomplish this he must collect an assortment of mythic elements and arrange them into an appropriate narrative.

Many posttribs in America have drawn upon Anglo-Israelism as their specific metanarrative. Unlike traditional Christians' belief that they have been chosen by God to inherit the role of ancient Israel, Anglo- (or British) Israelites view theirs as a genetic inheritance, an election not by grace but by race. In its simplest form, Anglo-Israelism extols the virtues of northern Europeans (English, German, Scandinavian, and Celtic), who, they believe, descended from the Ten Lost Tribes of Israel. The "Nordic races" bear the physical traits of the original Israelites who—physical anthropology to the contrary—were tall, blond, and blue-eyed. Dispersed by the Assyrians in the eighth century BC, various bands of them crossed the Caucasus (whereupon they came to be called "Caucasians") and eventually migrated to northern Europe, where one group, ever mindful of its lineage, called itself "Isaac's Sons" (or Saxons) and became the British Israelites. Ever restless, ever seeking their Promised Land, one branch of these, the descendants of Manasseh, son of Joseph, arrived in Massachusetts aboard the *Mayflower*. Once settled, they became a beacon of hope to all northern European Israelites, whom they then invited to regather in America.[30]

In America, Isaac's Sons began to encounter peoples of other lineages. To interpret these encounters, Anglo-Israelism, at first little more than an eccentric chauvinism, took on more sinister aspects. As discussed in Chapter 3, the myth of Noah had been reinterpreted in the antebellum South to explain the benign possibilities of inherited inequality. After Emancipation, white racism took another tack and sought an additional audience. The anonymously authored *Six Species of Man,* published in New York in 1866, appealed to more science-oriented Christians both in the North and in the South. Is it not illogical, it asked, to suppose that out of all the known mammals, the human is the only genus made up of a single species? After all, common sense shows that the several species of *Homo* are clearly differentiated. First of all, there is the Caucasian, the "great bearded and master species of humankind." The second is the Mongol, and then, in descending order, come the Malay, Indian, Esquimaux, and Negro. This, the author proposes, is the "great American doctrine of the diverse origin of human races."[31] The undisguised objective of this professedly "Anti-Abolition Tract" was, of course, to demarcate the "Negro" from the "Caucasian." "Negroes are strongly marked by their affinity to Mammalia," the author writes, and "for six thousand years [the Negro] has been a savage." This dating, a concession to the chronology of Bishop Ussher, indicates that the author places human speciation in antediluvian time—specifically, during the six days of Creation.

For the later followers of Anglo-Israelism, the same first four chapters of Genesis hold the key that unlocks the mystery of human destiny by now distinguishing between the human, the subhuman, and the satanic. The Southern antebellum myth of Ham and Japheth had justified white supremacy by appealing to biblical curses and blessings, but it decisively rejected as contrary to scripture the notions of separate human origins (polygenesis) and of human and infrahuman races. All human racial types, it maintained, are descended from Noah.[32] As it mutated in America after the Civil War and as it appears today in the Christian Identity movement, Anglo-Israelism assumed a more radical racism. (This movement does not consider the term "racism" negative or "racist" a slur.) According to this elaboration of Anglo-Israelism, the "colored" races did not come into being when Ham and his son Canaan were cursed, but are much older. They are, in point of fact, several hours older even than the white race of Adam, being among the "beasts of the earth" mentioned in Genesis 1:25. This means that when Noah filled his ark, besides pigs, sheep, and cattle, he had to round up a male and a female member of the black, yellow, and red races of soulless pre-Adamic humanoids in order to provide his future white descendants with serviceable beasts of burden. Only an Adamite has a soul and a conscience. This he proves when he blushes: "Adam in the original Hebrew is translated: 'to show blood in the face; turn rosy.'"[33]

If the Nordic people are the true Israelites, who, then, are those who claim to be descended from Abraham, Isaac, and Jacob? Encouraged by the rise of Nazism in the 1930s, some American Anglo-Israelites fashioned a curious tale: in the Garden of Eden, when Satan tempted Eve, he appeared to her as a preternaturally handsome white man, physically seduced her, and left his seed in her womb. This became her first-born son, Cain, a half-devil who expressed his satanic nature by murdering the true child of Adam and Eve, his half-brother Abel. God had already foretold this conflict when he said to the serpent: "And I will put enmity between thee and the woman, and between thy seed [Cain together with Eve's and Satan's descendants, the present-day Jews] and her seed [Abel, Seth, and the latter's legitimate Adamic descendants, the Nordic peoples]; it shall bruise thy head, and thou shalt bruise his heel [i.e., Adamites will eventually stamp out Satan's spawn, even though the latter will bite the foot that crushes it]" (Gen. 3:15). When Satan's firstborn was banished, his descendants, the Cainites, settled in central Asia where they called themselves Ash*ken*azim; another branch mentioned in the Bible as the *Ken*ites remained in the Middle East, where in later millennia they skulked about the borders of the original Israelite homeland. When the remnants of Judah returned from their captivity in Babylon in the sixth century, the latter branch of Cain infiltrated their leadership and became its rulers. Then, five centuries later, when Jesus appeared in order to call back the lost sheep of Israel, these were the Jews who crucified him. As for the

Jews of today, most of these are the descendants of the Asiatic branch of Cain who, calling themselves Khazars, craftily professed biblical Judaism in the eighth century AD. Then, after the Mongol invasions of the thirteenth century, they slipped stealthily into western Europe.

This narrative, in one or another of its variants, has provided the structure for an experience that all religions offer: personal transformation. If in the past one has felt weak and alone, lowly and worthless, one now learns that one is actually strong, noble, creative, and beautiful. Like every cultic conversion, this too leads the initiate from a liminal condition to a new status and an enhanced identity. Resembling the evangelicals' "born-again" experience, it prepares the neophyte to cope with social stresses in the specific terms outlined by the myth.

Whenever race replaces grace as the mark of divine election, a Darwinian imperative emerges: God saves only those of his elect who work to save their race. The fourteen words of David Lane have become a rallying cry: "We must secure the existence of our people and a future for White children."[34] To have a future, whites must not only produce racially pure children but also out-produce competing races. To accomplish this, they must counteract the centuries-old conspiracy of their racial enemies. The nonhuman races, led by the so-called Jews, pursue a three-pronged strategy: (1) to reduce the numbers of white babies being born, (2) to pollute the genetic purity of the next generation of whites, and (3) to prevent whites by law from resisting these trends.

The ultimate goal of the "Jews," these believers assert, has always been to exterminate the pure white race. No sooner had the descendants of Adam come to America than Satan's spawn followed them, setting in place their plan to exterminate the true human race here in the very land reserved by God to be their refuge. Step by step, this plan became reality. Using the propaganda of individual freedom, Jews began to transform America. Family planning, including abortion, was legalized to reduce the number of white offspring. The lifestyle choice of homosexuality was advertised to young whites to prevent them from growing up to become parents. Feminism, the seductive message of the serpent in the Garden of Eden, encourages wives to disobey husbands and young women to choose careers rather than marrying early and bearing children. Christian Identity white supremacists hold that the secretive Jewish conspiracy that currently rules America, known as the Zionist Occupied Government (the ZOG), supports family planning, gay rights, and radical feminism for whites while it also promotes the growth of the black population through welfare laws that reward teenage pregnancy and immigration laws that allow Asians, Africans, and Latin Americans to stream over our borders, their children educated in their own languages, and their views of the world advanced under the banner of multiculturalism.

Besides manipulating the birth rate, this Jewish conspiracy goes even further. It directly attacks the spiritual essence of the white race by genetically infecting the biological means by which its spirituality is transmitted: the white family. According to neo-Nazi elements in the Christian Identity movement, the Jews first bankrolled the slave trade just to flood the Aryan refuge of America with Africans, then fomented the Civil War to set them loose, and now agitate for the social and sexual mixing of the races. In the mid-twentieth century this entailed school integration, which has led to interracial dating and the production of nonwhite offspring. (It is an article of faith that a descendant of a mixed union can never be restored to whiteness, because it takes only one drop of nonwhite blood to mark a person as a member of one of the "mud races.") The adoption of nonwhite babies by whites also leads to "mongrelization," because these children grow up expecting to marry within their adoptive parents' race. To speed the breakdown of the white family, drugs are peddled in the street, tolerance in the churches, relativism in the classrooms, smut in the movies, and liberalism in the "jewspapers."

Finally, a third policy is set in place to ensure that these two other strategies succeed. It renders the beleaguered white race defenseless in their homes and communities by a de facto revoking of the first two articles of the Bill of Rights. The IRS has disallowed the tax-free status of religious organizations that speak out on political issues. Invoking "political correctness" and "hate speech" statutes, the enemies of the Christian Identity movement have blocked their access to the media and have tried to enjoin them from peaceably assembling to air their grievances. If this were not enough, the ZOG has attempted to criminalize the possession of all firearms by patriotic whites, while it turns a blind eye toward the nonwhite criminal class.

For its followers, the Christian Identity ideology resolves the contradiction between a religious injunction of love and a social habit of hate. The doctrine that Jews are half-devils intent on using "mud races" to destroy God's chosen race gives believers permission, finally, to indulge their nativist hatred of outsiders. What for some had been a distressing internal conflict is now converted into a guilt-free external conflict—one of grandiose apocalyptic proportions. Once race and homeland unite and tribal instincts reawaken, hatred becomes a racial virtue, violence becomes a patriotic duty, and whites who dissent from these views become "race-traitors."

If the white race is the True Israel accountable to God's biblical laws, then white violators must be punished with biblical severity. The example of Phinehas (or Phineas) is often cited. Shortly before the end of their forty years of wandering in the wilderness, the Israelites sinned by marrying Moabite women and eating meat sacrificed to alien gods, and the Lord demanded that Moses have every offender's head cut off and hung in the sun. Just as Moses was announcing this sentence, an Israelite appeared, accompanied by a local woman. Instantly, Phinehas "took a javelin in his hand . . . and thrust both of them through, the man of Israel, and the woman through her belly," and God made Phinehas's lineage to be priests forever (Num. 25:1–13). Attackers of abortion-clinic workers and of gay, lesbian, and mixed-race couples have often justified their violence as inspired by the example of Phinehas and have also referred to Revelation 2:14 as a later warning against the offenses mentioned in Numbers. Contemporary right-wing terrorists who feel biblically commissioned claim that unless they punish biblically cited sins, God will engulf them in the wrath to come and exclude them, too, from his kingdom.[35]

It should be noted that not all racist cults claim to be Christian. Neo-Nazis and Nazi skinhead groups are strongly antireligious. Yet their dualistic end-of-history scenario and their secret codes clearly draw upon Judeo-Christian apocalyptic, despite their Ragnarok rhetoric.[36] Rev. Richard Butler of the Aryan Nations, for example, was professedly Christian. At least his church, high in the Bitterroot Range of northern Idaho, declared as much— "The Church of Jesus Christ Christian." Sequestered from the evil influences of the ZOG, yet wired to the world through the Internet, Butler proclaimed the tenets of his Christian Identity creed: "Aryan Nations is the ongoing work of Jesus the Christ regathering His people, calling His people to a state for their nation to bring His Kingdom! We hail His Victory!" Following this Christianized version of "Sieg Heil!" he summarized his elaboration of the Anglo-Israelite homeland myth, then went on to refer to the ultimate battle:

> WE BELIEVE that there is a battle being fought this day between the children of darkness (today known as the Jews) and the children of light (Yahweh, The Everliving God), the Aryan Race, the true Israel of the bible. Revelations 17:10–11
>
> WE BELIEVE that there is a day of reckoning. The usurper will be thrown out by the terrible might of Yahweh's people, as they return to their roots and their special destiny. We know there is soon to

be a day of judgment and a day when Christ's Kingdom (government) will be established on the earth, as it is in heaven.[37]

As a result of a case argued by Morris Dees of the Southern Poverty Law Center, Butler lost his twenty-acre compound in September 2001. It was awarded to plaintiffs whom several of his skinhead guards had shot outside the compound. The then eighty-year-old Butler was prevailed upon to retire from his leadership role in the Aryan Nations by the younger insurgents Harold "Ray" Redfeairn (who died in 2003) and August Kreiss.

Race *and* Grace: A Two-Homelands Mythology

Nostalgia, that yearning to return home and to recover there one's true identity, is a powerful human motive that is deeply resonant in the Christian faith. The expression of this spiritual yearning is often drawn from that portion of the Old Testament associated with the Babylonian captivity and the exiles' longing for their country, which is symbolized by Mount Zion, the ancient fortified hill of Jerusalem.[38]

> By the waters of Babylon, there we sat down, yea, we wept when we remembered Zion. (Ps. 137:1)

> For the Lord shall comfort Zion: he will comfort all her waste places; and he will make her wilderness like Eden, and her desert like the garden of the Lord. . . . Therefore the redeemed of the Lord shall return, and come with singing unto Zion. (Isa. 51:3, 11)

> They shall ask the way to Zion with their faces turned hitherward, saying, Come, and let us join ourselves to the Lord in a perpetual covenant that shall not be forgotten. . . . [Thus saith the Lord:] I will bring Israel again to his habitation. (Jer. 50:5, 19)

Moving words of consolation such as these were usually accompanied by prayers for vengeance. The tenderly stirring Psalm 137 begins "By the waters of Babylon" and goes on to ask, "How shall we sing the Lord's song in a strange land?" It ends with the words: "O daughter of Babylon, who art to be destroyed: happy shall he be, that rewardeth thee as thou hast served us. Happy shall he be, that taketh and dasheth thy little ones against the stones"

(8–9). And in Jeremiah: "I will render unto Babylon and to all the inhabitants of Chaldea all their evil that they have done in Zion in your sight, saith the Lord. . . . As Babylon hath caused the slain of Israel to fall, so at Babylon shall fall the slain of all the earth" (Jer. 51:24, 49).

According to the Old Testament, the management of the world is a zero-sum game. No blessings may be distributed to one people without curses laid upon another people, no happy homecoming for one without lamentations for another, and—at the final Day of the Lord—no heavenly bliss for some without eternal torment for the rest. Fifty passages celebrate the vengeful aspect of this Deity toward the enemies of Israel. Yet he also brings suffering to his own people. In fact, he executes vengeance on their enemies *only* after he has made sure that his people have themselves been devastated by misfortune and lost all hope in their own power to defend themselves. Only then can they enter their promised homeland under a Joshua—or, under a Zerubbabel, return to it from Babylonian exile.

But now, thousands of years later, what of the original "People of the Book," the Jews? And what of the literal land of Israel? Christians have generally assumed that both Testaments of the Bible were ultimately written for *them* to read and understand. Having become the inheritors of biblical Israel, all the promises and threats God made to the patriarchs of old, when properly construed, have been transferred to them. According to "replacement theology," the divine homeland, the longed-for Zion—whether it is an earthly thousand-year kingdom or a timeless heavenly one—awaits the Christian faithful once "Babylon the great is fallen, is fallen, and is become the habitation of devils, and the hold of every foul spirit, and a cage of every unclean and hateful bird," as John ecstatically foretells (Rev. 18:2). For centuries theologians taught that the Jews had been cursed for rejecting Jesus and that their dispersion after the Romans destroyed the Second Temple was clear testimony of divine disfavor. When asked, "Does God still have a special regard for the Jews?" the traditional answer, for nearly two thousand years, was a simple "No."[39] Most Christians in the past, therefore, paid little attention to the role of the Jews in the cosmic finale.

Yet another view did persist. This tradition, which held that the Jews would convert to Christianity during the end times, was apparently first spread by the fourth-century Tibertine Oracle, one of the rambling poems known as the Sibylline Oracles. Through the Middle Ages this belief coexisted with others, e.g., that the Jews had crucified Jesus and that the Antichrist would be a Jew.[40] Pope Paul IV set up the Roman ghetto in 1555 expressly to proselytize Italian Jews, and by the end of that century, in a rare instance of agreement with the figure they themselves called the Antichrist, English Puritans declared that, yes, the restoration of the Jews to the Holy Land would be a necessary precondition for the Second Coming. Having seen in the Old Testament a theocratic system that they deemed a still-valid political model for themselves, some of them took their literalist logic one step further and interpreted the Old Testament prophecies of the restoration of Israel as still awaiting fulfillment. In New England, Increase Mather felt persuaded enough to write *The Mystery of Israel: Salvation Explained and Applyed* (1669).

The dispensational system, which has become a prominent part of premillennialist theology—a new foundation of fundamentalism—has much to say on the role of Jews in the end times. As John Nelson Darby and his American follower, Cyrus Scofield, saw it, the Church Age was a "great parenthesis," a pause of indefinite duration in God's providential design to reestablish the royal line of David and initiate the seventh and last dispensation, the messianic kingdom. What this meant was that the racially identified descendants of Abraham, Isaac, and Jacob, the Israelites, would someday enjoy the earthly kingdom they had already been promised.

According to this interpretation, Israel under Moses had entered into a covenant with God (Deut. 29–30), the "Palestinian Covenant," according to which their lease on the land of Canaan bound them through a regimen of blessings and curses to comport themselves as a "peculiar people" in the eyes of God. Though they later failed to uphold their obligations and caused God to scatter them among the nations, God would someday fulfill his promise. Reasoning from these legalistic principles, Darby devised a doctrine new to Christian eschatology: God had reserved *two* homelands for humanity. One would be the heavenly Zion to which only born-again Christians would be admitted by virtue of the grace Christ won during his First Coming. The other would be a thousand-year kingdom ruled over by the returned Christ, an *earthly* Zion to which only Jews would be admitted by virtue of their race. The Millennium would thus be a period in which the glorious promises of God to Abraham, Isaac, Jacob, Moses, and the later prophets would all be fulfilled. God's original chosen people would effectively rule the world from within their reestablished *just* kingdom, while the adopted children of God, born-again Christians, would be assumed into the *transcendent* kingdom of heaven.

But not all Jews would qualify to enjoy the earthly homeland. Cyrus Scofield filled in the details: for one thing, their dispersion would continue, pending their future repentance and the return of the Lord. Then would follow their restoration to the land, national conversion, judgment upon

Israel's oppressors, and finally national prosperity during the seventh dispensation, the Kingdom Age (the Millennium).[41] When he subsequently refers to these events in his explanatory notes, Scofield sometimes varies this order. In some instances, he says that the Jews will not repent and convert before returning to their biblical homeland. Because he was aware that Theodor Herzl had already begun organizing the Zionist movement (in 1897, twelve years before his annotated Bible appeared), Scofield must have realized that "unrepentant" Jews were most likely to arrive first in the biblical homeland. There is only one biblical answer for obduracy, of course, and Scofield knew exactly what that was. During the great worldwide tribulation, prior to the return of Christ, the "vortex" of violence will be "Jerusalem and the Holy Land," and this "involves the people of God who will have returned to Palestine in unbelief."[42] These unconverted Jews will have apparently found themselves in the right place at the wrong time—and with their papers not quite in order. Before Jerusalem becomes the world capital of the Kingdom Age, two-thirds of all regathered Israel will have to be killed.[43]

Only one-third of the population—the remnant—will survive to be converted to Christianity and reconciled to God in the person of the returning Messiah. "Jehovah will give Israel up," says Scofield, "till the believing remnant appears . . . and afterward the remnant [will] go as missionaries to Israel and to all the world."[44] This remnant he identifies as the 144,000 "sealed" Elect of Revelation 7:1–8. The strenuous ingenuity of Scofield and his followers has delineated the final fate of Jewry as follows. Most of the world's Jews will return to their ancient Promised Land, which of course will have to be enlarged to an area stretching from the Nile to the Euphrates, the dimensions promised to Abraham in Genesis 15:18. A third temple will have to be built on Mount Moriah. The old sacrifices will have to be reinstituted. A great war will then have to ensue in which God will punish both their oppressors and those among them who stubbornly refuse conversion. The one-third who accept Jesus will then go forth during the final months of the tribulation and preach the gospel to the few Jews remaining in the diaspora and to the unraptured multitude, who are given one last chance to be saved.

This final interpretation has been controversial, because other apocalyptic sects have preferred to imagine their own members as this army of saints. But staunch dispensationalists have maintained that at this point in the end times, the Jews reenter God's cosmic drama as major players. The immensely popular explainer of prophecy, Hal Lindsey, made this clear in 1973: "The fact that God redeems 144,000 literal Jews and ordains them His evangelists not only makes good sense but fits in with the counsel of God. . . .

So I say loud and clear: the 144,000 described here are not Jehovah Witnesses, or Mormon elders, or some symbol of the Church; they are Jews, Jews, Jews!"[45] And in 1997 he challenged his readers to visualize those "144,000 Hebrew Billy Grahams running around the world."[46]

Israelis have understandably mixed responses to the solid support that American dispensationalists such as Hal Lindsey, Jerry Falwell, and Pat Robertson pledge to Israel. Many question the agenda of those self-professed Christian Zionists who claim their love for Israel while asserting their belief that the Antichrist is a Jew or that Jews have a "stranglehold" on American culture. The latter assessment was that of no less a premillennialist than Billy Graham conferring with then President Richard Nixon in 1972. In this Oval Office tape, Graham went on to confide: "A lot of Jews are great friends of mine. They swarm around me, because they know I am friendly to Israel and so forth. But they don't know how I really feel about what they're doing to this country, and I have no power and no way to handle them."[47]

Israelis understand that their geopolitical situation is precarious. On the one hand, the religious Right in America has helped shape American foreign policy toward the Middle East by supporting pro-Israel candidates for the Congress and the presidency. On the other hand, this support has backed policies that have exacerbated conditions in Israel and the Occupied Territories.

Why, some have asked, if almighty God has determined the future, do American premillennialists need to have their own foreign policy? Why have some of them established an "embassy" in Jerusalem?[48] Why have they criticized those American leaders who, over several decades, have tried to arbitrate the Palestinian-Israeli conflict? One answer appears in Scofield's extended note to Genesis 15:18: "It has invariably fared ill with the people who have persecuted the Jew—well with those who have protected him. The future will still more remarkably prove this principle."[49] Dispensationalists no longer interpret "the Jew" in this passage as anyone who practices or identifies with Judaism, but as the state of Israel, and "people" as other nation-states. Therefore, it follows that America's "homeland security" is inextricably linked to that of Israel.

There is, however, another reason for their political activism. God's "timetable" may be a fixed sequence of events, but its tempo appears to be variable. For nearly two thousand years, during the great parenthesis of the Church Age, the "prophetic time-clock" has either ticked irregularly or stopped altogether. As Lindsey says, it "stalls" and then it "accelerates."[50] According to him, the "prophetic countdown" is always subject to stops and starts linked to human actions. When Satan inspires secular leaders to make peace, the clock slows down or even stops, but when God inspires true believers to work for the coming kingdom, the clock starts ticking again. This elastic clause saves his end-time doctrine from the fate of the nineteenth-century Millerites who attempted to specify the exact day of the Second Coming. Premillennialists' apocalyptic timing cannot be proven wrong, because when the going gets apocalyptic, the apocalyptic get going—the tribulation cannot begin until they rise in the Rapture and vanish to join Jesus in the sky. Only after they have safely exited will the precise and now unstoppable countdown to Armageddon begin.

Neither Christian nor Jew can hope to enter their separately designated homelands, however, if Israel makes peace with its neighbors. As Lindsey wrote, Israel is the "fuse of Armageddon."[51] Dispensational premillennialists have a programmatic foreign policy. The Jews *must* be assembled in Israel and remain surrounded by hostile nations. Their settlements *must* proliferate in the West Bank. Palestinians *must* be told that they have no rights to even an inch of biblical Israel. The fuse *must* smolder.

Especially since September 11, 2001, Christian Right leaders have seemed to make a special effort to characterize Islam as a benighted faith. When the former president of the Southern Baptist Convention, Jerry Vines, addressed the convention in St. Louis on June 10, 2002, he declared that "Islam was founded by Muhammad, a demon-possessed pedophile who had twelve wives—and his last one was a nine-year-old girl." Later that week, when Jerry Falwell was asked by interviewers on CNN's *Crossfire* to comment on this allegation, he responded: "I do know Dr. Vines very well as a humble man of God, a preacher of the Gospel for many years. And I didn't believe, when I was listening to him, that he was attacking Islam or Muslim people." Falwell added that "Muhammad, in fact, was guilty of massacring many, many thousands of Jews," and as for his private life, "I think pedophilia is not taking it beyond the limits of reality."[52] Having reconsidered the matter over the summer, Falwell announced on September 30, 2002, that Muhammad was apparently not only a pedophile but also a "terrorist." When he announced this on CBS's *60 Minutes,* he ignited even greater rage throughout Islamic countries, sparking violence between Muslims and Hindu nationalists in which nearly one hundred persons were injured and nine Muslims killed. Twelve days later, he expressed regret that his statements "were hurtful to the feelings of many Muslims. . . . I intended no disrespect to any sincere, law-abiding Muslim." He added: "I simply said what I do believe, that Muhammad is not a good example for most Muslim people."[53]

The reason Muslims take the words of preachers like Falwell and Robertson so seriously is that they understand that these men represent one of the base constituencies of the Republican Party. Furthermore, they believe, rightly or wrongly, that such men have access to President Bush. These anxieties, which are shared by many Europeans and Israelis as well, are hardly allayed when they read reports that quote the President as saying, "My administration has been calling upon all the leaders, in the—in the Middle East to do everything they can to stop the violence, to tell the different parties involved that peace will never happen"; "There needs to be a focused, coalition effort in the region against peace—I mean, against terror for peace"; and "You know, one of the hardest parts of my job is to connect Iraq to the war on terror."[54]

Kingdom Now!

An earthly homeland is a place in which the ethical values of the community, customarily voiced by religious leaders, are reconciled with the pragmatic workings of government. A secular regime that is in perfect conformity with a religious system and is envisioned as the *good kingdom* is one in which church and state are harmonized, *home* and *land* united in one nation under God, indivisible. When home and land are thus compounded and the nation "speaks with one voice," this voice of the people becomes indeed the voice of God. Such a divinely favored nation is consequently invincible. For "if God be for us, who can be against us?" (Rom. 8:31).

As the history of intentional communities testifies, however, this harmony is hard to sustain as the population grows in size from settlement to village to town—and proves impossible if it ever expands to the size of a sovereign nation. It is all a matter of scale. The voluntary goodwill and cheerful unanimity of the small community is reinforced by the fear of shame. Where people know one another's business and gossip circulates quickly, honesty is always the best policy, because it is always the only policy that can work. But when the population grows too large for peer oversight, security guards must be hired, and then police.

I have been arguing that no true unanimity of the communal and the governmental is attainable. Any attempt to construct it must end with a marriage of convenience, an unequal yoking, a sham consensus in which one level dictates the terms of the merger to the other. We are most familiar with the efforts of secular leaders to create civil-religious institutions by which to attribute to themselves and their policies the traditional ethics of the community. We have yet to examine a movement that, claiming to represent the community, seeks to dictate terms to the government in order to have its particular ethical agenda enforced by physical coercion. This presents a special problem, for, if the communal ideal is not modified by laws that allow for a margin of diversity in thought and private behavior, the communalized government is obliged to institute such measures as secret police, networks of informers, morality squads, show trials, humiliations, and public executions.

Religion has always expressed the ideals of the community through regulating the relationships of family members, proposing penalties here and hereafter for transgressive behavior, and fostering solidarity by extolling the altruistic examples of heroes, martyrs, and saints. But as the guardian of communal traditions, no single religion, I think it is fair to say, can abide a tolerance among its members for beliefs other than its own. Therefore, whenever a single religion attempts to impose its model upon a nation, it must promote itself as the only true voice of the communal level—of the heartland, the grassroots, the moral (or silent) majority, the salt of the earth, the "People." Any governmental regime that tolerates other beliefs disunites the sacral homeland and calls down God's wrath upon the nation.

This was the judgment that the televangelists Jerry Falwell and Pat Robertson issued on September 13, 2001, when they discussed the significance of the al Qaeda attack on New York City and Washington, D.C. Appearing on the Christian Broadcasting Network's *700 Club,* hosted by Robertson, Falwell said: "God continues to lift the curtain and allow the enemies of America to give us probably what we deserve." "Jerry, that's my feeling," Robertson replied. "I think we've just seen the antechamber of terror." Falwell then detailed his indictment:

> The abortionists have got to bear some burden for this because God will not be mocked. And when we destroy 40 million little innocent babies, we make God mad. I really believe that the pagans, and the abortionists, and the feminists, and the gays and the lesbians who are actively trying to make that an alternative lifestyle, the ACLU, People for the American Way—all of them who have tried to secularize America—I point the finger in their face and say, "You helped this happen."[55]

Interviewed the next day, Falwell restated his biblical position that America's "secular and anti-Christian environment left us open to our Lord's [decision] not to protect." In effect, God permitted the nineteen terrorists to succeed in order to chastise a stiff-necked and insufficiently Christian people. The lifting of a curtain, the antechamber of terror—such phrases might imply the cosmic showdown, the end of the world that premillennialists pray for. But in the context of 9/11, Falwell and Robertson suggested that this event might be the first in a series of divine chastisements directed at God's chosen nation, America, because its government has tolerated persons whose conduct is offensive to God. They implied that America must now purge itself of these offenders before God punishes it again.

A theocratic homeland, one in which the secular government is empowered to execute the ethos of one religious community, would finally be able to eliminate all those persons whose behavior offends God and provokes him to chastise his chosen people. The Bible tells us that he corrects his nation by removing his protective shield, thus making it vulnerable not only to its human enemies but also to the destructive forces of nature. The latter, traditionally known as acts of God, play a special role in American homeland mythology: when a natural disaster happens, it may be interpreted as collective punishment for a failure to weed out persons and groups who incite God's wrath. In a number of pronouncements, Pat Robertson has applied this Late Bronze Age theodicy to explain natural, as well as manmade, catastrophes. In 1998 he warned that God would devastate Orlando, Florida, for allowing Disney World to lease space for the "Gay Days" celebration and for flying rainbow flags from its light poles.[56]

As we have seen, biblical master narratives are politically useful when they put the fear of God into significant sectors of the population and persuade them that a particular course of action is divinely commanded. Waiting for the Rapture does not mobilize voters. From a political activist's point of view, the fear of God is desirable only when it can be channeled into a reflex of fight, not of flight. Unfortunately, the kinds of fight that the fear of God seems most often to instigate are scapegoating, intimidation of dissidents, and other campaigns of hatred in the name of holiness. Posttrib scenarios allow some evangelical Christians, like Robertson, to savor the prospect of a score-settling holy war at the end of history, but for others, a seven-year struggle followed by the Rapture is just not enough. Those who feel drawn to a really muscular Christianity hold that the only godly agenda is an ongoing postmillennialist Christian crusade for world domination.

One such agenda was formulated by Rousas John Rushdoony (1916–2001). The son of Armenian refugees from the Turkish genocide, he saw a need for Christians to consolidate political power. His system, which he called

Dominion Theology, shifted emphasis from the conversion of individual souls to the conversion of social institutions. Though it was rooted in conservative Presbyterianism, he offered its ideas to Christians of all denominations. Under the banner of "Christian Reconstruction," it first attracted sympathizers less for what it stood for than for what it stood against. All those troubled by the social upheavals of the 1960s and 1970s, the perceived breakdowns in racial arrangements, in sexual mores, in respect for parents, in patriotism, and in church attendance, were invited to join this movement regardless of whether they adhered to—or even knew—the creedal principles of its leadership.

Coming out of the older Calvinist/Reformed branch of Protestantism, rather than American Evangelicalism, Dominionism rejects premillennialist and dispensationalist expectations for the future. All the events portrayed in Revelation's first nineteen chapters were already completed by 70 AD, when Jerusalem was destroyed. Those living in the end times will see no horned beasts, no war in heaven, no Antichrist, no tribulation, no Armageddon. Staunchly postmillennialist, it calls Christians to reconstruct American society from the bottom up in preparation for Jesus's physical descent at the end of the world, when, instead of the Rapture, a worldwide revival will occur that will climax in the Last Judgment. Dominionism's reading of the biblical past is covenantal. Rather than a series of dispensations, or renegotiated contracts, there is but one body of law by which humans may be sanctified: the Law of Moses. This Law constitutes the one everlasting covenant between God and his people. When Jesus said that he had come to fulfill the Law (Matt. 5:17), he meant to restore it, not to supplant it, and, except for the ceremonial laws that Jesus abrogated, all its civil and moral commandments had remained in effect. The Old Israel, when it failed to recognize the divinity of Jesus, had been replaced by the New Israel, the Christian Church, the institution for which God in his Providence had always intended his Law. Unconverted Jews, no longer true Israelites, remain in enmity with God. Their practice of the Law can therefore never justify them in God's eyes or give them any role in the end-time drama.[57]

The rallying cry of "Kingdom Now" actually sums up Dominionism. The Dominionists' reasoning goes as follows: once Jesus rose from the dead, the dominion of Satan, begun with the Fall of Adam, was legally terminated and the world became the kingdom of God. Thereafter, the work of Christians became twofold: to spread this good news to unbelievers and to persuade themselves to act now as rulers of the world with Christ. The first task has always been easier than the second. Obviously, too many soft-minded

American Christians have still been turning the other cheek, forgiving their enemies, acting as peacemakers, and cultivating all those other beatitudinous virtues instead of seizing dominion—first over themselves, then their families, then their churches and civil institutions, then their homeland, and, finally, the entire world.

Though Dominionists profess to wrestle mainly with satanic principalities and the rulers of darkness, they also target flesh and blood. They do so by engaging in "imprecatory prayer," petitioning God to strike down their opponents with illness and death. For them this is an act of faith, for if they believe that the realization of Christ's kingdom on earth is God's will, then God should cast aside anyone who stands in its way. Not surprisingly, they vehemently oppose "hate speech" and "hate crimes" legislation. This prayerful holy war must be unrelenting, for Satan, though weakened, remains still active in his secular humanist agents. Therefore, as the Dominionists like to say, "The Kingdom is now, but not yet."

The plan that they have in mind for us they call Theonomy ("God's Law," *theos* + *nomos*). Rushdoony formulated this legal system in his more-than-800-page *Institutes of Biblical Law* (1973). This system, they maintain, was the original basis of American civil and criminal law and therefore supersedes the Constitution and all subsequent case law. The terms that Dominionists and their Christian conservative allies use to characterize their legislative agenda, e.g., "reconstruction," "restoration," and "reform," imply their wish to return to a status quo ante, an original Christian Americanism.[58]

Dominionists plan to reform criminal law by returning to the Mosaic commandments. Capital punishment would be extended beyond rape, kidnapping, murder, and treason to fornication, adultery, incest, homosexuality, abortion, witchcraft, astrology, heresy, apostasy, blasphemy, and Sabbath-breaking. The general criminalization of dissidents and "antinomians" would be based on the notion that disbelief in "The Kingdom" would be treason and, as such, a capital offense. Even children should sometimes be executed. The relevant passage is Deuteronomy 21:18–21: "If a man have a stubborn and rebellious son" who scorns reproof, his parents must denounce him to the elders, who will then have him stoned to death—"so shalt thou put evil away from among you; and all Israel shall hear, and fear." In crisp, modern, theonomic legalese, this reads: "Parents would be required to bring their incorrigible children before the judge and, if convicted, have them stoned to death."[59] For lesser crimes, such as thievery and disobedience, floggings might suffice. Most unhappy marriages would be dissolved—not by divorce, but by the execution of the wayward partner, thus permitting the righteous spouse to remarry. The prison system as it now exists would be abolished. Those convicted of noncapital crimes would instead be sentenced to seven years of slavery, during which they would recompense those whom they had offended.

Dominionists and allied conservative Christians are careful in their use of the word "theocracy." It tends to scare away Americans who still take pride in their independent spirit and libertarian privileges. It also brings to mind Islamic sharia law. Dominionists insist that the America they want is not a government by clergy, and they profess to uphold the separation of church and state. Their aim, however, is to Christianize the state and ultimately relegate its function to national defense and law enforcement, i.e., theonomy enforcement. Education and all other social programs would be run by the Church—*their* Church, the body of believers to whom Christ has granted earthly dominion.

Education has always been a primary concern for this movement. Rousas John Rushdoony regarded public education as a threat to parental (that is, paternal) authority and strongly supported homeschooling. But, in order to advance the kingdom, Dominionists encourage their sympathizers to undermine the public school system as well as other traditional American civic institutions from within. The following piece of advice was written by Rev. P. Andrew Sandlin, executive vice president of the Chalcedon Foundation:

> Infiltration. We need people to infiltrate institutions presently under the control of the Devil. We could start with the public schools. Of course, except in unusual cases, we should not send our own children to public schools; but courageous, Resistance-minded Christian educators need to secure posts in all levels of public education and reclaim their area for Christ. Obviously, while under the present humanistic yoke, they may have to operate covertly for a while. They may not be able to proclaim the Crown Rights of Jesus Christ. They should quietly subvert the humanistic system, however, by providing "acceptable alternatives" (red-blooded Biblical Faith). If they become a little too bold and incite the ire of the humanistic administration or school board, they should cry, "Violation of academic freedom!" in tones appropriate to the cry of "bloody murder!"[60]

The spirit that such advice reveals is unashamedly results-oriented, the end justifying the means. Furtive tactics of this sort call into question the claims by the Dominionists that they support the Constitution and the separation of church and state.

A notable aspect of this movement is its nostalgic identification with certain theocratic regimes of the past—particularly with John Calvin's Commonwealth of Geneva in the sixteenth century as well as, in the seventeenth century, with Cromwell's England and, most important, Puritan Massachusetts Bay. In his online publication *The Puritan Storm,* Rev. Jeff Ziegler says that his goal is "to use The Puritan Storm as a tool in the conversion of the American church from a slumbering, pietistic, wrecked vessel into a fully articulated Puritan fighting machine that will establish Christ as the Lord of this nation." In his article "Puritan Storm Rising," Ziegler predicts a "fuller acceptance of reconstructionism [Christian Reconstruction] across the parched domain of American Evangelicalism." He also foresees the "rise of a 'generalized' Puritan worldview," adding that the "'revival prayer movement' has 'wet [*sic*] the appetite' of many sincere saints who long for a 'golden age' of strapping Christianity."[61] However we interpret a "strapping Christianity," the phrase does indeed bring to mind the whipping posts of John Endicott and the Mather dynasty.

7

SECULAR MODERNISM, BIBLICAL STYLE

As I noted in my preface, the concept of master narrative was introduced by Jean-François Lyotard in 1979 with *The Postmodern Condition: A Report on Knowledge*. His two modernist master narratives, or "metanarratives," were scientific objectivity (the "speculative narrative") and social progress (the "emancipative narrative"). These were the founding principles, he said, of a cultural consensus that began to take shape in the seventeenth century and defined itself fully in the Enlightenment of the late eighteenth and early nineteenth centuries.

"Modernist master narrative" is a paradoxical phrase, because modernism was ideologically opposed to narrative explanations of either human or nonhuman phenomena, preferring instead to induce "natural laws" from verifiable and quantifiable data. Modernist principles of objective inquiry and human rights were themes that did, however, find expression in countless narratives read in books and journals, heard in popular oratory, and spread through such casual phrases as "It's only natural," "You can't stand in the way of progress," and "Everyone has a right to his own opinion." These principles—upon which actual narratives were constructed—were the tacit conclusions that hearers and readers felt that *they themselves* were deriving from these stories. If, as Voltaire said, "men use thought only to justify their misdeeds, and employ speech only to conceal their thoughts," then narrative is speech raised to an even higher level of deception, one at which speakers conceal the concealment of their thoughts by making them seem the thoughts of their audience.

By referring so broadly to "modernism," Lyotard evidently alluded to the old historical division between Antiquity, the Middle Ages, and the Modern

Era. Modernity therefore represented the repudiation not only of superstition and feudalism but also of those ethnic myths that seemed the legacy of that benighted past. He strove to reveal how bourgeois elites had encouraged science in order to enrich themselves on modern technology and had freed the rural poor in order to employ them in their urban factories. All this they had accomplished by using the demystifying narratives of modernism to re-mystify their control over the masses.

As the preceding six chapters would suggest, I find that applying Lyotard's model to American cultural history is problematic. I have instead proposed that the American master narratives, being biblical at base, are not modern at all but rather late medieval. If we characterize medieval culture as oral, narrative, land-rooted, and governed by a system of inheritable privilege, and modern culture as literate, analytic, cosmopolitan, and governed by an ideal of universal reason, we will recognize in America the significant continuance of that earlier culture. The postmodernist project that Lyotard defined as an incredulity toward modernist metanarratives makes more sense in a culture that has uncritically absorbed Enlightenment principles—in "Old Europe," as former U.S. Secretary of Defense Donald Rumsfeld once called it. But for most of the rest of the world, including eastern Europe, Asia, Muslim nations, and America, there is far more need for a modernist critique of premodern medievalism than for a postmodernist critique of a modernism that has as yet only shallowly taken root.

That the three-centuries-old conflict between biblical religion and Enlightenment science is by now a cultural cliché should not blind us to its historical and ongoing consequences. Most Americans, for example, accept the notion that the earth is billions of years old and that all life forms have evolved over time, yet most of them also believe that the same person who appears as the central character of the Bible created the earth and the entire universe for one purpose—to house the tiny family of man, or some even tinier group that calls itself a chosen people. And most Americans, it is also safe to say, do not look forward in Wigglesworthian glee to the incineration of the planet. Yet, according to polls, most profess to believe in the biblically described return of Jesus. Cognitive dissonances of truly cosmic proportions, it would seem, beset the collective American psyche.

I proposed earlier that narrative is the "talking cure" we humans have always resorted to when troubled by our contradictory beliefs. Whenever narrative is used to solve a societal problem, Lyotard maintains, it is customary for "such a question to solicit the name of a hero as its response: *Who* has the right to decide for society? Who is the subject whose prescriptions are norms for those they obligate?"[1] With that thought in mind, I will be looking for heroes, but not in the modernist avant-garde (where Lyotard sought them). I will be looking for them in the shadowy space between medieval and modern, between biblical authority and natural science, the space in which narrative is used to mitigate the distress of a cognitive dissonance of broad cultural significance.

In this final chapter, I will start with a reexamination of Lyotard's two modernist master narratives: first his "speculative narrative," focusing on the narrative of nature, and then his "emanicipative narrative," which I will split into the narrative of progress and the narrative of freedom. I will then propose a fourth narrative—that of judgment. For each of these I will nominate a hero, a character who has assumed "the right to decide for society" within the narratives that each metanarrative theme generates. These heroes will be persons willing to risk themselves by standing out from their communities and attracting the attention of the governmental elite. As I outline these modernist narratives, I will indicate how the concept of the American homeland that first emerged into the bracing dawn air of the Enlightenment was constructed, myth by myth, upon the deep foundation of medieval faith. Beneath the surface of secular modernism, the biblical master narrators have continued to ghostwrite the stories America tells itself.

The Narrative of Nature

When the Church reluctantly accepted Revelation into its biblical canon, it no doubt breathed a sigh of relief to announce that at least the age of prophecy had finally ended. Divinely inspired, John had cursed anyone who would add or remove any words from the "book of this prophecy" (Rev. 22:18–19). Humans were no longer called to be the spokesmen of God but henceforth only his witnesses. Hereafter, anyone who asserted that the Holy Spirit had inspired him or her to write an additional account of those realms and times veiled to human eyes would be declared anathema. Only the devil could inspire such a project.

The general rule that God had revealed the future only to the writers of the Bible had, according to tradition, only two exceptions: the gentile prophetesses, the Sibyls, and the gentile poet, Vergil.[2] But with the recovery of Greek literary texts in the fifteenth century came the Platonic notion (in the *Ion*) that all true poets are subject to divinely induced mantic fits, a notion that clothed them in the mantle of prophecy, at least among the learned.

For their own part, poets were eager to promote *furor poeticus,* recognizing all too well that if the license of sacred madness that had long protected the court fool were now extended to them, it would excuse whatever moral and doctrinal lapses might appear in their writings.

The dark-garbed magistrates of New England, however, would have nothing to do with inspired ravings of any sort. They were certainly not about to issue poetic licenses. For them, Wigglesworth had sprinkled into useful doctrine just the right amount of poetic sweetness for any righteous reader's palate. The soul God breathed into every child of Adam was a frail and wavering flame fed by no inborn pentecostal tongue of fire. He had not, certainly not, endowed any of them with a *genius,* that pagan *daimonion* that eighteenth-century bellelettrists would soon be claiming for themselves.

The similarities between poets and prophets were asserted from a different angle when, in 1753, Bishop Robert Lowth pointed out the poetic patterns of Hebrew verses. Timothy Dwight endorsed this view of biblical "literature" in 1772 by asking why his countrymen should "remain blind to Eloquence more elegant than *Cicero,* more grand than *Demosthenes;* or to Poetry more correct and tender than *Virgil.*"[3] As the distinctions between the two writing traditions gradually narrowed in the late eighteenth century, many began to suspect that, if the prophets wrote poetry, then it might indeed be possible for poets to write prophecy. If so, the age of prophecy had not at all concluded when John of Patmos penned his final *amen,* to which his Protestant translators centuries later appended their own emphatic "THE END."

One poet who not only claimed the role of poet-prophet but also strove to rewrite the Book of Revelation was William Blake. From all accounts capable of eidetic imagery, Blake could look outward and see mental images projected into space. He inferred that this power of "spiritual sensation," which he simply called "Imagination," had enabled the prophets of the Bible to see angels, devils, and God himself.[4] Were it not for our "finite organical perceptions," we all would always behold the infinite universe of spiritual beings. Blake liked to repeat the prayer of Moses: "would God that all the LORD's people were prophets, and that the LORD would put his spirit upon them" (Num. 12:29). Should we be able to cleanse the doors of perception, all of us, not only small children and visionary poets, would behold the spirit realm.

Few of the new British and American poets of the late eighteenth and early nineteenth centuries, however, claimed to have experienced full-blown waking visions or to have heard unearthly voices. They were confined to the outer world as it appears to the "organical perceptions," but they offset these

perceptions with inner states—moods, remembered feelings, intuitions—
in short, with aroused responses to what seemed to be messages encrypted
in natural phenomena. They never saw what others could not see, but they
sometimes felt what others had not yet learned to feel.

The poets of antebellum America were largely unaware of Blake, except
as an eccentric London engraver who wrote children's verse. The Romantic
poet that made the earliest and most lasting impression on them was William
Wordsworth, the master who strove to harmonize the inner with the outer
eye. America was, for these poets, their very own Lake Country—a text no
less readable than Wordsworth's, only writ exceedingly large. Here "Nature"
revealed herself as an alternative scripture open to all humanity, as fresh as
the day the Creator composed it. As John Locke had said, "In the beginning all the world was America."[5] Unlike the text of the Bible, which was a
series of miraculous interventions and dialogic responses to human asser-
tions of self-will, the text of nature was the result of the originating miracle.
This was the reality that, in response to God's command, had assembled itself
out of nothingness and had ever since remained the Creator's one, complete,
unedited testament.

Could it really be the Creator's intention to destroy this book? Even if it
was, even if these were the prophesied end times, was not God continuously
holding this text open for all to see, for all to study? The new science—from
Bacon through Newton and then beyond to the natural philosophers of the
eighteenth and nineteenth centuries—had placed its faith not only in the
stability of the Creation but also in its sacredness as the mirror of its Creator's mind. It was one of the great paradoxes of Western history that, thanks
to movable type and the spread of literacy, the rise of natural science had
coincided in the late sixteenth and early seventeenth centuries with the revival
of apocalypticism.

Here was a deep cultural rift: on the one hand, a medieval world animated by spiritual messengers, and on the other, a modern world governed
by physical laws. Here was a cognitive dissonance that the poet, as hero of
the nature narrative, had come to harmonize. Religion would somehow have
to accept that divine revelation had not stopped when John laid down his
pen; science, for its part, would have to share with poets the interpretation
of the natural world.

Neither of these two clashing orthodoxies could be happy with such a
compromise. No consistent belief system can tolerate a picking and choosing
among its first principles. Accommodation with positive science smacked of
the damnable position of the Church of Laodicea, which, being "lukewarm,

and neither cold nor hot," Jesus would soon spew out of his mouth (Rev. 3:16). To scientific materialists, on the other hand, any mixture of faith and fact was a soft-minded, wishful idealism. But for those who could neither turn their backs on Christianity nor renounce the advantages of modern science, the construction of an overarching cosmic mythology offered the only hope of relief. The resultant compromise, we should keep in mind, was a piece of wishful thinking, a dream that comes true only in the sense that any cultural construction ever "comes true." Formulated in such terms as "poetic inspiration" and "communion with nature," this construction soon revealed itself to be both spurious and serviceable, the two essential qualities of every genuine cultural cliché.

Wordsworth may have popularized the concept of wordless "communing," but a teenager from the hills of western Massachusetts was the first to bring this home to Americans. William Cullen Bryant's "Thanatopsis," first published in 1817 in the *North American Review,* memorably began: "To him who in the love of Nature holds / Communion with her visible forms, she speaks / A various language." The verb "commune" already meant to confer intently among unanimous parties. Nature and her lover, therefore, agree with one another, but what is the language they speak? Bryant explains, "for his gayer hours / She has a voice of gladness, and a smile / And eloquence of beauty, and she glides / Into his darker musings, with a mild / And gentle sympathy" (lines 3–7). She matches *his* every mood, apparently, with what he interprets as *her* own mood through the indexical gestures of her visible forms.

But Bryant was not satisfied with a broadly Wordsworthian consolation. Nature must teach, but more than that, she must have a voice equivalent to the very voice of God. Out of "all around— / Earth and her waters, and the depth of air,— / Comes a still voice" (lines 15–17), Bryant writes, with a pointed appropriation of that moment when Elijah, having fled from the wrath of King Ahab, found himself in a cave on Mount Horeb, where he hoped to commune with God. The Almighty announced his approach by a storm wind, an earthquake, and a fire, but he was not *in* these phenomena. Unlike Elijah's Lord, who revealed himself in a "still small voice," Bryant's divine Lady *is* the perceivable forms of this world. Moreover, her theophany is not a display of destructive power but is as quiet as her voice. Her message, too, which occupies the body of Bryant's poem, is not a death sentence on Ahab-like sinners but a view of death without the prospect of a judgment. Like all living beings, humans must die, but no divine retribution awaits them beyond the grave.

This natural state, which Rousseau, Marx, and Nietzsche in their very different ways posited as the guiltless, uncorrupted condition of primitive humanity, the Bible describes as the state of Adam before he sinned. Using the utopian myths available to them, Americans in the optimistic years following the War of 1812 began to visualize their virginal landscape both as the original paradise and as the ultimate peaceable kingdom, ignoring, in effect, the history between the expulsion of Adam and the Second Coming. The "howling wilderness" of the Puritans had now become the "plantations of God," as Ralph Waldo Emerson put it, and the dark wood, which had long been an allegorical setting for human perplexity, became instead a refuge from it.[6] A year or so later, with a respectful nod to his Calvinist heritage, the young Bryant also wrote: "The primal curse / Fell, it is true, upon the unsinning earth, / But not in vengeance." And so the denizens of this guiltless nature are forever gladsome: the birds "sing and sport / In wantonness of spirit; while below / The squirrel, with raised paws and form erect / Chirps merrily."[7] Insects, flowers, rocks, rivulet, and wind exhibit a manic seductiveness toward the wayfarer that recalls the animism of Faerie while anticipating the animation of Disney, but to Bryant and his hopeful generation, this is merely the way paradisiacal beings behave.[8]

Ever youthful (not the aging matron that seventeenth-century divines had pictured), Nature is either infused with the immanent spirit of God or at least inscribed by him with his intended meanings. All wild things are innocent and joyous, as are those peoples who dwell among them. The internal sense we use to commune wordlessly with nature is the same as, or similar to, the "moral sense," that innate faculty that induces all humans to recognize "natural law" as superior to the statutes of magistrates. The laws of nature, as the Enlightenment read them, constitute the cosmic government of God. No human government that tries to supersede them or suborn its people to violate them can long survive. Evil is an "unnatural" tendency, an idolatrous turning from God's creations to man's artifices. To those who saw themselves as citizens of the world, nature was the universal human homeland.

If what surrounds us is, in principle, the same universe that God created *in principio,* its meanings cannot be altered by human history. The world manifests itself as a multidimensional spatial entity here and now, rather than as a narrow time line. With that in mind, Emerson could propose that we "interrogate the great apparition that shines so peacefully around us."[9] The higher use of nature was as signifier, not as signified.

For seen in the light of thought, the world is always phenomenal. . . . Nature always speaks of Spirit. It suggests the absolute. It is a

perpetual effect. It is a great shadow pointing to the sun behind us.
. . . [T]he noblest ministry of nature is to stand as the apparition
of God. It is the organ through which the universal spirit speaks to
the individual, and strives to lead back the individual to it.[10]

Thus detached from history, the prophecy these poets derived from their
communings with nature was radically antiapocalyptic. New England Tran-
scendentalists would not have phrased it quite this way, but men like Emerson and Henry David Thoreau applauded when Walt Whitman did:

> I have heard what the talkers were talking, the talk of the beginning
>   and the end,
> But I do not talk of the beginning or the end.
>
> There was never any more inception than there is now,
> Nor any more youth or age than there is now,
> And will never be any more perfection than there is now,
> Nor any more heaven or hell than there is now.
>
> Urge and urge and urge,
> Always the procreant urge of the world.[11]

In the early nineteenth century, when Americans began to entertain the
notion of their land as a Garden of Eden and themselves as its guiltless gar-
deners, there was more than transcendentalism abroad in the land. Those
who were able to lay aside the warlike Canaan type together with its antitype, the Apocalypse, were able to wander into the wild because it was now
finally safe to do so. Their forefathers, justifying their conquest by an appeal
to biblical ethnic myths, had cleared the "howling wilderness" of its original
inhabitants, and now the generation that came after the War of 1812—at
least those east of the Alleghenies—could afford to elaborate a cosmic myth
of purity and power. The hapless tribes that had sided with Britain during
its latest attempt to win back its former colonies had been forced to trek
westward from New England, northern New York State, Pennsylvania, and
Virginia, leaving the woodlands finally safe for poets and painters. Without
the fear of the blood-curdling cry and the flying tomahawk, Americans
could now lay aside the book of Joshua, take up the *Lyrical Ballads,* and stroll
off alone through the forests primeval. Here was a land in which they could
finally feel at home. As for the Apocalypse, well, that fiery vengeance of God
must surely have been meant for some other, less innocent nation.

The Narrative of Progress

As a modernist concept, technological progress implies a departure from older cultural beliefs and practices. Yet American narratives of progress that feature the inventor as their hero reveal certain unmistakably medieval elements. In popular lore, successful inventors, especially those who used electrical energy, were deemed wonder-workers. From Benjamin Franklin to Samuel F. B. Morse, from Alexander Graham Bell to Thomas Edison, American inventors were linked to wizardry and the miraculous. When they demonstrated their devices, they drew the kind of audiences that attended public séances and magicians' performances.

But in the nineteenth century, an era of technological wonders, many Americans and Europeans also fantasized about a medieval world in which "wizard" and "miracle" were not mere figures of speech or puffery—a world in which faith was a self-justifying virtue, and men and women fervently believed. Mark Twain sensed this cultural ambivalence and sought to analyze it by transporting a Connecticut Yankee back in time to King Arthur's court—in effect, superimposing modernism upon medievalism.

Modernism is unthinkable without sophisticated machinery, which is itself unthinkable without energy sources. For thousands of years the principal source was fire, a useful but intractable element associated with the sky-gods. In the Bible, the most fearful image of God's wrath had always been his casting down of fire to consume the earth. "I am for certain informed, that this our City will be burned with fire from Heaven," says Bunyan's Christian.[12] After the Flood, God promised Noah that he would never again use water to destroy the living things of the earth. He did not say, though, that he would not destroy living things: nine chapters later, he demonstrated a different mode of attack. The first mention of "fire" in the Bible is associated neither with human usefulness nor with sacrificial offerings but with a kind of divine shock-and-awe blitzkrieg: "then the LORD rained upon Sodom and Gomorrah brimstone and fire from the LORD out of heaven" (Gen. 19:24).

The writers of the Bible imagined that somewhere high above the puny cities of man towered another city, the celestial City of God. The stars at night were the campfires of a mighty army that guarded this fortress; the wandering lights of sun, moon, and planets were angelic generals who surveyed these troops and reconnoitered the doings of mortals far below. Meteors, comets, and, most powerful of all, thunderbolts were the weapons in God's royal arsenal. But though its defenders were invincible, this citadel, like any earthly one, might also be subject to attack. For example the tower of Babel, the first city built after the Flood, having been designed to "reach unto heaven," posed such a threat to God's sovereignty that he had to use a linguistic stratagem to frustrate the project. For Book VI of *Paradise Lost,* Milton blended the siege of Olympus from Hesiod's *Theogony* with the rebellion of the satanic dragon in the Book of Revelation: interspersing classical imagery with references to an embattled army of "saints" with "palms," a "war in heaven," and a "bottomless pit," Milton leaves little doubt that this victory of God's lightning-wielding champion is but a foreshadowing of his final victory, which many Protestant readers then felt was imminent.

The two poets who have been most responsible for our imagery of hell differ radically as to its location. Dante places it within a roofed-over crater formed by the impact of Satan and his rebels when they were cast from heaven to earth, and Milton places this "penal fire" in an alternate universe. The popular image of hell is a mélange of the most horrendous details of both accounts—the fiery cavern under our feet and the bat-winged demons from outer space. Wherever hell is imagined to be, both versions agree that God created this prison house some time shortly before or after he created the world and that it is the unique place of eternal fire and brimstone. Here both versions are, from a biblical perspective, equally wrong: the Bible speaks of a subterranean place containing water and the dank abode of the dead (*sheol*) and later containing fire that, rather than rising up from below, is rained down from above. The sky, after all, is the proper site of eternal fires. According to Hellenistic astronomy, above the tenth sphere, the primum mobile, lay the empyrean, the pure, fiery dwelling place of the Immortals. Hellfire, in short, is *heaven*-fire cast to earth and left behind to burn the bodies of this sky-god's enemies forever.[13]

The power to wield celestial fire is the most fearsome attribute of any sky-god. In 2 Samuel 22:11–15 and in Psalm 18, Yahweh rides the black storm clouds, drops hailstones and coals of fire, and shoots arrows of lightning to defend his anointed one, David. As the antitype of David, Jesus, the "Son of David," when he returns, will also be accompanied by fire from heaven that will purge the dwellers of earth.[14] In the meantime, every thunderstorm that churns overhead gives mortals a foretaste of the crack of doom. "I used to be a person terrified with thunder," Jonathan Edwards recalled in his *Personal Narrative,* "and it used to strike me with terror when I saw a thunderstorm rising. But now, on the contrary, it rejoiced me. I felt God at the first appearance of a thunderstorm. And used to take the opportunity at such times to fix myself to view the clouds, and see the lightning play, and hear the majestic and awful voice of God's thunder, which often times was exceeding entertaining, leading me to sweet contemplations of my great and glorious God."[15]

Who among the ancients—indeed, who among Edwards's own generation—could have dreamed that the tiny crackle sometimes emitted from a cat's brushed fur was a phenomenon in any way related to the theophanic voice of God and to that most awesome instrument of his wrath, the thunderbolt? What we now know as static electricity had long been a subject of intellectual speculation. For centuries, investigators had been curious to understand why amber (in Greek, *elektron*) and other substances could produce sparks when rubbed. This property, which William Gilbert in 1600 named "electricitie," was a force that certain materials could conduct and other materials retain. Once loaded, or "charged," with this force, such materials could be made to "discharge" it under proper conditions—producing a crackling spark and, if the experimenter came too close, a perceptible "shock." In the seventeenth and early eighteenth centuries, machines were constructed to magnify these effects, using friction applied to a variety of substances. The Abbé Nollet in 1746 remarked how similar the atmospheric illumination during a thunderstorm was to the effects produced by electrical machines. Six years later, Benjamin Franklin—with his audacious kite and key—proved that the two phenomena were, in principle, identical.

For some eighty years, the only functional consequence of Franklin's research was to be the lightning rod. The practical and cultural effects of this simple device were prodigious, however. Soon all buildings, secular and religious, were assured a large measure of protection against a force since measured by scientists to generate five times the heat of the surface of the sun. To those, like Edwards, for whom the storm was an expression of God's sovereignty, this invention seemed a virtual disarming of the Almighty. Though insurance underwriters hence would still refer to them as "acts of God," lightning strikes soon lost their supernatural aspect. Readers and writers found it increasingly difficult to take the notion of a thunderbolt-hurling deity with any seriousness, though as an element in the gothic novel and the melodrama it still retained some of its uncanny aura. When Edwards's grandson, Timothy Dwight, stretched for the biblical sublime in *The Conquest of Canaan* (1788), he slipped so many fulgurant jaculations into his pages that John Trumbull advised booksellers to supply a lightning rod with every copy.[16]

The human mastery of the "fire from heaven" seemed to prove that mankind had transitioned from a medieval to a modern world. But this achievement and the shift it portended brought with them a certain mood of apprehension. Kant had heralded the inventor-statesman Franklin as the "new Prometheus," and in 1778 the French economic reformer Turgot penned the line "Eripuit cœlo fulmen sceptrumque tyrannis"—"He snatched the lightning from heaven and the scepter from tyrants"—in his honor.[17] In an age of classical reference and republican fervor, this double snatching recalled the image of the rebel Titan who defied Zeus by stealing the fire from heaven to serve humanity. Those who followed in the footsteps of Franklin were hailed as enemies of ignorance and superstition, torchbearers of the Enlightenment, benefactors of humanity. It took little imagination for readers to understand that the Olympian in this modernized fable was a stand-in for the irascible, jealous god of the Old Testament, that version of the Deity that Blake would set down in his poetic notebook as "Nobodaddy." "Cover your heaven, Zeus, with cloud-vapor and, like a boy beheading thistles, practice your strength on oaks and mountain peaks," says Goethe's Prometheus in the poem of the same name. The old gods survive only on the fears and hopes of the ignorant, he says, but for his part he will create a race "to suffer, to weep, to enjoy, and be glad—and to ignore you, as do I!" Shelley's *Prometheus Unbound* depicts not only the liberation of the fire-thief but also the dethronement of Jupiter, the tyrannical god of lightning. In the new Promethean age of self-governing man, "the lightning is his slave," and the universe, from "the heaven's utmost deep" to the "abyss," lays bare its ancient secrets (lines 818–24).[18]

Prometheus, the titanic inventor, continued to personify the progress of science in the nineteenth and twentieth centuries, a progress that also seemed to come at the expense of the storm-god whose ancient powers, one by one, were expropriated: his power to speak over great distances, to illuminate the darkness, to propel objects, to traverse land and sky at furious speeds, and to incinerate enemies. Led by advances in electrical technology, these awesome attributes of the god of the Apocalypse would come to serve the children of Prometheus, at least those who could afford them. No longer the uncanny agent of the Almighty, electrical energy has become our indispensable, everyday collaborator—our "slave," as Shelley asserted with a flourish.

In the 1830s the construction of the electrical motor and the electrical telegraph transformed this force from a danger that humans could tame with Franklin's magic rod to a resource they could exploit. The motor was still rudimentary, still unable to compete with the steam engine, but the telegraph, which required less of an electric charge, was a device they quickly put to use. Thanks to steam power, the United States became a nation of fast-growing cities along the Erie Canal, the shores of the Great Lakes, and down the Ohio and Mississippi Rivers, and a network of railroads began moving westward toward national borders as yet undetermined. The electric telegraph followed the railroads in the 1840s and created an immeasurably swifter network, a network of words.

When Morse demonstrated his version of the telegraph before the U.S. Congress in 1844, the particular words he transmitted over a wire from Washington to Baltimore came from an episode in the book of Numbers. Having learned that the Israelites were marching toward his kingdom on their way to Canaan, the king of Moab asked the prophet Balaam to obtain from God a curse against them, but God told Balaam: "thou shalt not curse the people: for they are blessed" (Num. 22:12). God subsequently induced the entranced prophet himself to pronounce a blessing on the invaders, which included the exclamation "What hath God wrought!" (23:23). Though Morse may not have meant this phrase to convey a specific biblical message, his hearers had to have recalled that famous conversion of a curse into a blessing, of judgment into justification. The fire from heaven that God had reserved to incinerate the world had now been made the means by which the New Israel would fulfill its Manifest Destiny and build its millennial Promised Land. It was God's will, Morse seemed to be saying, that Congress should underwrite his version of the electric telegraph. After all, his invention had been God's own idea all along.

Others made little pretense of creaturely humility. Alexander Jones, in his exuberant history of the electric telegraph (1852), declared: "Electricity is the poetry of science; no romance—no tales of fiction excel in wonder its history and achievements. Viewed in its terrible atmospheric manifestations, no element would seem less likely to be brought under the control of man, and, in feebler currents, made to do his bidding than it: yet such is the result."[19] His book concludes in a spirit no less Promethean: "Future investigators must disclose new discoveries in electricity, applicable to new and important purposes, conducive alike to the advancement of man's power over matter, of his elevation of intellect and higher civilization. 'CANST THOU SEND LIGHTNINGS, THAT THEY MAY GO, AND SAY UNTO THEE, HERE WE ARE?'"[20] Jones referenced that quote as simply "Job," reminding his readers of God's challenging voice out of the whirlwind. He left it to the reader to reply, "Yes, now *I* can."

As the demand for electrical energy grew in America and Europe, not only for telegraphic and, later, telephonic and radio communications but also for machinery, lighting, and mass transit, devices had to be invented to generate this power, e.g., storage cells (batteries) and large steam-powered generators (dynamos). Such practical uses notwithstanding, electrical energy retained some of its premodern mythic aura, and the inventors wielding it were revered as virtual wizards. In that famous chapter of his *Education,* "The Virgin and the Dynamo," Henry Adams meditates on energy and its symbols.[21] For Adams as a cultural historian, energy is measured by its effect on human activity. If men had been mobilized to build vast cathedrals because they felt irresistibly attracted to a symbol (that is, the Virgin Mary), that symbol constituted an energy. "Symbol or energy," he wrote, "the Virgin had *acted as* the greatest force the Western world ever felt, and drawn men's activities to herself more strongly than any other power, natural or supernatural had ever done."[22] The dynamo, as Adams sensed its import, represented an opposite force—that of outward, centrifugal entropy. This produced in him a conflict, a cognitive dissonance: there, in the "great hall of dynamos" in the Paris Exposition of 1900, he found himself overcome with religious awe and, despite its faceless inhumanity, he felt an impulse to pray to this machine.

Though he knew that the two symbols were similarly potent, Adams could not, or would not, attempt to reconcile them. The dynamo, soundlessly revolving its huge wheel "at some vertiginous speed," was a man-made dispenser of lightning bolts and, though he does not mention it, a potent symbol of the fierce god of the Apocalypse.[23] In Adams's mind, America had celebrated its triumph over the feminine and the sexual by creating, in the dynamo, its own secular male deity of expansionism. His nation could never fathom the energy that the Virgin once evoked: "An American Virgin would never dare command."

The Narrative of Freedom

Adams's model for an American virgin was perhaps too specific—a slight, pale girl holding an infant, a medieval icon fashioned out of tinted glass. There was, however, one prominent American icon that Adams had not considered. Virginal, but after the manner of a Valkyrie or a Roman Minerva, this woman cradled a book instead of a child and with her other arm upraised a "torch, whose flame / Is the imprisoned lightning," as Emma Lazarus said. The Virgin of Chartres, a woman clothed with the sun, glowed translucently, but the virgin of New York harbor—an opaque colossus of stone, steel, and copper—projected into the darkness her own dynamo-generated light. Furthermore, as every schoolchild learns, this figure does indeed dare to command. "Give me your tired, your poor," she declares to the tyrannical regimes across the sea. As *Liberty Enlightening the World,* Frédéric-Auguste Bartholdi's statue embodied the consonances that America then craved, the reconciliation of tradition with science. Like Moses coming down from the Mount, Liberty held a tablet-like book, and her brow sent forth light.[24] As a daughter of the Enlightenment, her book was inscribed with the date "July 4, 1776" and she held aloft the torch of Reason. At her feet lay broken links of chain and a call to the world to send its "huddled masses yearning to breathe free."

"The State resorts to the narrative of freedom every time it assumes direct control over the training of the 'people,' under the name of the 'nation,' in order to point it down the path of progress," says Lyotard, summarizing the motive behind this narrative.[25] But what form would such a narrative actually take? Like the two preceding modernist narratives, it will begin at a low point (corresponding to phase 3 of Tzvetan Todorov's cycle) and show the people's movement upward (into phase 4), which in this metanarrative marks a movement from servitude to freedom. It will also need its own hero, one who will lead or advise or encourage the people in their collective action. In America, this has always been the role of the president, the commander in chief, a person who occupies an elective office yet possesses a sacred aura associated with inherited kingship. Despite his foibles, he will be viewed, like a medieval monarch, as "God's Anointed." This narrative will need other characters as well, antagonists who oppose this people's liberation and allies that serve the hero's noble cause; it will accordingly be marked by setbacks and advances. It may also include the abduction narrative as an important subplot. Here, as I described it in Chapter 5, the national leader assumes the role of redeemer, the person sworn to liberate the captive and destroy the tyrant.

The Israelites' flight from Egypt and their wanderings in the wilderness formed the first part of a larger epic that concluded with their conquest of their Promised Land. The second part of this extended chronicle had provided important models for the English colonists, whose later successes against British forces and their Indian allies reminded them of Joshua's campaigns against the Canaanites. During the so-called Era of Good Feelings (1817–23) following its second defeat of England in 1815, America settled into secure possession of the land, and the Edenic myth of nature that I outlined above began to take hold and partly displace the Exodus myths.

By 1865, the imagery of a suffering people escaping tyranny and marching forward toward their Promised Land was once again usable. But this biblical master narrative needed some tailoring before it could fit. The ranks of marchers on this journey had been swollen by freed slaves and by new arrivals who demanded their piece of this Garden of Eden or Promised Land.

As they soon learned, however, the garden was securely walled, a "No Tres-passing" sign nailed to the gate. And as for *their* Promised Land, that lay somewhere in the future. The myth of nature, the land of America as a Gar-den of Eden to be enjoyed without guilt here and now, presupposed a sin-less possessor. Only an Adam and Eve *before* their Fall could enjoy such a blessing. For the resident underclass, white and black, and the newcomers whose lot more closely resembled that of the expellees from Eden, some *other* myth was needed. The freedom narrative needed to be restyled for a diverse and unruly multitude. According to this revision, the present land of hard-ships was to be only gradually replaced by a future land, a Promised Land. For those to whom the latter myth was preached, America was to remain a place of wandering, a wilderness that would someday, in one's children's lifetime perhaps, become a "land flowing with milk and honey." In the mean-time, like the Israelites, they must march on, overcoming temptations, obeying their divinely appointed leaders, and patiently undergoing toil and suffering. The metanarrative of freedom, and every narrative based on it, is not meant to reach phase 5, the (re-)establishment of a just and prosperous social order. It is the story of an escape from bondage, but not from trials and suffering. The people, now a "nation," are directed to the path of free-dom, encouraged by the hope of progress, but their story always ends short of their goal. The rallying cry "Freedom is on the march" is more properly stated as "Freedom *is* the march."

The American narrative of freedom has been so systematically revised by the Exodus master narrative that the "march of freedom" has become an unquestioned axiom. If we think we are wanderers in a wilderness, we may not know where we are, but we will know one thing: we must not stay where we now find ourselves. Any political leader who promises to "get this coun-try [state, municipality, school district, and so on] moving again," to "push on," or to "stay the course" will be applauded and, moreover, assumed to know where that course will take us.

Under these narrative-governed conditions, an accepted leader will wear the invisible mantle of Moses. The rhetorical power of this narrative is such that any person in authority, it seems, can parry challenges by enunciating that magical verb form, "go forward," as in "we must resolutely go forward to overcome these obstacles" or "I say we put the past behind us and go for-ward." Any reference to the future gains vigor and conviction, apparently, when it has tagged onto it or dangled from it the participle "going forward," as in "This era of partisan infighting must end, going forward"—or, to use a popular variant, "We will succeed, moving forward."

In the latter half of the nineteenth century and the first half of the twentieth, those two biblical master narratives, Eden (disguised as the secular narrative of nature) and Exodus (disguised as the secular narratives of progress and freedom), legitimated most of the narratives that gave popular expression to America's homeland mythology. Those two biblical master narratives were, however, difficult to reconcile. It seemed as though two images of the nation had been inserted at the tip of the American stereoscope in the decades following the Civil War. One tintype was of God's Country with its virgin forests, fruited plains, and purple mountains; the other, a desolation of felled trees, steel rails, and coal mines. With one eye its citizens saw mansions, gardens, and smiling children, while with the other they saw textile mills, stooplaborers, and sweatshops. However hard they tried, they could not bring this double image into a single, three-dimensional focus. All the while, both post- and premillennialists assured their congregations that the blur they saw when they tried to reconcile these two Americas was only temporary: Eden and the goal of Exodus, the Promised Land, were, after all, merely types of the glorious kingdom soon to be established on earth. Good Christians would simply have to continue gazing into that glass darkly until the glorious day dawned when the lion and lamb would lie down together.[26]

The common theme in both the Eden and the Exodus myths is compensation. *Who* gets *what*, and *when?* Answers to this question seem to center on the cultural idea of the holiday, which I introduced in Chapter 4. First, two uncontroversial premises: a holiday is time off from work, and time off from work, being culturally defined, is subject to class distinctions. As though they were the prelapsarian lords of creation, the wealthy, if they choose, are free to be always on holiday. Their free time is designated as "leisure." When those, on the other hand, who have inherited the destiny of the fallen Adam choose to absent themselves from work, this time is designated "idleness." Leisure is time *for.* Idleness is time *from.* Leisure is a positive state, but idleness connotes the absence of a normative aspect. We speak of "idle" (not "leisurely") machinery, because machines are, by definition, instruments of labor.[27] Only during designated holidays can workers' time off rise to the rank of leisure. Only then can the wanderers in the wilderness savor a foretaste of the paradisiacal realm into which their betters seem to have been born.

Those who enjoy this Edenic foretaste of the millennial kingdom all their lives also command the means to justify their ownership of nature by cultural persuasion. As they explain it, prosperity is the just reward of virtue, and the wealth of the few actually benefits the many—who, generation by generation, are slowly but surely moving toward their Promised Land, the ultimate consumer economy. In the process, it is only just that they accept the jobs available to them. As this version of freedom is promulgated, class identity and social role are mythically reinforced. The wealthy, who derive their identity from the ownership of nature and their presumption of innocence, derive their social role from managing the accumulation of wealth and by promoting the freedom narrative. Members of the working class who regard themselves as the potentially wealthy see themselves as moving along toward some ultimate, dimly envisaged future. Eden and the road to the Promised Land will, after all, soon blend into some millennial homeland in which all will be equally blessed. In the interim, the essential difference between the narrative of nature and the narrative of freedom is that for one class, the promised reward is here and now; for the other, it is a dream deferred.

The vast majority of America's citizenry are told to aspire to the current status of the elite—or at least to believe fervently that their descendants will someday achieve it. Lee Greenwood's popular patriotic song "God Bless the USA" is a kind of pledge of allegiance to this narrative: even if he were to wake up tomorrow and find that everything he had worked for all his life was gone, he would just gather up his wife and children and start over again, grateful that the flag fluttering overhead "still stands for freedom." Then the martial refrain: "I'm proud to be an American / Where at least I know I'm free!" Most Americans think they understand the meaning of such sentiments and cannot understand why foreigners to whom we offer to export this way of life cannot quite "get" it. Perhaps we haven't examined the freedom narrative closely enough ourselves. It's that blur of small print down there at the bottom of the American social contract.

The Narrative of Judgment

A population in ethnic flux poses problems for any homeland mythology. During the period 1820 to 1930, the United States was the goal of an estimated 60 percent of global immigration. In 1820, only 8,000 aliens arrived on these shores; in 1840, 48,000; in 1850, 370,000; and in 1880, 457,000. Between 1905 and 1914, the rate averaged 1,000,000 per year.[28] Infected, as many immigrants were thought to be, with the contagion of corrupt cultures abroad, their moral disorders would need to be treated with public education and curbed by just laws. Even so, some were destined never to convert to an American (white, Anglo-Saxon, Protestant) system of values.

Those who could not or would not accept the curative process of assimilation would need to be monitored, quarantined, expelled, or dealt with even more severely.

Liberty, whose own manacles lay broken at her feet, cast upon the liberated newcomers a strict schoolteacherly gaze, extending to those who passed through her "golden door" into the slums of lower Manhattan the promise of freedom but also the threat of coercion. Just as to the biblical kingdom of God many were called but few were chosen, not all the "wretched refuse" she called to the new Republic of Man would merit the full fruits of citizenship. Original sin and predestination may have lost doctrinal force in the minds of most nineteenth-century Americans, but the fall of man as an individual option was still very much believed in. The Tree of Life grew tall in this regulated Paradise, but so did the Tree of the Knowledge of Good and Evil.

Liberty Enlightening the World could therefore represent Justice—not blindfolded at all, but as eagle-eyed as the doomsday Judge. Her torch could light the way for those yearning to breathe free, but her "imprisoned lightning," that ancient instrument of doom, could still strike dead the irredeemable reprobate. In the 1880s, as America celebrated this symbol of the modern (electrically powered) enlightenment, a new application for this energy was being debated. Mark Twain alluded to it in *A Connecticut Yankee in King Arthur's Court* (1889) when he had his hero string up an electrified fence, a device he called "silent lightning" that eventually slew 25,000 of his technologically backward besiegers. In the summer of the next year, the first electric chair was put to use.

Promoted as a swifter, cleaner, more enlightened alternative to hanging, this device became the ultimate apocalyptic weapon in the armory of criminal justice. R. T. Irvine, the physician who oversaw its first use at the state prison at Auburn, New York, begins an encyclopedia article on "Electrocution" by expressing his abhorrence of that term ("a barbarous newspaper coinage which has come into common use"—*electrical* + *execution,* a portmanteau word). This pet peeve out of the way, he warms to his task of describing the apparatus used on "one Kemmler, a murderer, who was executed at Auburn, Aug. 6, 1890." A totally state-of-the-art piece of engineering, it used a "stationary engine, an alternating-current dynamo and exciter, a voltameter with extra resistance coil, calibrated for a range from 30 to 2,000 volts, etc." The electricity generated by the dynamo and engine, which were "located in one of the prison shops, several hundred feet from the execution room," terminated in two electrodes. One was attached to the top of the head, and the other to the base of the spine, "the nerve tissues [of which] contain an excess of saline moisture," Dr. Irvine informs us, "and hence are among the best conductors, while the amount of organic matter in the live bone also renders it a fairly good conductor."[29]

As we have seen, electricity drew its considerable cultural energy from the Bible, where it was described as the most dreaded weapon of the Divine Judge. It had been brought safely to earth in the eighteenth century. Then in the nineteenth and twentieth centuries, while facilitating the wonders of invention celebrated in the narrative of progress, it now had become the instrument of human judges. Was it more efficient or "humane" than other judicial killing machines then in use? Though penologists have disagreed, one thing is certain: the electric chair has long occupied a unique place in the American imagination. Ever since its first use, it has seemed to satisfy the public's desire for retribution in a ritual that vindicated the divine right of the state to take the lives of malefactors. Each time the wall switch was lowered, this ritual reconfirmed the probity of law-abiding citizens, who, because they were not the reprobate condemned to die, could regard themselves as the elect. Through their representatives—that is, newspaper reporters and prison officials—they could witness the spasms of the malefactor as the saved would one day witness the spectacular agonies of the damned.[30] The pleasure of spectatorship, we need to recall, was a traditional feature of the apocalyptic scenario, but because the Apocalypse is not a fiction for believers, the empathetic imagination is never evoked to bridge the distance between spectator and sufferer. As one preacher later phrased it: "Thank God, I will get a view of the Battle of Armageddon from the grandstand seats of heaven. All who are born again will see the Battle of Armageddon, but it will be from the skies."[31]

Righteous *Schadenfreude* like this has also been a major element in tales of crime and punishment, and particularly in the detective novel, a genre we may especially associate with the secularization of apocalyptic themes and imagery. Stephen Knight has traced this literary form to the *Newgate Calendar,* which first appeared in 1773. In installments over the next four decades, this immensely popular series of books recounted the often short, always nasty, careers of British rogues. Each edition offered the reader a set of cautionary biographies of men and women who had rejected the prayers and counsel of their families and become public enemies. While not innately evil, these criminals became infected with a moral disease of which the body social must eventually purge itself through imprisonment, transportation, or execution. All of the malefactors were brought to justice and confessed their crimes; many were so wracked with guilt that they acknowledged the correctness of their sentences.[32] Such stories reinforced the "twin beliefs that we are all

Christian at heart and that our society is integral and at root a single healthy body."[33] The bond between government and community, rich and poor, was dramatized by this common effort to expose the criminal. From this perspective, class resentment would be counterproductive, and class warfare suicidal.

In the *Newgate Calendar* the prime agent of detection was the moral populace, but as this genre developed in the nineteenth century, the figure of the solitary detective began to emerge. In the now-familiar formula, he (or in some twentieth- and twenty-first-century series, *she*) is called upon by members of the community to investigate a crime, almost invariably a murder.[34] Intent on discovering the sources and minute details of evil, he eventually triumphs, forcing the criminal to expose his misdeeds in a public confession. This ratiocinative searcher of hearts is a separate and superior being. He serves the interests of his community but is no mere representative of it.[35]

The detective novel, which is of course not unique to American culture but popular in other apocalyptically troubled countries as well, belongs to a larger class of narratives. This class includes all those narratives in which a righteous person or community is victimized by evil persons and is saved by a strong, virtuous stranger. Versions of this ancient mythic plot appear in the labors of Hercules, the Grail legends, and, with less muscle than miracle, in the legends of the saints. In these tales we find a lone fighter struggling to uphold a cultural good against forces intent on destroying it. In short, we find heroic myth embedded within ethnic myth—and both narrative discourses deployed to celebrate a just kingdom, an ideal homeland.

Tales conforming to the narrative of judgment reemerged in the nineteenth century in response to some of the more dismaying aspects of industrial capitalism. As Tennyson, in England, was elegizing the passing of an earlier, nobler age in *The Idylls of the King* and, in Germany, Wagner was moving on from *Lohengrin* and *Tannhäuser* toward the blazing *Twilight of the Gods,* America was beginning to imagine its own chivalric apocalypse centered on its own heroic horseman, the cowboy. This agent of retributive justice was, and is, the heroic savior of an oppressed community, a hero with a thousand names: Natty Bumppo, Tom Mix, the Lone Ranger, Superman, Rambo, Captain Kirk, and the Terminator, to name but a few.[36]

Taking Joseph Campbell's concept of the "classical monomyth" as their model, Robert Jewett and John S. Lawrence set out to define the "distinctively *American monomyth*":

> The monomythic superhero is distinguished by disguised origins, pure motives, a redemptive task, and extraordinary powers. He

originates outside the community he is called to save, and in those exceptional instances when he is resident therein, the superhero plays the role of an idealistic loner. His identity is secret, either by virtue of his unknown origins or his alter ego, his motivation a selfless zeal for justice. By elaborate conventions of restraint, his desire for revenge is purified. Patient in the face of provocations, he seeks nothing for himself and withstands all temptations. Sexual fulfillment is renounced for the duration of the mission. The purity of his motivations ensures moral infallibility in judging persons and situations. When threatened by violent adversaries, vigilantism is the answer, restoring justice and thus lifting the siege of paradise. To accomplish this mission without incurring blame or causing undue injury to others, superhuman powers are required. The aim of the superhero is unerring. In the most dangerous trials he remains utterly cool and thus divinely competent.[37]

Jewett and Lawrence acknowledge that this hero has some Christlike aspects but associate them exclusively with the Jesus of the Gospels. Had they appreciated the foundational character of the Apocalypse myth in American culture, they might have recognized that the variants of what they call the American monomyth are fictionalizations of the judgment narrative that shield us from the terror of its master narrative, the Apocalypse. The American Western—in novel, film, and early radio versions—bears several other interesting resemblances to the Book of Revelation. Both feature scenes of horsemen and cavalry charges. In Revelation, the references to horses and riders occur fourteen times, whereas in all the preceding books of the New Testament, only one such reference appears. The single reference to "wilderness" had seemed especially significant ever since the earliest Puritan times, when ministers and magistrates declared the True Church under attack from the red dragon of hostile Indian tribes. The Indians, of course, also corresponded to the armies of the Great Beast encircling the elect.

The narrative of judgment is the generic model for at least four subgenres: (1) tales of criminal "lowlife" such as we read in the police-blotter columns of local newspapers and view on tabloid-style TV docudramas; (2) tales of murderers and sociopaths that detectives and other sleuths track down; (3) tales of gangsters and prosperous mobsters that district attorneys prosecute; and (4) tales of shadowy conspiracies investigated at a higher governmental level. Narratives that depict this latter investigative level (e.g., fictive and historical accounts of international intrigue) most clearly carry over into modern discourse various premodern, biblically inspired, cultural attitudes toward such topics as heresy, witchcraft, and other cabals deemed dangerously subversive.

A survey of events occurring in the year 1693 reveals trends that suggest that England and the Continent were turning away from cultural assumptions to which New England still resolutely clung. In 1693, Louis XIV was consolidating his power in Versailles, and LaFontaine was issuing his long-awaited third book of fables. In England, John Locke, having completed his major works on the philosophy of mind and of government, was beginning his treatise *The Reasonableness of Christianity.* In the Age of Dryden, that long, genial afterglow of the Restoration, the Puritan tumult of midcentury seemed part of a distant past. Indeed, the topic of interest to Londoners early in 1693 was the young comedic wit William Congreve, whose first comedy, *The Old Bachelor,* had drawn excited crowds to the Theatre Royal in Drury Lane. New England, however, insisted on preserving its traditions of spiritual warfare. In 1693, one year after the witch trials and executions in Salem, Cotton Mather published *The Wonders of the Invisible World,* introducing his account of the events as follows:

> The New Englanders are a people of God settled in those, which were once the devil's territories; and it may easily be supposed that the devil was exceedingly disturbed, when he perceived such a people here accomplishing the promise of old made unto our blessed Jesus, that He should have the utmost parts of the earth for His possession. . . . The devil thus irritated, immediately tried all sorts of methods to overturn this poor plantation: and so much of the church, as was fled into this wilderness, immediately found the serpent cast out of his mouth a flood for the carrying of it away. I believe that never were more satanical devices used for the unsettling of any people under the sun, than what have been employed for the extirpation of the vine which God has here planted, casting out the heathen, and preparing a room before it. . . . Wherefore the devil is now making one attempt more upon us; an attempt more difficult, more surprising, more snarled with unintelligible circumstances than any that we have hitherto encountered. . . . We have been advised by some credible Christians yet alive, that a malefactor, accused of witchcraft as well as murder, and executed in this place more than forty years ago, did then give notice of an horrible plot against the country by witchcraft, and a foundation of witchcraft

then laid, which if it were not seasonably discovered, would probably blow up, and pull down all the churches in the country. And
we have now with horror seen the discovery of such a witchcraft!
An army of devils is horribly broke in upon the place which is the
center, and after a sort, the firstborn of our English settlements.

Here indeed is pure evil of the highest order, an evil conspiracy not only of
flesh and blood but also of principalities, of powers, and of rulers of the
darkness of this world. Mather's statement may seem to modern or postmodern ears the product of a benighted or perhaps diseased mind, but when
New Englanders first read it, most accepted it as a quite plausible explanation. The notion that the righteousness of their cause had itself provoked
the malevolence of unseen forces and the belief that God's justice would prevail on their behalf reflect a premodern narrative of judgment, one derived
from apocalyptic prophecy. We can easily identify with Mather's representation of free-floating dread. In the twenty-first century, Americans have been
told that that they are at war, a perpetual war "against terror," and, for their
own good, must allow a secretive government to monitor their private lives.

"Hark Ye Yet Again,—The Little Lower Layer"

When I began this inquiry into the compound noun "homeland," I suggested
that a tension has always existed between the meanings represented by "home"
and "land." I went on to propose that in American culture, whenever these
two mutually resistant concepts were brought together closely, a cognitive dissonance ensued that only some biblically modeled myth, be it civil-religious
or secular-modern, could temporarily relieve. In this concluding section, I
will first analyze the rhetorical process by which even patently false narratives can achieve believability when biblically masked—and then review the
rationales for doing so.

    As I proceeded to chronicle the tensions between home and land by cross-
referencing politics and history with biblical narratives, I found myself encountering, now and again, one particular rhetorical device: metaphor. In
an earlier book, *Authority Figures,* I had analyzed several "metaphors of mastery," among them the shepherd and helmsman figures. In each of these, a
single, superior agent is contrasted with an aggregation of subordinates whose
welfare he is sworn to preserve. The shepherd's work is one of lonely vigi-
lance; the sheep have only to follow and cluster and graze. The helmsman

knows the weather, the currents, and the stars; the passengers' lives are in his hands. The shepherd says, "Trust me." The helmsman vows to "stay the course." The relationship between these agents and their charges appears, at first glance, to offer an allegory of the relationship between the government and community, providing these abstract systems with narrative concreteness. Metaphor and narrative ought to be somehow connected, but when a narrative is as metamorphic as homeland mythology, allegory seems too simple a solution and too weak a link.

In Chapter 1 of this book, I cited George Lakoff's 1991 article "Metaphor and War," in which he demonstrated how *realpolitik* could be translated into metaphors and sold to the public as scenarios. Lakoff did not address *how* metaphors could manage to mutate into narratives, however. Before I venture to answer this question, I should say a few words about metaphor and its inherent quirkiness.

The two terms of an effective metaphor come from radically different semantic domains, and each term performs a different function. The main topic, A (also called the target, or tenor), is usually a complex or obscure entity, while B (the source, or vehicle) is more concrete, familiar, and imaginable. Though it is extracted from a wholly different context, once it is "mapped onto" A, B clarifies certain aspects of A. But because these two terms are so disparate, this is only a partial clarification. No more than a few of B's entailments will ever correspond to the properties of A, so some properties of A will remain unrevealed. For example, in the metaphor "a king is a shepherd," "shepherd" carries in its situational context such features as *sheep, predators, pastures,* and *protectiveness,* features traditionally associated via metaphor with kingship.[38] Yet there are other features of shepherding—e.g., the coercion of a blindly obedient herd and the shearing, slaughtering, and roasting of individual members. To prevent these from contaminating the concept of kingship, other words, verbs such as *feed* and *lead* and nouns such as *trust* and *care* are customarily added to the formula.

Heads of state and those who profit from government are motivated to stabilize these metaphors by pre-scripting those aspects of B that are to be mapped onto A. According to Lakoff, we map just so much knowledge from the source domain (B) onto the target domain (A) as is consistent with the properties of that target. For example, one is expected to know enough about kingship to know what pastoral entailments illuminate kingship and what entailments one should ignore.[39] But to the extent that our concept of kingship is constituted by the traditional pastoral metaphor, we find ourselves trapped in a hermeneutical circle: we know that A (kingship) possesses these positive properties, which correspond to and accept those entailments from B (shepherding), because B has revealed that A possesses them. Circular arguments like this are rarely detected, however, when they are enshrined in pre-scripted, or "dead," metaphors.

Citizens who assume that traditional metaphors like this are abbreviated social contracts are often deceived. Having bought into the pastoral metaphor, they feel assured of wise leadership and loving protection, only to discover that they have signed up for periodic shearings and eventual slaughter. I. F. Stone spoke to this issue when he wrote:

> Now, government lies, but it doesn't like to lie literally. Because a literal, flat and obvious lie tends to be caught up. So, what they do is, they become the masters of the disingenuous statement, of phrasing something in such a way that the honest, normal and unwary reader gets one impression—that he is supposed to get. And then, three months later, when he discovers it's not true and he goes back to complain, they say, "That isn't what we said. Look at it carefully." You look at it carefully, and sure enough, it was really double-talk, it didn't say exactly what you thought.[40]

Sophistical phrasings and weasel words are one layer of double-talk, but metaphor and metaphor-generated narrative can constitute a "little lower layer" of duplicity.[41]

So far, we have observed how metaphor makers can design them to signify pre-scripted meanings by controlling what entailments of B are mapped onto A and how, from time to time, they can take advantage of the unwary and apply other entailments by a process akin to "bait and switch." A ruler, for example, can shear his herd of financial security, health benefits, and privacy rights, keep them in ignorance, lead them about aimlessly, and drive them to the abattoir of war—all without abandoning his pastoral role.

Premodern metaphors, such those of the shepherd and the helmsman, persist, but metaphors suited to modernist narratives are more effective. One of them, aligned with the narratives of freedom, progress, and judgment, obscures the gap between the governmental and communal levels by linking them through metaphor, thereby mapping onto government the moral concerns of communal living. In his 1991 article, Lakoff named this the "state-as-person metaphor system":

> A state is conceptualized as a person, engaging in social relations within a world community. Its land-mass is its home. It lives in a

neighborhood, and has neighbors, friends and enemies. States are seen as having inherent dispositions: they can be peaceful or aggressive, responsible or irresponsible, industrious or lazy. . . .

Strength for a state is military strength. Maturity for the person-state is industrialization. Unindustrialized nations are "underdeveloped," with industrialization as a natural state to be reached. Third-world nations are thus immature children, to be taught how to develop properly or disciplined if they get out of line. Nations that fail to industrialize at a rate considered normal are seen as akin to retarded children and judged as "backward" nations. Rationality is the maximization of self-interest. . . .

Violence can further self-interest. It can be stopped in three ways: Either a balance of power, so that no one in a neighborhood is strong enough to threaten anyone else. Or the use of collective persuasion by the community to make violence counter to self-interest. Or a cop strong enough to deter violence or punish it. The cop should act morally, in the community's interest, and with the sanction of the community as a whole.

Morality is a matter of accounting, of keeping the moral books balanced. A wrongdoer incurs a debt, and he must be made to pay. The moral books can be balanced by a return to the situation prior to the wrongdoing, by giving back what has been taken, by recompense, or by punishment. Justice is the balancing of the moral books.

War in this metaphor is a fight between two people, a form of hand-to-hand combat. Thus, the US sought to "push Iraq back out of Kuwait" or "deal the enemy a heavy blow," or "deliver a knock-out punch." A just war is thus a form of combat for the purpose of settling moral accounts.[42]

Once a government's actions can be framed in communal terms, they can be moralized through narrative, i.e., through a linear series of episodes featuring nations-as-persons engaged in an epic conflict of wills—deception and revelation, strike and counter-strike, crime and punishment, disorder and pacification, captivity and redemption. The self-defense and rescue scenarios that I referred to earlier (pp. 19–20) were available to Bush I in 1991 and reused by Bush II in 2003. The metaphorical framing of the state-as-person, dwelling within a community of nations, lays bare the foundational metaphor upon which homeland mythology and all its narratives are ultimately based: *government-as-community,* or *land-as-home.*

This metaphor clearly involves a transfer of pre-scripted entailments. Those who employ this metaphor attribute to *their* government the traits of an exemplary homeowner, a pillar of his community, an arbitrator among his less temperate neighbors, an upholder of fair play, and a trouncer of bullies. As for other governments, they are metaphorized as either friends who help him or enemies who eventually learn to respect him. Used in the context of modern nation-states, this metaphor generates all the classes of narratives I discussed earlier in this chapter—all except the narrative of nature. The reason is this: the narrative of nature involves issues of territory and extractable resources, the very items that modern governments rapaciously covet and, when strong enough, expropriate from others. Accordingly, when communal traits are mapped onto government in the discourse of "public diplomacy," no such issue as petroleum is highlighted or spun into narrative, for the exemplary homeowner is materially secure, thank you very much, and has no designs whatsoever on the property of his neighbors.

The process that has generated homeland mythology, however, is even subtler than this. It all began by linking those two concepts, home and land, by forming the conceptual metaphor "land is home," a variant of "government is community." But before the two contrasting concepts could become fully united, they had to dissolve their metaphorical relationship. How this happens I first suggested in Chapter 3, when I sought to explain the rhetorical power of reversible metaphors, such as those that use as terms the concepts of religion and war. If, as Lakoff and his colleagues have argued, a normal metaphor transfers meaning in one direction only, from source (or vehicle) to target (or tenor), then a reversible metaphor, I concluded, is not merely a defective metaphor. It is not a metaphor at all, but an equation. In "Metaphor and War," Lakoff implied that the state-as-person metaphor could indeed be reversed: "There is a metonymy that goes hand-in-hand with the State-as-Person metaphor: /*THE RULER STANDS FOR THE STATE.*/ Thus, we can refer to Iraq by referring to Saddam Hussein, and so have a single person, not just an amorphous state, to play the villain in the just war scenario. It is this metonymy that was invoked every time President Bush said 'We have to get Saddam out of Kuwait.'"

I would take this a step further and subordinate "the ruler stands for the state" metonymy to the metaphor "The person is the state" (or, less formally phrased, the "person-as-state" metaphor). According to this formulation, a person—any person—is significantly characterized by the political structures of the country in which he or she lives.[43] However one regards the governmental system of a given state—as noble, villainous, inefficient, benighted, and so on—the traits that define these stereotypes will be transferable to the citizen, and especially to the ruler. When the person-as-state and the state-as-person metaphors coexist in public discourse, they interact in such a way that the vital differences between the two constituent terms become obscured and their specific meanings more and more difficult to conceptualize.

More fundamental yet than "The person is the state," however, is "Community is government." When this and its own mirror image ("Government is community") are allowed to operate in the political unconscious, their two terms cancel out their differences and the two metaphors become one simple, mind-numbing equation. The slogans of the ruling party in Orwell's *1984* were likewise equations that could be read backwards or forwards: WAR IS PEACE, FREEDOM IS SLAVERY, and IGNORANCE IS STRENGTH. These were an outward affirmation of an inward mental exercise called "doublethink," defined as "the power of holding two contradictory beliefs in one's mind simultaneously, and accepting both of them."[44]

The irreconcilability of communal ethos with governmental praxis is a deeply human knowledge. The cognitive dissonance that dual allegiance to these codes condemns us to is an ancient human infirmity. Tragic narratives acknowledge this predicament, but the homeland narratives I have commented on in this book pretend to overcome this knowledge and heal this infirmity by asking Americans to reject facts, deny their own experience, and trust their leaders as divinely chosen, thereby obeying the maxim IGNORANCE IS STRENGTH.

In recent years, two allied ideologies—Christian conservatism and the imperial presidency—have applied this Orwellian maxim to the task of blurring the distinctions between community and government. Christian conservatism has sought to invest the communal level with what it sees as the proper trappings of government, e.g., sovereignty, protectiveness, and coercive strength. Should it succeed in applying the governmental model to families and local institutions, it could justify an array of paternalistic social policies, including the revocation of female reproductive rights, censorship of the media, workhouses for the poor, church-controlled social welfare, home-schooling, and corporal punishment for children—in short, the Dominionist agenda of Christian Reconstruction. The imperial presidency, for its part, has sought to enhance its inherent attributes while at the same time clothing itself in the traditional attributes of community, such as moral clarity, "compassionate conservatism," a belief in hard work and "playing by the rules," and, above all, a biblical faith in the God of History and his covenant with America. Narrative plays an essential role in this ideological cross-dressing and is particularly necessary to the down-home masquerade of an imperial presidency, which, as a complex system superordinate to persons, cannot promote itself unless it somehow manifests itself in human figures portrayed as living their lives on the communal level. The saints of civil religion are the personae whom presidents point out in the gallery and extol during State of the Union addresses. As a discourse, narrative must have characters, of course. But narratives that mean to demonstrate the fusing of the governmental and the communal levels must have *heroic* characters, men and women who are called to serve purposes that transcend communal ethos without violating it.

Lakoff referred to the metaphor-generated narratives that Bush I and II employed to sell their two Gulf Wars as "fairy tales," and indeed they are. As I have argued, though, they derive their legitimating authority not from Hans Christian Andersen and the Brothers Grimm but from biblical master narratives. Beneath these scenarios, and buttressing them, are such narratives as the conquest of Canaan, the Babylonian captivity, the apocalyptic redemption of the Church, and the establishment of the kingdom of God. Belief begets beliefs, or may be made to do so, if the talking points are adhered to: "See, in my line of work you got to keep repeating things over and over and over again for the truth to sink in, to kind of catapult the propaganda." So said George Bush, explaining how difficult it was to convince the elderly to privatize their Social Security accounts.[45] If American credulity had not been cultivated for generations and extolled as a virtue, the deceptions of the Bush/Cheney administration could not have survived their first unmasking. They would have blown away like pieces of fluff and, with them, the credibility of their authors.

As I have tried to show in this chapter, lying beneath the secular American narratives of modernism is a little lower layer of premodern (that is, medieval Christian) narratives. But to understand the cultivation of credulity as public policy, we need to delve into a layer even lower—that of classical antiquity, whose political philosophy has proved extremely relevant to modern circumstances, as Leo Strauss and other scholars have revealed. When a ruling elite seeks to persuade the many to act against their own best interests, it must first gain the trust of the many before abusing it. In doing so, the elite must rely on an unwavering political base, for, as George Bush explained, "You can fool some of the people all of the time and those are the ones you want to concentrate on."[46] The governing class must therefore inculcate a homeland myth in which it is represented as united, heart and soul, with the commons.

As Strauss taught his neoconservative disciples, the foundations of Western political philosophy were set in place by the teachings of Plato's Socrates. In the *Republic,* Socrates first divides the citizenry of his prospective city into two classes, the guardians and the workers, roughly equivalent to the governmental and communal levels. Then, as the state evolves, the guardian class splits into the rulers, or "perfect guardians," and the auxiliaries, who become the police and professional military (the *epikouroi*). Now there are three classes: those few who have the ability to reason things out in free debate, those who believe the conclusions of the reasoners, and those who have little capacity either to reason or to believe.[47] The reasoners who speak, being the wisest, have the natural right to rule the state; the hearers are its natural defenders; and the third class, the artisans and farmers, are the producers of its material wealth.

The wise rulers, advised by philosophers, depend most directly on the second class to protect the state from foreign foes and pacify the unruly rabble, whose only aims are carnal pleasure and self-enrichment. To this end, Socrates encourages rulers to devise "one noble lie," one master narrative that is no mere parable or analogy but a story meant to be religiously believed. The falsehood that Socrates proposes is a version of an old legend according to which the original citizens of a given city emerged, like plants, out of its very soil.[48] This noble lie had four parts. First, the people had to be persuaded that their former life had been a dream. Second, they would be told that they had lain asleep in the earth and had just been birthed out of their motherland; henceforth they should regard the city-state as their true mother and their fellow citizens as their true brothers. Third, they must be made to believe that while they slept in their earthy womb, some god had inserted within each of them a small amount of gold, silver, or one of the baser metals, copper or iron. If they had been given gold, they would be raised to be rulers and philosophers; if silver, they would be military men, dedicated to upholding the laws of the city; if any admixture of copper or iron, they would become artisans or farmers. Fourth, though occasionally a son born in one class might be identified as belonging to another, no one rightfully belonging to the working class could aspire to guardian status. To foreclose that possibility, a divine oracle was to be fabricated that would declare: "When guarded by copper or iron, the city shall perish."

Socrates admits that this pious fraud would be hard to sell at first, but, after a generation or two, even the rulers might believe it. The new city, Kallipolis ("our fair city"), would by then be a going concern, and this founding myth would refer to the ancestral past. The keepers of this heritage, the auxiliaries (*epikouroi*), would evidently be the second class, the prime allies of the ruling class. Here and elsewhere in the dialogues, they are characterized as courageous, spirited, zealous for honor, and incapable of critical thinking. In the place of logical reasoning (*logos*), they deploy readymade opinions (*doxai*). They begin as blank as white wool, and then, dyed permanently in the laws they are taught, they become dyed-in-the-wool conservatives, as it were.[49] These credulous enforcers of the noble lie are also likened to trained guard dogs, or, in accordance with the pastoral metaphor, to sheepdogs: "In our city we have made the auxiliaries into dogs obedient to the rulers—to the shepherds of the city."[50]

This "noble lie" sounds rather crude to our ears. The first and third parts of it, the dream and the metals stories, apparently did seem a bit much even to Socrates and his young disciples—though they agreed that the legends might eventually gain acceptance. But part two, the autochthony story, could not have seemed odd to them at all. Athens, no less than Thebes, prided itself in its belief that its people were descended from men who had erupted from the very soil of its city.[51]

Homeland myths, as Socrates and his young friends conclude, do not have to be rational to be believed. Given their talking points, the auxiliaries will see to it that the masses fall in line and choose to act against their own best interests even to the extent of sacrificing their lives to vindicate their leaders' policies. The common folk are inherently trusting creatures, so, for the good of the state, a ruler must lead them as a shepherd leads his flock.

One cohort of auxiliaries that governments have always sought to recruit have been religious leaders. By representing the praxis of a given regime as consonant with the ethos of the community, these allies are uniquely positioned to harmonize the homeland. But, as recent American history illustrates, religious leaders can sometimes prove as politically naive as their congregations. In the early months of 2001, the Bush administration set up the White House Office of Faith-Based and Community Initiatives with the reported purpose of funneling money to community groups engaged in social services. As it turned out, however, its underlying aim was to persuade its principal beneficiaries, conservative evangelical pastors, to mobilize support for Republican candidates. As its first head, John DiIulio, soon learned, his main job was to serve the needs not of organizers of soup kitchens and after-school programs, but of the political staffers who worked under Karl Rove's watchful eye. After six months he left the OFBCI and waited a year before publicly exposing this policy. In a letter dated October 24, 2002, to the investigative reporter Ron Suskind, DiIulio outlined how the White House had misused this noble-sounding program simply to promote far-right electoral politics. The political staffers that did so he dubbed "Mayberry Machiavellis," implying that they were a breed of down-home cynics determined to exploit religion for political advantage.[52]

Then, in October 2006, David Kuo, a former deputy director of this same White House Office of Faith-Based and Community Initiatives, came out with a book-length exposé of this program. In *Tempting Faith,* Kuo corroborated DiIulio's account of underfunded and over-politicized compassion and added one other telling bit of information: White House senior and middle-level staffers held their Christian allies in derisive contempt.

> They knew the "nuts" were politically invaluable, but that was the extent of their usefulness. . . . National Christian leaders received hugs and smiles in person and then were dismissed behind their backs and described as "ridiculous," "out of control," and just plain "goofy." The leaders spent much time lauding the president, but they were never shrewd enough to do what Billy Graham had done three decades before, to wonder whether they were being used. They were.[53]

Whether the deliberate deception occurs between individuals or between social groups, lying and believing are correlative behaviors. Moreover, no one can deceive another unless the deceived maintains a twofold belief: one, that the speaker's statement is true, and two, that the speaker *believes* it is true. A lie is therefore both a misrepresentation of the truth and a betrayal of a social bond. A lie that speakers represent to themselves as a "noble lie" is meant to serve a higher good, a good that they think cannot be attained without deception. When this good is deemed to be the maintenance of national unity, the lie must be carefully concealed, as we have seen, in a web of metaphor-threaded narratives, for it is no less than the secret key that locks together *home* with *land,* governmental expedience with community values. But once a noble lie of this magnitude is disclosed, this key turns in the lock—and the terrible chasm between the praxis of the sovereign state and the ethos of the communal level yawns wide for all to see.

As we have seen, noble lies and homeland mythologies are not uniquely American. Plato's Socrates casually discourses on fantasies that were culturally specific to ancient Greece, fables that, to us, seem patently absurd. The neoconservative strategists who came to power in 2001 made the most of homeland fantasies specific to a biblically imbued American constituency.

To the Greeks, ours would appear equally absurd—barbaric, as they might say—yet *not incredible.*

In quite another spirit, that of mythopoeic *truth*-telling, I will herewith conclude with a fantasy of my own. Suppose some time-traveler should appear in a Platonic dialogue on statecraft, a character called the American Stranger. (I imagine him looking like Bill Kristol, but you may imagine whomever you prefer.) Welcomed into their circle, he listens respectfully as Socrates and his pupils discuss the need for a courageous citizenry, men instructed in such a way as to be willing to fight and die for the good of the homeland. Poets who, like Homer, sometimes disparage the motives of kings and speak of the afterlife as a wretched state must never be permitted to undermine this courage, and they should therefore be sent away from the ideal homeland.

The Stranger agrees that not all narratives build good character. Rulers may sometimes be foolish and venal, but to say so will disturb public order. Death may be a nothingness in which virtue goes unrewarded and vice unpunished, but to say so will cruelly deprive the people of their hope. He then offers to share with them his own faraway nation's founding myth, a sacred tale without which his government could not keep its workers patient with injustice and its military undismayed amid the horrors of war. Unlike the Greeks' myth of homegrown founders, the American founding myth tells of wanderers, divinely led migrants who invade and dispossess the native population. The Stranger begins his national myth in the distant past:

> Once, long ago and far away, a man called Abram heard God's voice telling him to journey to a foreign land. Though he would live there as a stranger and a sojourner, his descendants would someday possess this land. This they eventually did, having killed and scattered its original inhabitants. But afterwards, because they displeased God and rejected his son, they lost this land. So God chose a second people as his favorites, a people whom he also told to journey to another foreign land, especially reserved for them, a vast new land that they would eventually possess, having killed and scattered its original inhabitants. Now, so long as they neither displease God nor reject his son, who is soon to come a second time, they will reign with him for a thousand years in an earthly paradise.

"By Zeus," exclaims Socrates, "that is a noble tale indeed, but do the citizens believe it?"

"Of the few who know it, many believe it. Of the many who do not know it, many also believe it, we think, because they believe the other tales we make for them out of this one tale. Our citizens, you see, require stories they can believe in. Without such stories they would be hopeless and depraved."

"When ordinary citizens make up stories and tell them to one another, we call these 'lies,'" Socrates says, "and regard this behavior as shameful. On the other hand, rulers have the natural right to tell lies with which to deceive enemies and citizens alike for the welfare of the state.[54] Do you agree?"

"I do indeed."

"Would it not then be unjust for rulers to reveal the truth about the noble lies they tell their citizens?"

"It would be most unjust," replies the Stranger. "A just government must never deprive its citizens of their salutary tales. Moreover, when it refers to these tales, it must never use the word 'lie,' but use instead the word 'truth.' For there are different truths for different people: one truth for philosophers, a similar truth for rulers, a different truth for the auxiliaries, and a quite different truth for that many-headed beast, the people."

"That is a wise policy indeed," says Socrates. "And now, since we understand one another well, I propose that we conclude our discourse."

NOTES

PREFACE

1. Richard Cooper, "General Casts War in Religious Terms," *Los Angeles Times,* October 16, 2003.

2. Jay Rosen, "Public Journalism as a Democratic Art," http://www.imdp.org/artman/publish/article_23.shtml (a revised version of a talk delivered at the Projects Seminar on public journalism of the American Press Institute, Reston, Virginia, November 11, 1994).

3. She made this remark on NBC's *The Today Show,* January 27, 1998.

4. Interview with George W. Bush by David Horowitz, *Salon,* May 6, 1999, http://www.salon.com/news/feature/1999/05/06/bush/index.html.

CHAPTER I

1. See also William Safire, "Homeland," On Language, *New York Times Magazine,* January 20, 2002, 12.

2. The significance of this event was considerable, because a scant two weeks earlier the British forces had taken Washington, D.C., and burnt down the entire Capitol, an attack of even greater extent and ferocity than that inflicted on the Pentagon on September 11, 2001. The banner celebrated in Francis Scott Key's poem had been designed to link the local to the national by representing the union of the separate states—*e pluribus unum,* the singular from the plural. But plural usage did not fade away, despite the motto. Writing to Ralph Waldo Emerson in 1856, Walt Whitman could assure him that "the United States . . . are founding a literature." Only after the Civil War was it considered grammatically correct to use a singular verb with "the United States of America." While the distinction between individual states and the federal government does not logically match that between "home" and "land," advocates for both jurisdictions have always exploited these terms in their political rhetoric. The federal government, projecting itself as the "*land* of the free," has promoted nationwide standards of health, education, and civil rights; the states, claiming to know the real needs of their people, have represented themselves as the "*home* of the brave" in their resistance to outside interference.

3. The lyric "Home, Sweet Home," written by the New York–born actor and poet John Howard Payne (1791–1852), had sold over 100,000 copies of sheet music even before it appeared in his opera *Clari, Maid of Milan* at London's Covent Garden in 1823. Popularized by Jenny Lind, by the 1850s it had swept America. Its appeal was such that on December 12, 1862, the eve of the Battle of Fredericksburg, a regimental band struck up the melody—and Union and Confederate soldiers, massed for battle along the Rappahannock, stood up and tearfully sang the words together, a scene that the young Winslow Homer sketched in oils. Among the first songs recorded on Edison's phonograph, it provided no less than six hit records between 1891 and 1915. D. W. Griffith's first feature-length film, *Home, Sweet Home* (1914), used it for a theme.

4. These, needless to say, were the magic words that transported Dorothy back from the palace of Oz to Aunty Em's cozy kitchen in Kansas.

5. If the phrase "God bless you," said in response to a sneeze, represents a prayer that the sneezer

not contract some debilitating disease (the plague? tuberculosis?), perhaps "God bless America" is a formula felt to avert some analogous misfortune in the body politic.

6. See Frans de Waal's *Our Inner Ape* (New York: Riverhead Books, 2005).

7. See Robin Dunbar, *Grooming, Gossip, and the Evolution of Language* (Cambridge: Harvard University Press, 1998), and S. Mithen, *The Prehistory of the Mind* (London: Phoenix Books, 1996).

8. Though I would prefer to use BCE (Before the Common Era) and CE (Common Era), I will use the traditional Christian dating abbreviations, because they will be consistent with most of the texts to which I will refer.

9. Bellah had already published an essay, "Religious Evolution" (in *Beyond Belief: Essays on Religion in a Post-Traditional World* [New York: Harper and Row, 1970]), in which he listed an additional two stages: the early modern, beginning with the Protestant Reformation, and the modern, beginning with Kant. The author's dropping of the two more recent stages may reflect his second thoughts regarding the hopeful 1960s teleology of that essay. Robert N. Bellah, *Varieties of Civil Religion* (New York: Harper and Row, 1980).

10. Émile Durkheim, *Elementary Forms of Religious Life,* trans. Carol Crosman (New York: Oxford University Press, 2001), 427.

11. See V. Gordon Childe, *Man Makes Himself* (London: Watts, 1936), and T. D. Price and G. M. Fineman, eds., *Foundations of Social Inequality* (Madison, Wis.: Prehistory Press, 1995).

12. The Genesis story goes on to tell us that farmer Adam's first begotten, like him a "tiller of the earth," murdered his brother, a pastoralist. Like Adam, Cain was cursed with survival and with progeny: his first son, Enoch, was the first builder of a city. We understand—as did the ancient compilers of this myth, no doubt—that cities are built by agriculturalists, not shepherds.

13. See Arnold J. Toynbee's abridged *A Study of History* (New York: Oxford University Press, 1947), 164–87.

14. Colin Turnbull, *The Mountain People* (London: Jonathan Cape, 1973), quoted in Hugh Brody, *The Other Side of Eden: Hunters, Farmers, and the Shaping of the World* (New York: North Point Press, 2000), 140. Hunter-gatherers have complex languages and knowledge that they store in oral narratives. They have no writing—not because they are incapable of symbolization, but because they have no need to store it in graphic forms. Only a society that needs to keep inventories and send coded messages over considerable distances needs writing. A fully developed agricultural economy produces food surpluses that must be centrally managed. It therefore requires accountants and couriers. Once a ruler could encode his voice in graphic symbols, it was no longer necessary for him to harangue an assembly of followers or to survey his territory in person. He could rule at a distance, transmitting commands to far-dispersed economic and military embassies, and in return receive precise accountings of taxes, tribute, work levies, and population numbers from lands he would never need to see.

15. See Arnold Ludwig's *King of the Mountain: The Nature of Political Leadership* (Lexington: University Press of Kentucky, 2002).

16. As I noted in the Preface, the governmental/communal distinction that I develop in this chapter parallels, in some respects, the distinction Ferdinand Tönnies made between society (*Gesellschaft*) and community (*Gemeinschaft*). See his *Community and Society,* trans. C. P. Loomis (Ann Arbor: Michigan State University Press, 1957).

17. See Numa Denis Fustel de Coulanges, *The Ancient City: A Study on the Religion, Laws, and Institutions of Ancient Greece and Rome* (New York: Doubleday Anchor, 1956), 122–26.

18. For a discussion of this metaphor, see my *Authority Figures: Metaphors of Mastery from the Iliad to the Apocalypse* (Lanham, Md.: Rowman and Littlefield, 1996), 17–39 and passim.

19. Coke's timely, oft-repeated dictum appeared in this seventeenth-century jurist's report, "The Case of Sutton's Hospital." For more on this case, see Steve Sheppard's *Selected Writings of Sir Edward Coke,* 3 vols. (Indianapolis, Ind.: Liberty Fund, 2004). The second quote was attributed to the Tory politician Edward Thurlow, cited by John Poynder in his *Literary Extracts* (London: J. Hatchard and Son, 1844–47), 1:268.

20. "Nixon's Views on Presidential Power: Excerpts from an Interview with David Frost," *New York Times,* May 20, 1977, A16.

21. G. K. Chesterton, *What I Saw in America* (New York: Dodd, Mead, 1922), 14.

22. Bellah has defined it as "a collection of beliefs, symbols, and rituals with respect to sacred things and institutionalized collectively." Though it is derived from Christianity, this religion is "neither sectarian nor in any specific sense Christian," according to him. It is a national faith that emerged in the early Republic, but it was never "felt to be a substitute for Christianity. There was an implicit and quite clear division of function between the civil religion and Christianity." Rather more austere than devotional, American civil religion has been "much more related to order, law, and right than to salvation and love." It finds its models in the Old Testament and the Book of Revelation, and among its archetypes are "Exodus, Chosen People, Promised Land, New Jerusalem, Sacrificial Death and Rebirth." See Robert N. Bellah, "Civil Religion in America," in *Religion in America,* ed. Bellah and William G. McDonald (Boston: Beacon Press, 1968), 9–13, 20. As will soon become apparent, my definition of "civil religion" differs from Bellah's 1960s definition (as do most others' subsequent definitions, including Bellah's own). I see civil religion as the calculated use of religious references to induce broad and diverse sectors of the community to unite in support of governmental policies.

23. Dwight David Eisenhower's remark in the *New York Times,* December 23, 1952, is quoted in Will Herberg, *Protestant-Catholic-Jew* (Garden City, N.Y.: Doubleday, 1955), 97. The circle of American religion was not, of course, widened without some incidents of bigotry and communal violence. The motive for inclusion was political prudence rather than religious conviction.

24. In his *Totem and Taboo,* trans. James Strachey (1913; New York: Norton, 1962).

25. *Civilization and Its Discontents* [New York: Norton, 1961], 37–39, 109–10. Applying psychoanalytic principles to this issue, he asked: What might correspond to a collective super-ego and a collective id? On the individual level, a sure sign for Freud that the super-ego has been all too successful is the appearance of neurotic lassitude, the condition that overtakes the ego when it must survive with less aggressive energy at its command. Another sign is a diminishment of the sex drive caused by the requirement that a portion of it be diverted into non-libidinal love—for example, parental love, sympathy with others, and loyalty to the group. In the Western tradition this altruism is embodied in the command "Thou shalt love thy neighbor as thyself," which Freud finds to be a problematic ideal. "If he is my friend's son," yes. If he is one of those "belonging to me," yes, "but if he is a stranger to me and cannot attract me by any worth of his own . . . , it will be hard for me to love him" (*Civilization and Its Discontents,* 65–66). Of course, Freud is interpreting these words of Jesus as contemporary liberal Christians did, as binding on all "civilized" nations as well as neighborhoods. The actual text that Jesus cited suggests he indeed meant the "son of my friend" and not some notion of universal humanity: "Thou shalt not avenge, nor bear any grudge against the *children of thy people,* but thou shalt love thy neighbor as thyself" (Lev. 19:18, italics added).

26. Freud, *Civilization and Its Discontents,* 68–70.

27. Leon Festinger, Henry W. Rieken, and Stanley Schachter, *A Theory of Cognitive Dissonance* (Palo Alto: Stanford University Press, 1957), 3.

28. Ibid.

29. Freud, *Civilization and Its Discontents,* 76–92.

30. As Lev Vygotsky said, this speech is abbreviated. If we were to externalize this speech, it might reveal itself as proverbs and exempla, i.e., short pieces of encapsulated counsel that may well include contradictions ("Look before you leap," "He who hesitates is lost") and cautionary portraits ("Don't be like your cousin," "When you're ready to give up, remember your grandfather"). See Vygotsky's *Thought and Language,* trans. E. Hanfmann and G. Vakar (Cambridge: MIT Press, 1971), 43, 47, 131, 139–49.

31. See J. Barkow, L. Cosmides, and J. Tooby, *The Adapted Mind: Evolutionary Psychology and the Generation of Culture* (New York: Oxford University Press, 1992).

32. From this divisive perspective, the noun "community" has come to mean "minority group," as in the "handicapped community" or the "immigrant community." The adjective "communal" has come to refer to its opposite—to local groups in ancient feuds, as in "communal violence broke out again in Cyprus" (or Rwanda or Northern Ireland or Afghanistan or Iraq).

33. According to some archaeologists, the stage between communally organized societies and governmental (hierarchical) systems may be termed "transegalitarian" society. During this phase, strong

leaders emerged whom these archaeologists call "aggrandizers." See Peter Bogucki, *The Origins of Human Society* (Oxford: Blackwell Press, 1999), 205–58.

34. By "governing individuals," I mean not only the actual rulers and administrators but also the members of those favored groups who may be persuaded to identify with the quasi-heroic individualism of the powerful.

35. Lakoff called these narratives "scenarios," but would later refer to them as "master-narratives." See George Lakoff, "Metaphor and War: The Metaphor System Used to Justify the War in the Gulf." An introduction to his essay notes, "This paper was presented on January 30, 1991 in the midst of the Gulf War to an audience at Alumni House on the campus of the University of California at Berkeley. An earlier version had been distributed widely via electronic mail, starting on December 31, 1990." See *Viet Nam Generation Journal* 3, no. 3 (1991), online at http://www3.iath.virginia.edu/sixties/HTML_ docs/Texts/Scholarly/Lakoff_Gulf_Metaphor_1.html. Text made available by The Sixties Project, sponsored by Viet Nam Generation Inc. and the Institute of Advanced Technology in the Humanities at the University of Virginia at Charlottesville.

36. The utility of a fallback scenario was evident during the summer of 2003, as journalists and congressional critics began reacting to the apparently inaccurate claims the second Bush administration had made in regard to Iraq's WMDs. The self-defense scenario began to be hedged by the rescue scenario. In a speech in Elizabeth, New Jersey, on June 15, 2003, Bush railed against his critics: "There are some who would like to rewrite history—revisionist historians is what I like to call them." The next day, speaking at Northern Virginia Community College, he again blasted the "revisionists," reminded his audience that Saddam was now "no longer a threat," and added with emphasis, "The people of Iraq are free." Mike Allen, "President Assails Iraq War Skeptics: Prewar Intelligence Record Defended," *Washington Post,* June 18, 2003, A13.

37. According to the Harris Poll (October 2004), 62 percent believed that there had been "strong ties" between Saddam Hussein and al Qaeda; 41 percent believed that he helped plan the 9/11 attacks. Harris found on February 18, 2005, that 64 percent believed the "strong ties" theory and 47 percent believed that Saddam had conspired with the terrorists. As late as September 2006, 31 percent still believed the connection (Times/CBS poll).

38. Franklin Graham, son of the evangelist Billy Graham, made this remark at the dedication of a church in Wilkesboro, North Carolina; several weeks later (November 16, 2001) it was broadcast on *NBC Nightly News.*

CHAPTER 2

1. Augustine of Hippo, *Confessionum libri tredecim* (Leipzig: Teubner, 1898), 11.17.

2. A later prophet, Muhammad, was to have a monarchist interpretation of this turning point in Israelite history. In the Koran, the people call for a king expressly to lead them into battle in the cause of Allah, yet too often prove cowardly and falsely murmur against the ruler God chose for them (2:246–47).

3. The Hebrew word, *segad,* appears only in Daniel. The common word used for honoring a divinity, invisible or in physical form, is *shachah.* Because the king himself "reveres" (*segad*) Daniel (2:46), the word implies profound respect, but not necessarily divine honors. Whatever it meant, however, this obeisance was a violation of Mosaic law.

4. The fact is clear that Daniel and his three friends were treated in Babylon with respect *as Jews* (see Dan. 1:8–20, 2:46–47).

5. John J. Collins, "Daniel, Book of," *Anchor Bible Dictionary,* ed. David Noel Freedman (New York: Doubleday, 1992), 2:29–37.

6. *New English Bible* (New York: Oxford University Press, 1976), Apocrypha, 109. The Wisdom of Solomon is classified as apocryphal by Jews and Protestants, but accepted as canonical by Catholics.

7. From a governmental point of view, the issue here is one of controlling space without physically occupying it. This problem long predated governments, of course. The semiotics of territoriality begins with indexical signs, such as the excretions used by animals to mark their range. With humans

came iconic signs, such as the visual representations of absent owners, and symbolic signs, such as writing and other conventional signs (e.g., emblems and flags). Eventually icon and symbol were combined to form massive stone and metal presences. These have proven so powerful that wars, both ancient and modern, have been fought not merely against human enemies, but against monuments as well. In the cultural spaces between opponents lie the semiotic extensions of each, the pillars, statues, and inscriptions—in recent times, the fashions, foods, and films—that render absent authority magically present. These therefore must be toppled, demolished, and effaced. In Daniel we are not told what Nebuchadnezzar's statue represented, but it has been traditionally assumed to be a god (Antiochus had set up a number of Greek divinities in Judea). But Cyrus Scofield, reading this episode in the context of the Book of Revelation with its focus on the cult of the emperor, identifies it as a statue of Nebuchadnezzar himself, who, as a type of the beast, was attempting "to unify the religions of his empire by self-deification" (see Cyrus I. Scofield, ed., *The New Scofield Study Bible* [New York: Oxford University Press, 1967], 902). See also Jesper Svenbro's *La parole et le marbre: Aux origines de la poétique grecque* (Lund, Sweden: Studentlitteratur, 1976) and *Phrasikleia* (Paris: Éditions La Découverte, 1988).

8. The Pharisees themselves came back the same day to ask a follow-up question: "What is the great commandment of the law?" He answered, quoting Deuteronomy 6:5: "Thou shalt love the Lord thy God with all thy heart, and with all thy soul, and with all thy mind." Then, quoting Leviticus 19:18, he added that the "second is like unto it, thou shalt love thy neighbor as thyself. On these two commandments hang all the law and the prophets" (Matt. 22:36–40). What had made Jesus's preaching so unsettling was his separation of the community from the state and his attempt to reconcile the former to the transcendent level, the government of God, the true homeland. The kingdom of this world had no moral principles to offer its subjects, for only at the communal level does morality, summed up in the "second greatest commandment," operate. The ethos of the Gospels was simple and, in the context of Romanized Judea, conspicuous: "By this shall all men know that ye are my disciples, if ye have love one to another" (John 13:35).

9. See Simon Price's *Rituals and Power: The Roman Imperial Cult in Asia Minor* (New York: Cambridge University Press, 1984).

10. Expressions such as "generation to come" (Deut. 29:22; Pss. 78:4, 6, and 102:18) and "time to come" (Prov. 31:25; Eccles. 1:11; Isa. 30:8) actually mean the "generation behind" and the "time behind." The Hebrew word for "end," *acharith,* connotes ultimate behindness rather than some ultimate point of progression. This view of time has a logic that we find traces of in languages other than Hebrew. In Latin, *primus,* like our "first," is a superlative, meaning the "most forward." *Secundus* (from the verb *sequor*) means "following." These initial ordinals show a clear directionality and suggest that all Latin numbers were conceived of as following behind the number one. Yet nowadays we tend to regard the second in any series as proceeding from the first and leading on in the direction of the third. Every subsequent number in this series seems to us to assume lead position in the procession. Similarly, in modern English, when we use the expression the "following day," we do not suppose that Tuesday, for example, if it actually did follow Monday, would need to move in the direction of Monday. We commonly say that Monday comes "before" Tuesday and Tuesday "after" Monday—without realizing that this puts Monday in the lead of a procession and Tuesday as logically following behind it into the past.

11. Tzvetan Todorov, *Genres in Discourse* (New York: Cambridge University Press, 1990), 29.

12. Arnold van Gennep, *Rites of Passage* (Chicago: University of Chicago Press, 1966), 10–12.

13. The shadow metaphor implies a light intercepted by a body. The rituals of the Old Law were a "shadow of things to come; but the body is of Christ" (Col. 2:17). The full situational context of this metaphor might be visualized as follows: the observer is turned in traditional Jewish fashion toward the storied past, symbolized by the west, while dawn lightens in the east; the observer is aware that, as the sun appears above the horizon behind him, there is a person approaching him out of that blinding light, a person whose shadow stretches beyond him into the west. Christian apocalyptic thus takes the river metaphor of time and converts it into a river of light. This implies that a light somehow shining *out of the future* shone upon Jesus in the first century and projected his shadow backward into the fourteenth century of the Patriarchs and Moses ("Your father Abraham rejoiced to see my day: and he saw it and was glad" [John 8:56]) and beyond them all the way back to Adam.

14. "[W]hereas there is plenty of Jewish propaganda against Babylon and Greece and Rome, there is not a single Jewish text, biblical or rabbinic, directed against the Persians" (Norman Cohn, *Cosmos, Chaos, and the World to Come: The Ancient Roots of Apocalyptic Faith* [New Haven: Yale University Press, 1993], 223). The Jewish community of the captivity must have noted the resemblance of the "Day of Yahweh" to the final battle between Ormuzd and Ahriman, and the religious traditionalists in the two nations must have felt united in their enmity toward Hellenism. For a sober assessment of Persian influence on Jewish apocalyptic, see John Collins, *The Apocalyptic Imagination: An Introduction to the Jewish Matrix of Christianity* (New York: Crossroad, 1987), 22–26.

15. Theodor Gaster, *The Dead Sea Scriptures in English Translation* (New York: Anchor Books, 1976), 281–310.

16. The Kittians, or Chittim, were originally the Cypriots, so named for their coastal city of Citium. See Numbers 24:24; Isaiah 23:1, 12; and Daniel 11:30.

17. Gaster, *Dead Sea Scriptures*, 282, 296–97. Bracketed text represents Gaster's reconstruction of lacunae.

18. Norman Cohn, *The Pursuit of the Millennium: Revolutionary Millenarians and Mystical Anarchists of the Middle Ages* (New York: Oxford University Press, 1990), 14; Paul Boyer, *When Time Shall Be No More: Prophecy Belief in Modern American Culture* (Cambridge, Mass.: Harvard University Press, 1994), 49.

19. Boyer, *When Time Shall Be No More*, 51.

20. Ibid., 60–61.

21. Bernard McGinn attributes the earliest example of this polemic to the Dominican friar Arnold in the late 1240s. See his *Visions of the End* (New York: Columbia University Press, 1979), 175–76.

22. See John Neville Figgis, *The Divine Right of Kings* (1896; New York: Harper, 1965), 9–11, 40–45; Cohn, *Pursuit of the Millennium*, 16–21, 53–58.

23. See James West Davidson, *The Logic of Millennial Thought: Eighteenth Century New England* (New Haven: Yale University Press, 1977).

24. John Cotton, *The Churches Resurrection, or the Opening of the Fift and Sixt Verses of the 20th Chap. of the Revelation* (London: Henry Overton, 1642). See also Cotton, *An Exposition Upon the Thirteenth Chapter of the Revelation* (London: Livwel Chapman, 1655).

25. Moses Lowman, *Paraphrase and Notes upon the Revelation of St. John*, paraphrased by James West Davidson in *The Logic of Millennial Thought*, 145–48.

26. Stephen J. Stein, "Transatlantic Extensions: Apocalyptic in Early New England," in *The Apocalypse in English Renaissance Literature: Patterns, Antecedents, and Repercussions*, ed. C. A. Patrides and Joseph Wittreich (Ithaca: Cornell University Press, 1982), 287.

27. Robert Henry Charles, *A Critical and Exegetical Commentary on the Revelation of St. John* (New York: Scribner, 1970), clxxxiv.

28. Such a vision of the future lends to the passage of time an urgency that many observers find lacking in Catholic cultures. In Protestant eyes, at least, Catholics have an underdeveloped work ethic, expressed in a resistance to tight scheduling and a willingness to indulge themselves without a sense of guilt. This generalization, if it has a value, may be explained by Catholics' belief that they are now enjoying the spiritual security of the millennium, that Christ is present now in the Church, his Mystical Body, and that through the sacraments they remain in communion with God.

29. Davidson, *The Logic of Millennial Thought*, 44. Mede's magnum opus was *Clavis apocalyptica* (1627), translated as *Key of the Revelation* (1643).

30. Quoted in Boyer, *When Time Shall Be No More*, 66.

31. James H. Moorhead sides with those who hold that before the Civil War, most Americans were united in militant apocalypticism and little moved by doctrinal dissension on this matter. See Moorhead's *American Apocalypse: Yankee Protestants and the Civil War, 1860–1869* (New Haven: Yale University Press, 1978), 9. Ruth Bloch, however, dates the beginning of millennialist dissension in America as the 1790s; see *Visionary Republic: Millennial Themes in American Thought, 1756–1800* (Cambridge: Cambridge University Press, 1985), 130–31.

32. The word *patria* had two meanings in medieval Latin: the kingdom of heaven and one's native

region. See Johann Huizinga, "Patriotism and Nationalism in European History," from *Men and Ideas,* trans. James S. Holmes and Hans van Marle (Princeton: Princeton University Press, 1970), 104–6. The former meaning, which the Gospels, the Epistles of Paul, and the pronouncements of the Church Fathers affirm, was consistently promulgated through the Middle Ages. Aquinas regularly used *patria* (homeland) to mean heaven. The last verse of the hymn "Verbum supernum," sung at the Feast of Corpus Christi, is a prayer that God will grant us life without end *in patria.* For another reference to the heavenly *patria,* see also Peter Abelard's celebrated hymn "O quanta, qualia sunt illa sabbata."

33. Harry S. Stout, "Word and Order in Colonial New England," in *The Bible in America: Essays in Cultural History,* ed. Nathan O. Hatch and Mark A. Noll (New York: Oxford University Press, 1982), 23.

34. Ibid., 25–26.

35. Ibid.

36. John Winthrop, *A Model of Christian Charity* (1630).

37. See the *New Scofield Study Bible,* 24 (note to Gen. 15:18).

38. William McLoughlin, *Revivals, Awakenings, and Reform: An Essay on Religion and Social Change in America, 1607–1977* (Chicago: University of Chicago Press, 1978), passim, esp. 212; Stephen D. O'Leary, *Arguing the Apocalypse: A Theory of Millennial Rhetoric* (New York: Oxford University Press, 1994), 171.

39. See "President Delivers 'State of the Union,'" http://www.whitehouse.gov/news/releases/2003/01/20030128-19.html.

40. Stephen Mansfield, *The Faith of George W. Bush* (New York: Tarcher, 2003).

41. Simon Freeman, "The Truth About God and George," *(London) Times Online,* October 7, 2005, http://www.timesonline.co.uk/article/0,,11069-1815665,00.html. The Palestinian official Nabil Shaath, who was a witness to this statement, reported that indeed these were the President's words, but that he, personally, interpreted them in a figurative sense.

42. Jack Brubaker, "Bush Meets with Amish Group During July Campaign Stop," *Mennonite Weekly Review,* August 2, 2004. Despite his attempts to win over the Amish, the Bush reelection campaign lost the state of Pennsylvania in November.

43. "Revisionist history," a term associated with Holocaust denial, in this context suggests that critics of this war refused to believe that Saddam Hussein had brutally suppressed the Kurds and Shi'ites. Rice introduced this phrase during an interview on NBC's *Meet the Press;* see Audrey Hudson, "Powell, Rice Defend Iraq Arms Charges," http://washingtontimes.com/national/20030609-122702-8383r.htm. The president's remarks were made before a group of businessmen gathered in Elizabeth, New Jersey, on June 16, 2003, and were released by the White House Press Secretary. See "President Meets with Small Business Owners in New Jersey," http://www.whitehouse.gov/news/releases/2003/06/20030616-2.html.

44. On January 20, 2005, concluding his second Inaugural Address, Bush declared, "America, in this young century, proclaims liberty throughout all the world, and to all the inhabitants thereof. Renewed in our strength—tested, but not weary—we are ready for the greatest achievements in the *history of freedom.*" See "President Sworn-In to Second Term," http://www.whitehouse.gov/news/releases/2005/01/20050120-1.html. Addressing U.S. troops in Germany on February 23, 2005, he assured them: "You're a part of the *history of freedom* and peace." See the transcript at http://edition.cnn.com/TRANSCRIPTS/0502/23/lt.01.html. The next day, in Slovakia, a member country of the "Coalition of the Willing" that had contributed some 106 men to the Iraq war effort, he said: "I'm proud to stand in this great square, which has seen momentous events in the history of Slovakia and the *history of freedom*"; see "Transcript: Bush Addresses Slovak People," http://www.washingtonpost.com/wp-dyn/articles/A49680-2005Feb24.html?sub=AR. Addressing the World Affairs Council in Washington, D.C., on December 12, 2005, he linked that phrase with that other political cliché, "turning point": "There's still a lot of difficult work to be done in Iraq, but thanks to the courage of the Iraqi people, the year 2005 will be recorded as a turning point in the history of Iraq, the history of the Middle East and the *history of freedom*"; see Liza Porteus, "Bush Addresses Challenges to Iraqi Democracy," http://www.foxnews.com/story/0,2933,178409,00.html. (All italics in this note have been added.)

45. See "President Commemorates Veterans Day, Discusses War on Terror," November 11, 2005, http://www.whitehouse.gov/news/releases/2005/11/20051111-1.html.

46. In other words, if there were mistakes, they were not strategic, but tactical—not on the presidential but the military level. See the press conference transcript at http://www.whitehouse.gov/news/releases/2005/12/print/20051219-2.html.

47. Bob Woodward, investigative reporter and author of *Plan of Attack*, in a discussion with Mike Wallace on CBS's *60 Minutes*, March 15, 2004. His interview with the president took place on December 11, 2003; see "Woodward Shares War Secrets," http://www.cbsnews.com/stories/2004/04/15/60minutes/main612067.shtml.

48. "Remarks at Town Hall Event at the University of Sydney's Conservatorium of Music," http://www.state.gov/secretary/rm/2006/63166.htm. Speaking with Bill O'Reilly on September 14, 2005, on the coverage of the war, she assessed the current state of Iraqi society and also zoomed out to take in the grander sweep of history: "It is easier to put a picture on television of a suicide bomb than to show the process that is going on where people are registering to vote. . . . The political process has been moving inexorably along. . . . They are going to make it. I'm enough of a student of history to know that everything that is a major historical change—of any kind—is messy and violent and difficult." See the transcript of the interview at http://www.state.gov/secretary/rm/2005/53155.htm.

49. See "President Bush Speaks to United Nations," http://www.whitehouse.gov/news/releases/2001/11/print/20011110-3.html.

CHAPTER 3

1. Josephus, when discussing Deuteronomy as the "second law (book)," translated *torah* (law) as *politeia*, which would have brought to mind Plato's *Politeia* (*The Republic*). Dean McBride Jr., "Polity of the Covenant People: The Book of Deuteronomy," *Interpretation* 41 (1987): 229–30.

2. According to Calvin's marginal notes included in the Puritans' Geneva Bible, Israel, Canaan, or Jerusalem were all understood as "temporal" signs of the invisible "Kingdom of Christ." Readers learned that Joshua was important to them not as a conquering soldier of the Lord but because he "doth represent Jesus Christ the true Joshua, who leadeth us into eternal felicitie, which is signified unto us by this land of Canaan." See Calvin's note to Joshua 1:1 in *The Geneva Bible* (Ozark, Mo.: L. L. Brown Publishing, 1999).

3. The result was often an unstable mix of highly volatile tropes. In Edward Johnson's *Wonder-Working Providence of Sions Saviour*, the "Souldiers of Christ" escape from the bondage of "old England," where they had been *"Oppressed, Imprisoned and scurrilously derided,"* in order to "re-build the most glorious Edifice of Mount *Sion* in the Wildernesse." There they would cry out to all the world: "prepare yee the way of the Lord, make his paths strait, for behold hee is comming againe, he is comming to destroy the *Antichrist*, and give the whore double to drinke the very dregs of his wrath." From chapters 1 and 12 of Johnson's *Wonder-Working Providence* (1654), reprinted in Perry Miller and Thomas H. Johnson, eds., *The Puritans: A Sourcebook of Their Writings*, rev. ed. (New York: Harper Torchbooks, 1963), 1:144, 147–48.

4. Here Oakes recalls not only Winthrop's celebrated use of the "city on a hill" from Matthew 5:14 but also the next verse: "Neither do men light a candle, and put it under a bushel, but on a candlestick; and it giveth light unto all that are in the house." Cotton Mather in his introduction to *Magnalia Christi Americana* (1702) invokes end-time prophecy when he explicitly identifies the light provided by the "New England Israel" with the candles of the Revelation (1:12–13, 20): "Behold, ye *European* Churches, there are Golden Candlesticks, [more than *twice Seven times Seven!*] in the midst of this *Outer Darkness*. . . . And let us humbly speak it, it shall be *Profitable* for you to consider the *Light* which from the midst of this *Outer Darkness* is now to be Darted over unto the other side of the *Atlantick Ocean*." Reprinted in Miller and Johnson, eds., *The Puritans*, 1:167. Urian Oakes, "New England Pleaded with and Pressed to Consider Those things which Concern her Peace," in *Nationalism and Religion in America: Concepts of American Identity and Mission*, ed. Winthrop S. Hudson (New York: Harper and Row, 1970), 40–41.

5. Timothy Dwight, "A Valedictory Address . . . at Yale College, July 25, 1776," in *Nationalism and Religion in America*, ed. Hudson, 60–61.

6. Ezra Stiles, "The United States Elevated to Glory and Honor, a sermon . . . at the anniversary election, May 8, 1783," in *Nationalism and Religion in America,* ed. Hudson, 63–70. The key text for the sermon was Deuteronomy 26:19, God's promise of glory to Israel above all the nations.

7. No wonder the books of Joshua and Revelation were not recommended to, and rarely adapted for, young readers. See Allene Phy, "The Bible as Literature for Children," in *The Bible and Popular Culture in America,* ed. Phy (Philadelphia: Fortress Press, 1985), 172–73.

8. George Lakoff and Mark Turner, *More than Cool Reason: A Field Guide to Poetic Metaphor* (Chicago: University of Chicago Press, 1989), 131–33; Zoltán Kövecses, *Metaphor: A Practical Introduction* (New York: Oxford University Press, 2002), 102–4.

9. Quoted in Ernest Lee Tuveson, *Redeemer Nation: The Idea of America's Millennial Role* (Chicago: University of Chicago Press, 1968), 59.

10. This quote, which is nothing less than a foreign policy statement in myth form, extols a newborn Messiah (born on the Fourth of July, 1776) who will grow to be the leader of the end-time war. Borrowing the language of the Prologues in Shakespeare's *Henry the Fifth,* we are asked to visualize this young king as he reclaims his rightful kingdom in an action that is called a "progress." This word combines the older meaning of a royal journey with the new meaning of an irresistible process of social advancement, an Enlightenment concept that, once merged with apocalyptic Christianity, produces postmillennialism. David Austin, "The Downfall of Mystical Babylon," in *The Millennium,* ed. Austin (Elizabethtown, N.J., 1794), 353, quoted in Tuveson, *Redeemer Nation,* 117.

11. James Ussher (1581–1656) was a founder of the Irish Protestant church and a prominent scholar. His famous biblical chronology was published in 1650–54 in two volumes. It has become the standard system of dating for many conservative Protestant sects.

12. Godly sovereigns would wield this authority most visibly in foreign wars. To borrow from Jean Rostand, at home, when you kill one man, you are a murderer. But abroad, if you kill millions, you are a conqueror. If you kill all of them, you are a god. Rostand put it this way in *Pensées d'un biologiste* (Paris: Stock, 1978): "On tue un homme, on est un assassin. On tue des millions d'homme, on est conquérant. On les tue tous, on est un dieu" (116).

13. Herman Melville, *White Jacket, or The World in a Man-of-War,* ed. Harrison Hayford, Hershel Parker, and Thomas Tanselle (Evanston, Ill.: Northwestern University Press, 1970), 157.

14. Melville, *White Jacket* (conclusion of chap. 36), quoted in Tuveson, *Redeemer Nation,* 156–57.

15. Joseph Conrad, *Heart of Darkness,* Norton Critical Edition (New York: Norton, 1988), 16. Marlow's aunt quotes from Luke 10:7. The entire commission of Jesus to the seventy disciples (Luke 10:2–16) is worth examining in order to grasp the religious dimension of colonialism.

16. In his perceptive study of Genesis-based American ethnic myths, *Noah's Curse: The Biblical Justification of American Slavery* (New York: Oxford University Press, 2002), Stephen Haynes teases out the tangled justification for the displacement and immiserization of Native Americans. See especially 142–45, in which he examines the biblical imagination of the segregationist clergyman Benjamin Palmer as exercised in a sermon delivered in 1901.

17. Timothy Dwight, "America," in *The Major Poems of Timothy Dwight,* ed. William J. McTaggart and William K. Bottorff (Gainesville, Fla.: Scholars' Facsimiles and Reprints, 1969), 3.

18. This and the following extracts from Dwight's *Conquest of Canäan* appear in *Major Poems,* 60–62.

19. "Victims" here implies no compassion. The word does not signify a wrongly persecuted group but rather a *justly* condemned race: "cursed be Canaan." The concept is similar to "devoted," which originally meant designated for destruction as an offering to God, as in "None devoted, which shall be devoted of men, shall be redeemed; but shall surely be put to death" (Lev. 27:29). The practice referred to here is uncomfortably close to human sacrifice.

20. In Miller and Johnson, eds., *The Puritans,* 1:138–39 (italics added).

21. "Starting from Paumanok," line 245, in Whitman, *Leaves of Grass and Other Writings,* ed. Michael Moon (New York: Norton, 2002), 24.

22. "Seul," "An Indian Tale," *Godey's Lady's Book,* January 1858, 45.

23. Scofield, *New Scofield Study Bible,* note to Genesis 6:4, 13.

24. Quoted in Thomas Virgil Peterson, *Ham and Japheth: The Mythic World of Whites in the Antebellum South* (Metuchen, N.J.: Scarecrow, 1978), 143.

25. Haynes, *Noah's Curse,* 74–75.

26. Modern scholars concur, but for another reason. The curse is concentrated on Canaan, as the progenitor of the people whom the Israelites expelled from their Promised Land. He was called the son of Ham, because Canaan, the country, had been a client state of Egypt (Ham, or Kem in Egyptian). The servitude of Canaan—the Gibeonites at least—is referred to in the prophecy.

27. Samuel Adolphus Cartwright, *Essays, Being Inductions Drawn from the Baconian Philosophy Proving the Truth of the Bible and the Justice and Benevolence of the Decree Dooming Canaan to Be Servant of Servants* (1843), 9–11. In Peterson, *Ham and Japheth,* 99–100. The America that the antebellum South imagined as the fulfillment of the Noachic prophecy was in fact a racial order structured as the pronoun paradigm, as I outlined it in *Authority Figures* (1–18). In its idealization of plantation life, the first person, the master of a heavenly blessed realm, is the sole speaker; the second person is the docile servant, the permanent child whose obedience now atones for the offense to *patria potestas* that his ancestor long ago committed. The Indian, as third person, however, has now acquired the character that European folklore assigned to the Jew—that of a sad, devious, resentful, and irredeemable wanderer, an outsider forced by law into designated reservations.

28. Quoted in Peterson, *Ham and Japheth,* 98.

29. Ibid., 24.

30. Ibid., 149.

31. Robert Bellah, *The Broken Covenant: American Civil Religion in Times of Trial* (New York: Seabury Press, 1975), 6.

32. Douglas Robinson, *American Apocalypses: The Image of the End of the World in American Literature* (Baltimore: Johns Hopkins University Press, 1985), 2.

33. John F. Wilson, *Public Religion in American Culture* (Philadelphia: Temple University Press, 1979), 59–62, lists Adams (May 9, 1798); Madison (Sept. 1813 and Jan. 1815); Lincoln, who proclaimed three such days during the Civil War; and Wilson, who did likewise during the First World War. Such days were also proclaimed after the deaths of presidents Harrison, Lincoln, and Garfield. After Wilson, the custom of national "humiliation" vanished, a development worth exploring. George W. Bush's proclamation of "Days of Prayer and Remembrance" to mark the one-year anniversary of September 11, 2001, implied no need for national moral self-examination.

34. William Blake in *America: A Prophecy* was not the only one to make these connections. These were standard rhetorical gestures used by pro-independence preachers, politicians, and journalists in the colonies and in the early republic.

35. In his letter to James Madison dated September 6, 1789, Jefferson suggested that liberty demands that unless each succeeding American generation rewrites the Constitution, the dead would rule the living.

36. John Adams, from his letter to Abigail Adams, July 3, 1776, in "Correspondence Between John and Abigail Adams," *Adams Family Papers: An Electronic Archive,* The Massachusetts Historical Society, http://www.masshist.org/DIGITALADAMS/AEA/letter/. (By the two ends of the continent, Adams probably meant the seaboard from Maine to Georgia.) July 4 that year fell, by coincidence or design, on the old-style date for Midsummer's Day. Those who had resisted the change from the Julian to the (popish) Gregorian calendar in 1752 would be ringing bells, shooting guns, and leaping about bonfires on what was now the day or eve of July 4. Rebels could claim this as support for their cause. If challenged, independence-sympathizers could explain that they were celebrating the traditional eve and day of St. John.

37. Ralph Waldo Emerson, "Remarks at a Meeting for the Relief of the Family of John Brown," in *The Complete Works of Ralph Waldo Emerson,* Centenary Edition, ed. E. W. Emerson (Boston: Houghton Mifflin, 1903–4), 11:317.

38. Harriet Beecher Stowe, *Uncle Tom's Cabin* (New York: Oxford University Press, 2002), 456.

39. Fredric Jameson, from his foreword to Jean-François Lyotard, *The Postmodern Condition: A Report on Knowledge,* trans. Geoff Bennington and Brian Massumi (Minneapolis: University of Minnesota Press, 1984), xi–xii.

CHAPTER 4

1. Boyer, *When Time Shall Be No More*, 62, 182, 318.

2. Revelation 3:3 and 16:15. See also 1 Thessalonians 5:2.

3. Joseph Mede, in his *Key of the Revelation* (English translation, 1643), supported the interpretation on which the premillennialist position was based, asserting that John's prophetic narrative in chapters 4–9 covers the same time as chapters 10–22. The Apocalypse was simply too packed with episodic detail to be narrated as a single series of events. As Michelangelo's fresco depicts it, chapter 20 alone involves many events happening at once in various places. John's entire vision, however, so overwhelmed the prophet that no linear narration could adequately convey it. This required the prophet in chapter 10 to go back in time to describe from different angles the same, already narrated events. This also explains most of the repetitions of numeration and motif. According to Mede's system, the opening of the seventh seal and the Last Judgment are actually synchronous events. There is no lag in the divine onslaught, no millennial intermission. When we "synchronize" these two passages, we learn that, yes, Doomsday will come as a thief in the night and that many will be dragged out of their beds to a military tribunal and a summary execution. For a perceptive discussion of Mede's impact on American millennialism, see Davidson, *The Logic of Millennial Thought*, 43–48. He speculates, on the authority of the OED, that Mede coined the verb "synchronize."

4. Robinson, *American Apocalypses*, 37.

5. Theodicy, or as Milton defined it, "to justify the ways of God to man," was a growing issue in Protestant Europe. As the divine rights of kings and prelates came under attack, the arbitrary sovereignty of the biblical Deity also came to be questioned. Leibniz (Voltaire's Dr. Pangloss) was only one of many to confront this issue.

6. Michael Wigglesworth, *The Day of Doom, Or, A Poetical Description of the Great and Last Judgment: With Other Poems* (1662), from the 6th edition (1715; Newburyport, Mass.: E. Little, 1811), Early American Imprints, 2nd series, no. 24443.

7. Wigglesworth's imagination is unspecific: do these infants step forward, toddle, crawl? And when these infants speak, do they talk like babies? He doesn't say. Like the folk portraits of his day, these infants are apparently to be imagined as miniature adults.

8. Wigglesworth, *Day of Doom*, 117 (from Mather's funeral sermon for Wigglesworth). Though its popularity waned in the mid-eighteenth century, when Franklin's *Way to Wealth* nudged it from first place in book sales, it did go through at least twelve separate editions from 1662 to 1828. Since then, its readership steadily dropped. A history of colonial American literature published in 1876, the centennial year and the heyday of the postmillennialist Social Gospel movement, voiced what most of Wigglesworth's later readers must have concluded: *The Day of Doom*, "with entire unconsciousness, attributes to the Divine Being a character the most execrable and loathsome to be met with, perhaps, in any literature, Christian or pagan." Moses Coit Tyler, *History of American Literature, 1607–1765*, quoted in *The Bible and Popular Culture*, ed. Phy, 166–67.

9. John Bunyan, *The Pilgrim's Progress* (New York: Oxford University Press, 1984), 8.

10. In Part 2, published in 1684, Bunyan recounts a similar allegorical journey taken by the pilgrim's wife, Christiana, and her two children.

11. Many of Edwards's congregation and subsequent readers would also be familiar with the image of death knocking at the door from Horace's ode "Solvitur acris hiems": "Pallida mors aequo pulsat pede pauperum tabernas / regumque turris" (1. 4. 13–14).

12. Wigglesworth, *Day of Doom*, 102.

13. Ibid. 97.

14. Davidson, *Logic of Millennial Thought*, 13, 14, 15.

15. Richard A. Proctor, "Meteor," *American Cyclopaedia* (New York: D. Appleton, 1881), 11:433.

16. Quoted in Boyer, *When Time Shall Be No More*, 81.

17. Quoted in Timothy Weber, *Living in the Shadow of the Second Coming: American Premillennialism, 1875–1925* (New York: Oxford University Press, 1979), 53.

18. Ibid.

19. The other four were the inerrancy of Scripture, the virgin birth, the vicarious atonement, and

the physical resurrection of Jesus. These were spelled out in the twelve-volume publication *The Fundamentals: A Testimony to the Truth* (Chicago: Testimony Publishing, 1910–15).

20. Davidson, *Logic of Millennial Thought*, 13, 61, 76.

21. Premillennialists have argued among themselves about when in this seven-year tribulation the Rapture will occur—before, during, or after it. Most now believe that it will occur *before*.

22. O'Leary, *Arguing the Apocalypse*, 81.

23. Joseph F. Rutherford, *Vindication* (Brooklyn, N.Y.: Watchtower Bible and Tract Society, 1931), 1:338.

24. Joseph F. Rutherford, *The Kingdom Is at Hand* (Brooklyn, N.Y.: Watchtower Bible and Tract Society, 1944), 350.

25. See Stephen W. Nissenbaum, *The Battle for Christmas* (New York: Knopf, 1996), and Penne L. Restad, *Christmas in America: A History* (New York: Oxford University Press, 1995).

26. This, according to some social historians (e.g., Stephen Nissenbaum), marked an unhealthy decline in community. This may be true, for, though every home is the essential center of communal activity, if this activity does not extend beyond the center, the local community may suffer. On the other hand, the old-fashioned Christmas, with its wassailers and open houses, may have served no healthier purpose than does the modern end-of-year office party—to enact a temporary and wholly symbolic leveling of social ranks.

27. As Ralph Waldo Emerson said, "infancy is the perpetual Messiah, which comes into the arms of fallen men, and pleads with them to return to paradise." See Emerson, *Nature*, in *Selections from Ralph Waldo Emerson*, ed. StephenWhicher (Cambridge, Mass.: Riverside Editions, 1957), 53.

28. The authorship of *A Visit from Saint Nicholas* has recently been questioned. See Don Foster, *Author Unknown: On the Trail of Anonymous* (New York: Henry Holt, 2000). Using stylistic evidence, Foster argues that the true author of this poem was Henry Livingston (1757–1823), a New Yorker and an associate justice of the Supreme Court.

29. Nissenbaum, *Battle for Christmas*, 73. Santa is still used as a threat for preschoolers: "If you don't mind what I say, Santa's not gonna bring you anything for Christmas." Store Santas still ask children if they have been good, and the lump of coal in the stocking is still believed to be a possibility, even though most American children have never seen this mineral product.

30. The evolution of the Saint Nicholas figure from bishop to Santa is, needless to say, more complicated than this. I am concerned here only to note his function in the construction of the "unapocalypse." For a detailed account, see Nissenbaum's carefully researched *Battle for Christmas*.

31. Saint Nicholas had been the patron saint of New York for forty years already, having been jocularly so designated by commercial boosters in order to exploit the city's Dutch history. Washington Irving later made his contributions in his mythicized *History of New York* (1810), inducing the New-York Historical Society to hold its annual meetings on December 6. See Restad, *Christmas in America*, 45–56.

32. The most often quoted apologist for this pious fraud was Francis Church of the *New York Sun*. When, in the fall of 1897, a child wrote that her friends had been saying that Santa Claus is not real and that she wanted the newspaper to tell her the truth, he answered her on the editorial page: "Virginia, your little friends are wrong. They have been affected by the scepticism of a sceptical age. They do not believe except what they see" (Francis Pharcellus Church, from his editorial first printed in *The Sun*, September 12, 1897). More readers then than now would have recognized here an allusion to the passage in John's Gospel where Thomas, encountering the risen Christ, says: "Except I see the print of the nails . . . , I will not believe" (John 20:25). Francis Church thereby implies that belief in Santa Claus and belief in Christ require the same kind of faith. He then explains what kind of faith this is: without belief in Santa Claus, "there would be no childish faith . . . , no poetry, no romance to make tolerable this existence. . . . Not believe in Santa Claus! You might as well not believe in fairies." The editorial, with its shift of implied addressee from child to adult to child again, demonstrates the dual target of the Santa myth. There is a "veil covering the unseen world," he tells his readers, both young and old, and "only faith, poetry, love, romance, can push back that curtain." We are left to conclude that nothing but a most resolute suspension of disbelief can reveal the beings that make tolerable this existence and that, whoever they are, they somehow all participate in Santahood.

33. Mikhail Bakhtin, *Rabelais and His World* (Bloomington: Indiana University Press, 1984), 15.

34. When Vergil envisioned such a new beginning, he alluded to the final age predicted by the Cumaean Sibyl when the goddess of Justice and the kingdom of Saturn (*Saturnia regna*) would return to earth (Eclogue 4.5–6). The Roman Saturnalia (December 17–23) was itself a public ritual based on this myth. Coming, as it did, just before the winter solstice, it marked the end of one annual cycle and the beginning of another.

35. With minor variations, this is identical with Isaiah 40:3–4.

36. See also the so-called Dives and Lazarus parable (Luke 16:19–26).

37. This holiday apparently absorbed features of an earlier British commemoration, Guy Fawkes Day (November 5), a festival that celebrated the foiling of the Catholic plot to bomb Parliament. Celebrated in pre-Revolutionary Boston as "Pope's Day," it could be used to divert internal class resentments toward the foreign agents of the papal Antichrist. See Len Travers, *Celebrating the Fourth: Independence Day and the Rites of Nationalism in the Early Republic* (Amherst: University of Massachusetts Press, 1997), 34–35. Yet apocalyptic rhetoric can be difficult to control, for, once external dangers subside, the same demagoguery can be turned inward—as it was during the English Civil War.

38. These followed a fixed order: cannon firing and church bells, a procession, a prayer, an ode (an original poem to be sung by all assembled), and an oration (including, in order, the causes of the war, distinguished persons, aid from France, blessings of republican government, and need for public virtue). Feasting followed, marked by earnest toasting, and finally, in the evening, bell-ringing, cannon firing, horse races, and fireworks. The whole ceremony resembled a Sabbath service in which the congregation here represented the "political Elect." Ibid., 49–50.

39. Ibid., 221, 67. Even today we hear the media town criers admonishing us to have a "safe and sane Fourth."

40. Francis Blake, "Oration on Independence, July 4, 1796," in *The Columbia Orator*, ed. Caleb Bingham (Boston: J. H. Frost, 1832), 236–37. Blake alludes to passages in Matthew 23:11, Revelation 7:1, and Luke 2:14.

41. Dwight, "A Valedictory Address . . . at Yale College," 60–61. His grandfather, Jonathan Edwards, felt confident that this epoch would begin in the year 2000. According to Bishop Ussher's chronology, the kingdom of God would appear on earth in October 1996. Most Americans then, unfortunately, were too absorbed in President Bill Clinton's sexual misadventures to notice when the auspicious date came and went.

CHAPTER 5

1. The abduction of Demeter's daughter, Persephone, by Hades was associated with the Eleusinian cult, an immensely popular Greek mystery religion. Both Homeric epics build upon this theme: the *Iliad* is preceded by the abduction of Helen, and the *Odyssey* concludes with the return of the avenging hero and the rescue of Penelope. A major portion of the Hindu epic, the *Ramayana*, is devoted to the abduction of Sita by the demon-king Ravana and Sita's rescue by her divine husband, Rama. We find this narrative of the captive damsel also in the tales of Perseus, St. George, Ruggiero and Angelica in Ariosto's *Orlando Furioso*, and Walter Scott's *Ivanhoe*. In medieval legends, abducted ladies rescued by doughty knights—e.g., Lancelot and Guinivere in the Arthurian romances—is a familiar theme.

2. For sixty-two years (1891–1953), the Watchtower Society taught that Jehovah lived in the Pleiades—on the star Alcyone, to be precise. See *Studies in Scripture* 3 (1891); *International Bible Students Souvenir Convention Report* (1914): 252–53; *Golden Age*, Sept. 10, 1924, 793–94; and *Reconciliation* (1928): 14.

3. Erich von Däniken, *Chariots of the Gods? Unsolved Mysteries of the Past* (1968; rpt., New York: Berkley Publishing Group, 1999), 10.

4. Ibid., 35.

5. Ibid., 36. Homophobes from outer space?

6. Ibid., 11. Later he shares with us his thought "that a group of Martian giants perhaps escaped to earth to found the new culture of *homo sapiens* by breeding with the semi-intelligent beings living there" (129). "Questions, questions, questions," he murmurs on page 88.

7. Ibid., 43–44 (italics added).

8. William Bramley, *The Gods of Eden* (New York: Avon, 1993), 137–39.

9. Ibid., 142.

10. Cited in Douglas Curran, *In Advance of the Landing: Folk Concepts of Outer Space* (New York: Abbeville, 1985), 10.

11. Hal Lindsey, *Planet Earth—2000 AD: Will Mankind Survive?* (Beverly Hills, Calif.: Western Front, 1997), 68.

12. "UFOs: A Christian Response," as featured on CBN's *Newswatch Today,* April 26, 1996.

13. A segment of *The 700 Club* (from July 8, 1997) as reported by Skipp Porteous of *Freedom Writer,* http://www.ifas.org/press/aliens.html (accessed 8/23/02; italics added). Christians who choose to identify unidentified flying objects as demons have more than one biblical text to support their theory. Paul spoke of Satan as the "prince of the power of the air." Therefore, "we wrestle not against flesh and blood, but against principalities, against powers, against the rulers of the darkness of this world, against spiritual wickedness in high places" (Eph. 2:2, 6:12). The latter phrase, *en tois epouraniois* in Greek, literally means "in the heavens," for in Paul's cosmos all supernatural beings, God and his angels *and* Satan and his, hover high above the earth. Christian UFOlogists would add that, though Satan is still up there, he is now reconnoitering the earth, where he is preparing to make his last stand. As Revelation prophesies: "And there was war in heaven: Michael and his angels fought against the dragon. . . . And the dragon was cast out, that old serpent, called the Devil, and Satan, which deceiveth the whole world: he was cast out into the earth, and his angels were cast out with him" (12:7, 9). ("Into," of course, is Elizabethan English for "onto"—the demonic powers are to be expelled from the heavens and driven down onto the earth.) "Woe to the inhabiters of the earth and of the sea! For the devil is come down unto you, having great wrath, because he knoweth that he hath but a short time" (12:12). Robertson's clear suggestion that Christians are authorized by God to "dispose of" UFO enthusiasts had to have pleased that fringe of the Christian Right that condones violence in obedience to what it understands as the inspired laws of Moses. On August 22, 2005, on *The 700 Club,* Robertson—for whom killing often seems a religious imperative—recommended "taking out" Venezuelan president Hugo Chavez. See the Associated Press story "Robertson: U.S. should assassinate Venezuela's Chavez," http://www.cnn.com/2005/US/08/23/robertson.chavez.1534/index.html.

14. Michael Barkun, *Religion and the Racist Right: The Origins of the Christian Identity Movement* (Chapel Hill: University of North Carolina Press, 1994), 158–59.

15. C. L. Turnage, *Sexual Encounters with Extraterrestrials: A Provocative Examination of Alien Contacts* (Santa Barbara, Calif.: Timeless Voyager Press, 2001). Cynthia Turner, a member of the Ancient Astronaut Society, links such evils as teenage pregnancy and gun-control initiatives to the efforts of those offspring of hybridizing extraterrestrials that infiltrated the federal government during the Clinton administration.

16. According to ancient Jewish marriage customs, the marriage vows are said in the home of the bride, and then the groom departs and prepares a chamber for himself and her in his father's house. At some indeterminate time in the future, he returns at midnight with a shout and the sound of shofars to steal away his bride.

17. For example, the Californian visionaries George Van Tassel and George King. Van Tassel received word of the existence of the Ashtar Command, a pantheon of gods and goddesses in saucers, including Lord Sananda (Jesus Christ), who watched over the earth; King revealed the messages of Master Aetherius and the other Cosmic Masters who told him how he and his followers could escape the imminent atomic doomsday. See Daniel Wojcik, *The End of the World as We Know It: Faith, Fatalism, and Apocalypse* (New York: New York University Press, 1999), 185–87. Hollywood quickly exploited the saucer craze and helped craft its now familiar imagery. From 1950 to 1958, it produced no fewer than fifteen films in which saucer-driven aliens befriended or threatened earthlings. Some early examples: *Flying Disc Man from Mars* (1950); *The Thing* and *The Day the Earth Stood Still* (1951); *The War of the Worlds* (1953), and *Killers from Space* (1953).

18. Leon Festinger, Henry W. Rieken, and Stanley Schachter, *When Prophecy Fails: A Social and Psychological Study* (Minneapolis: University of Minnesota Press, 1956), 130.

19. Ibid., 133.

20. As noted above, George Van Tassel, revelator of the Ashtar Command, also spoke of a principal director of the Command called Sananda. The fact that Sananda was the principal contact of the Seekers in 1954 suggests that Van Tassel's message had by then reached the Upper Midwest. He, too, reported that the "space brothers" would help the believers escape a great flood that would inundate the Midwest. Festinger et al. neglect to factor into the Seekers' psychological resiliency following their failed prophecy the support they may have felt or actually received from like-minded channelers around the country.

21. Festinger, Rieken, and Schachter, *When Prophecy Fails*, 134.

22. James Brooke, "The Day a Cult Shook a Tiny Town," *New York Times*, March 30, 1997, 17.

23. Ibid.

24. Ibid.

25. [M. H. Applewhite], "'95 Statement by an E.T. Presently Incarnate," originally posted to the Internet on October 11, 1995, and slightly edited in January 1997. This and other Web-posted documents from this group are currently available at http://religiousmovements.lib.virginia.edu/nrms/heavensgate_mirror/index.html.

26. Yrsody, "The Way Things Are," April 7, 1996, http://religiousmovements.lib.virginia.edu/nrms/heavensgate_mirror/book/a13.htm. The resemblance to Scientology's doctrine of discarnate extraterrestrials ("Thetans") lodged within the body is worth noting. This and other statements of Do's students appeared in the online book *How and When Heaven's Gate May Be Entered*. ("Yrsody," three identifying consonants followed by "-ody," is typical of the names taken by cult members. Perhaps, like "Do" and "Ti," there is a musical allusion here—"mel-*ody*.")

27. Immanuel Velikovsky's *Worlds in Collision* (Garden City, N.Y.: Doubleday, 1950) attempted to associate ancient ecological disasters on earth with encounters with comets, and he used ancient texts, such as Exodus, to prove that human concepts of the divine were based on these planetary events. Zecharia Sitchin took several steps further and hypothesized that the planet Nibiru, with an orbit intersecting that of Mars and Earth, returns to Earth's vicinity every 3,600 years and brings with it its technologically superior humanoids, the Anunnaki (the names are Sumerian). Needless to say, it is due to rendezvous with Earth *very* soon. For Sitchin, see http://www.world-mysteries.com/pex_2.htm.

28. Whitley Strieber, *Communion: A True Story* (New York: Avon, 1988).

29. Daniel Wojcik rightly concludes that Heaven's Gate's "basic theology . . . largely consists of vernacular and personal interpretations of Christian doctrine" (*End of the World*, 183). In Revelation, the divine injunction "to overcome" clearly implies the readiness to lay down one's life in order to give witness to one's faith. For them, their final act was not so much a "suicide" as it was a martyrdom, i.e., a witnessing believed to ensure their individual salvation.

30. Jwnody, "'Away Team' from Deep Space Surfaces Before Departure," April 8, 1996, http://religiousmovements.lib.virginia.edu/nrms/heavensgate_mirror/book/a20.htm.

31. The Usenet posting can be found at http://www.mt.net/~watcher/cultrep.html. At a press conference on October 24, 1989, Louis Farrakhan announced that he had had an encounter with an alien and had learned that Elijah Muhammad, founder of the Nation of Islam, now lives on a UFO mothership where he is preparing the downfall of the white race, the apocalyptic end of its 6,000-year domination (Donna Kossy, *Kooks* [Portland, Ore.: Feral House, 1994], 27).

32. "One Year Later, Heaven's Gate Suicide Leaves Only Faint Trail," *CNN Interactive*, March 25, 1998, http://www.cnn.com/US/9803/25/heavens.gate/.

33. A partial transcript of the comments of Jerry Falwell and Pat Robertson (September 13, 2001) appears on Beliefnet, http://www.beliefnet.com/story/87/story_8770_1.html. For Robertson's advice to the citizens of Dover, see FOX News, "Robertson: God May Smite Down Town That Voted Out Anti-Evolution School Board," November 11, 2005, http://www.foxnews.com/story/0,2933,175247,00.html.

34. *Confessions*, 7.10.16.

35. Just as there is no contradiction between a square and a cube, or a circle and a sphere, there is no essential contradiction between God's supernatural kingdom as the Bible reveals it and man's natural world as science observes it. Imprisoned in matter, we are like the citizens of Edwin Abbott's Flatland,

who were blind to the existence of three-dimensional reality and consequently bewildered whenever a hyperdimensional phenomenon intersected their plane. Edwin A. Abbott, *Flatland: A Romance of Many Dimensions* (1884; New York: Dover, 1992).

36. A recent effort to demythicize the Bible, published by the United Synagogue of Conservative Judaism, is entitled *Etz Hayim: Torah and Commentary,* edited by David Lieber (Philadelphia: Jewish Publication Society of America, 2001). "Etz Hayim" means "Tree of Life" in Hebrew.

37. Writing, when it came along, began to tip the balance of information, quantitatively at least, from the extraordinary to the ordinary. Clear-eyed observers over time tend to encounter more and more patterned repetition than novelty in the behavior of things and, as I pointed out earlier in regard to history, writing can and does preserve the repetitive as easily as the unique. Over the past three millennia, the observation of nature has amassed, catalogued, and organized into theories and laws so much ordinary data that the once demonstrative divine has lost its major *monstra.*

38. Increase Mather, *Kometographia, Or a Discourse Concerning Comets* (Boston, 1683).

39. Donald Holbrook, Donald Barnhouse, and William Smith, all quoted in Boyer, *When Time Shall Be No More,* 116–19.

40. Ibid., 127.

41. As though to fulfill Lindsey's futurist prophecies, George W. Bush's Pentagon in 2006 used "Divine" to name a series of tests intended to gauge the explosive effect of nuclear bombs on underground facilities: Divine Strake, Divine Warhawk, Divine Hellcat, and Divine Hates.

42. See Gershom Gorenberg, *The End of Days: Fundamentalism and the Struggle for the Temple Mount* (New York: Oxford University Press, 2002), and Boyer, *When Time Shall Be No More,* 193–99.

43. As Gorenberg has noted, leading American evangelicals seldom identify their doctrine as a recent theological system created by John Nelson Darby 150 years ago and spread by the Plymouth Brethren and the branch that called itself the Exclusive Brethren. See Gorenberg's *End of Days.*

44. Hal Lindsey, *Planet Earth: The Final Chapter* (Beverly Hills, Calif.: Western Front, 1998), 149. See also Lindsey's apparent source, Seymour M. Hersh, *The Samson Option: Israel's Nuclear Arsenal and American Foreign Policy* (New York: Random House, 1991).

45. Mary White Rowlandson, *A Narrative of the Captivity and Restoration of Mrs. Mary Rowlandson,* ed. Frederick Lewis Weiss (Boston: Houghton Mifflin, 1930).

46. See Jill Lepore, *The Name of War: King Philip's War and the Origins of American Identity* (New York: Knopf, 1998).

47. In *Popular American Literature of the 19th Century,* ed. Paul C. Gutjahr (New York: Oxford University Press, 2001), 974, 1014–15.

48. See Lepore, *The Name of War,* and June Namias, *White Captives: Gender and Ethnicity on the American Frontier* (Chapel Hill: University of North Carolina Press, 1993).

49. See Alan Gallay, *The Indian Slave Trade: The Rise of the English Empire in the American South, 1670–1715* (New Haven: Yale University Press, 2002).

50. Ira Berlin, *Many Thousands Gone: The First Two Centuries of Slavery in North America* (Cambridge: Harvard University Press, 1998).

51. H. Bruce Franklin, *M.I.A., or, Mythmaking in America* (Brooklyn, N.Y.: L. Hill Books, 1992). See also Elliot Gruner, *Prisoners of Culture: Representing the Vietnam POW* (New Brunswick, N.J.: Rutgers University Press, 1993) and Susan Katz Keating, *Prisoners of Hope: Exploiting the POW-MIA Myth in America* (New York: Random House, 1994).

52. Tad Tuleja, "Closing the Circle: Yellow Ribbons and the Redemption of the Past," in *Usable Pasts: Traditions and Group Expressions in North America* (Logan: Utah State University Press, 1997), 311–28. The fact that this narrative could quickly braid the strands of several popular songs, a story about a released convict, and a John Wayne movie into a custom that most Americans under thirty believe has always been observed testifies to its intense cultural potency.

53. See David C. Martin, "New Light on the Rescue Mission," *Newsweek,* June 30, 1980.

54. See "Operation Urgent Fury" at SpecialOperations.com for useful links: http://www.specialoperations.com/Operations/grenada.html.

55. The United States military reported 18 dead and 116 wounded. See "Frequently Asked Questions,

Grenada, Operation Urgent Fury," Naval Historical Center, http://www.history.navy.mil/faqs/faq95-1. htm.

56. Susan Schmidt and Vernon Loeb, "She Was Fighting to the Death," *Washington Post*, April 3, 2003.

57. José Martinez, "Inside the Daring Nighttime Raid," *New York Daily News*, April 3, 2003.

58. Todd Purdum, "The Invasion of Iraq," interview on PBS's *Frontline*, January 29, 2004; transcript available at http://www.pbs.wgbh/pages/frontline/shows/invasion/interviews/purdum.html.

59. Dick Cheney, interview on NBC's *Meet the Press*, March 16, 2003.

60. For the transcript of these remarks, see "President Bush Announces Major Combat Operations in Iraq Have Ended," http://www.whitehouse.gov/news/releases/2003/05/20030501-15.html. The final reference in the speech is to Isaiah 49:9 (New International Version). Isaiah 40–55, the work of "Second Isaiah," as scholars have named him, deals with the thoughts and emotions of the Babylonian captives whom Cyrus freed to return to Judah. These chapters are a favorite source for liberationist rhetoric. See David Austin's use of Isaiah in Chapter 3.

61. This xenophobic sleight-of-hand is difficult to pull off without invoking biblical absolutes. The notion that whenever alien forces have sought to harm white Christian Americans it has been out of envy or pure evil or, as George W. Bush explained, "because they hate our freedom" has for centuries been a popular belief. In religious terms, the Redeemer Nation must also be the suffering redeemer, the Christlike victim.

CHAPTER 6

1. See Susan Niditch, *Oral World and Written Word: Ancient Israelite Literature* (Louisville, Ky.: Westminster John Knox Press, 1996).

2. I am aware that some who define "text" narrowly may find "oral text" a contradiction in terms. Rather than speaking of "oral discourse" or "orature" (as opposed to "literature"), I prefer to term all stored verbal compositions (differences in storage methods notwithstanding) "texts," because the storage of such information is the primary distinction between verbal artifacts and the everyday use of language. See Walter Ong, *Orality and Literacy: The Technologizing of the Word* (New York: Methuen, 985), 10–15, for a lively discussion of this matter. See also my *Authority Figures*, 122–28.

3. Of course, narrative is not restricted to oral communication. Like poetic meter, narrative is a mnemonic form that has survived the leap from orality to literacy and has continued to function in ways as old as human speech itself.

4. Dunbar, *Grooming, Gossip*.

5. See Jack Goody, *The Logic of Writing and the Organization of Society* (New York: Cambridge University Press, 1986).

6. By *primary* orality Ong meant preliterate culture; by *secondary* orality he meant the new, audiovisual media-produced orality that now competes with the print media.

7. By the phrase "narrative logic," I have in mind the second meaning of "logic" as *Webster's Third International Dictionary* defines it: "Something that convinces or proves or that obviates argument or makes argument useless and that is by its nature quite apart from or beyond or opposed to the use of reason as a means of arriving at decisions or settling disputes or attaining truth." Though the lexicographer was probably thinking of a nonverbal instrument, like a six-shooter slammed onto a poker table, this definition perfectly fits narrative when it is used to establish truth without resorting to rational argument.

8. In Homer, when a fighter is presented with three options (a trilemma), he must either consult his inner spirit (the *thumos*) or wait to be saved by a divinity. See my *Authority Figures*, 73–85. As for cognitive dissonance, the function of oral narrative and myth is to mask it. Oral culture overcomes guilt by externalizing it in shame and scapegoating.

9. Ron Suskind, "Without a Doubt," *New York Times Magazine*, October 17, 2004.

10. American Dialect Society, "Truthiness Voted 2005 Word of the Year," January 6, 2006, http://www.americandialect.org/index.php/amerdial/truthiness_voted_2005_word_of_the_year/.

11. "Stephen Colbert," interview by Nathan Rabin, *A. V. Club,* January 25, 2006, http://www.avclub.com/content/node/44705. "The Colbert Report" began broadcasting on October 17, 2005.

12. This transcript is a slightly improved version of the "Re-Improved Colbert Transcript" posted by Frederick on the Daily Kos Web site, April 30, 2006, http://www.dailykos.com/story/2006/4/30/1441/59811.

13. Thomas Jefferson, *Notes on the State of Virginia,* from Query XIX, *Manufacturers.* The Beast of the Apocalypse for Jefferson may also be the multiheaded Beast that Plato chose to symbolize the appetitive soul of the Tyrant (*Republic,* Book IX, 588b–589d3).

14. Even the holy city of Jerusalem, being manmade and earthly, is corruptible. In Revelation 11:8, it is in fact associated with Sodom.

15. Revelation 17:6; 18:2, 7, 9, 11, 17; 19:3, 6.

16. David Rosenbaum, "Nixon Tapes at Key Time Now Drawing Scant Interest," *New York Times,* December 14, 2003.

17. See Boyer, *When Time Shall Be No More,* 118.

18. Ibid., 283. Using the same numerical values, Church also found that "MARK OF BEAST" and "COMPUTER" also added up to 666.

19. Ibid., 253.

20. The word comes from the Latin *castellum,* which in turn comes from *castrum* (pl. *castra*), "military camp." It meant, therefore, a fixed encampment, a stronghold, a fortified outpost.

21. For "safe room" advice, see http://www.nononsenseselfdefense.com/saferoom.html.

22. Joseph L. Conn, "God, Guns, and the GOP," in *Church and State,* November 1998, 4.

23. Boyer, *When Time Shall Be No More,* 121, 148.

24. Eric A. Miller and Steve A. Yetiv, "The New World Order in Theory and Practice," *Presidential Studies Quarterly* (March 2001); Jay Whitley, "The New World Order," http://www.greenapple.com/~ricfinke/NWO.html.

25. On Satan's "liberal agenda," see David Bay, "Disarmament, Last Stage Before New World Order," http://www.cuttingedge.org/ce1067.html.

26. Obviously, not all angry premillennialists are men, and not all are equally angry. Relatively few are prepared to act out their fantasies. But those whom I have categorized as "angry men" would say that they could understand, and even admire, those who do act them out. Moreover, not every angry man shares the same imaginary script; that is, each one's apocalyptic worldview has a slightly different admixture of reactionary elements. Details of farm, castle, and kingdom imagery are traceable in each angry man's cultural palimpsest, but each man chooses them in a kind of "mix-and-match" procedure.

27. This issue is an old one. The separatists who wrote the Dead Sea Scrolls tell us that they expected to launch an all-out attack on the Romans and their collaborators as soon as the heavenly host appeared in the sky. Then, fighting alongside angels, they would totally destroy their oppressors. These ancient zealots correspond in this respect to contemporary posttribulationists, whose own writings seem as much influenced by the Essene as by the Johannine prophecies.

28. Pat Robertson, *The End of the Age* (Dallas: Word Publishing, 1995).

29. See their homepage, http://christianexodus.org; see also "Fringe Group Hopes to Create an Officially 'Christian' South Carolina," *Church and State,* September 2004, 20.

30. Some sources for this belief include Richard Brothers, *A Revealed Knowledge of Prophecies and Times* (1794); John Wilson, *Our Israelitish Origins* (1840); and Edward Hine, *Forty-Seven Identifications of the British Nation with the Lost Tribes of Israel* (1874). Only the latter two are acknowledged by contemporary Anglo-Israelites.

31. Anonymous, *The Six Species of Man,* Anti-Abolition Tracts no. 5 (New York: Van Evrie, Horton, 1866). In *Popular American Literature,* ed. Gutjahr, 772, 755.

32. Peterson, *Ham and Japheth,* 24–25.

33. Richard Butler on the Aryan Nations Web site, July 1998.

34. David Lane, in the early 1980s, organized the Colorado branch of the Aryan Nations and a number of other white-power groups, including The Order; he was convicted of involvement in the

murder of Alan Berg, a Denver talk-show host, and in armed robbery. He is currently serving a sentence of 190 years.

35. Buford O'Neal Furrow, who on August 10, 1999, opened fire on a group of Jewish children in Los Angeles and later murdered a Filipino American postman, identified himself as a member of the "Phineas Priesthood" pledged to kill Jews and nonwhites.

. 36. Members of such groups may use codes such as "88," signifying HH (the eighth letter of the alphabet), it in turn meaning "Heil Hitler!" The code "14" refers to David Lane's "Fourteen Words" slogan, mentioned above. "RaHoWa" is the acronym for "Racial Holy War," their version of Armageddon. For a useful overview, see Chip Berlet, "White Supremacist, Antisemitic, and Race Hate Groups in the U.S.: A Genealogy," http://www.publiceye.org/racism/white-supremacy.html.

37. See the Aryan Nations Web site, http://www.nidlink.com/%7Earyanvic/index-E.html.

38. When Solomon built his Temple on nearby Mount Moriah, it too was referred to as "Zion."

39. In 1980, speaking at the National Briefing Convention of the Republican Party in support of Ronald Reagan's candidacy, Bailey Smith, then president of the Southern Baptist Convention, stoutly reconfirmed this doctrine when he declared, "God Almighty does not hear the prayer of a Jew." E. Glenn Hinson, "Reconciliation and Resistance," *Wesleyan Theological Journal* 37, no. 1 (2002): 26.

40. This belief was restated as recently as January 1999, when Rev. Jerry Falwell, speaking at an evangelical conference in Tennessee, assured the assembled that the Antichrist was alive today and was undoubtedly a Jew. See Sonja Barisic, "The Antichrist Is Alive Now, Falwell Suggests," *Milwaukee Journal Sentinel*, January 17, 1999.

41. Cyrus I. Scofield, *New Scofield Study Bible*, 250 (note to Deut. 30:3).

42. Ibid., 1337 (note to Rev. 7:14).

43. Ibid., 966–78 (note to Zech. 12:1, 13:8).

44. Ibid., 949 (note to Mic. 5:3).

45. Hal Lindsey, *There's a New World Coming: A Prophetic Odyssey* (Santa Ana, Calif.: Vision House, 1973), 121. For my references to Lindsey's Christian Zionism, I am indebted to chapter 6 of Stephen Sizer's extensive Web-posted analysis, "Hal Lindsey: The Father of Apocalyptic Christian Zionism," http://www.cc-vw.org/articles/hallindsey.htm.

46. Hal Lindsey, *The Apocalypse Code* (Beverly Hills, Calif.: Western Front, 1997), 118.

47. David Firestone, "Billy Graham Responds to Lingering Anger Over 1972 Remarks on Jews," *New York Times*, March 17, 2003.

48. The International Christian Embassy Jerusalem (ICEJ) has been housed since 1980 in a building on Brenner Street near the Israeli prime minister's residence. Before it was confiscated in 1948, it had been the home of the family of the late Edward Said.

49. Scofield, *New Scofield Study Bible*, 25.

50. Lindsey, *Late Great Planet Earth*, 76, and Lindsey, *Israel and the Last Days* (Eugene, Ore.: Harvest House, 1983), 166.

51. Lindsey, *Late Great Planet Earth*, 44.

52. See "Muslims Angered by Baptist Criticism," *CNN.com/Inside Politics*, June 13, 2002, http://www.cnn.com/2002/ALLPOLITICS/06/13/cf.crossfire. Abe Foxman of the B'nai Brith Anti-Defamation League, which in the past had welcomed evangelical support for Israel, promptly denounced Vines's inflammatory remarks.

53. Allan Cooperman, "Falwell Remarks Trigger Anti-U.S. Reaction," *Washington Post*, October 16, 2002.

54. These remarks were made, respectively, in Crawford, Texas, on August 13, 2001 (this appears on many Internet sites but without a verifiable source other than reporter Michael Shively); Crawford, Texas, on March 30, 2002 (see "President Calls on World Leaders to Condemn Terrorism," with a transcript available at http://www.whitehouse.gov/news/releases/2002/03/20020330-1.html); and his interview with CBS News's Katie Couric on September 6, 2006, with a transcript at http://www.cbsnews.com/stories/2006/09/06/eveningnews/main1979106.shtml.

55. John F. Harris, "God Gave the U.S. 'What We Deserve,' Falwell Says," *Washington Post*, September 14, 2001, C03.

56. See "Robertson Warns of Peril to Follow Gay Days," *Milwaukee Journal Sentinel,* June 10, 1998. Robertson has promoted himself as one who, Abraham-like, walked with God and by his prayers twice prevailed with the Almighty to spare his company headquarters in Virginia Beach, Virginia, from hurricanes (from Gloria in 1985, and from Felix in 1995). In 2003, when Hurricane Isabel turned landward, he assured the locals that he could avert it, but for some reason it slammed directly through Virginia Beach on September 18. See "Pat Robertson's Contradictory Theology," *Media Matters for America,* May 2, 2005, http://mediamatters.org/items/200505020002.

57. "The god of Judaism is the devil. The Jew will not be recognized by God as one of the chosen people until he abandons his demonic religion and returns to the faith of his fathers—the faith which embraces Jesus Christ and His Gospel." See David Chilton, *The Days of Vengeance: An Exposition of the Book of Revelation* (Fort Worth, Tex.: Dominion Press, 1984), 127.

58. See, for example, the Religious Freedom *Restoration* Act of 1993 (to permit sectarian prayer and the display of the Ten Commandments in public schools), struck down by the Supreme Court in 1997 and reintroduced in 2003; the Constitution *Restoration* Act of 2005 (to limit judicial powers to rule on governmental advocacy of religion); and the Houses of Worship Free Speech *Restoration* Act of 2005 (to permit churches to electioneer on behalf of political candidates without losing their tax-exempt status).

59. Mark Rushdoony, *Chalcedon Report* 252 (1986). Mark Rushdoony is the son of the founder and currently in charge of his father's think tank, the Chalcedon Foundation in Vallecito, California. "Chalcedon" alludes to the Church Council of Chalcedon (451), which declared Christ to be true Man and true God, thereby acknowledging his dominion over the spiritual and the material realms.

60. Andrew Sandlin, "Join the Resistance," *Puritan Storm,* http://forerunner.com/puritan/PS.Join_the_Resistance.html.

61. Jeff Ziegler, "Puritan Storm Rising," *Puritan Storm,* http://www.forerunner.com/puritan/PS.Puritan_Storm_Rising.html.

CHAPTER 7

1. Lyotard, *The Postmodern Condition,* 30.

2. The Sibyls had been inspired to announce a messianic age preceded by a catastrophic purging of the earth, and Vergil had been inspired to foretell in his Fourth Eclogue the birth of a child who would usher in a golden age of peace and harmony. Because the Sibyls had been prophetesses who wrote poetry and Vergil had been a poet who wrote prophecy, the linkage of the two textual traditions was already in place by the fifteenth century, when the generation of Lorenzo Valla and Marsilio Ficino reintroduced the Greek classics into Europe. Up to that point, poets could not pretend to gaze into the future or venture to unearthly realms, except via the conventions of dream-vision and allegory and only for the purposes of Christian edification.

3. "On the History, Eloquence, and Poetry of the Bible," in *The Major Poems of Timothy Dwight,* 545. Cited in Lawrence Buell, *New England Literary Culture: From Revolution Through Renaissance* (New York: Cambridge University Press, 1986), 169.

4. See his letter to Rev. Dr. Trusler, August 23, 1799. William Blake, *The Complete Poetry and Prose of William Blake,* ed. David B. Erdman (Berkeley and Los Angeles: University of California, 1982).

5. John Locke, *The Second Treatise on Government,* ed. Thomas Preston Peardon (New York: Liberal Arts Press, 1952), 49, 1.

6. Emerson, *Nature,* 24.

7. Bryant, *Inscription for the Entrance to a Wood,* 11–13, 17–20. See *The Poetical Works of William Cullen Bryant* (New York: Russell and Russell, 1967).

8. Cf. Milton, *Paradise Lost,* IV.205–357, which describes the "sporting lion" dandling the kid "in his paw," the gamboling bears and tigers, and the "unwieldy elephant" straining to amuse Adam and Eve by wreathing his "lithe proboscis."

9. Emerson, *Nature,* 22.

10. Ibid., 48–49.

11. Whitman, "Song of Myself," 38–45, in *Leaves of Grass* (1892 edition).

12. For scattered agricultural communities in valleys and on alluvial plains, flooding is the most dreaded danger, but for densely populated trading and manufacturing centers, fire is the greater fear. In the urbanized Hellenistic and Roman periods, the ultimate catastrophe was visualized as a conflagration. The fiery finale presented in the Book of Revelation is arguably less incendiary than the cosmic finale of the Stoics.

13. Fundamentalist Christians maintain that the fiery hell referred to in the Gospels as the "fires of Gehenna" and in Revelation as the "lake of fire" does not yet exist. The myriad unsaved souls, dead and alive, will have to wait until the Last Judgment to know the pains that God will create for them then. As for Satan, Scofield writes that "the notion that he reigns in hell is Miltonic, not biblical" (*New Scofield Study Bible*, 1350 n. 2). He is the ruler of the rulers of "this world" and is still somewhere aloft in the "heavens."

14. Not only will his victory be gained by the fire of heaven, but it will itself theophanically *resemble* it: "For as the lightning cometh out of the east, and shineth unto the west; so shall also the coming of the Son of man be" (Matt. 24:27).

15. *The Works of Jonathan Edwards*, ed. Perry Miller (New Haven: Yale University Press, 1957–2006). In Hebrew, the common word for voice is *qol*. Depending on the context, a *qol* could be the speaking voice of a man or woman or the cooing of a turtledove. But in a storm the *qol* is God's reverberating voice as he hurls his fiery weaponry at the mountaintops.

16. Kenneth Silverman, *Timothy Dwight* (New York: Twayne, 1969), 28.

17. This is said to be derived from a fragment of Ctesias in the Photii Bibliotheca that refers to a fountain in India whose waters could avert thunderbolts. A more likely source for Turgot's Enlightenment sentiment, however, is Manilius, who in celebration of the power of human reason to dispel superstition, wrote: "Eripuitque Jovi fulmen viresque tonandi / et sonitum ventis concessit, nubibus ignem" (And it snatched from Jupiter the lightning and the power to thunder, / and attributed the noise to the winds, the fire to the clouds). See *Astronomica* 1.104–5 (my translation).

18. In these poems, Goethe and Shelley celebrated an antiapocalyptic apocalypse, a cosmic revolution that was to liberate the children of Prometheus from the terrors of an alien god, that "Jove in the clouds," as Wallace Stevens was to describe him, that being who had had an "inhuman birth." Prometheus became the mythic personification of a revolutionary *éclaircissement* that had demystified both the *éclair* and the *éclat* of a tyranny. In the context of this classical myth, Prometheus unseats a pagan deity. But because the name "Jove" (or "Jupiter") had been commonly substituted for the biblical God in formal rhetoric for several centuries, the extollers of an unbound Prometheus were, *sub rosa*, rejoicing over the downfall of a vengeful version of God.

19. Alexander Jones, *A Historical Sketch of the Electric Telegraph: Including Its Rise and Progress in the United States* (New York: Putnam, 1852), v.

20. Ibid., 188.

21. Adams, *The Education of Henry Adams: An Autobiography* (Boston: Houghton and Mifflin, 1918), 388–89.

22. Ibid., 385 (italics added).

23. God the Father and God the returning Son are conspicuously absent from Adams's presentation of the Virgin. In terms of electrical polarity, a dynamo functions as a positive pole; insofar as she draws human energy to herself, Adams's Virgin functions as a negative pole. This polarity prompted a theological analogy in the mid-nineteenth century: God the Father as the inexhaustible generator of creative energy, and Mother Nature as the receiver of this metamorphic potency. These polar opposites attract. "The world is charged with the grandeur of God," said Hopkins. As in an electrical storm, the positively charged mass of ions in the cumulus is not "angry" with the negatively charged terrain below it. It merely needs to restore a mutual electrical balance. So too, the Creator of the universe desires only to share his superabundant energy with his Creation. If Adams was ever tempted to use this electrical paradigm to reconcile the Virgin with the Dynamo, he did not say so.

24. Ruth Wisse, in an article first published in *Commentary* in 1990, observed that "'Liberty Enlightening the World,' as the statue was originally entitled, was iconographically quite complicated. The

torch in the lady's right hand (which for a time did practical duty as a lighthouse) represented the flame of reason which had sparked the Enlightenment and ignited the French Revolution. The tablets in her left hand linked the American Declaration of Independence to the Tablets of the Law at Sinai, while her majestic crown of thorns or rays evoked both martyred Christ and prophetic Moses." This article, under the title "The Hebrew Imperative," was posted on the Web site of The National Center for the Hebrew Language.

25. Lyotard, *The Postmodern Condition,* 32.

26. These two American myths, that of nature (as Eden) and that of progress and freedom (as an Exodus to a Promised Land), have continued to generate a complex cognitive dissonance expressed in numerous contradictory public policy goals. How, for example, can America reconcile its belief in absolute property rights while preserving the integrity of the environment, its need for clean water and safe air while demanding low-priced and abundant energy, and its faith in freedom of opportunity with its hunger for cheap labor at home and abroad?

27. The derivation of "leisure" from the Norman French and "idleness" from the Old English recalls the same class disparities that are revealed in the synonyms *pork* and *swine, mutton* and *sheep, beef* and *cow,* and *farm* and *field.*

28. These numbers (rounded off) include only persons of European origin, not those from Asia, Canada, and the West Indies. In addition, we should note that in 1865, four million former slaves joined the free labor force. See the Bureau of the Census, *Historical Statistics of the United States* (Washington, D.C.: The Bureau, 1976), pt. 1.

29. R. T. Irvine, "Electrocution," *Johnson's Universal Cyclopaedia* (New York: D. Appleton, 1897), 3:59–61. The fire that a Promethean age had stolen from heaven and placed in the service of mankind had many a use, both symbolic and practical. What God hath wrought was an energy that sped messages across North America and under the Atlantic to the Old World. Biologists spoke of it as the animating force of all life. Emerson, in a famous phrase, had imagined himself closing an electrical circuit: "I become a transparent eyeball; I am nothing; I see all; the currents of the Universal Being circulate through me; I am part or parcel of God" (*Nature,* 21). These "floods of life stream around and through us" (ibid., 24). We experience that vitality "by virtue of which a man is the conductor of the whole river of electricity" (Emerson, "The Poet," in *Selections,* ed. Whicher, 240). For some more recent research into this matter, see Richard Moran, *Executioner's Current: Thomas Edison, George Westinghouse, and the Invention of the Electric Chair* (New York: Knopf, 2003), and Mark Essig, *Edison and the Electric Chair* (New York: Walker, 2003).

30. For a carefully researched and subtly argued treatment of the relation between biblical literalism (and its apocalyptic agenda) and the strict constructionism of Reagan-era appointments to the federal judiciary, see Vincent Crapanzano's *Serving of the Word: Literalism in America from the Pulpit to the Bench* (New York: New Press, 2000).

31. Carl McIntyre, quoted in Boyer, *When Time Shall Be No More,* 136. On the relation between the scenery of Revelation and that of Roman games, see J. Massyngberde Ford, *Revelation: Introduction, Translation, and Commentary* (Garden City, N.Y.: Doubleday, 1975), 74, 218. John of Patmos may have visualized himself in the grandstand seats of the amphitheater of Ephesus.

32. The gallows confession was a common theme in the broadside ballads of the seventeenth and eighteenth centuries. Not even eternal torment was fully edifying if not preceded by it. As Wigglesworth put it: "sinners have nought to say, / but that 'tis just, and equal most / they should be damned for aye."

33. Stephen Knight, *Form and Ideology in Crime Fiction* (Bloomington: Indiana University Press, 1980), 13.

34. Cf. the popular documentary TV "cops" shows that pit decent and polite police officers against those enemies of society who, most viewers probably feel, would surely not be missed if some punishment could be found to fit their crimes.

35. In this respect, he corresponds to the warrior-judge of the Apocalypse, the "Son of man" who, as John Collins remarked, "is not a personification of the righteous community, but is conceived, in mythologic fashion, as its heavenly Doppelganger" (see *The Apocalyptic Imagination*). Though his study

of the apocalyptic genre has nothing to do with nineteenth-century fiction, Collins's reference is germane to our present inquiry. The doppelgänger, a separately existing, suddenly appearing replica of oneself, was a theme made popular by writers as diverse as Jean Paul, E. T. A. Hoffmann, Poe, Longfellow, Oliver Wendell Holmes, Guy de Maupassant, Fyodor Dostoyevsky, Conrad, and Henry James. Because the doppelgänger fantasy coincided with the phenomenon of double consciousness, it may well represent the hallucinated projection of one dissociated element—and insofar as double consciousness was invested with apocalyptic imagery, the doppelgänger was a personalized image of the returning Judge of the World. The fact that the perceived personality of the visitor may, depending on the text, be that of a mentor, an avenger, a destroyer, a savior, or a blend of several of these actors does not disqualify him from serving in this apocalyptic role. After all, when the messianic hero suddenly appears at the cosmic crime scene, he too will be perceived in similarly various ways by different viewers.

36. In this discussion of fictions, I realize that I am not giving proper weight to the importance of cinematic fiction in twentieth-century American culture. Yet some of what I say in reference to prose fiction can apply to film as well. One whole genre, the "disaster film," is obviously based on apocalyptic apprehensions.

37. Robert Jewett and John Shelton Lawrence, *The American Monomyth* (Garden City, N.Y.: Doubleday, 1977), 195–96.

38. See my *Authority Figures,* 19–39.

39. Lakoff and Turner, *More than Cool Reason,* 131–33; Kövecses, *Metaphor,* 102–4.

40. Cited by Mitchell J. Freedman on the Web page "American Rebels and You . . . ," http://www.thenation.com/doc/20030929/letter.

41. Ahab to Starbuck in Herman Melville, *Moby Dick* (Indianapolis: Bobbs-Merrill, 1964), 221.

42. Lakoff, "Metaphor and War."

43. This trope is at least as old as Herodotus and was the metaphor that Plato played with in book 9 of his *Republic.*

44. Orwell, *1984* (New York: Plume Books, 2003), 35.

45. From a Social Security "conversation" in Greece, New York, on May 24, 2005. What he meant by "catapult the propaganda" is unclear, but this expression remained in the copy released by his press secretary. See "President Participates in Social Security Conversation in New York," http://www.whitehouse.gov/news/releases/2005/05/20050524-3.html.

46. This remark he made before the Gridiron Club in Washington, D.C., on March 31, 2001. See "Bush Mocks Bush," BBC News, March 25, 2001, http://news.bbc.co.uk/2/hi/americas/1241240.stm. It purports to be a piece of advice given to him by a veteran Texas politician when he was running for governor.

47. This of these three is aligned to a psychic center (or "soul"), which in the *Republic* and other dialogues Plato locates in the head, the chest, and the abdomen, respectively. See *Timaeus* 71a1–72c1; *Phaedrus* 253d4–e5; *Sophist* 263d7–8; and *Republic* 435e–436a3, 547e3–548a1, 571–72, 580d7–589d3. This tripartition conforms to the pronoun paradigm—*I* and *We* who speak, *You* who listen, and *They* who are talked about but are excluded from the speech situation. (See the Preface, xii above.)

48. *Rep.* 3.414–15. Socrates alludes here to the legend of Cadmus, the Phoenician prince who, in his quest to recover his sister Europa, wandered into Greece and one day encountered and slew a dragon. On the advice of Athena, he removed the dragon's teeth and sowed them in the ground. Soon, fully armed warriors arose and began battling one another until only five remained alive. These Cadmus chose as co-founders of his new city, Thebes. Plato returned to this story in the *Laws* and pointed out that Theban children grow up believing this story, a factor that accounts for the fierce cohesiveness of this city.

49. *Rep.* 3.429–30. The phrase evidently entered English from North's translation of Plutarch's *Lives,* which perhaps derived it from this passage in the *Republic.*

50. *Rep.* 440c–d; for the guard dogs and sheepdogs, see 416a and 375c–76.

51. Cecrops, their first king, appeared in just this miraculous manner, as did a later king, Erechtheus. As an ethnic myth, autochthony flatters those who regard themselves as legitimate occupiers of a particular place vis-à-vis newcomers or resident aliens. Cf. the *Panegyricus* of Isocrates, published in 380 BC: "For it is admitted that our city is the oldest and the greatest in the world and in the eyes of

all men the most renowned. But noble as is the foundation of our claims, the following grounds give us even a clearer title to distinction: [24] for *we did not become dwellers in this land by driving others out of it, nor by finding it uninhabited, nor by coming together here a motley horde composed of many races;* but we are of a lineage so noble and so pure that throughout our history we have continued in possession of the very land which gave us birth, since *we are sprung from its very soil* and are able to address our city by the very names which we apply to our nearest kin; [25] for we alone of all the Hellenes have the right to call our city at once nurse and fatherland and mother" (italics added). During the race riots that exploded in Cronulla, a recreation area south of Sydney, Australia, in December 2005, native-born whites taunted persons they identified as Muslims with the chant, "We grew here, you flew here." This nativism prompted some Aboriginal Australians to comment, "We growed here, you rowed here." Its use in Athenian funeral oratory also suggests that interment in the motherland might have served a consolatory purpose, a return to the national womb. Thucydides alludes to this in his funeral oration (*Peloponnesian War,* 2.36). See also the Platonic (or Pseudo-Platonic) dialogue *Menexenus,* in which Socrates reports a funeral oration delivered by Aspasia, wife of Pericles, in which she, too, mentions this belief: the Athenians' "ancestors were not strangers, nor are these their descendants mere sojourners whose fathers have come from another country; but they are the children of the soil, dwelling and living in their own land. And the country which brought them up is not like other countries, a stepmother to her children, but their own true mother; she bore them and nourished them and received them, and in her bosom they now repose." As for the manipulation of oracles, this was a perennial suspicion, though difficult to prove.

52. With DiIulio's consent, Suskind promptly made his letter public. The ensuing furor apparently induced the writer to have second thoughts: he recanted and contritely apologized for his words. See Joe Conason, "'Mayberry Machiavellis'—Shutting Down a Truth-Teller," *The New York Observer,* December 4, 2002, and Ron Suskind, "Why Are These Men Laughing?" *Esquire,* January 1, 2003.

53. David Kuo, *Tempting Faith: An Inside Story of Political Seduction* (New York: The Free Press, 2006), 229–30. Though neither DiIulio nor Kuo regarded George W. Bush as insincere in his professions of faith, they did question the character of his appointees.

54. *Rep.* 3.389.

BIBLIOGRAPHY

Abbott, Edwin A. *Flatland: A Romance of Many Dimensions.* 1884. Reprint, New York: Dover, 1992.

Abrams, Meyer. *Natural Supernaturalism: Tradition and Revolution in Romantic Literature.* New York: Norton, 1971.

Adams, Henry. *The Education of Henry Adams: An Autobiography.* Boston: Houghton and Mifflin, 1918.

Ahearn, Edward J. *Visionary Fictions: Apocalyptic Writing from Blake to the Modern Age.* New Haven: Yale University Press, 1996.

Alverson, Hoyt. *Semantics and Experience: Universal Metaphors of Time in English, Mandarin, Hindi, and Sesotho.* Baltimore: Johns Hopkins University Press, 1994.

Arguet, Roland. *Cruelty and Civilization: The Roman Games.* London: Routledge, 1996.

Austin, David. "The Downfall of Mystical Babylon." In *The Millennium,* ed. David Austin. Elizabethtown, N.J., 1794.

Awad, Louis. *The Theme of Prometheus in English and French Literature: A Study in Literary Influences.* Cairo: Imprimerie Misr, 1963.

Bakhtin, Mikhail. *Rabelais and His World.* Bloomington: Indiana University Press, 1984.

Barkow, J., L. Cosmides, and J. Tooby. *The Adapted Mind: Evolutionary Psychology and the Generation of Culture.* New York: Oxford University Press, 1992.

Barkun, Michael. *Millennialism and Violence.* Portland, Ore.: Frank Carr, 1996.

———. *Religion and the Racist Right: The Origins of the Christian Identity Movement.* Chapel Hill: University of North Carolina Press, 1994.

Barnett, James. *American Christmas: A Study in National Culture.* New York: Macmillan, 1954.

Bellah, Robert N. *Beyond Belief: Essays on Religion in a Post-Traditional World.* New York: Harper and Row, 1970.

———. *The Broken Covenant: American Civil Religion in Times of Trial.* New York: Seabury Press, 1975.

———. *Varieties of Civil Religion.* New York: Harper and Row, 1980.

Bellah, Robert N., and William G. McDonald, eds. *Religion in America.* Boston: Beacon Press, 1968.

Bercovitch, Sacvan, ed. *The End of the World.* Vol. 14 of *A Library of American Puritan Writings: The Seventeenth Century.* New York: AMS Press, 1982.

———. *Typology and Early American Literature.* Amherst: University of Massachusetts Press, 1972.

Berlin, Ira. *Many Thousands Gone: The First Two Centuries of Slavery in North America.* Cambridge: Harvard University Press, 1998.

Bingham, Caleb, ed. *The Columbian Orator.* Boston: J. H. Frost, 1832.

Blake, Francis. "Oration on Independence, July 4, 1796." In *The Columbian Orator,* ed. Caleb Bingham, 234–37. Boston: J. H. Frost, 1832.

Blake, William. *The Complete Poetry and Prose of William Blake.* Edited by David B. Erdman. Berkeley and Los Angeles: University of California, 1982.

Bloch, Ruth. *Visionary Republic: Millennial Themes in American Thought, 1756–1800.* Cambridge: Cambridge University Press, 1985.

Bloom, Harold. *The American Religion: The Emergence of the Post-Christian Nation.* New York: Simon and Schuster, 1992.

———. *Omens of Millennium: The Gnosis of Angels, Dreams, and Resurrection.* New York: Riverhead Books, 1996.

Bogucki, Peter. *The Origins of Human Society.* Oxford: Blackwell, 1999.

Boman, Thorleif. *Hebrew Thought Compared with Greek.* Philadelphia: University of Pennsylvania Press, 1960.

Boyer, Paul. *When Time Shall Be No More: Prophecy Belief in Modern American Culture.* Cambridge: Harvard University Press, 1992.

Bramley, William. *The Gods of Eden.* New York: Avon, 1993.

Brandon, Ruth. *The Spiritualists: The Passion for the Occult in the Nineteenth and Twentieth Centuries.* New York: Knopf, 1983.

Brody, Hugh. *The Other Side of Eden: Hunters, Farmers, and the Shaping of the World.* New York: North Point Press, 2000.

Brooke, James. "The Day a Cult Shook a Tiny Town." *New York Times,* March 30, 1997.

Bryant, William Cullen. *The Poetical Works of William Cullen Bryant.* New York: Russell and Russell, 1967.

Buell, Lawrence. *New England Literary Culture: From Revolution Through Renaissance.* New York: Cambridge University Press, 1986.

Bunyan, John. *The Pilgrim's Progress.* New York: Oxford University Press, 1984.

Bush, Douglas. *Mythology and the Romantic Tradition in English Poetry.* New York: Norton, 1967.

Charles, Robert Henry. *A Critical and Exegetical Commentary on the Revelation of St. John.* New York: Scribner, 1970.

Chesterton, G. K. *What I Saw in America.* New York: Dodd, Mead, 1922.

Childe, V. Gordon. *Man Makes Himself.* London: Watts, 1936.

Chilton, David. *The Days of Vengeance: An Exposition of the Book of Revelation.* Fort Worth, Tex.: Dominion Press, 1984.

Cohn, Norman. *Cosmos, Chaos, and the World to Come: The Ancient Roots of Apocalyptic Faith.* New Haven: Yale University Press, 1993.

———. "Medieval Millenarism: Its Bearing on the Comparative Study of Millenarian Movements." In *Millennial Dreams in Action: Essays in Comparative Study,* ed. Sylvia L. Thrupp, 31–43. The Hague: Mouton, 1962.

———. *The Pursuit of the Millennium: Revolutionary Millenarians and Mystical Anarchists of the Middle Ages.* New York: Oxford University Press, 1990.

Collins, Christopher. *Authority Figures: Metaphors of Mastery from the Iliad to the Apocalypse.* Lanham, Md.: Rowman and Littlefield, 1996.

———. *The Poetics of the Mind's Eye: Literature and the Psychology of Imagination.* Philadelphia: University of Pennsylvania Press, 1991.

———. *Reading the Written Image: Verbal Play, Interpretation, and the Roots of Iconophobia.* University Park: Pennsylvania State University Press, 1991.

Collins, John. *The Apocalyptic Imagination: An Introduction to the Jewish Matrix of Christianity.* New York: Crossroad, 1987.

Comens, Bruce. *Apocalypse and After: Modern Strategy and Postmodern Tactics in Pound, Williams, and Zukofsky.* Tuscaloosa: University of Alabama Press, 1995.

Conrad, Joseph. *Heart of Darkness.* Norton Critical Edition. New York: Norton, 1988.

Crapanzano, Vincent. *Serving of the Word: Literalism in America from the Pulpit to the Bench.* New York: New Press, 2000.

Cross, Whitney R. *The Burned-over District: The Social and Intellectual History of Enthusiastic Religion in Upper New York State, 1800–1850.* Ithaca: Cornell University Press, 1950.

Curran, Douglas. *In Advance of the Landing: Folk Concepts of Outer Space.* New York: Abbeville, 1985.

Daniels, Rev. W. H., ed. *Moody: His Words, Works, and Workers.* New York: Nelson and Phillips, 1877.

Davidson, James West. *The Logic of Millennial Thought: Eighteenth Century New England.* New Haven: Yale University Press, 1977.

Dennett, Daniel C. *Darwin's Dangerous Idea: Evolution and the Meanings of Life.* New York: Simon and Schuster, 1996.

de Waal, Frans. *Our Inner Ape.* New York: Riverhead Books, 2005.

Drury, Shadia B. *Leo Strauss and the American Right.* London: Palgrave Macmillan, 1999.

———. *The Political Ideas of Leo Strauss.* 1988. Reprint, London: Macmillan, 2005.

Dunbar, Robin. *Grooming, Gossip, and the Evolution of Language.* Cambridge: Harvard University Press, 1998.

Durkheim, Émile. *Elementary Forms of Religious Life.* Translated by Carol Crosman. New York: Oxford University Press, 2001.

Dwight, Timothy. *The Major Poems of Timothy Dwight.* Edited by William J. McTaggart and William K. Bottorff. Gainesville, Fla.: Scholars' Facsimiles and Reprints, 1969.

———. "A Valedictory Address . . . at Yale College, July 25, 1776." In *Nationalism and Religion in America: Concepts of American Identity and Mission,* ed. Winthrop S. Hudson, 60–61. New York: Harper and Row, 1970.

Edwards, Jonathan. *The Works of Jonathan Edwards.* Edited by Perry Miller. New Haven: Yale University Press, 1957–2006.

Emerson, Ralph Waldo. *Nature.* In *Selections from Ralph Waldo Emerson,* ed. Stephen Whicher. Cambridge, Mass.: Riverside Editions, 1957.

———. "The Poet." In *Selections from Ralph Waldo Emerson,* ed. Stephen Whicher. Cambridge, Mass.: Riverside Editions, 1957.

———. "Remarks at a Meeting for the Relief of the Family of John Brown." In *The Complete Works of Ralph Waldo Emerson,* Centenary Edition, ed. E. W. Emerson, vol. 11. Boston: Houghton Mifflin, 1903–4.

Essig, Mark. *Edison and the Electric Chair.* New York: Walker, 2003.

Festinger, Leon, Henry W. Rieken, and Stanley Schachter. *When Prophecy Fails: A Social and Psychological Study.* Minneapolis: University of Minnesota Press, 1956.

———. *A Theory of Cognitive Dissonance.* Palo Alto: Stanford University Press, 1957.

Figgis, John Neville. *The Divine Right of Kings.* 1896. Reprint, New York: Harper, 1965.

Ford, J. Massyngberde. *Revelation: Introduction, Translation, and Commentary.* Garden City, N.Y.: Doubleday, 1975.

Foster, Don. *Author Unknown: On the Trail of Anonymous.* New York: Henry Holt, 2000.

Franklin, H. Bruce. *M.I.A., or, Mythmaking in America.* Brooklyn, N.Y.: L. Hill Books, 1992.

Frend, W. H. C. *Martyrdom and Persecution in the Early Church*. New York: Oxford University Press, 1967.

Freud, Sigmund. *Civilization and Its Discontents*. New York: Norton, 1961.

———. *Totem and Taboo*. Translated by James Strachey. 1913. Reprint, New York: Norton, 1962.

Fuller, Robert C. *Mesmerism and the American Cure of Souls*. Philadelphia: University of Pennsylvania Press, 1982.

———. *Naming the Antichrist: The History of an American Obsession*. New York: Oxford University Press, 1995.

Fustel de Coulanges, Numa Denis. *The Ancient City: A Study on the Religion, Laws, and Institutions of Ancient Greece and Rome*. New York: Doubleday Anchor, 1956.

Gallay, Alan. *The Indian Slave Trade: The Rise of the English Empire in the American South, 1670–1715*. New Haven: Yale University Press, 2002.

Gaster, Theodor. *The Dead Sea Scriptures in English Translation*. New York: Anchor Books, 1976.

Goody, Jack. *The Logic of Writing and the Organization of Society*. New York: Cambridge University Press, 1986.

Gorenberg, Gershom. *The End of Days: Fundamentalism and the Struggle for the Temple Mount*. New York: Oxford University Press, 2002.

Grabo, Carl. *A Newton Among Poets: Shelley's Use of Science in "Prometheus Unbound."* Chapel Hill: University of North Carolina Press, 1930.

Gruner, Elliot. *Prisoners of Culture: Representing the Vietnam POW*. New Brunswick, N.J.: Rutgers University Press, 1993.

Gutjahr, Paul C., ed. *Popular American Literature of the 19th Century*. New York: Oxford University Press, 2001.

Haines, Richard F. *UFO Phenomena and the Behavioral Scientist*. Metuchen, N.J.: Scarecrow, 1979.

Halsell, Grace. *Prophecy and Politics: Protestant Evangelists on the Road to Nuclear War*. Westport, Conn.: Lawrence Hill, 1986.

Hartman, Geoffrey H. *Wordsworth's Poetry, 1787–1814*. New Haven: Yale University Press, 1971.

Hatch, Nathan O., and Mark A. Noll, eds. *The Bible in America: Essays in Cultural History*. New York: Oxford University Press, 1982.

Haynes, Stephen. *Noah's Curse: The Biblical Justification of American Slavery*. New York: Oxford University Press, 2002.

Herberg, Will. *Protestant-Catholic-Jew*. Garden City, N.Y.: Doubleday, 1955.

Hersh, Seymour M. *The Samson Option: Israel's Nuclear Arsenal and American Foreign Policy*. New York: Random House, 1991.

Hesiod. *Theogony*. Translated by Norman O. Brown. Indianapolis: Bobbs-Merrill, 1953.

Hinson, E. Glenn. "Reconciliation and Resistance." *Wesleyan Theological Journal* 37, no. 1 (2002).

Hudson, Winthrop S., ed. *Nationalism and Religion in America: Concepts of American Identity and Mission*. New York: Harper and Row, 1970.

Huizinga, Johann. "Patriotism and Nationalism in European History." In *Men and Ideas*, trans. James S. Holmes and Hans van Marle, 104–6. Princeton: Princeton University Press, 1970.

Irvine, R. T. "Electrocution." In *Johnson's Universal Cyclopaedia*, 3: 59–61. New York: D. Appleton, 1897.

Jefferson, Thomas. *Notes on the State of Virginia*. Chapel Hill: University of North Carolina Press, 1954.

Jewett, Robert, and John Shelton Lawrence. *The American Monomyth*. Garden City, N.Y.: Doubleday, 1977.

Jones, Alexander. *A Historical Sketch of the Electric Telegraph: Including Its Rise and Progress in the United States*. New York: Putnam, 1852.

Keating, Susan Katz. *Prisoners of Hope: Exploiting the POW-MIA Myth in America*. New York: Random House, 1994.

Kermode, Frank. *The Sense of an Ending: Studies in the Theory of Fiction*. New York: Oxford University Press, 1967.

Knight, Stephen. *Form and Ideology in Crime Fiction*. Bloomington: Indiana University Press, 1980.

Kossy, Donna. *Kooks*. Portland, Ore.: Feral House, 1994.

Kövecses, Zoltán. *Metaphor: A Practical Introduction*. New York: Oxford University Press, 2002.

Kuo, David. *Tempting Faith: An Inside Story of Political Seduction*. New York: The Free Press, 2006.

Lakoff, George. "Metaphor and War: The Metaphor System Used to Justify the War in the Gulf." *Viet Nam Generation Journal* 3, no. 3 (1991). http://www3.iath.virginia.edu/sixties/HTML_docs/Texts/Scholarly/Lakoff_Gulf_Metaphor_1.html.

Lakoff, George, and Mark Turner. *More Than Cool Reason: A Field Guide to Poetic Metaphor*. Chicago: University of Chicago Press, 1989.

Lepore, Jill. *The Name of War: King Philip's War and the Origins of American Identity*. New York: Knopf, 1998.

Lewis, James, ed. *The Gods Have Landed: New Religions from Other Worlds*. Albany: State University of New York Press, 1995.

Lindsey, Hal. *The Apocalypse Code*. Beverly Hills, Calif.: Western Front, 1997.

———. *Israel and the Last Days*. Eugene, Ore.: Harvest House, 1983.

———. *The Late Great Planet Earth*. New York: Bantam, 1973.

———. *Planet Earth: The Final Chapter*. Beverly Hills, Calif.: Western Front, 1998.

———. *Planet Earth—2000 AD: Will Mankind Survive?* Beverley Hills, Calif.: Western Front, 1997.

———. *There's a New World Coming: A Prophetic Odyssey*. Santa Ana, Calif.: Vision House, 1973.

Locke, John. *The Second Treatise on Government*. Edited by Thomas Preston Peardon. New York: Liberal Arts Press, 1952.

Ludwig, Arnold. *King of the Mountain: The Nature of Political Leadership* . Lexington: University of Kentucky Press, 2002.

Lyotard, Jean-François. *The Postmodern Condition: A Report on Knowledge*. Translated by Geoff Bennington and Brian Massumi. Foreword by Fredric Jameson. Minneapolis: University of Minnesota Press, 1984.

Mansfield, Stephen. *The Faith of George W. Bush*. New York: Tarcher, 2003.

Marty, Martin. *Pilgrims in Their Own Land: 500 Years of Religion in America*. Boston: Little, Brown, 1984.

Mather, Increase. *Kometographia, Or a Discourse Concerning Comets*. Boston, 1683.

McBride, Dean, Jr. "Polity of the Covenant People: The Book of Deuteronomy." *Interpretation* 41 (1987): 229–44.

McDonald, John. *Isaiah's Message to the American Nation: A New Translation of Isaiah, Chapter XVIII, With Notes Critical and Explanatory.* Albany, N.Y.: E. and E. Hosford, 1814. Facsimile reprint, New York: Arno Press, 1977.

McGinn, Bernard. *Antichrist: Two Thousand Years of the Human Fascination with Evil.* San Francisco: HarperSanFrancisco, 1994.

———. *Visions of the End.* New York: Columbia University Press, 1979.

McLoughlin, William. *Revivals, Awakenings, and Reform: An Essay on Religion and Social Change in America, 1607–1977.* Chicago: University of Chicago Press, 1978.

Melville, Herman. *Moby Dick.* Indianapolis: Bobbs-Merrill, 1964.

———. *White Jacket, or The World in a Man-of-War.* Edited by Harrison Hayford, Hershel Parker, and Thomas Tanselle. Evanston, Ill.: Northwestern University Press, 1970.

Mendel, Arthur P. *Vision and Violence.* Ann Arbor: University of Michigan Press, 1992.

Miller, Perry, and Thomas H. Johnson, eds. *The Puritans: A Sourcebook of Their Writings.* Rev. ed. 2 vols. New York: Harper Torchbooks, 1963.

Mithen, S. *The Prehistory of the Mind.* London: Phoenix Books, 1996.

Moorhead, James H. *American Apocalypse: Yankee Protestants and the Civil War, 1860–1869.* New Haven: Yale University Press, 1978.

Moran, Richard. *Executioner's Current: Thomas Edison, George Westinghouse, and the Invention of the Electric Chair.* New York: Knopf, 2003.

Namias, June. *White Captives: Gender and Ethnicity on the American Frontier.* Chapel Hill: University of North Carolina Press, 1993.

The New English Bible. New York: Oxford University Press, 1976.

Nietzsche, Friedrich. *The Birth of Tragedy* and *The Genealogy of Morals.* Translated by Francis Golffing. Garden City, N.Y.: Doubleday, 1956.

Niditch, Susan. *Oral World and Written Word: Ancient Israelite Literature.* Louisville, Ky.: Westminster John Knox Press, 1996.

Nissenbaum, Stephen W. *The Battle for Christmas.* New York: Knopf, 1996.

———. *Christmas in Early New England, 1620–1820: Puritanism, Popular Culture, and the Printed Word.* Worcester, Mass.: American Antiquarian Society, 1996.

Oakes, Urian. "New England Pleaded with and Pressed to Consider Those Things Which Concern Her Peace." In *Nationalism and Religion in America: Concepts of American Identity and Mission,* ed. Winthrop S. Hudson, 40–41. New York: Harper and Row, 1970.

O'Leary, Stephen D. *Arguing the Apocalypse: A Theory of Millennial Rhetoric.* New York: Oxford University Press, 1994.

Ong, Walter. *Orality and Literacy: The Technologizing of the Word.* New York: Methuen, 1985.

Orwell, George. *1984.* New York: Plume Books, 2003.

Patrides, C. A., and Joseph Wittreich, eds. *The Apocalypse in English Renaissance Literature: Patterns, Antecedents, and Repercussions.* Ithaca: Cornell University Press, 1984.

Penton, M. James. *Apocalypse Delayed: The Story of Jehovah's Witnesses.* 2nd ed. Toronto: University of Toronto Press, 1997.

Peterson, Thomas Virgil. *Ham and Japheth: The Mythic World of Whites in the Antebellum South.* Metuchen, N.J.: Scarecrow, 1978.

Phy, Allene, ed. *The Bible and Popular Culture in America.* Philadelphia: Fortress Press, 1985.

———. "The Bible as Literature for Children." In *The Bible and Popular Culture in America,* ed. Allene Phy, 170–84. Philadelphia: Fortress Press, 1985.

Poynder, John. *Literary Extracts.* London: J. Hatchard and Son, 1844–47.

Price, Simon. *Rituals and Power: The Roman Imperial Cult in Asia Minor.* New York: Cambridge University Press, 1984.

Price, T. D., and G. M. Fineman, eds. *Foundations of Social Inequality.* Madison, Wis.: Prehistory Press, 1995.

Proctor, Richard A. "Meteor." *American Cyclopaedia,* 11:433. New York: D. Appleton, 1881.

Restad, Penne L. *Christmas in America: A History.* New York: Oxford University Press, 1995.

Robertson, Pat. *The End of the Age.* Dallas: Word Publishing, 1995.

Robinson, Douglas. *American Apocalypses: The Image of the End of the World in American Literature.* Baltimore: Johns Hopkins University Press, 1985.

Rosen, Jay. *What Are Journalists For?* New Haven: Yale University Press, 2001.

Rostand, Jean. *Pensées d'un biologiste.* Paris: Stock, 1978.

Rowlandson, Mary White. *A Narrative of the Captivity and Restoration of Mrs. Mary Rowlandson.* Edited by Frederick Lewis Weiss. Boston: Houghton Mifflin, 1930.

Rutherford, Joseph F. *The Kingdom Is at Hand.* Brooklyn, N.Y.: Watchtower Bible and Tract Society, 1944.

———. *Vindication.* Vol 1. Brooklyn, N.Y.: Watchtower Bible and Tract Society, 1931.

Scofield, Cyrus I., ed. *The New Scofield Study Bible.* New York: Oxford University Press, 1967.

"Seul." "An Indian Tale." *Godey's Lady's Book,* January 1858.

Sharlet, Jeff. "Through a glass darkly." Harpers Magazine, Dec. 2006.

Sheppard, Steve. *Selected Writings of Sir Edward Coke.* 3 vols. Indianapolis: Liberty Fund, 2004.

Shepperson, George. "Comparative Study of Millenarian Movements." In *Millennial Dreams in Action: Essays in Comparative Study,* ed. Sylvia L. Thrupp. The Hague: Mouton, 1962.

Siefker, Phyllis. *Santa Claus, Last of the Wild Men: The Origins and Evolution of Saint Nicholas, Spanning 50,000 Years.* Jefferson, N.C.: McFarland, 1997.

Silverman, Kenneth. *Lightning Man: The Accursed Life of Samuel B. F. Morse.* New York: Knopf, 2003.

———. *Timothy Dwight.* New York: Twayne, 1969.

Stein, Stephen J. "Transatlantic Extensions: Apocalyptic in Early New England." In *The Apocalypse in English Renaissance Literature: Patterns, Antecedents, and Repercussions,* ed. C. A. Patrides and Joseph Wittreich, 266–89. Ithaca: Cornell University Press, 1984.

Stout, Harry S. "Word and Order in Colonial New England." In *The Bible in America: Essays in Cultural History,* ed. Nathan O. Hatch and Mark A. Noll, 19–38. New York: Oxford University Press, 1982.

Strozier, Charles B. *Apocalypse: On the Psychology of Fundamentalism in America.* Boston: Beacon Press, 1994.

Stiles, Ezra. "The United States Elevated to Glory and Honor, a sermon . . . at the anniversary election, May 8, 1783." In *Nationalism and Religion in America: Concepts of American Identity and Mission,* ed. Winthrop S. Hudson, 63–70. New York: Harper and Row, 1970.

Stowe, Harriet Beecher. *Uncle Tom's Cabin.* New York: Oxford University Press, 2002.

Strieber, Whitley. *Communion: A True Story.* New York: Avon, 1988.

Svenbro, Jesper. *La parole et le marbre: Aux origines de la poétique grecque.* Lund, Sweden: Studentlitteratur, 1976.

———. *Phrasikleia.* Paris: Éditions La Découverte, 1988.

Thrupp, Sylvia L., ed. *Millennial Dreams in Action: Essays in Comparative Study.* The Hague: Mouton, 1962.

Todorov, Tzvetan. *Genres in Discourse.* New York: Cambridge University Press, 1990.

Tönnies, Ferdinand. *Community and Society.* Translated by C. P. Loomis. Ann Arbor: Michigan State University Press, 1957.

Toynbee, Arnold J. *A Study of History.* Abridged. New York: Oxford University Press, 1947.

Travers, Len. *Celebrating the Fourth: Independence Day and the Rites of Nationalism in the Early Republic.* Amherst: University of Massachusetts Press, 1997.

Tuleja, Tad. "Closing the Circle: Yellow Ribbons and the Redemption of the Past." In *Usable Pasts: Traditions and Group Expressions in North America*, ed. Tad Tuleja, 311–28. Logan: Utah State University Press, 1997.

———, ed. *Usable Pasts: Traditions and Group Expressions in North America.* Logan: Utah State University Press, 1997.

Turnage, C. L. *Sexual Encounters with Extraterrestrials: A Provocative Examination of Alien Contacts.* Santa Barbara, Calif.: Timeless Voyager Press, 2001.

———. *War in Heaven! The Case for Solar System War.* Santa Barbara, Calif.: Timeless Voyager Pres, 1998.

Turnbull, Colin. *The Mountain People.* London: Jonathan Cape, 1973.

Turner, Victor. *Ritual Process: Structure and Anti-Structure.* Chicago: Aldine, 1969.

Tuveson, Ernest Lee. *Redeemer Nation: The Idea of America's Millennial Role.* Chicago: University of Chicago Press, 1968.

Van Gennep, Arnold. *Rites of Passage.* Chicago: University of Chicago Press, 1966.

Velikovsky, Immanuel. *Worlds in Collision.* Garden City, N.Y.: Doubleday, 1950.

Von Däniken, Erich. *Chariots of the Gods? Unsolved Mysteries of the Past.* 1968. Reprint, New York: Berkley Publishing Group, 1999.

Vygotsky, Lev. *Thought and Language.* Translated by E. Hanfmann and G. Vakar. Cambridge: MIT Press, 1971.

Weber, Timothy. *Living in the Shadow of the Second Coming: American Premillennialism, 1875–1925.* New York: Oxford University Press, 1979.

Whitman, Walt. *Leaves of Grass and Other Writings.* Edited by Michael Moon. New York: Norton, 2002.

Wigglesworth, Michael. *The Day of Doom, Or, A Poetical Description of the Great and Last Judgment: With Other Poems.* 1662. Newburyport, Mass.: E. Little and Co., 1811 (from the 6th edition, 1715). Early American imprints, 2nd series, no. 24443.

Wilson, John F. *Public Religion in American Culture.* Philadelphia: Temple University Press, 1979.

Wojcik, Daniel. *The End of the World as We Know It: Faith, Fatalism, and Apocalypse.* New York: New York University Press, 1999.

INDEX